Brief Contents

A Note to Students from Miriam Moore

Since 1991, I have taught writing, grammar, reading, and ESL in a variety of places, including two universities, an Intensive English program, two community colleges, and even a chicken-processing plant! In each place, I have tried to share my love of words with students, and I have learned by listening to their words, the rhythms of their speech, their questions, and their frustrations.

Words, and the ways we put them together, help us accomplish ordinary tasks and, as our skills improve, some incredible feats: getting a date, making a sale, convincing the boss to try a new idea, changing a law, or solving a long-standing problem. The words we use to read and write can also help us to think more creatively, more deeply, and more effectively. In the ninth edition of *Real Writing*, I want to help you see the value of language skills like reading and writing and the power of practicing them together. Sure, it takes time and attention to learn new words, understand them when you read, and master rules for combining and punctuating them accurately. But in the end, after working for these skills, you will begin to see *them* working for *you*. It will be worth the effort.

I applaud your decision to take this course, and I wish you every success.

Ninth Edition

Real Writing with Readings

Paragraphs and Essays for College, Work, and Everyday Life

Susan Anker

Miriam Moore
The University of North Georgia

bedford/st.martin's
Macmillan Learning

Boston | New York

Vice President: Leasa Burton
Program Director, English: Stacey Purviance
Director of Content Development: Jane Knetzger
Executive Development Editor: Jane Carter
Assistant Editor: Paola García-Muñiz
Director of Media Editorial: Adam Whitehurst
Media Editor: Sarah Gatenby
Marketing Manager: Amy Haines
Senior Director, Content Management Enhancement: Tracey Kuehn
Senior Managing Editor: Michael Granger
Senior Manager of Publishing Services: Andrea Cava
Senior Content Project Manager: Lidia MacDonald-Carr
Senior Workflow Project Manager: Susan Wein
Production Supervisor: Lawrence Guerra
Director of Design, Content Management: Diana Blume
Interior Design: Claire Seng-Niemoeller, Heather Marshall
Cover Design: William Boardman
Text Permissions Editor: Allison Ziebka-Viering
Text Permissions Researcher: Elaine Kosta, Lumina Datamatics, Inc.
Director of Rights and Permissions: Hilary Newman
Photo Researcher: Krystyna Borgen, Lumina Datamatics, Inc.
Director of Digital Production: Keri deManigold
Advanced Media Project Manager: Rand Thomas
Project Management: Lumina Datamatics, Inc.
Project Manager: Vanavan Jayaraman, Lumina Datamatics, Inc.
Editorial Services: Lumina Datamatics, Inc.
Copyeditor: Angela Morrison
Indexer: Michael Ferreira
Composition: Lumina Datamatics, Inc.
Cover Image: Lew Robertson/DigitalVision/Getty Images
Printing and Binding: King Printing Co., Inc.

Library of Congress Control Number: 2021930565

ISBN 978-1-319-24827-7 (Student Edition)
ISBN 978-1-319-24828-4 (Loose-leaf Edition)

Printed in the United States of America.
3   4   5   6   26   25   24   23

Acknowledgments

*Text acknowledgments and copyrights appear at the back of the book on page 563, which
constitutes an extension of the copyright page. Art acknowledgments and copyrights appear on
the same page as the art selections they cover.*

For information, write: Bedford/St. Martin's, 75 Arlington Street, Boston, MA 02116

Contents

Thematic Contents

Preface

The first aim of *Real Writing with Readings* has always been to support academic literacy and success for all students in developmental writing, regardless of their skill level or level of preparedness. *Real Writing* achieves this goal by communicating to students that good writing skills are both essential and attainable. When they have this perspective, students can start fresh, reframing the writing course for themselves not as an irrelevant hoop to jump through but as a central gateway—a potentially life-changing opportunity, worthy of their best efforts. In large and small ways, *Real Writing* is designed to help students prepare for their futures. It connects the writing class to their other courses, to their real lives, and to the expectations of the larger world.

This powerful message is underscored in **Achieve with *Real Writing***, courseware that provides students with an engaging and structured online learning environment in which to practice and improve their writing. The writing tools in Achieve connect them back to the text so that it can guide them as they write. These tools also scaffold the writing process—from drafting to peer review and source check to reflection and revision—encouraging students to understand what experienced writers already know: that effective writing can be learned and that it is an important component to success in college and career.

In Profiles of Success, we provide inspirational portraits of former students, now in the workplace, who reflect on the varied, important ways they use writing on the job. These profiles are accompanied by real samples of the kinds of writing these professionals use at work. A diverse collection of both student and professional readings further encourage students to see the big picture, giving them a context and an appreciation for how they will apply what they're learning. *Real Writing*'s practical, real-world approach puts writing in a real-world context and links writing skills to students' own goals in and beyond college.

New to This Edition

The new Ninth Edition includes carefully developed features, paired with Achieve, to help students become better readers and writers in college and beyond.

- **Readings that reflect students' lived experience:** The readings in this new edition represent a diverse array of voices and perspectives (including selections by Nneka M. Okona, Eugene Robinson, and Steven Thrasher) and address relevant and relatable topics, from "ghosting" to the relationship between happiness and success to the complexities of patriotism for Black Americans. The goal is to make sure students see themselves in the writers and reading selections in the text and help students hone their critical reading and thinking skills while also engaging with topics that are relevant and important to them. In Achieve, instructors can also assign prebuilt, auto-graded multiple-choice quizzes to check reading comprehension and motivate students to complete the assigned reading.

- **A more balanced approach to writing and grammar instruction:** Part 1 on the writing process now includes a separate chapter on revision that asks students to focus on what is—and what isn't—working in their writing, with special attention to unity, development, and coherence. The grammar coverage retains its friendly, accessible tone and ample opportunity for practice, with new Chapter Quizzes at the end of each chapter in Parts 3 and 4. (These quizzes are auto-graded in Achieve.) The grammar coverage has been streamlined to focus on the "Four Building Blocks of Effective Sentences"—sentence fragments, run-on sentences and comma splices, subject-verb agreement, and other verb problems—as well as on editing for clarity, cohesion, and conventions. Coverage of pronoun reference has also been updated to reflect contemporary usage on questions like using the singular *they* and making writing inclusive. Together, these revisions demonstrate the text's balanced approach to writing instruction that puts equal emphasis on developing clear, focused, well-organized paragraphs and essays while also providing ample instruction and practice in writing clear, appropriate, grammatically correct sentences. In Achieve, instructors will find tools for students who need extra help with grammar, including diagnostics that generate personalized study plans to provide instruction targeted to each student's identified growth areas. Feedback links to the e-book provide students with point-of-need support within the context of their own writing. And auto-graded quizzes for each chapter in Parts 3 and 4 as well as LearningCurve activities on topics that frequently affect multilingual writers and other developmental writers, such as sentence structure and parts of speech (articles, nouns, prepositions, verbs), give students frequent opportunities for practice.

- **Easier-to-follow coverage of the "Four Basics" for each rhetorical mode:** In each of the Part 2 chapters, a new numbering system and boldface words at the beginning of each item highlight the Four Basics of a successful paragraph or essay:

1. Main idea

2. Primary support (key reasons, examples, or characteristics)

3. Secondary support (details and evidence to support each reason, example, or characteristic)

4. Organization (with coverage of transitions and new graphic organizers in each Part 2 chapter to show students how writing is structured in each rhetorical mode)

These numbered Four Basics are now carried throughout the chapter, leading to a simplified, easier-to-understand "Paragraphs versus Essays" graphic that shows students how to recognize and apply the Four Basics to their own writing. Achieve reinforces the Four Basics by providing a rubric and interactive assessment activity using the text's sample student paragraph, so students can first practice giving feedback based on key criteria for assessment without worrying about hurting the feelings of a classmate. The Writing Tools in Achieve scaffold peer review using the Four Basics to help students learn how to assess their own writing and that of their classmates, while allowing instructors to monitor and manage every step of the peer review process to ensure that students stay on track.

- **New "Reading Strategies in Action" activities:** Following the readings in each Part 2 chapter, the Reading Strategies in Action prompts ask students to apply one or more of the reading strategies introduced in Part 1 to the reading they're doing in the text. These reading strategies are reinforced by LearningCurve, which offers activities on active, critical, and interpretive reading; reasoning and logical fallacies; and recognizing the key parts of the rhetorical situation (topic, purpose, audience) for students who need extra help.

- **An Updated MLA Appendix:** Writing research papers is an extremely important part of many college courses. With that in mind, we provide instructions for citing sources in MLA style based on the Ninth Edition of the *MLA Handbook* (2021), with model citations for students completing research assignments. Achieve also provides a useful tutorial that helps students understand what they do and don't need to cite and a LearningCurve activity on MLA citation ("Working with Sources") that can help students practice what they're learning in a low-stakes environment, where they can try again if they make a mistake.

Core Features

Successful and popular features of earlier editions of *Real Writing* remain, with revisions based on suggestions from many insightful instructors and students—and now, enhanced by Achieve.

- **A Comprehensive Teaching and Learning Package:** *Real Writing* combines carefully curated readings, writing samples, writing assignments, grammar instruction, critical thinking coverage, and reading coverage in one convenient volume, reducing the time spent pulling together materials from various sources and allowing instructors to focus on what matters most: their students. With Achieve, instructors also have access to extra practice activities (auto-scored with immediate feedback) that they can assign to students who need additional support.

- **Writing Practice:** Not only does *Real Writing* feature a number of student model paragraphs and essays, workplace writing, and professional readings, it also asks students to write their own paragraphs and essays in multiple assignments throughout the book, assignments that help students translate their writing skills to the real world. Each rhetorical mode chapter features a step-by-step writing guide and checklist that students can refer to when completing their writing assignments. In Achieve, each of these writing assignments is prebuilt and fully customizable, including rubrics that connect back to the Four Basics, reinforcing the drafting, feedback, and revision loop.

- **The Four Basics and Four Building Blocks of Effective Sentences:** This approach breaks the writing process down into logical steps, focusing on the Four Basics of each rhetorical mode as well as four of the key topics in grammar (sentence fragments, sentence run-ons and comma splices, subject-verb agreement, and other verb problems). In Achieve, instructors can reinforce the Four Building Blocks with LearningCurve, adaptive game-like quizzing that helps students focus on the material they need the most help with.

- **A Chapter on Critical Thinking, Reading, and Writing Processes:** Chapter 1 introduces the processes of thinking, reading, and writing critically, providing the tools students need to tackle challenging readings and to produce the thoughtful writing that will help them succeed in first-year composition, in all their other college classes, and on the job. Activities following each reading in the text ask students to read critically. Writing assignments ask students to apply what they've learned, so they can summarize without plagiarizing, use evidence to support main ideas, synthesize information with their own ideas, and evaluate their own writing and the writing of their classmates. In Achieve, instructors can assign LearningCurve activities on active, critical, and interpretive reading; reasoning and logical fallacies; and recognizing the key parts of the rhetorical situation (topic, purpose, audience) for extra practice.

- **Mode-Appropriate Grammar-in-Context Feature:** This feature, which appears in each of the Part 2 chapters, allows students to practice their grammar skills within the context of real-life applications and their own writing. When instructors use editing marks to provide feedback on writing assignments in Achieve, students are supported with resources that help them understand and improve their own writing.

Bedford/St. Martin's Puts You First

From day one, our goal has been simple: To provide inspiring resources that are grounded in best practices for teaching reading and writing. For more than 40 years, Bedford/St. Martin's has partnered with the field, listening to teachers, scholars, and students about the support writers need. No matter the moment or teaching context, we are committed to helping every writing instructor make the most of our resources—resources designed to engage every student.

How Can We Help You?

- Our editors can align our resources to your outcomes through correlation and transition guides for your syllabus. Just ask us.
- Our sales representatives specialize in helping you find the right materials to support your course goals.
- Our learning solutions and product specialists help you make the most of the digital resources you choose for your course.
- Our *Bits Blog* on the Bedford/St. Martin's English Community (**community.macmillan.com**) publishes fresh teaching ideas regularly. You'll also find easily downloadable professional resources and links to author webinars on our Community site.

Contact your Bedford/St. Martin's sales representative or visit **macmillanlearning .com** to learn more.

Digital and Print Options for Real Writing, *Ninth Edition*

Choose the format that works best for your course, and ask about our packaging options that offer savings for students.

Digital

- *Achieve with* Real Writing, *Ninth Edition.* Achieve puts student writing at the center of your course and keeps revision at the core, with a dedicated composition space that guides students through drafting, peer review, Source Check, reflection, and revision. Fully editable prebuilt assignments support the book's approach and an e-book is included. To order *Achieve with Real Writing (1 Term, printed access card)*, use ISBN 978-1-319-41388-0. For details, visit **macmillanlearning.com/college/us/achieve/english.**
- *Popular e-book formats.* For details about our e-book partners, visit **macmillanlearning.com/ebooks**.
- *Inclusive Access.* Enable every student to receive their course materials through your LMS on the first day of class. Macmillan Learning's Inclusive Access program is the easiest, most affordable way to ensure all students have access to quality educational resources. Find out more at **macmillanlearning.com/inclusiveaccess.**

Print

- *Paperback.* To order the paperback edition, use ISBN 978-1-319-24827-7. To order Achieve packaged with the paperback version, use ISBN 978-1-319-47216-0.
- *Loose-leaf edition.* This format does not have a traditional binding; its pages are loose and hole-punched to provide flexibility and a lower price to

students. To order the loose-leaf version, use ISBN 978-1-319-24828-4. To order Achieve packaged with the loose-leaf version, use ISBN 978-1-319-47218-4.

Your Course, Your Way

No two writing programs or classrooms are exactly alike. Our Curriculum Solutions team works with you to design custom options that provide the resources your students need. (Options below require enrollment minimums.)

- *ForeWords for English.* Customize any print resource to fit the focus of your course or program by choosing from a range of prepared topics, such as Sentence Guides for Academic Writers.

- *Mix and Match.* With our simplest solution, you can add up to 50 pages of curated content to your Bedford/St. Martin's text. Contact your sales representative for additional details.

Instructor Resources

You have a lot to do in your course. We want to make it easy for you to find the support you need—and to get it quickly.

Instructor's Annotated Edition of *Real Writing with Readings,* Ninth Edition (ISBN 978-1-319-40722-3), includes teaching tips and answers to all the practice activities in the text.

Instructor's Manual for Teaching with Real Writing with Readings, Ninth Edition, is available as a PDF that can be downloaded from **macmillanlearning .com** and is also available in Achieve. In addition to practical suggestions for teaching *Real Writing with Readings,* the Instructor's Manual includes a sample syllabus and a variety of class schedules, Lexile levels for all the readings in the text, tips for new instructors and for working with developmental writers and readers, and much more.

Achieve with *Real Writing,* Ninth Edition, makes for a comprehensive teaching package, making available the teaching tips and answers to all the practice activities (from the Instructor's Annotated Edition) as well as the Instructor's Manual all in one place (and visible only to instructors).

Part 1

How to Write Paragraphs and Essays

IGOR SOKOLOV/500PX/GETTY IMAGES

Critical Thinking, Reading, and Writing

Making Connections

Learning Outcomes   In this chapter, you will learn to

- List habits for success in college.
- Identify and practice parts of the critical thinking process.
- Define and apply steps in the critical reading process.
- Define and apply steps in the critical writing process.

If you are reading this chapter, you probably just started a college writing course, and you might not know what to expect. What will the teacher require? What will class be like? How do I get through this course — and all my courses — successfully?

Students come to college with different types of experiences and backgrounds. What may be common knowledge to you about how to be a successful student may be a new idea to another student. Before starting any course, it is important to recognize what your instructor expects and put yourself into a mind set that will help create a successful college experience for you.

In this chapter, you will learn about some common expectations that college writing instructors have of their students: being prepared, thinking critically, reading carefully and critically, and writing critically about **texts** (which can include readings and images) and problems. Some of these expectations may be familiar to you, and some may be new. It is important not only to be aware of these expectations, but also to know that you will not be alone as you work to achieve them. A writing class is, in fact, a writing community; in a writing class, you will collaborate with others to develop writing skills and meet your instructor's expectations. At times, you may find the experience of sharing your writing uncomfortable, but learning to work with others to brainstorm, draft, revise, and edit papers will help you become a stronger writer. By understanding your role in this community and the ways it can support you as a writer and student, you will be better equipped for success in this and other courses.

Preparing for Success

All students can benefit from thinking carefully about the strategies that will help them become successful in class. During the first week of class, your instructor should provide a syllabus or other document listing expectations and policies. Not all policies and expectations will be the same because every instructor and every course is different, but most share the basic expectations outlined in this chapter. You should be aware of these policies and expectations as you start this course because your instructor will expect you to understand and adhere to them throughout the semester.

> **PRACTICE 1-1**   **Learn More about Your Own Preparedness**
>
> Take the Student Preparedness Quiz. How many of these strategies for success do you already employ? Why have you chosen to use them? If you haven't used one of them, why not? Would you be willing to try? Why or why not?
>
> After assessing your preparedness, discuss your responses with one or two other students. What strategies do they use? What do their choices tell you about the way different people learn and participate in a class?

Student Preparedness Quiz: Are you ready for success in college?

Do You . . .	Always	Sometimes	Never
Treat your coursework as seriously as you would a job? Think of your coursework as a job that can lead to bigger and better things.	❑	❑	❑
Commit to the time required for the course? In a face-to-face class, arrive on time and stay the full class session. For online classes, log in regularly and schedule enough time to complete all your assigned tasks with care.	❑	❑	❑
Prepare for class? This includes doing homework and completing reading assignments. In college, some instructors will not accept late homework, and you cannot participate in discussions if you have not read assigned material.	❑	❑	❑

Do You . . .	Always	Sometimes	Never
Connect to others in class? In face-to-face classes, exchange contact information with a classmate so you can study together or get assignments if you must miss class. In your online class, check your learning management system (or LMS) for assignments, and ask your instructor about creating online study groups.	❏	❏	❏
Communicate often with your instructor? Alert your instructor if you must miss classes or activities, or if you are confused about a grade, a reading, a lecture, or a class discussion. Visit your instructor during office hours or make an appointment.	❏	❏	❏
Read and keep the syllabus? The syllabus includes the instructor's policies on attendance, grading, and late work. It may also include important due dates.	❏	❏	❏
Participate in class? Ask and answer questions regularly. Do not be afraid of making a silly comment or giving the wrong answer in class or in an online discussion. That is part of the learning process.	❏	❏	❏
Listen and take notes? Listen carefully to your instructor, but do not try to write down every word. Instead, watch the instructor. Important points are often signaled with a hand gesture, a note on the board, or a change in the instructor's tone of voice.	❏	❏	❏
Reduce distractions? Keep focused by sitting near the front of the class, turning off social media, and closing extra windows.	❏	❏	❏
Schedule your time wisely? Don't wait until the last minute to begin work on an assignment. Instead, chunk assignments and set aside time every week to work on each part.	❏	❏	❏

Students who are prepared also set long-term and short-term goals and connect coursework to their future plans. Goals give you a reason to attend class and a tangible aim to work toward. You may already know what degree you want to pursue in college and what type of job you want in the future. To achieve these long-term goals, set shorter-term goals — steps that help you get where you want to go.

PRACTICE 1-2   Looking Ahead to Degree Goals

Whether or not you have decided what you want to major in, you should still think about which majors interest you and what the graduation requirements are. The course requirements for each major will appear on your college website, but it will be better still to sit down with your academic adviser to plan a course sequence.

If you are like most students, you are juggling a lot of important priorities, and having a plan to reach your goals will help you achieve them. Write a paragraph about your academic or degree goals using these questions as a guide:

- What do you think you might major in?
- What courses will you need for that major?
- What courses will you take next?
- What kinds of reading and writing assignments will be required for these courses?
- Why is this class important for your degree?

As you write, think about how this writing class connects to your degree plans.

PRACTICE 1-3   Looking Ahead to Career Goals

You may or may not know what your career goals are at this point. Answering the following questions in a few sentences can help jump-start your thinking. As you write, think about how this writing course connects to your plans:

- What field might you like to work in after completing your college coursework?
- What kinds of additional degrees or certifications might you need to obtain to work in that field?
- In this field, how is writing used? (Reports? Memos? Charts?)
- In this field, how is reading used? (Computer records? Articles? Guidebooks?)
- Why is this course important for your career?

Thinking Critically

College instructors expect students to think critically about course concepts and assignments. But what is critical thinking?

Imagine you are the supervisor of a small, family-owned business. Recently, one of the owners hired a new employee whom you are asked to train during your shift. The new employee shows up 15 minutes late in a wrinkled and stained uniform, didn't call in advance about a problem with the start time, and doesn't seem in any hurry to find you or anyone else to check in with. What assumptions have you made about the kind of employee this person will be? Why do you think that?

Thinking critically means that you do not stop with your first impressions and assumptions. Critical thinking requires you to recognize the iceberg principle. Only about 10 percent of an iceberg is visible above the surface of the ocean; the remaining 90 percent is hidden from view. But that 90 percent has a tremendous impact on what is going on above the surface. Similarly, you may not be fully aware of what is motivating your reactions in a situation. When you think critically, you pause to explore what is hidden below the surface of what you read or see, along with your reactions to it. Such pauses help you keep an open mind, see new perspectives, find alternatives, and make better decisions.

The Critical Thinking Process

Be alert to assumptions made by you and others.

Question those assumptions.

Consider and **connect** various points of view, even those different from your own.

Keep an open mind; avoid rushing to conclusions.

Assumptions — ideas or opinions that we do not question and that we automatically accept as true — can get in the way of critical thinking. Here are some assumptions you might make about the new employee:

Lateness shows the new employee is careless.

The messy uniform shows the new employee is sloppy.

Not contacting anyone about being late shows the new employee is unreliable.

Not immediately apologizing for being tardy shows the new employee will cause problems at work.

In college, work, and everyday life, we often hold assumptions that we are not even aware of. By identifying these assumptions, stating them, and questioning them, we are more likely to see reality and act more effectively.

In the case of the new employee, perhaps the person did not know the correct start time for the shift. Or perhaps the employee was in a minor car accident on the way to work, a fender-bender that led to both the uniform and cell phone being drenched in coffee? In that case, the employee could not have called ahead and would need a few minutes after arrival to clean up and get ready for work. There could be several possible causes for the employee's tardiness and appearance, and our initial assumptions could be incorrect.

When questioning assumptions, it can help to try to get a bit of distance from them. Imagine what people with entirely different points of view might say. You might even try disagreeing with your own assumptions. Take a look at the following examples.

Questioning Assumptions

Situation	Assumption	Questions
College: I saw from the syllabus that I need to write five essays for this course.	This course may be too difficult for me.	What have other students done to pass? What obstacles might be getting in my way and how might I work around them?
Work: Two of my coworkers just got raises.	My own raise is just around the corner.	Did my coworkers accomplish anything I did not? When were their last raises, and when was mine?
Everyday Life: My friend has been acting strangely toward me lately.	I must have done something wrong.	Is it possible my friend's behavior has nothing to do with me? What else might be going on in my friend's life?

You need to be aware not only of your own assumptions but also of assumptions in what you read, see, and hear. For example, bottled-water labels and advertising might suggest directly or indirectly that bottled water is better than tap water. Think carefully about the evidence provided to support this assumption. What other sources of information could be consulted to either support, disprove, or call into question this assumption? However confidently a claim is made, never assume it is 100 percent correct and cannot be questioned.

PRACTICE 1-4   **Thinking Critically**

What assumptions are behind each of the images below? Write down as many as you can identify. Then write down questions about these assumptions, considering different points of view.

COURTESY OF BETH CASTRODALE

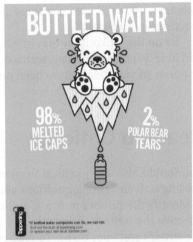

DI MASSIMO GOLDSTEIN/DIGO BRANDS

COURTESY OF BETH CASTRODALE

COURTESY OF BETH CASTRODALE

In addition to assumptions, be aware of **biases**, one-sided and sometimes prejudiced views that prevent you or others from seeing multiple perspectives. Here is just one example:

> As a manager, I don't hire people over fifty; after all, no one older than fifty can pick up new skills quickly.

Others could contradict this extreme statement with experiences or additional information to show that reality is more nuanced or complicated than this statement allows. Biases like these prevent the manager from seeing other perspectives and possibilities.

Be on the lookout for bias in your own views and in whatever you read, see, and hear. When a statement seems one-sided or extreme, ask yourself what facts or points of view might have been omitted.

Reading Critically

You should also apply critical thinking to reading. **Critical reading** begins with reading actively (asking questions and taking notes) and paying careful attention to identify the author's purpose, audience, main idea, and support. Consider how effective the writer's support is and look out for assumptions and biases (both the writer's and your own). To read critically, you must also reflect and consider how your experiences confirm, contradict, expand, or complicate what the writer says. The critical reading process is outlined in the box below.

The Critical Reading Process

Preview the text, skimming to identify the context and the topic.

Read the text actively, looking for and annotating the main idea and support.

Pause to **question** and **interpret** the text, taking notes as you read.

Review the text using reading strategies and your notes, and **respond** to it.

Preview the Text

The first step in the critical reading process is **previewing**. The roots of this word can help you understand what it means: you look ("view") before ("pre") to get a general sense of the **rhetorical context**, what a reading is about (the topic), who it is written for (audience), and why it was written (purpose). You may also be able to determine the main ideas and key supporting details as you skim through a text quickly. When you preview, you also make connections with the topic and determine why you are reading the text (to get information needed for an assignment, make a choice about a political candidate, or just pass time while waiting for an appointment, for example).

To preview a reading, skim through it quickly, paying attention to the following elements:

- **Source:** The source or location of publication (online magazine, newspaper, Facebook, class handout) can help you identify the writer's purpose.

- **Author:** Information about the author can help you evaluate the purpose and accuracy of the information.

- **Title:** The title or subject line can help you determine the topic and main idea.

- **Headings:** Subtitles, headings, or captions often reveal the major supporting details.

- **Marginal notes:** Definitions or comments in the margins (sidebars) often highlight key terms or major supporting details.

- **Visuals:** Charts, graphics, or photos illustrate the main idea by giving specific details.

- **Bold words:** Words or phrases in bold often show the ideas that the writer wants to emphasize.

- **Summaries:** A short summary, also called a *headnote* or *abstract* (a type of summary found in many scholarly publications), may appear at the beginning of a reading and indicate the topic, main idea, and major supporting points.

Once you have identified the rhetorical context of the text, consider your own reasons for reading: Why are you reading the piece? What do you already know about the topic? What else do you need to know? Choose a guiding question — a question you think the reading might answer — to help you stay focused as you read.

Read the Text: Find the Main Idea and Support

If you have previewed a reading, you have already begun to read actively. Active readers recognize that looking at words or images on a page or screen is not the same as reading those words or images. As the name suggests, active readers act: They ask questions (using their minds, their voices, or their hands as they write or type), and they write to read better — they annotate a reading by making notes and adding words or images that will help them make sense of what they are reading. After previewing a reading, active readers read the text carefully and attentively to identify the main point and supporting details.

Main Idea and Purpose

The **main idea** of a text is the central idea the author wants to communicate. The main idea is related to the writer's **purpose**, which can be to explain, demonstrate, persuade, or entertain. Writers often introduce their main idea early, so read the first few paragraphs with special care. Use these hints to help you identify the writer's main idea:

- Don't confuse the topic and the main idea. The main idea tells you what the writer says about the topic. To make sure you have identified the main idea and not just the topic, complete this sentence:

The writer is saying that _____.

- The main point is often the answer to the guiding question you created when previewing the reading.

- A reading has only one main point. Make sure you identify the main idea of the entire reading, not a supporting detail. (Don't focus on only one or two paragraphs; look at the entire text.)

- The main point (or thesis) may be stated or implied. When the main point is stated directly, you can highlight or double-underline it. If the main idea is only implied (not stated directly), write the main point in your own words, either in the margins of the text or your notebook.

> ### PRACTICE 1–5   Finding the Main Idea
>
> Read each of the following paragraphs. Then write the main idea in your own words.
>
> 1. Making a plan for your college studies is a good way to reach your academic goals. The first step to planning is answering this question: "What do I want to be?" If you have only a general idea—for example, "I would like to work in the health-care field"—break this large area into smaller, more specific subfields. These subfields might include working as a registered nurse, a nurse practitioner, or a physical therapist. The second step to planning is to meet with an academic adviser to talk about the classes you will need to take to get a degree or certificate in your chosen field. Then map out the courses you will be taking over the next couple of semesters. Throughout the process, bear in mind the words of student mentor Ed Powell: "Those who fail to plan, plan to fail." A good plan boosts your chances of success in college and beyond.
>
> 2. Networking is a way businesspeople build connections with others to get ahead. Building connections in college also is well worth the effort. One way to build connections is to get to know some of your class-mates and to exchange names, phone numbers, and email addresses with them. That way, if you cannot make it to a class, you will know someone who can tell you what you missed. You can also form study groups with these other students. Another way to build connections is to get to know your instructor. Make an appointment to visit your instructor during office hours. When you go, ask questions about material you are not sure you understood in class or problems you have with other course material. You and your instructor will get the most out of these sessions if you bring examples of specific assignments with which you are having trouble.

Support

Support is the details that show, explain, or prove the main idea. Authors might use statistics, facts, definitions, examples, and scientific results for support. Or they might use memories, stories, comparisons, quotations from experts, and personal observations. As you read, annotate by underlining major supporting details.

> **PRACTICE 1-6**   **Identifying Support**
>
> Go back to Practice 1-5 and underline the support for the main ideas of each passage in the practice.

Not all support that an author offers in a piece of writing is effective. When you are reading, ask yourself what information the author is including to help you understand or accept the main idea. Is the support (evidence) valid and convincing? If not, why not?

Pause to Question and Interpret

Critical readers also take time to pause and think during the reading process. If you race through a reading without stopping to consider what you are reading, you may not fully understand the author's point, mistaking a minor detail for the main idea or misunderstanding the author's purpose. If you read too quickly, you may accept or reject the writer's position too quickly, without understanding or evaluating the reasons behind that position. Pause regularly to question and interpret what you read, and, if needed, reread a sentence or paragraph.

Make Notes to Summarize, Capture Your Reactions, and Ask Questions

When you pause, ask yourself, "What is the writer saying here?" and make a note of your answer.

- Use quick marks to indicate your reactions to ideas in the text:
  - I agree. (✓)
  - I disagree. (✗)
  - I don't understand. (?)
  - I need to remember this. (!)
- Note any examples of an author's assumptions or biases.
- Jot down any additional notes or questions.
- Ask: Why did the writer include this information? Why is it important?

Paraphrase

If you are struggling with any particular sentence in the text, try **paraphrasing** it. Paraphrasing is a reading strategy that explains a key sentence by rephrasing it in a way that you can understand, using your own words. If you have read carefully and critically, you should be able to explain the writer's meaning for yourself and for others. Here are three tips to help you effectively paraphrase key points from your reading:

Tip 1: Do not copy the main idea or major supporting details when you take notes. Doing so may lead to plagiarism, using other's words or ideas without acknowledgment (see Chapter 4).

Tip 2: Focus on explaining the writer's point. Think about what the writer says for each point and imagine you are explaining that point to one of your friends. Here is one way to begin your paraphrase: "In other words, the writer is saying that . . ."

Tip 3: Avoid faulty paraphrases. There are two kinds of faulty paraphrases:

- Paraphrases that copy the writer's point and change just one or two words. This is sometimes called *patchwriting*, because it patches pieces of the original together with just a few new words.
- Paraphrases that substitute synonyms for key words from the original.

Both types of faulty paraphrase cause problems for readers and writers, so let's look at an example of each one.

Below is an original sentence from Amanda Jacobowitz's essay "A Ban on Water Bottles: A Way to Bolster the University's Image" (p. 16) followed by a patched-together paraphrase, a synonym-substitution paraphrase, and an appropriate paraphrase.

Original

"However, I can't help but wonder if the university's ban on the sale of water bottles is more about appearance and less about decreasing the environmental impact of our student body."

Patched-together paraphrase, with parts from the original highlighted

Amanda says she has to wonder if the university's ban on selling water bottles shows more concern about appearance and less interest in decreasing the environmental impact that the student body makes.

Synonym-substitution paraphrase, with synonyms highlighted

> She has to question whether the school's prohibition on the sale of water bottles is more about image and less about reducing the environmental effects of our student population.

In both cases, do you see how close the sentence structure and language are to the original? These faulty paraphrases would not be acceptable in written work. Consider instead the following:

Appropriate paraphrase

> In her essay "A Ban on Water Bottles: A Way to Bolster the University's Image," Amanda Jacobowitz questions the motivation behind her university's decision to stop selling water bottles on campus; she thinks the school might actually want to boost its image as an environmentally friendly campus, not get students to change habits that harm the environment.

While some of the individual words are the same in this paraphrase, the student taking these notes has not borrowed Amanda Jacobowitz's structure or longer strings of words.

Review and Respond

After reading, take a few minutes to look back and review. First, make sure you can identify the main point and major supporting details of the piece. If you have paraphrased key points from the reading, review those paraphrases and discuss them with others in your class.

Once you have identified the writer's main point, go over your guiding question, your notes, and your other questions, and make connections with what you have read. Ask yourself, "What interested me? What did I learn? How does it fit with what I know from other sources? How does it fit with my own experiences?" When you have reviewed your reading in this way and fixed it well in your mind and memory, it is much easier to respond in class discussion and writing assignments.

A Critical Reader at Work

Read the following piece to see how one student applied the process of critical reading to an essay on bottled water. The student previewed the reading to identify a guiding question, read to find the main idea and supporting details, and paused after each paragraph to think and make notes.

Amanda Jacobowitz

A Ban on Water Bottles: A Way to Bolster the University's Image

Amanda Jacobowitz is a student at Washington University and a columnist for the university's publication *Student Life*. The following essay appeared in the Forum section of *Student Life*, which publishes editorials, letters, and opinions.

Preview: Essay is probably an opinion piece; topic is banning water bottles.

Guiding question: What does the author think about the ban on bottled water?

Par. 1: Larger main idea (not stated directly): (1) the ban is ineffective, and (2) there are better ways to protect the environment.

Par. 2: Why not just drink from a water fountain? You don't have to have a bottle.

Par. 3: Examples of other common forms of waste

Par. 4: Examples of other ways to protect the environment

Lately, I am always thirsty. Always! I could not figure out why until I realized that the bottled water I had purchased continuously throughout my day had disappeared. At first I was just confused. Where did all the water bottles go? Then I learned the simple explanation: The University banned water bottles in an effort to seem environmentally friendly.

2   Ideally, given the ban on selling water bottles, every student on campus should now take the initiative to carry a water bottle, filling it up throughout the day at the water fountains on campus. Realistically, we know this has not [happened] and will not happen. As a somewhat environmentally conscious person, I have tried to bring a water bottle with me to classes, but have rarely succeeded in this effort. Instead, although I have never been too much of a soda drinker, I find myself reaching for a bottle of Coke out of pure convenience. We can't buy bottled water, but we can buy soda, juice, and other drinks, many of which come in plastic bottles. I am sure that for most people — particularly those who give very little thought to being environmentally conscientious — convenience prevails and they purchase a drink other than water. Wonderful result. The university can pride itself on being more environmentally friendly, with the fallback that its students will be less healthy!

3   Even if students are not buying unhealthy drinks, any benefit from the reduction of plastic water bottles could easily be offset by its alternatives. Students are not using their hands to drink water during meals. They are using plastic cups — cups provided by the university at every eatery on campus. Presumably no person picks up a cup, drinks their glass of water, and then saves that same cup for later in the day. That being said, how many plastic cups are used by a single student in a single day? How many cups are used by the total campus-wide population daily, yearly? This plastic-cup use must equate to an exorbitant amount of waste as well.

4   My intent is not to have the university completely roll back the water-bottle ban, nor is my intent for the university to level the playing field by banning all plastic-drink bottles. I'm simply questioning the reasons for specifically banning bottled water of all things. Why not start with soda bottles — decreasing

the environmental impact, as well as the health risks? There are also many other ways to help the environment that seem to be so easily overlooked.

5   Have you ever noticed a patch of grass on campus that's not perfectly green? I can't say that I have. The reason: the sprinklers. Now, I admit that I harbor some animosity when it comes to the campus sprinklers; I somehow always manage to mistakenly and inadvertently walk right in their path, the spray of water generously dousing my feet. However, my real problem with the sprinklers is the waste of water they represent. Do we really need our grass to be green at all times?

Par. 5: Another example: eliminate water waste.

6   The landscaping around our beloved Danforth University Center (Gold LEED Certified) is irrigated with the use of rainwater. There is a 50,000-gallon rainwater tank below the building to collect rain! I admit, this is pretty impressive, but what about the rest of the campus? What water is used to irrigate and keep green the rest of our 169 acres on the Danforth campus?

Par. 6: Town/city water, I assume? What's her point here?

7   I understand that being environmentally conscious is difficult to do, particularly at an institutional level. I applaud the Danforth University Center and other environmental efforts the university has initiated. However, I can't help but wonder if the university's ban on the sale of water bottles is more about appearance and less about decreasing the environmental impact of our student body. The water-bottle ban has become a way to build the school's public image: We banned water bottles; we are working hard to be environmentally friendly! In reality, given the switch to plastic cups and the switch to other drinks sold in plastic bottles, is the environmental impact of the ban that significant? Now that the ban has been implemented, I certainly don't see the university retracting it. However, I hope that in the future the university focuses less on its public image and more on the environment itself when instituting such dramatic changes.

Par. 7: Is it really about public image? What would a university administrator say?

> **PRACTICE 1-7**   **Responding**
>
> Look back at the images on page 9. Then review the reading by Amanda Jacobowitz. What assumptions does she make about bottled water? What evidence, if any, is provided to support these assumptions? On the basis of your own observations, would you like to see bottled water banned or not banned at your college? Why or why not?

Writing Critically about Readings, Visuals, and Problems

In college, instructors will ask you to use your critical thinking and reading skills to complete different kinds of writing assignments. In Chapters 2 through 6, you will learn about the process of writing paragraphs and essays. In Chapters 7 through 15, you will explore different techniques for developing an essay, such as narration and illustration. Regardless of the techniques you use, you must apply critical thinking to write about readings, images, or problems.

Write Critically about Readings

College professors ask you to write critically about readings to show your understanding of course content. When you write critically about readings, you summarize, analyze, synthesize, and evaluate, and, in doing so, you answer questions like those in the box below.

The Critical Writing Process

Summarize

- What is important about the text?
- What is its purpose; what is the big picture?
- What are the main ideas and key support?

Analyze

- What elements have been used to convey the main idea?
- Do any elements raise questions? Do any key points seem missing or undeveloped?

Synthesize

- What do other sources say about the text's topic?
- How does your own (or others') experience affect how you see the topic?
- What new point(s) might you make by bringing together all the different sources and experiences?

Evaluate

- Based on your application of summary, analysis, and synthesis, what do you think about the material you have read?
- Is the work successful? Does it achieve its purpose?
- Does the author show any biases? If so, do they make the piece more effective or less effective?

Summary

A **summary** is a condensed, or shortened, version of something — often, a longer piece of writing, a movie or television show, a situation, or an event. A summary paragraph presents the main idea, support, and organizational pattern of a longer piece of writing, stripping the information down to its essential elements. A summary is a logical final step in the reading process: It expresses what you have learned about the important features of a text in your own words.

A summary has these features:

- A topic sentence that names the title and author of the selection and states its main idea

- Major supporting details
- References to the author with descriptive verbs that describe what the writer says in the text (See the list of verbs below.)
- The author's final observations or recommendations
- New language that does not borrow extensively from the original text (See the discussion of paraphrase on p. 14.)

Verbs Introducing What the Writer Says

argue	ask	assert	claim
demand	deny	explain	imply
point out	suggest		

Caroline Bunker Rosdahl and Mary T. Kowalski

Excerpt from *Textbook of Basic Nursing*

This excerpt comes from a chapter that discusses some of the stresses that families can face, including divorce.

Adults who are facing separation from their partners — and a return to single life — may feel overwhelmed. They may become preoccupied with their own feelings, thereby limiting their ability to handle the situation effectively or to be strong for their children. The breakdown of the family system may require a restructuring of responsibilities, employment, childcare, and housing arrangements. Animosity between adults may expose children to uncontrolled emotions, arguments, anger, and depression.

2   Children may feel guilt and anxiety over their parents' divorce, believing the situation to be their fault. They may be unable to channel their conflicting emotions effectively. Their school performance may suffer, or they may engage in misbehavior. Even when a divorce is handled amicably, children may experience conflicts about their loyalties and may have difficulties making the transition from one household to another during visitation periods.

3   Experts estimate that approximately 50 percent of all children whose parents divorce will experience another major life change within three years: remarriage. The arrival of a stepparent in the home presents additional stressors for children. Adapting to new rules of behavior, adjusting to a new person's habits, and sharing parents with new family members can cause resentment and anger. When families blend children, rivalries and competition for parental attention can lead to repeated conflicts.

Below is a summary of the textbook excerpt. The main idea is double-underlined, and the supporting points are underlined. The verbs the writer has used to introduce the main idea and support are circled.

> Although divorce seriously affects the people who are splitting up, Rosdahl and Kowalski point out that the couple's children face equally difficult consequences, both immediately and in the longer term. In the short term, according to the authors, children may blame themselves for the split or feel that their loyalty to both parents is divided. The authors further assert that these negative emotions can affect children's behavior at school and elsewhere. Later on, if one or both of the parents remarry, the children may have trouble adjusting to the new family structure.

Analysis

An **analysis** breaks down the points or parts of something and considers how they work together to make an impression or convey a main idea. When writing an analysis, use verbs like those below that show what the writer does or what strategies the writer uses.

Verbs Introducing Writing Strategies

analyze	classify	compare	contrast	define
describe	emphasize	evaluate	express	identify
illustrate	list	narrate	present	

You might also consider points or parts that seem to be missing or that raise questions in your mind.

Here is an analysis of the excerpt from the *Textbook of Basic Nursing*. The main idea is double-underlined, and the supporting points are underlined. The verbs that show what Rosdahl and Kowalski are doing are circled. Note also how the writer raises questions about the textbook excerpt in the second paragraph.

> We all know that divorce is difficult for the people who are splitting up, but Rosdahl and Kowalski address the effects of divorce experienced by children of divorce, both right after the split and later on. The authors identify several possible results of divorce on children, including emotional and behavioral difficulties and trouble in school. They also list the stresses that remarriage can create for children.
>
> The authors rightly emphasize the negative effects that divorce can have on children. However, I found myself wondering what a divorcing couple could do to help their children through the process. Also, how might parents and stepparents help children adjust to a remarriage? I would like to examine these questions in a future paper.

Synthesis

A **synthesis** pulls together information from multiple sources or experiences to make a new point. Below is a synthesis of the textbook material on divorce. Because the writer wanted to address some of the questions she raised in her analysis, she incorporated additional details from published sources and from people she interviewed. These sources are highlighted. Her synthesis of this information helped her arrive at a fresh conclusion in paragraph 5. Note that the writer has included a list of her sources, her **Works Cited**, following paragraph 5. (For more about creating a list of works cited, see the appendix "Citing Research Sources in MLA Style" at the end of the text.)

In the *Textbook of Basic Nursing*, Rosdahl and Kowalski focus on the problems faced by children of divorce, both right after the split and later on. According to the authors, immediate problems can include emotional and behavioral difficulties and trouble in school. Later on, parents' remarriage can create additional stresses for children (92). Although the authors discuss the impact of divorce on all parties, they do not suggest ways in which parents or stepparents might help children through the process of divorce or remarriage. However, other sources, as well as original research on friends who have experienced divorce as children or adults, provide some additional insights into these questions. 1

A website produced by the staff at the Mayo Clinic recommends that parents come together to break the news about their divorce to their children. The website also suggests that parents keep the discussion brief and free of "ugly details." In addition, parents should emphasize that the children are in no way to blame for the divorce and that they are deeply loved. As the divorce proceeds, neither parent should speak negatively about the other parent in the child's presence or otherwise try to turn the child against the ex-spouse. Finally, the site recommends counseling for parents or their children if any problems around the divorce persist. 2

Sharon Leigh and colleagues from the University of Missouri Extension also address the problems that can arise for children after their parents remarry. Specifically, their article describes several things that stepparents can do to make their stepchildren feel more comfortable with them and the new family situation. One strategy is to try to establish a friendship with the children before assuming the role of a parent. Later, once stepparents have assumed a more parental role, they should make sure they and their spouse stand by the same household rules and means of discipline. With time, say the authors, the stepparents might also add new traditions for holidays and other family gatherings to help build new family bonds while respecting the old ones. 3

4   To these sources, I added interviews with three friends—two who are children of divorce and one who is both a divorced parent and a stepparent. The children of divorce said that they experienced many of the same difficulties and stresses that Rosdahl and Kowalski described. Interestingly, though, they also reported that they felt guilty, even though their parents told them not to, following the advice given by the Mayo Clinic. As my friend Kris said, "For a long time after the divorce, every time my dad and I were together, he seemed distracted, like he wished I wasn't there. I felt bad that I couldn't just vanish." Dale, the stepparent I interviewed, liked the strategies suggested by Leigh, Jackson, and Clark, and he had actually tried some of these approaches with his own stepchildren. However, as Dale told me, "When you're as busy as most parents and kids are these days, you can let important things fall by the wayside—even time together. That's not good for anyone."

5   Thinking back on Kris's and Dale's words and everything I've learned from the other sources, I have come to conclude that divorced parents and stepparents need to make sure they build "together time" with their own children and/or stepchildren into every day. Even if this time is just a discussion over a meal or a quick bedtime story, children will remember it and appreciate it. This approach would help with some of the relationship building that Leigh, Jackson, and Clark recommend. It would also improve communication, help children understand that they are truly loved by *all* their parents, and assist with the process of post-divorce healing.

Works Cited

Leigh, Sharon, et al. "Foundations for a Successful Stepfamily." Updated by Kim Leon, *MOspace,* Apr. 2007, www.mospace.umsystem.edu /xmlui/bitstream/handle/10355/51356/gh6700-2007.pdf?sequence= 1&isAllowed=y.

Mayo Clinic Staff. "Children and Divorce: Helping Kids after a Breakup." *Mayo Clinic,* 14 May 2011, www.mayoclinic.org/healthy-lifestyle/ childrens-health/in-depth/divorce/art-20047788.

Rosdahl, Caroline Bunker, and Mary T. Kowalski. *Textbook of Basic Nursing*. 9th ed., Lippincott Williams & Wilkins, 2008.

Evaluation

An **evaluation** is the result of critical thinking: a thoughtful judgment about something based on what you have discovered through your summary, analysis, and synthesis. To evaluate something effectively, apply the questions from the

Critical Reading Process (p. 10) and the Critical Writing Process (p. 18) boxes. You will want to refer to these questions as you work through later chapters of this book and through readings from other college courses.

Here is an evaluation of the excerpt from the *Textbook of Basic Nursing*:

> In just a few paragraphs, Rosdahl and Kowalski give a good description of the effects of divorce, not only on the former spouses but also on their children. The details that the authors provide help to clearly communicate the difficulties that such children face. In the short term, these difficulties can include emotional and behavioral problems and trouble in school. In the longer term, if one or both of a child's parents remarry, the child faces the stress of dealing with a new and different family. Although the authors do not specifically address ways that parents and stepparents can ease children into divorce and/or new families, other sources—such as the websites of the University of Missouri Extension and the Mayo Clinic, as well as people I interviewed—do get into these issues. In the end, I think that Rosdahl and Kowalski present a good overview of their subject in a short piece of writing that was part of a larger discussion on family stresses.

PRACTICE 1-8   **Writing Critically about "A Ban on Water Bottles"**

As you work through this exercise, refer to the Critical Writing Process box on page 18.

1. **Summary:** Summarize "A Ban on Water Bottles," Amanda Jacobowitz's essay on pages 16–17.

2. **Analysis:** Whether you agree or disagree with Jacobowitz, write a paragraph analyzing the points she presents.

3. **Synthesis:** Read additional opinion pieces or blog postings about banning bottled water. In one paragraph, state your position on the subject based on your reading. Also explain the range of opinions on the subject.

4. **Evaluation:** Write a paragraph that evaluates Jacobowitz's essay.

Write Critically about Visuals

Images play a huge role in our lives, and it is important to think critically about them just as you would about what you read or hear. Whether the image is a photograph, illustration, a graphic, or an advertisement, you need to be able to "read" it. You can apply the same critical reading skills of summary, analysis, synthesis, and evaluation to read a visual.

Look carefully at the images of water bottles on page 9. Then consider how to read a visual using the critical thinking skills you have learned.

Summary

To summarize a visual, ask yourself what the big picture is. What is going on in the image? What is the main impression or message (the main idea)? What is the purpose? How is this purpose achieved (the support)? To answer these questions, consider the dominant elements, figures, and objects used in visuals.

Dominant Elements   Artists, illustrators, and advertisers may place the most important object in the center of an image. Or they may design visuals using a **Z pattern**, with the most important object in the top left and the second most important object in the bottom right. In English and many other languages, people read printed material from left to right and from top to bottom, and the Z pattern takes advantage of that pattern. Because of these design strategies, the main idea of a visual can often be determined by looking at the center of the image or at the top left or bottom right.

Figures and Objects   The person who creates an image has a purpose (main idea) and uses visual details to achieve (or support) that purpose. In a photograph, illustration, or painting, details about the figures and objects help create the impression the artist wants to convey. (Here, the term *figures* refers to people, animals, or other forms that can show action or emotion.) When studying any image, ask yourself the following questions:

- Are the figures from a certain period in history?
- What kind of clothes are they wearing?
- What are the expressions on their faces? How would I describe their attitudes?
- Are the figures shown realistically, or are they shown as sketches or cartoons?
- What important details about the figures does the creator of the image want me to focus on?

PRACTICE 1–9   **Summarizing a Visual**

Focus on the public service announcement from the Nebraska Safety Council on the next page and answer the following questions:

1. What is the big picture? What is going on?

2. What is at the center of the ad?

3. What is the ad's purpose?

4. What are the most important details in the piece?

COURTESY OF THE NATIONAL SAFETY COUNCIL, NEBRASKA

PUT DOWN THE PHONE AND NO ONE GETS HURT.

Analysis

To analyze a visual, focus on its parts (figures, objects, any text included), and ask yourself how they contribute to the message or main impression. Consider the background; the use of light and dark; and the colors, contrasts, textures, and sizes. Think also about how the designer of the image made choices to target a specific audience.

PRACTICE 1–10   Analyzing a Visual

Focus on the public service announcement from the Nebraska Safety Council (above) and answer the following questions:

1. What elements are placed in large type? Why?

2. How do all the features in the ad contribute to the main impression?

3. Which features seem to be chosen to appeal to a specific audience?

Synthesis

To synthesize your impressions of a visual, ask yourself what the message seems to be, using your summary and analysis skills. Consider how this message relates to what else you know from experience and observation.

> **PRACTICE 1–11**   **Synthesizing Your Impressions of a Visual**
>
> Focus on the public service announcement from the Nebraska Safety Council on page 25 and answer the following questions:
>
> 1. What is the ad's central message?
>
> 2. How does this message relate to what you already know or have heard or experienced?
>
> 3. How might this message be presented for other audiences?

Evaluation

To evaluate an image, ask yourself how effective it is in achieving its purpose and conveying its main idea or message. What do you think of the image, using your summary, analysis, and synthesis skills? Consider any biases or assumptions reflected in the image.

> **PRACTICE 1–12**   **Evaluating a Visual**
>
> Focus on the public service announcement from the Nebraska Safety Council on page 25 and answer the following questions:
>
> 1. What do you think about the ad, especially its visual elements?
>
> 2. Does the creator of the ad seem to have any biases? Why or why not?
>
> 3. Is the ad effective, given its purpose and the main idea it is trying to convey? Why or why not?

Write Critically about Problems

In college, at work, and in everyday life, we often need to "read" situations to make important decisions about them. This process, known as *problem solving*, can also involve summarizing, analyzing, synthesizing, and evaluating. Let's look at the key steps in the process.

1. Summarize the problem.

    Try to describe it in a brief statement or question.

> **Example:** My ten-year-old car needs a new transmission, which will cost at least $1,000. Should I keep the car or buy a new one?

2. Analyze the problem.

Consider possible ways to solve it, examining any questions or assumptions you might have.

> **Example:**
>
> *Assumption:* I need to have a reliable car.
>
> *Question:* Is this assumption truly justified?
>
> *Answer:* Yes. I can't get to school or work without a reliable car. I live more than 15 miles from each location, and there is no regular public transportation to either place from my home.
>
> **Possible Solutions:**
> - Pay for the transmission repair.
> - Buy a new car.

3. Synthesize information about the problem.

Consult various information sources to get opinions about the possible solutions.

> **Examples:**
> - My mechanic
> - Friends who have had similar car problems
> - Car advice from print or web sources
> - My past experience with car repairs and expenses

4. Evaluate the possible solutions and make a decision.

You might consider the advantages and disadvantages of each possible solution. Also, when you make your decision, you should be able to give reasons for your choice.

> **Examples (considering only advantages and disadvantages):**
> - Pay for the transmission repair.
>
>   *Advantage:* This option would be cheaper than buying a new car.
>
>   *Disadvantage:* The car might not last much longer, even with the new transmission.
>
> - Buy a new car.
>
>   *Advantage:* I will have a reliable car.
>
>   *Disadvantage:* This option is much more expensive than paying for the repair.

Final Decision: Pay for the transmission repair.

Reasons: I do not have money for a new car, and I do not want to take on more debt. Also, two mechanics told me that my car should run for three to five more years with the new transmission. At that point, I will be in a better position to buy a new car.

> **PRACTICE 1-13**   **Solving a Problem**

Think of a problem you are facing now — in college, at work, or in your everyday life. On a separate sheet of paper, summarize the problem. Next, referring to the previous steps, write down and analyze possible solutions, considering different sources of information. Then write down your final decision or preferred solution, giving reasons for your choice.

Chapter 1 Review

1. What is the critical thinking process?

2. What are the four parts of the critical reading process?

3. What are the four major steps of writing critically about readings and visuals?

4. Without looking back in the chapter, define the task of synthesizing in your own words.

Reflect and Apply

1. Can you think of a time when you or someone you know did not read a document or visual critically? What happened?

2. Talk to someone who has taken courses in your major or who is working in your field. What documents or visuals will you need to be able to read for your major or your career?

3. Did the information in this chapter confirm, contradict, or complicate your expectations for college writing courses? Explain.

Writing Basics

Audience, Purpose, Form, and Process

In this chapter, you will learn to

- Explain how audience, purpose, tone, and form influence writing.
- Identify similarities and differences between paragraphs and essays.
- Explain steps in the writing process.
- Use a rubric to evaluate writing.

Writing — whether in college or in the workplace — varies in form and style. Regardless of the situation, four elements shape effective writing. Keep them in mind whenever you write.

Four Basics of Effective Writing

1 Effective writing is appropriate for the situation, including audience, purpose, form, and tone.

2 It results from a thoughtful process that includes prewriting, drafting, revising, editing, and proofreading.

3 It makes a clear, definite point.

4 It provides organized support that shows, explains, or proves the main idea.

This chapter addresses the first basic of effective writing in detail and provides an overview of the writing process (the second basic). This chapter also shows you how grading tools called **rubrics** can help you focus as you work through the writing process.

Chapters 3–6 explain the steps of the writing process in detail:

- Chapter 3 focuses on finding and clarifying the main point (the third basic).
- Chapter 4 shows how to find and organize strong support (the fourth basic).
- Chapter 5 demonstrates how to write a complete draft.
- Chapter 6 completes the writing process by showing you how to revise.

Understanding Audience, Purpose, Genre, and Tone

Your **audience** is the person or people who will read what you write. Whenever you write, always have at least one real person in mind as a reader. Think about what that person already knows and needs to know to understand your main idea. In college, your audience is usually your instructor, but your instructor may ask you to write for a different audience, perhaps someone who is not familiar with your class and your assignments. Be careful to provide background information (also called *context*) that your reader will need to understand what you write.

The **purpose** of a piece of writing is the reason for writing it. Understanding your purpose for writing is the key to writing successfully, particularly as writing tasks become more complex. In college, your instructor typically will want you to demonstrate that you understand the content of the course, so your purpose for writing often will be to explain something by describing or analyzing it or to make a convincing case. To understand the purpose of a particular assignment, be sure to read instructions and exam questions critically, highlighting words that tell you what your instructor wants to see in your writing. In Part 2 (Chapters 7–15), you will learn more about words that instructors use in different kinds of writing assignments.

Understanding your audience and your purpose helps you to select the most appropriate genre and tone for your writing. **Genres** (or common writing types) used by college writers include essays, lab reports, texts, emails, and résumés. **Tone** is the attitude (*friendly, confident, irritated*) conveyed by the words you use; readers can hear your attitude in the tone of your writing. **Level**, or *register,* is how formal or informal your writing is.

The form, tone, level, and content of your writing will vary depending on your audience and purpose: A paper for a course or an assignment at work tends to be objective and formal, whereas a message to a friend or classmate might sound friendly or snarky and informal. Read the following three notes, which describe the same situation but are written for different audiences and purposes.

Situation: Marta woke up one morning feeling strange, and her face was swollen and red. She immediately called her doctor's office and made an appointment. Marta's mother was coming in a few minutes to stay with Marta's children, so Marta asked a neighbor to watch the children until her mother got there. Marta then texted her mother explaining why she had already left. When she got to the doctor's office, she was feeling better, and, since the doctor was running late, she decided not to wait. The nurse asked her to write a brief description of her symptoms for the doctor to read later. Before leaving the doctor's office, however, Marta also wanted to make sure that her instructor knew why she would be late to class, so she also sent her professor a quick email.

Marta's text to her mother: Not feeling well, going 2 Dr. I'm OK. Don't worry. TY for watching the kids.

Marta's note to her doctor: When I woke up this morning, my face was swollen, especially around the eyes, which were almost shut. My lips and skin were red and dry, and my face was itchy. However, the swelling seemed to go down quickly.

Marta's email to her professor:

Dr. Smith,

I woke up feeling ill this morning and made an appointment with my doctor. I thought I might need to miss class, but I am now feeling better and will manage to make it to class. I am leaving the doctor's office right now and should be at school very shortly. I apologize for any inconvenience this may cause.

Sincerely,

Marta

PRACTICE 2–1   **Comparing Marta's Notes**

Read Marta's three notes and discuss the following questions:

1. How does Marta's note to her mother differ from the one to her doctor? How does the one to her doctor differ from the one to her instructor?

2. How do the different audiences and purposes affect what the notes say (the content) and how they say it (the tone and level)?

3. Which note has the most detail and why?

As these examples show, we communicate with family members and friends differently than we communicate with people in authority (like doctors, instructors, or other professionals) — or we should. Marta's text to her mother is extremely informal; it not only uses incomplete sentences but also abbreviations because the two women know each other well and are used to speaking casually to each other. Because Marta's purpose is to get quick information to her mother and to reassure her, she does not need to provide a lot of details. In contrast, Marta's note to her doctor uses more formal language because the relationship is more formal. Also, the note to the doctor is more detailed because the doctor will be making treatment decisions based on it. Finally, the email to the instructor is the most formal because Marta wants to maintain a professional relationship with her instructor.

> **PRACTICE 2-2** **Writing for a Formal Audience**
>
> A student, Terri Travers, texted a friend to complain about being removed from a criminal justice course due to a hold on her account. Rewrite the email as if you were Terri and you were writing to Professor Widener. The purpose is to ask whether the professor would reconsider allowing you into the class given that you signed up early, have the necessary grades, and took care of the hold as soon as you could.
>
> I cant believe that they took me out of widener's cj class 😔.
> You and luis said he is the best and i need this class lol.
> Gonna email him now.

Understanding Paragraph and Essay Form

In college, professors often assign paragraphs and essays as homework assignments, course projects, or exams. Each of them has a basic structure.

Paragraph Form

A **paragraph** is made up of the topic sentence, the body sentences, and the concluding sentence.

Paragraph Part	Purpose of the Paragraph Part
1 The **topic sentence**	States the **main idea**; often the first sentence of the paragraph
2 The **body sentences**	Support (show, explain, or prove) the main idea with **supporting sentences** and **details** (facts, stories, examples, descriptions, comparisons, definitions, and so on)
3 The **concluding sentence**	Reminds readers of the main idea and often makes an observation

Read the paragraph that follows with the paragraph parts labeled.

1 Following a few basic strategies can help you take better notes, an important skill for succeeding in any course. **2** First, start the notes for each class session on a fresh page of your course notebook, and record the date at the top of the page. Next, to improve the speed of your note taking, abbreviate certain words, especially ones your instructor uses regularly. For example, abbreviations for a business course might include *fncl* for financial, *svc* for service, and *mgt* for management. Finally, don't try to write down every word instructors say. Instead, look for ways to boil down extended explanations into short phrases. For instance, if a business instructor says, "A profit-and-loss statement is a report of an organization's revenue and expenses over a specific financial period; often, P-and-Ls are used to determine ways to boost revenue or cut costs, with the goal of increasing profitability," you might write down something like, "P&L: rpt of revenue + expenses over a specific period. Used to boost rev or cut costs." Although you do not need to record every word of every lecture, listen for clues that indicate when a point is important enough to write down. Instructors might raise their voices or use signal phrases such as "It's important to remember" or "Bear in mind." Instructors may also repeat important points more than once. **3** By carefully listening to and writing down key points in class, you are not just getting notes to study later; you are also beginning to seal this information into your memory.

1 Topic sentence
2 Body sentences

3 Concluding sentence

Essay Form

An **essay** is a piece of writing that examines a topic in more depth than a paragraph. A short essay may have four or five paragraphs. A long essay may have many pages, depending on what the essay needs to accomplish, such as persuading someone to do something, using research to make a point, or explaining a complex concept. An essay includes an introduction, the body paragraphs, and the conclusion.

Essay Part	Purpose of the Essay Part
1 The **introduction**	Draws readers in and states the main idea (**thesis**) generally in a single, strong statement; may be a single paragraph or multiple paragraphs
2 The **body paragraphs**	Support (show, explain, or prove) the essay's main idea (thesis) with three or more **supporting paragraphs**; for each body paragraph, include a **topic sentence** (which states the paragraph's main idea and supports the thesis) and **supporting details**, such as facts, stories, examples, descriptions, comparisons, definitions, or other types of evidence (which support the paragraph's main idea)
3 The **conclusion**	Reminds readers of the main idea and draws the essay to a satisfying close; often summarizes and reinforces the support

Read the essay that follows with the essay parts labeled.

1 Introduction with **thesis**

1 You know all the emotions that come with taking tests: nervous anticipation before the exam starts, an adrenaline rush as the time allotted ticks down, and waves of relief when the test is finished. The process repeats days or weeks later, when professors announce that exams have been graded. Your anxiety rises as the instructor calls each name or walks from desk to desk, returning each paper. You may sweat a little as you ask yourself, "How did I do this time?" A strong score makes you elated, but a low grade may leave you frustrated, angry, or defeated. You can build your test-taking confidence — and reduce test-taking anxiety — by adjusting your study strategies, both in and out of class, before the next scheduled exam.

2 Body paragraphs

2 First, take a careful look at how you are taking notes in class. Begin by making sure you can see and hear well; if you cannot see the screen or hear the instructor clearly, change seats. Also consider your level of distraction. If you find it difficult to stay focused on what the instructor is saying, identify your distractors and try to reduce them: Move away from chatty classmates, put the phone away, or take notes by hand instead of on the laptop. Also, don't try to write down every word that the instructor says or copy every note written on the slides. If the instructor is willing to share lecture notes or slides, print these before class and use them to take notes. If not, listen for the professor's clues about what is most important: "This is critical," "You need to know," or "Keep in mind." If the instructor refers to a course website or a textbook, make a note of pages or links to review later.

2 Second, be strategic and proactive with your notes after you leave class. Within a day of the class session, go back and review your notes while the material is still fresh in your mind. Rewrite the notes, if needed, or clarify the notes to explain abbreviations and incomplete sentences that you may have jotted down during class. If you do not look at the notes for several days, you may not understand what you wrote when it is time to study for a test. Annotate your notes as well, making notes of questions, key points, important definitions, and concepts that are not clear. Be ready to ask questions in the next class, if possible, or to drop by the instructor's office during office hours to clarify your notes. Some students find that typing the notes and adding headings in bold helps them organize the course material and makes studying easier. Finally, use your notes to review assigned readings: The notes will help you know how to focus your attention while rereading, and you can add examples and details from the reading to help you support the key points you identified from class.

3 Whether you are in class or at home, the key to studying effectively is having a strategic plan: Take notes, organize them, review them regularly, and ask questions. If you practice good note taking and review your notes every two or three days, you will not need to cram for a test the night before. Instead, you can spend one or two hours making a final review of the notes, taking breaks every 30 minutes, and eating well. You can also get a good night's sleep instead of relying on caffeine for an all-night study binge. You may still encounter a few nerves on the day of the test, but you won't panic. You will be prepared — and confident.

3 Conclusion

Understanding the Writing Process

The diagram that follows shows the four stages of the **writing process**. These are all the steps you need to follow to write well. The rest of the chapters in Part 1 cover every stage except editing (presented in Parts 3 and 4). You will practice each stage, see how another student completed the process, and write your own paragraph or essay.

The Writing Process

When you prewrite, you will generate ideas for your writing (Chapter 3), considering your audience and your purpose (pp. 30–32), and use these ideas to identify support for your main point (Chapter 4). In drafting, you will arrange your main ideas and support to make an outline (Chapter 5) and write a complete draft of your paper (Chapter 5). Once you have a draft, you will read it critically and get feedback from others so that you can **revise** to make your draft clearer and more convincing for your readers (Chapter 6). Finally, you will edit carefully to make sure sentences are complete and accurate (Chapters 16–20); words are precise and appropriate (Chapters 21–23); sentences and paragraphs connect smoothly (Chapter 6, 24); spelling, punctuation, and capitalization are accurate (Chapters 25–28). As the arrows in the chart suggest, you won't always go in a straight line through the four stages; for example, you may need to circle back to generate ideas if you find that you need more supporting evidence as you draft or revise.

Understanding Grading Criteria

When you complete the writing process and submit a paper, your instructor may use a rubric, a list of the elements on which a paper will be graded. Some professors use one rubric for several assignments, whereas others may use assignment-specific rubrics. If your instructor provides a rubric, review it before you begin writing. Use the rubric to set draft goals (targets for the first or second version of your paper) and to determine when you are ready to submit the paragraph or essay for a final grade. The following sample rubric shows you some of the elements you may be graded on:

	1–Falls Below Expectations	2–Nearly Meets Expectations	3–Meets Expectations	4–Exceeds Expectations
Main Idea	Main idea is vague or missing.	Main idea needs focus or clarification.	Main idea is clear and focused.	Main idea is worded effectively and provides a clear focus for the writing.
Support	Support is missing, inaccurate, or disconnected from the main idea.	Support is underdeveloped or weakly connected to the main idea.	Support is clearly related to the main idea and includes details or examples.	Support is logical, detailed, and developed enough to make the point clear to the reader.
Organization	There is no clear pattern of organization.	There is a pattern of organization, but the paper is choppy—it does not move smoothly from one idea to the next.	The paper is logically organized, with clear transitions from one part to the next.	The paper is logically organized, with transitions and variations in sentence structure to move the reader smoothly from one idea to the next.
Language Use	Significant problems in sentence structure or word choice make the paper difficult to read throughout.	Some problems with clarity in sentence structure or word choice make text difficult to read in places.	Sentence structure is clear but simple; word choice is accurate but tone may need attention.	Sentence structure is varied and clear; word choice is specific and appropriate to the context.
Grammar and Mechanics	The paper has not been edited for appropriate and accurate language choices.	The paper shows some evidence of editing, but major problems with grammar or mechanics make the paper hard to understand.	The paper is carefully edited with only minor problems in grammar or mechanics.	The paper is carefully edited, with very few problems in grammar or mechanics.

To use a rubric when you are writing, first consider the assignment. You will not focus on everything in the rubric as you start. Instead, use the first two or three rows of the rubric to set goals for your first draft. (For more on first-draft goals, see Chapter 5.)

For example, Marissa, whose paragraph appears below was given the following assignment:

> Write a paragraph about something you enjoy doing. Your paragraph should have a topic sentence and enough details about the activity so that a reader who knows little about it will have an idea of why you enjoy it. Edit your paragraph carefully before you submit it.

She set the following goals for her first draft:

- A clear topic sentence
- Enough support to make the main idea clear for readers

Read her first-draft paragraph, and then decide how to evaluate it using the rows in the rubric for Main Idea and Support.

Paragraph

> In my spare time, I enjoy talking with my friend Karen. I know Karen since we ten, so we have growed up together and been through many things. Like a sister. We can talk about anything. Sometimes we talk about problems. Money problems, problems with men. When I was in a difficult relationship, for example. We both have children and we talk about how to raise them. Things are different then when we kids. Talking with a good friend helps me make good decisions and patience. Especially now that my son is a teenager. We talk about fun things, like what were going to do on the weekend, what clothes we buy. We tell each other good jokes and make each other laugh. These conversations are as important as talking about problems.

PRACTICE 2–3   Using a Rubric

Use the rubric on page 36 to determine a score (1–4) for Main Idea and Support: Did Marissa achieve her goals for the first draft? If not, what could she do to improve the next draft?

Now look at the remaining sections of the rubric (Organization, Language Use, and Grammar and Mechanics). Based on the first draft of the paragraph, how can Marissa improve her organization, language use, and grammar/mechanics? Write two to three sentences that explain your assessment and advice to Marissa.

In Chapters 3, 4, and 5, you will learn more about the first three rows of the rubric and how to set draft goals based on them. The chapters in Part 2 (Chapters 7–15) show how the rubric criteria of Main Idea, Support, and Organization apply to specific writing strategies so that you can practice setting draft goals and writing different kinds of papers. The chapters in Parts 3 and 4 (Chapters 16–28) will show you how to improve your editing skills and set editing goals related to grammar and mechanics. At the end of the book is a list of correction symbols that your instructors are likely to use when marking grammar and language problems that need to be edited.

Chapter 2 Review

1. In your own words, define *audience, purpose, genre,* and *tone.*

2. What are the three parts of a paragraph? Of an essay?

3. What are the stages of the writing process?

4. What are four of the grading criteria often evaluated in rubrics?

Reflect and Apply

1. Think about writing you have done for work or other courses. What genres did you write (a lab report, inventory report, or self-evaluation, for example)? What was the purpose of each piece? How did the form, purpose, and audience affect the tone and level of formality of your language?

2. In Chapter 1, you learned that reading is a process, and in this chapter, you learned that writing is a process. How are those processes similar? How is reading involved in the writing process?

3. Have your instructors ever given you a rubric for writing assignments? Did the rubric help you understand how to complete the assignment effectively? Explain.

Finding Your Topic and Drafting Your Thesis Statement

Making a Point

Learning Outcomes In this chapter, you will learn to

- List the features of a good topic.
- Practice three strategies for narrowing a topic.
- Identify and practice prewriting techniques.
- List features of an appropriate topic sentence or thesis statement.
- Draft a topic sentence or thesis statement.

Good writing makes a clear, definite point. As you begin the writing process, you will find and narrow a topic so that you can develop your point.

Understanding What a Topic Is

A **topic** is who or what you are writing about. It is the subject of your paragraph or essay. In many classes, you will be writing about readings or about subjects that your instructor assigns. Sometimes, however, you may be allowed to choose your own topic. A good topic for an essay is one that

- Interests you and your readers
- Is narrow enough to be developed in the space allowed
- Fulfills the requirements of the assignment

To select a good topic, you need to ask questions about your assignment and your own interests:

- How long should the assignment be?
- How formal is the assignment?

- Is the topic specified, or am I allowed to choose it? Is there a list of suggested or banned topics?
- Does the assignment specify a particular type of paper such as narrative, argument, or cause-and-effect?
- Does the assignment specify an audience for the paper?

Your answers will help you determine an appropriate topic.

Once you have analyzed your assignment, make a list of possible topics that might fulfill the assignment requirements. Review that list carefully, asking the questions that appear in the box below about each topic choice. You should have a good topic if you are able to answer "yes" to each question.

Questions for Finding a Good Topic

- Does the topic interest me? If so, how is it relevant to me?
- Do I know something about the topic? Do I want to know more?
- Is the topic specific enough for the assignment (a paragraph or a short essay)?
- Is the topic interesting for the audience specified in the assignment?

> **PRACTICE 3–1**   **Finding a Good Topic**
>
> Select one category from the following list (or a topic given by your instructor). Choose an example of that category that is relevant to you.
>
> | | |
> |---|---|
> | Local music groups | Sports |
> | Problems of working students | A personal goal |
> | Activities or hobbies | A time when I took a big risk |
> | My proudest moment | My ideal job |
> | An issue in the news | Social media influencers |
>
> Now, ask the "Questions for Finding a Good Topic" about the topic you have selected. If you answer "no" to any of them, keep looking for a topic or modify your topic. Share your topic choice with your instructor or class members.

With the general topic you have chosen in mind, read this chapter and complete all the Practice activities. When you finish the chapter, you will have an appropriate topic and a preliminary topic sentence or thesis statement, as well as some ideas for your next steps.

Narrowing a Topic

If your instructor assigns a broad topic, it may at first seem uninteresting, unfamiliar, or too general. It is up to you to find a good, specific topic based on the general one. Whether the topic is your own or assigned, you need to narrow and explore it. To **narrow** a general topic, focus on smaller parts of it until you find a specific topic that will interest you and your reader and that will also be appropriate to your assignment. Here are some ways to narrow a general topic.

Divide the General Topic into Smaller Categories

A general topic usually includes several smaller categories; for example, personal goals could include health goals, education goals, and financial goals. These smaller categories may help you identify a narrow topic for your paper.

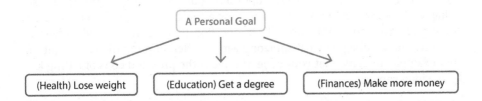

Think of Specific Examples from Your Life

To narrow your general topic, you might also brainstorm examples of the topic based on your own experiences.

General Topic	Crime
	The contractor who took money but didn't repair our roof
	When I had my wallet stolen by two kids
	The email scam that my grandmother lost money in
General Topic	Social Media
	Instagram accounts for my cats
	Managing all my accounts (from Instagram to TikTok)
	Copyright strikes on my YouTube channel

Think of Specific Examples from Current Events

Another option for narrowing a topic is to consider current events.

General Topic	**Political Activism**
	Running for a local office
	Registering new voters through outreach events
	How politicians use social media
General Topic	**Responding to Pandemics and Disasters**
	Risks faced by first responders
	What does FEMA do?
	How to set up a food drive

Question Your Assumptions

Questioning assumptions—an important part of critical thinking (see Chapter 1)—can be a good way to narrow a topic. First, identify any assumptions you have about your topic. Then question them, playing devil's advocate; in other words, imagine what someone with a different point of view might say. For example, imagine that your general topic is the pros and cons of letting kids play video games.

Possible Assumptions	Questions
Video game pros:	
Kids get rewarded with good scores for staying focused. ➔	Does staying focused on a video game mean that a kid will stay focused on homework or in class?
Video games can teach some useful skills. ➔	What types of skills does the game teach? How am I defining *useful*?
Video game cons:	
Video games make kids more violent. ➔	Is there really any proof for an increase in violence? What do experts say?
Video games have no real educational value. ➔	Didn't my niece say that some video game helped her learn to read?

Next, ask yourself what assumptions and questions interest you the most. Then focus on those interests.

When you have found a promising topic for a paragraph or essay, be sure to test it by using the "Questions for Finding a Good Topic" (p. 40). You may need to narrow and test your ideas several times before you find a topic that will work for the assignment.

A topic for an essay can be a little broader than one for a paragraph because essays are longer. But think carefully before expanding an essay topic too much: An essay should develop ideas in depth with examples and details, not introduce a broad topic without support.

Read the following examples of how a general topic was narrowed to a more specific topic for an essay and an even more specific topic for a paragraph.

General Topic		Narrowed Essay Topic		Narrowed Paragraph Topic
Internships	→	How internships can help you get a job	→	One or two important things you can learn from an internship
Social media	→	Popularity of social media among preteens	→	Should there be an age limit for social media use?
Getting healthy	→	Eating the right foods	→	Healthy snacking on a college-student budget
A great vacation	→	A family camping trip	→	What I learned on our family camping trip to Michigan

PRACTICE 3–2   **Narrowing a General Topic**

Use one of the four methods discussed above (pp. 41–43) for narrowing the topic you devised in Practice 3–1 (or another topic). Then ask yourself the "Questions for Finding a Good Topic" (p. 40). Share your narrowed topic with your instructor and members of your class.

Exploring Your Topic

Prewriting techniques, or **invention strategies,** can give you ideas at any time during your writing: to find a topic, to explore what you want to say about the topic, and to support what you decide to say about the topic. Ask yourself these questions: What interests me about this topic? What do I know? What do I want to say? Then use one or more of the prewriting techniques to find the answers. No one uses all these techniques; writers choose the ones that work best for them.

Prewriting Techniques

- Freewriting
- Listing/brainstorming
- Discussing
- Clustering/mapping
- Keeping a journal

When prewriting, your goal is to come up with as many ideas as possible. Do not say, "Oh, that's stupid" or "That won't work." Just get your brain working by writing down all the possibilities.

A student, Chelsea Wilson, was assigned to write a short essay. She chose to write on the general topic of a personal goal, which she narrowed to "Getting a college degree." The following pages show how she used prewriting techniques to explore her topic.

Freewriting

Freewriting is like having a conversation with yourself. To freewrite, write down everything you can think of about your topic without stopping for at least five minutes. Do not go back and cross anything out, and do not worry about using correct grammar or spelling; just write.

Chelsea Wilson's Freewriting

So I know I want to get a college degree even though sometimes I wonder if I ever can make it because it's so hard with work and my two-year-old daughter and no money and a car that needs work. I can't take more than two courses at a time and even then I hardly get a chance to sleep if I want to do any of the assignments or study. But I have to think I'll get a better job because this one at the restaurant is driving me nuts and doesn't pay much so I have to work a lot with a boss I can't stand and still wonder how I'm gonna pay the bills. I know life can be better if I can just manage to become a nurse. I'll make more money and can live anywhere I want because everyplace needs nurses. I won't have to work at a job where I am not respected by anyone. I want respect, I know I'm hardworking and smart and good with people and deserve better than this. So does my daughter. No one in my family has ever graduated from college even though my sister took two courses, but then she stopped. I know I can do this, I just have to make a commitment to do it and not look away.

After freewriting, Chelsea read her freewriting, and she noticed two themes: Her current job is not meeting her financial or family needs, and college is a path to a better life and more respect.

Listing/Brainstorming

Listing, or **brainstorming**, is when you *list* all the ideas about your topic that you can think of. Write as many as you can in five minutes without stopping.

Chelsea Wilson's Listing/Brainstorming

GETTING A COLLEGE DEGREE

want a better life for myself and my daughter

want to be a nurse and help care for people

make more money

not have to work so many hours

could live where I want in a nicer place

good future and benefits like health insurance

get respect

proud of myself, achieve, show everyone

be a professional, work in a clean place

Discussing

Many people find it helpful to discuss ideas with another person before they write. As they talk, they get more ideas and immediate feedback. After you review your freewriting and brainstorming, consider finding a partner so that you can talk about your ideas.

If you and your discussion partner both have writing assignments, first explore one person's topic and then the other's. When your partner is talking, listen carefully and ask questions if you want more details or clarification. Try to identify and question any assumptions your partner seems to be making (pp. 42–43). Then change roles. When your partner is asking questions or identifying your assumptions, listen with an open mind, and take notes.

Clustering/Mapping

Clustering, also called **mapping**, is like listing except that you arrange your ideas visually. Start by writing your narrowed topic in the center. Then answer the following questions around the narrowed topic:

- Why?
- What interests me?
- What do I want to say?

Using Chelsea's clustering, which follows, as a model, write three answers to these questions. Keep branching out from the ideas until you feel you have fully explored your topic. Note that when Chelsea filled in "Why?" "What interests me?" and "What do I want to say?" she had lots of reasons and ideas that she could use in her writing assignment.

Keeping a Journal

Setting aside a few minutes on a regular schedule to write in a journal will give you a great source of ideas when you need them. What you write does not need to be long or formal. You can use a journal in several ways:

- To record and explore your personal thoughts and feelings
- To comment on things that happen, to you personally or in politics, in your neighborhood, at work, in college, and so on
- To explore situations you do not understand (As you write, you may figure them out.)
- To keep track of your opinions on movies, television shows, music, or books

Writer Joan Didion described her journaling this way: "I write entirely to find out what I'm thinking, what I'm looking at, what I see, and what it means. What I want and what I fear."

Chelsea did all these things in the following journal entry:

Another day of overtime, stress, and not enough time with Emma. I didn't finish the math assignment from last week, and I know I've got to get this done. I am wondering if I should just wait on school for a while, maybe until Emma's a little older. But will I have more time then? I am afraid if I quit now, I will never come back again. And Emma and me will be stuck in the same place with the same hours and no money. I'm afraid she won't respect me and she will want to leave as soon as she can. Why wouldn't she wanna leave? I do! I want out of this mess . . . and the degree is the only way. I won't let her down. I'm gonna snuggle with Emma now and set my clock 30 minutes early for tomorrow. I will finish that math, and maybe see about the on-campus tutoring.

PRACTICE 3-3   **Exploring Your Narrowed Topic**

Use two or three prewriting techniques to explore the narrowed topic you identified in Practice 3-2.

Understanding What a Main Idea Is: Topic Sentence and Thesis Statement

Once you have narrowed your topic and generated ideas from your prewriting, review your topic choice carefully by asking yourself these questions:

- Does the topic I've narrowed interest me and my potential readers?
- Is it specific?
- Can I write about it in a paragraph or essay (whichever has been assigned)?
- Have I generated things to say about the topic?

When Chelsea Wilson reviewed her topic choices and ideas, she could answer "yes" to each question, and she felt confident she was ready to move to the next step in writing a paper: narrowing her topic and pulling together the ideas from her prewriting.

Chelsea Wilson's Narrowed Topic (Paragraph and Essay)

General topic: *a personal goal*

Narrowed topic (for a paragraph): *why I want to get a nursing degree*

Narrowed topic (for an essay): *the many benefits of getting a college degree*

Chelsea Wilson's Summary of Ideas from Her Prewriting

Ideas for a paragraph: *why I want to get a nursing degree*

make more money

get a better job

become a respected professional

live where I want

Ideas for an essay: *the many benefits of getting a college degree*

get a job as a nurse

make more money

be a good role model for my daughter

be proud of myself

If you are confident in your narrowed topic and the ideas you have generated, you are ready to draft the main idea of your paper. Every good piece of writing has a **main idea** — what the writer wants to get across to the readers about the topic or the writer's position on that topic. A **topic sentence** (for a paragraph) and a **thesis statement** (for an essay) express the writer's main idea. Because the topic sentence or thesis statement controls a paragraph or essay, it should have some basic features as shown below.

Basics of a Good Topic Sentence or Thesis Statement

- It is specific enough to develop within the assigned length (paragraph or essay).
- It contains a single main idea.
- It is an idea you can show, explain, or prove.
- It fits the context, audience, and purpose.

One strategy for writing an effective topic sentence or thesis with these basic characteristics is to use the following template:

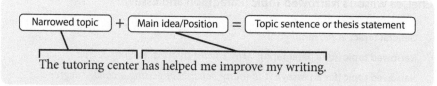

The tutoring center has helped me improve my writing.

The **main idea/position** is what you want to say about the narrow topic, and it is sometimes called the *controlling idea*.

If you have trouble coming up with a main idea or position, look back over the prewriting you did. For example, when Chelsea Wilson looked over her prewriting about getting a college degree (see pp. 41–47), she realized that several times she had mentioned the idea of more options for employment, living places, and chances to go on to be a nurse. She could also have chosen to focus on the topic of respect or on issues relating to her young daughter, but she was most drawn to write about the idea of *options*. Here is how she stated her main idea.

Chelsea Wilson's Main Idea

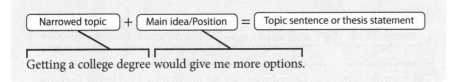

Narrowed topic + Main idea/Position = Topic sentence or thesis statement

Getting a college degree would give me more options.

PRACTICE 3–4   Finding the Topic Sentence and Main Idea

Read the paragraph that follows, and highlight the topic sentence. Practice annotation (see Chapter 1) by identifying the narrowed topic and the main idea.

> A recent survey reported that employers consider communication skills more critical to success than technical skills. Employees can learn technical skills on the job and practice them every day. But they need to bring well-developed communication skills to the job. They need to be able to make themselves understood to colleagues, both in speech and in writing. They need to be able to work cooperatively as part of a team. Employers cannot take time to teach communication skills, but without them an employee will have a hard time.

PRACTICE 3–5   Identifying Topics and Main Ideas

In each of the following sentences, highlight the topic and underline (or highlight in a different color) the main idea about the topic.

Example: Rosie the Riveter was the symbol of working women during World War II.

1. Discrimination in the workplace is alive and well.
2. The oldest child in the family is often the most independent and ambitious child.

3. Gadgets created for left-handed people are sometimes poorly designed.

4. Presidential campaigns bring out dirty politics.

5. Walking away from a mortgage has become a financial survival strategy for some homeowners.

As you get further along in your writing, you may go back several times to revise the topic sentence or thesis statement based on what you learn as you develop your ideas. Look at how one student revised the example sentence on page 48 to make it more detailed:

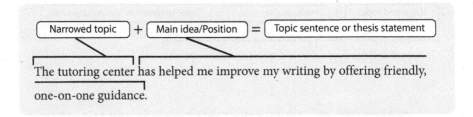

Chelsea Wilson's Revised Main Idea

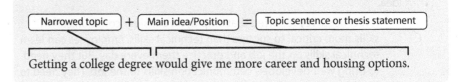

Developing a Good Topic Sentence or Thesis Statement

The explanations, examples, and exercises in this section will help you understand the basic features of a topic sentence or thesis statement and practice writing them effectively.

It Is Specific Enough to Develop within the Assigned Length

As you develop a topic sentence or thesis statement, think carefully about the length of the assignment. You must be able to address your main idea within the length of the paragraph or essay assigned.

Sometimes, a main-idea statement can be the same for a paragraph or essay. Often, however, a topic sentence for a paragraph is much narrower than a thesis statement for an essay, simply because a paragraph is shorter and allows less development of ideas. (See the chart on p. 43 for examples of related paragraph and essay topics.) In Chelsea's case, she decided that reasons for getting a nursing degree would be enough to cover in one paragraph.

Chelsea Wilson's Topic Sentence

My goal is to become a nurse.

For an essay, however, Chelsea knew she could cover more of the benefits and options that a college degree would offer, so she chose a broader thesis.

Chelsea Wilson's Thesis Statement

Getting a college degree will give me more career and housing options.

PRACTICE 3–6   **Writing Sentences to Fit the Assignment**

Using the following example as a guide, write a thesis statement for the narrowed essay topic and a topic sentence for the narrowed paragraph topic.

Example:

Topic: Sports

Narrowed for an essay: Competition in school sports

Narrowed for a paragraph: User fees for school sports

Possible thesis statement (essay): *Competition in school sports has reached dangerous levels.*

Possible topic sentence (paragraph): *This year's user fees for participation in school sports are too high.*

1. **Topic:** Public service opportunities
   Narrowed for an essay: Volunteering at a homeless shelter
   Narrowed for a paragraph: My first impression of the homeless shelter
   Possible thesis statement (essay):
   Possible topic sentence (paragraph):

2. **Topic:** A personal goal
   Narrowed for an essay: Getting healthy
   Narrowed for a paragraph: Eating the right foods
   Possible thesis statement (essay):
   Possible topic sentence (paragraph):

3. **Topic:** A great vacation

   Narrowed for an essay: A family camping trip

   Narrowed for a paragraph: A lesson I learned on a family camping trip

   Possible thesis statement (essay):

   Possible topic sentence (paragraph):

Some topic sentences or thesis statements are too broad for either a short essay or a paragraph. A main idea that is too broad is impossible to show, explain, or prove within the space of a paragraph or short essay. Chelsea Wilson, for example, knew that the importance of a college degree would be part of her main idea. But her first attempt was much too broad for the essay assignment. She could not possibly support such a broad concept in a paragraph or essay. She would have more success by narrowing her topic sentence or thesis statement down.

Too broad:	College is important to me.
Narrower:	Getting a college degree will give me more career and housing options.

PRACTICE 3-7   Focusing Topic Sentences That Are Too Broad

Three of the following topic sentences are too broad, and two of them are okay. In the space to the left of each item, write "B" for too broad or "OK" for just right. Rewrite the three weak sentences to make them more focused.

Example: B Life can be tough for soldiers when they come home.

We are not providing our returning soldiers with enough help in readjusting to civilian life.

1. ___ A review of the history of public transportation explains all of the problems cities currently face in providing transportation.

   Revision:

2. ___ Because of state budget cuts, county schools have cut services and programs that are critical for success of students with disabilities.

   Revision:

3. ___ Navigating college can be challenging in the twenty-first century.

   Revision:

4. ___ Like any other student my age, I would like to be successful.

   Revision:

5. ___ A positive attitude improves students' ability to function, their inter-actions with others, and their stress levels.

Revision:

One way to make sure your topic sentence or thesis statement is focused enough to fit the length of your assignment is to include a preview of what you are planning to say in the rest of the paragraph or essay. Just be certain that every point you preview is closely related to your main idea.

Preview: Working college students have to learn how to juggle many responsibilities: doing a good job at work, getting to class regularly and on time, being alert in class, and doing the homework assignments.

Preview: Getting a college degree will give me more job opportunities, allow me to find a safer place to live, and help me be a role model for my daughter.

It Is an Idea You Can Show, Explain, or Prove

The opposite of a main idea that is too broad for an assignment is a sentence that is too narrow. If a main idea is so obvious that it does not need support or if it states a simple fact, you will not have much to say about it.

Obvious:	The Toyota Prius is a top-selling car.
	Many people like to take vacations in the summer.
Revised:	Because of rising gas costs and concerns about the environmental impact of carbon emissions, the Toyota Prius is a top-selling car.
	The vast and incredible beauty of the Grand Canyon draws crowds of visitors each summer.
Fact:	Employment of medical lab technicians is projected to increase by 11 percent between 2018 and 2028.
	Three-hundred cities worldwide have bicycle-sharing programs.
Revised:	Population growth and the creation of new types of medical tests mean the employment of lab technicians should increase by 11 percent between 2018 and 2028.
	Bicycle-sharing programs are popular, but funding them long term can be challenging for cities with tight budgets.

Here is an example of a statement that is too specific for Chelsea's main idea; it would not give her anything else to show or prove:

Fact (too narrow):	A nursing degree requires at least two years of full-time study.
Broader:	The opportunities that a nursing degree will give me are worth the time it takes to get the degree.

Although facts and obvious statements do not work effectively as main ideas, that does not mean those statements are worthless. Don't discard them after you revise your main idea; you may be able to use these statements as you develop support for your main idea. You will learn more about support in Chapter 4.

> **PRACTICE 3–8**   **Writing Sentences with Ideas You Can Show, Explain, or Prove**
>
> Revise the following sentences so that they contain an idea you could show, explain, or prove.
>
> **Example:** Leasing a car is popular.
>
> Leasing a car can help save money: There are fewer costs to get the car, maintenance costs are less, and there is no interest to pay on a loan.
>
> 1. Texting while driving is dangerous.
>
> 2. My monthly rent is $1,200.
>
> 3. Health insurance rates rise every year.
>
> 4. Many people in this country work for minimum wage.
>
> 5. Technology is becoming increasingly important.

It Contains a Single Main Idea

Your topic sentence or thesis statement should focus on only one main idea. Two main ideas can weaken the focus of the writing.

Topic sentence with two main ideas: High schools should sell healthy food instead of junk food, and they should start later in the morning.

The two main ideas are underlined. Although both are good main ideas, together they split both the writer's and the reader's focus. The writer would need to give reasons to support each idea, and the ideas are completely different.

Topic sentence with a single main idea: High schools should sell healthy food instead of junk food.

OR

High schools should start later in the morning.

> **PRACTICE 3–9   Writing Sentences with a Single Main Idea**
>
> In each of the following sentences, underline the main idea(s). Put an **✗** next to sentences with two main ideas.
>
> **Example: Shopping at secondhand stores is a fun way to save money, and you can meet all kinds of interesting people as you shop. ✗**
>
> 1. My younger sister, the baby of the family, was the most adventurous of my four siblings.
>
> 2. Servicing hybrid cars is a growing part of automotive technology education, and dealers cannot keep enough hybrids in stock.
>
> 3. My brother, Bobby, is incredibly creative, and he takes in stray animals.
>
> 4. Pets can actually bring families together, and they require lots of care.
>
> 5. Unless people conserve voluntarily, we will deplete our water supply.

It Fits the Context, Audience, and Purpose

A topic sentence or thesis statement should also fit the context, audience, and purpose of the writing assignment. In some areas of study, called *disciplines*, writers are expected to state a thesis directly at the beginning of the essay:

Direct:	Everyone should exercise to reduce stress, maintain a healthy weight, and feel better overall.
Direct:	The number of justices on the Supreme Court should remain at nine, with no additions, to best preserve objectivity and continuity for future court decisions.

Writing in other disciplines, however, may expect writers to announce their purpose or main idea:

Announced:	In this paper, **I will review evidence** to support a low-fat diet, even in one's 20s or 30s.
Announced:	Because of recent court cases, **I argue that** the number of justices should be expanded to at least fifteen.

Writing for different disciplines may also vary in the location of thesis statements or topic sentences. Writers in some fields place a thesis at the end of the introduction, whereas others may put it in the body of the essay or at the end. Similarly, readers in some disciplines expect to see topic sentences at the beginning of every paragraph, but readers in other disciplines may expect subtitles to show sections of the essay. In such cases, topic sentences may be implied and not directly stated. Because of these differences in the expected form and location of a topic sentence or a thesis, it is important to read instructions carefully and study models provided by your instructor. If you are not sure what the expectations are, ask.

Writing Assignment: Write Your Own Topic Sentence or Thesis Statement

If you have worked through this chapter, you should have a good sense of the features that make for an effective topic sentence or thesis statement.

WRITING ASSIGNMENT

Write a topic sentence or thesis statement using the topic you chose in Practice 3-1 or one of the following topics:

Community service	A holiday or family tradition
A local problem	A strong belief
Dressing for success	Bullying
Movie franchises	Exciting experiences
Saving money	Juggling many responsibilities
Interviewing for jobs	Friendship
Music	Conservation/recycling on campus
Sexual harassment	Professional athletes

To develop your main idea, follow the process you have learned in this chapter:

1. Make sure you have a strong topic. Refer to "Questions for Finding a Good Topic" (p. 40).

2. Narrow the topic for the assignment. Use the strategies for narrowing topics on pages 41–43.

3. Explore the topic with prewriting techniques (pp. 43–47).

4. Draft a main idea statement (topic sentence or thesis statement), using the "Basics of a Good Topic Sentence or Thesis Statement" (p. 48).

After writing your topic sentence or thesis statement, complete the checklist that follows.

CHECKLIST

Evaluating Your Main Idea

Have I written a statement that

☐ includes my point and the main idea I want to make about it?

☐ is narrow and specific enough to address within the paragraph or essay assigned?

☐ is an idea I can show, explain, or prove?

☐ addresses a single main idea?

☐ fits the context, audience, and purpose of the assignment?

Coming up with a good working topic sentence or thesis statement is the foundation of the writing you will do. Now that you know what you want to say, you are ready to learn more about how to show, explain, and prove your main idea to others. The next chapter, Supporting Your Point, helps you make a strong case, consider what your readers need to know, and provide sufficient details and examples in your paragraph or essay.

Chapter 3 Review

1. What are four questions that can help you find a good topic?

2. How can you narrow a topic that is too broad or general?

3. What are some prewriting techniques for exploring your topic?

4. What are the basic features of a topic sentence or thesis statement?

Reflect and Apply

1. Think about writing you have done for work or other courses. How did you choose your topic?

2. Many students struggle with writer's block—getting stuck during the process of writing. You also may have experienced writer's block. How can the invention strategies listed in this chapter help you overcome writer's block?

3. Many students see writing as a solitary activity: one person composing alone. But as you have seen in this chapter, some prewriting techniques involve collaboration. What are the advantages of working with a partner early in the writing process?

4. Scholar and writer Mina Shaughnessy said that a writer "gets below the surface of a topic." When it comes to exploring a topic, what do you think getting "below the surface" means?

Supporting Your Point

Finding Details, Examples, and Facts

Learning Outcomes   In this chapter, you will learn to

- List the features of strong support.
- Practice three strategies for generating support.
- Develop secondary support.

In Chapter 3, you learned how to narrow a topic and develop a strong topic sentence (for a paragraph) or thesis statement (for an essay) that states your main idea clearly. If you stop there, however, your readers are unlikely to accept your main idea. You need to provide support.

Understanding What Support Is

Support is the collection of examples, facts, or other evidence that shows, explains, or proves your main idea. **Primary supporting points** are the major ideas that back up your main idea, and **secondary supporting points** give details to back up your primary support.

Key Features of Good Support

Without support, you *state* the main idea, but you do not *show*, *explain*, or *prove* the main idea. Consider these unsupported statements:

> The amount shown on my bill is incorrect.
>
> I deserve a raise.
>
> I need a vacation.

The statements may be true, but without good support, they are not convincing. If you sometimes get papers back with the comment "You need to support/develop your ideas," the suggestions in this chapter will help you. Keep in mind that the same point repeated several times is not support. It is just repetition. Support requires specific evidence such as facts, data, and examples.

Repetition, not support:	The amount shown on my bill is incorrect. You overcharged me. It didn't cost that much. The total is wrong.
Support:	The amount shown on my bill is incorrect. I ordered the bacon-cheeseburger plate, which is $6.99 on the menu. On the bill, the order is correct, but the amount is $16.99.

As you develop support for your main idea, make sure it has the three basics of good support.

Three Basics of Good Support

- The support relates directly to your main idea. (Remember that the purpose of support is to show, explain, or prove your main idea.)
- It is appropriate for your readers and tells them what they will need to know.
- It gives readers enough specific details so that they can see what you mean.

Support in Paragraphs versus Essays

Again, primary supporting points are the major reasons and ideas that back up your main idea. In both paragraphs and essays, it is important to add enough details (secondary support) about the primary support to make the main idea clear to readers. In the following paragraph, the topic sentence is underlined twice, the primary supporting points are underlined once, and the details for each supporting point are in italics.

When I first enrolled in college, I thought that studying history was a waste of time. <u>But after taking two world history classes, I have come to the conclusion that these courses count for far more than some credit hours in my college record.</u> <u>First, learning about historical events has helped me put important current events in perspective.</u> *For instance, by studying the history of migration around the world, I have learned that immigration has been going on for hundreds of years. In addition, it is common in many countries, not just the United States. I have also learned about ways in which various societies have debated immigration, just as Americans are doing today.* Second, history courses have taught me about the power that individual people can have, even under very challenging circumstances. *I was especially inspired by the story of Toussaint L'Ouverture, who, in the 1790s, led enslaved people to rise up in the French colony of Saint-Domingue, transforming it into the independent nation of Haiti. Although L'Ouverture faced difficult odds, he persisted and achieved great things.* The biggest benefit of taking history courses is that they have encouraged me to dig more deeply into subjects than I ever have before. *For a paper about the lasting influence of Anne Frank, I drew on quotations from her famous diary, on biographies about her, and on essays written by noted historians. The research was fascinating, and I loved piecing together the various facts and insights to come to my own conclusions.* To sum up, I have become hooked on history, and I have a feeling that the lessons it teaches me will be relevant far beyond college.

Anne Frank (1929–1945): A German Jewish girl who fled to the Netherlands with her family after Adolf Hitler, leader of the Nazi Party, became chancellor of Germany. In 1944, Anne and her family were arrested by the Nazis, and she died in a concentration camp the following year.

Did you notice that the primary supporting points are more specific than the topic sentence, and the secondary supporting points are more specific than the primary supporting points? The primary supporting points, for example, include general nouns, such as *events* or *people*, while the secondary support gives specific examples of each of these: immigration and Toussaint L'Ouverture. *Toussaint L'Ouverture* is a proper noun: It is a name written with a capital letter. Proper nouns are specific, and they may be used to illustrate general nouns.

In an essay, each primary supporting point, along with its supporting details, is developed into a separate paragraph. (See "Chelsea Wilson's Draft Paragraph," pp. 74–75 and "Chelsea Wilson's Draft Essay," p. 82, both in Chapter 5.) To develop the previous paragraph into an essay, each underlined point could be turned into a topic sentence that would be supported by the italicized details. The writer would want to add more details and examples for each primary supporting point. Here are some possible additions:

- **For primary supporting point 1:** More connections between history and current events (one idea: the rise and fall of dictators in past societies and in the modern Middle East)

- **For primary supporting point 2:** More examples of influential historical figures (one idea: the story of Joan of Arc, who, in the fifteenth century, led the French to victories over English armies)

- **For primary supporting point 3:** More examples of becoming deeply engaged in historical subjects (one idea: fascination with the work of the Tuskegee airmen in World War II)

Supporting a Main Idea and Avoiding Plagiarism

To generate support for the main idea of a paragraph or essay, try one or more of the following strategies.

Three Quick Strategies for Generating Support

1. **Circle an important word or phrase** in your topic sentence (for a paragraph) or thesis statement (for an essay) and freewrite (Chapter 3) about it for a few minutes. As you work, refer back to your main idea to make sure you're on the right track.

2. **Reread your topic sentence or thesis statement and brainstorm.** Write down the first thought you have. Then write down your next thought. Keep going.

3. **Use another prewriting technique** (discussing or clustering) while thinking about your main idea and your audience. Write for 3 to 5 minutes.

In Chapter 3, you saw how Chelsea Wilson developed a topic sentence. To generate support, Chelsea used brainstorming to create a list of possible supporting points.

Chelsea Wilson's Supporting Points (Draft)

Topic sentence: My goal is to become a nurse.

Primary supporting points:

nurses help people and I want to do that	role model
jobs all over the country	pride in myself and my work, what I've done
good jobs with decent pay	good benefits
good setting, clean	nice people to work with
a profession, not just a job	may get paid to take more classes—chance for further professional development
opportunity, like RN	uniform so not lots of money for clothes
bigger place, more money	I'll be something
treated with respect	

> **PRACTICE 4-1**   **Generating Supporting Ideas**
>
> Use one of the three quick strategies for generating support to come up with primary and secondary supporting evidence for one of the topics listed below (or your own topic sentence or thesis statement). Because you will need a good supply of reasons and evidence to support your main idea, try to generate at least a dozen possible ideas for primary supporting points and details. Keep your answers because you will use them in later practice activities in this chapter.
>
> 1. Some television shows challenge my way of thinking instead of numbing my mind.
> 2. Today there is no such thing as a "typical" college student.
> 3. Learning happens not only in school but throughout a person's life.
> 4. Practical intelligence cannot be measured by grades.
> 5. I am an excellent candidate for the job.

For some assignments, you may not be able to find enough support from your own experience. In that case, you may need to do some research, usually online or in your college's library. If you use research to find facts or examples to support your main idea, make sure that you take notes about the source of the information. You must be able to show readers where you found the information, and you need to avoid **plagiarism**—using ideas or words written by someone else as your own, without acknowledging where the information comes from. Writers who plagiarize, either on purpose or by accident, risk failing a course or losing their jobs and damaging their reputations.

To avoid plagiarism, take careful notes on every source you might use in your writing, whether your source is in print (like books, magazines, and newspapers), broadcast over the airwaves (like an interview on a TV talk show or podcast), or accessed online (like from a website or online news site).

When recording information from sources, take notes in your own words (paraphrase), unless you plan to use direct quotations. In that case, make sure to record the quotation word for word and include quotation marks around it, both in your notes and in your paper. When you use material from other sources— whether you directly quote, paraphrase, or summarize—you must provide the information readers will need to identify and locate the source for themselves. For more detailed information about paraphrasing, see Chapter 1; for more about citing and documenting sources, see the Appendix.

Select the Best Primary Support

After you have generated possible support, review your ideas to find the best ones to use as primary support. Here you take control of your topic, shaping the way readers will see it and the main idea you are making about it. These ideas are yours, and you need to sell them to your audience. The following steps can help:

1. Read the ideas you have generated carefully.

2. Select the three to five primary supporting points that will be clearest and most convincing to your readers, providing the best examples, facts, and observations to support your main idea. If you are writing a paragraph, these points will become the primary support for your topic sentence. If you are writing an essay, they will become topic sentences of the individual paragraphs that support your thesis statement.

3. Cross out ideas that are not closely related to your main idea.

4. If you find that you have crossed out most of your ideas and do not have enough left to support your main idea, use one of the three strategies on pages 43–47 (Chapter 3) to generate more.

When Chelsea Wilson reviewed her list of possible supporting points, she knew she needed to eliminate some ideas.

Chelsea Wilson's Supporting Points (Revised)

nurses help people and I want to do that

jobs all over the country

good jobs with decent pay

~~good setting, clean~~

a profession, not just a job

opportunity, like RN

bigger place, more money

treated with respect

role model

pride in myself and my work, what I've done

~~good benefits~~

~~nice people to work with~~

may get paid to take more classes—chance for further professional development

~~uniform so not lots of money for clothes~~

~~I'll be something~~

PRACTICE 4-2   Selecting the Best Primary Support

Refer to your response in Practice 4-1. Of your possible primary supporting points, choose three to five that you think will best show, explain, or prove your main idea to your readers. Write down your three to five points.

Add Secondary Support

Once you have selected your best primary supporting points, you need to flesh them out for your readers. Do this by adding secondary support—specific examples, facts, observations, and so on—to back up your primary supporting points. You may also decide that some of the ideas on your list are related to others; in that case, a more general concept may be a primary supporting point, while the related specific ideas can serve as secondary support.

Chelsea noticed that some of her notes were related to the same subject, so she arranged them into clusters. Each cluster included a more general idea first (the primary supporting point) followed by an indented list of more specific details and examples (the secondary support).

Chelsea Wilson's Primary and Secondary Support (Draft)

good job	pride/achievement
decent pay	a job that helps people
jobs all over the country	treated with respect
opportunity for the future (like RN)	I'd be a role model
may get paid to take more classes	a profession, not just a job

Next, Chelsea took the notes she made and organized them into primary support and supporting details. Notice how she changed and reorganized some of her supporting details.

Chelsea Wilson's Primary and Secondary Support (Revised)

Primary support: Being an LPN is an excellent job.

   Supporting details:

   The pay is regular and averages about $40,000 a year.

   I could afford to move to a bigger and better place with more room for my daughter.

   I could work fewer hours.

Primary support: Nursing is a profession, not just a job.

   Supporting details:

   Nurses help care for people.

   Nursing is an important job, giving to the world.

   Nursing offers future opportunities, like becoming an RN with more money and responsibility.

   People respect nurses.

Primary support: Being a nurse will be a great achievement for me.

   Supporting details:

   I will have worked hard and met my goal.

   I will respect myself and be proud of what I do.

   I will be a good role model for my daughter.

> **PRACTICE 4-3** **Adding Secondary Support**
>
> Using your answers to Practice 4-2, write your three best primary support-ing points in the spaces below. Then, after reading each of them carefully, write down at least three supporting details for each one. For examples of secondary support, see the example paragraph on pages 60–61.
>
> Primary support point 1:
>
>   Supporting details:
>
> Primary support point 2:
>
>   Supporting details:
>
> Primary support point 3:
>
>   Supporting details:

Writing Assignment: Write Your Own Support

If you have worked through this chapter, you should have developed a set of primary supporting points as well as more specific examples, facts, statistics, or other details to demonstrate your main idea (topic sentence or thesis statement).

> **WRITING ASSIGNMENT**
>
> Develop primary and secondary support using your topic sentence or thesis statement from Chapter 3 or one of the following:
>
>   It is important for future [name of profession] to write well.
>
>   Learning to disagree politely can make workplaces more effective.
>
>   Going to college is/is not essential.
>
>   People who do not speak "proper" English are discriminated against.
>
>   Most of us could/could not live without technology today.
>
> After developing your support, complete the following checklist.

CHECKLIST

Evaluating Your Support

- ☐ All of my supporting points consider my readers and what they need to know about my main idea.
- ☐ All my primary supporting points are directly related to my main idea.
- ☐ My secondary supporting points include examples, facts, and observations that will make sense to my readers.

Once you have pulled together your primary supporting points and secondary supporting details, you are ready for the next step: drafting a paragraph or essay based on a plan. For more information, see Chapter 5.

Chapter 4 Review

1. What is support?

2. What are the three basics of good support?

3. What are three strategies for generating support?

4. Once you have selected your primary supporting points, what should you add?

Reflect and Apply

1. Think about writing you have done for work or other courses. How did you find support for those texts? How did you know when you had enough support?

2. How can reading help you in the process of generating support?

3. Karin generated support for a paragraph about the qualities of an ideal teacher. For her second supporting point, she wrote this:

   Primary support: A great teacher cares about her students and wants them to learn.

   Secondary support: Her students are important to her, and she is concerned about them and their progress. For example, she hopes they will do well.

   Do you think Karin has provided strong secondary support for this point? Why or why not?

4. Look back at the essay by Amanda Jacobowitz on pages 16–17. What are her primary supporting points? What are her secondary supporting points? How does she use proper nouns (beginning with capital letters) to provide specific supporting details?

5

Drafting

The First Complete Version

Learning Outcomes In this chapter, you will learn to

- Set goals for the first draft of a paper.
- Identify three organizational strategies for drafts.
- Outline a draft.
- Write a draft paragraph or essay.

If you have worked through Chapters 3 and 4, you should have generated a strong topic sentence or thesis statement, as well as several supporting points and details. Although you have written quite a bit, you have not yet organized all of your ideas into a single piece of writing, which is the next step in the writing process.

Understanding What a Draft Is

A **draft** is a version of all your ideas put together in a piece of writing. When you are drafting, your text begins to take shape. Keep in mind that your first draft is not final; you can still make changes to your content, organization, and style. Many writers set **draft goals** to help them stay focused as they begin to write. Rubrics such as the one in Chapter 2 (p. 36) can help you create your draft goals, or you may use the features listed on the next page as goals for your draft.

> ## Goals for a First Draft
>
> - Include a topic sentence (paragraph) or thesis statement (essay) with a clear main idea.
> - Provide primary support and secondary support (details that show, explain, or prove the main idea).
> - Organize the supporting evidence clearly and logically (by time, space, or order of importance, for example).
> - Include a concluding sentence or paragraph that makes an observation or emphasizes the importance of the main idea.

(Notice that a paragraph or essay with these characteristics follows the conventions discussed in Chapter 2 for a standardized paragraph, p. 33, or a standardized essay, pp. 34–35.) Two good first steps for drafting a paragraph or essay are to arrange the ideas that you have generated in an order that makes sense and to write a plan (or outline) for your draft.

Arranging Your Ideas

In writing, **order** means the sequence in which you present your ideas: what comes first, what comes next, and so on. There are three common ways of arranging your ideas:

1. Time (or *chronological*) order
2. Space order
3. Order of importance or emphasis

Read the paragraph examples that follow. In each paragraph, the **1** main idea, **2** primary support, **3** secondary support, and **4** conclusion are highlighted.

Use Time Order to Write about Events

Use time (or *chronological*) order to arrange points according to when they happened. Time order works best when you are writing about events.

Example Using Time Order

1 Officer Meredith Pavlovic's traffic stop of August 23, 2020, was fairly typical of an investigation and arrest for drunk driving. **2** First, at around 12:15 a.m. that day, she noticed that the driver of a blue Honda Civic was acting suspiciously. 3 The car was weaving between the left and center lanes of Interstate 93 North near exit 12. In addition, it was proceeding at 45 mph in a 55 mph zone. 2 Therefore, Officer Pavlovic took the second step of pulling the driver over for a closer investigation. 3 The driver's license showed that the driver was twenty-six-year-old Paul Brownwell. Brownwell's red eyes, slurred speech, and alcohol-tainted breath told Officer Pavlovic that Brownwell was very drunk. But she had to be absolutely sure. 2 Thus, as a next step, she tested his balance and blood alcohol level. 3 The results were that Brownwell could barely get out of the car, let alone stand on one foot. Also, a Breathalyzer test showed that his blood alcohol level was 0.13, well over the legal limit of 0.08. 4 These results meant an arrest for Brownwell, an unfortunate outcome for him, but a lucky one for others on the road that night.

Use Space Order to Describe Objects, Places, or People

Use **space order** to arrange ideas so that your readers picture your topic the way you see it. Space order usually works best when you are writing about a physical object, a place, or a person's appearance. You can move from

- Top to bottom or bottom to top
- Near to far or far to near
- Left to right or right to left
- Back to front or front to back

Example Using Space Order

1 I was gazing at my son's feet in awe. 2 There were ten toes, and they were no bigger than my fingernail. 3 How could something so small be moving so quickly? Staring at those little toes squirming around as I tried to put socks on them, 2 I had to laugh because the chubby little tree trunks that his dad and I call legs decided to get in on the action. 3 Those full kicks that I had felt for the past several months and that had felt like someone performing kung-fu on my internal organs were now free and he clearly enjoyed that open space. 2 Nothing, however, could prepare me for that tubby little belly. 3 So small, round, and smooth—yet it bounced up and down with each giggle, burp, and cry. 2 Two large sausage-like appendages turned into arms 3 with long, slender fingers and fingernails that were no larger than the head of a pin, or so it appeared. 2 But what did all that matter when the true beauty perched right atop his nonexistent neck: 3 that gorgeous, round head covered with brown peach fuzz, sticking up in all directions. 4 Add all the pieces together, and all you see is love.

Use Order of Importance to Emphasize a Particular Point

Use **order of importance** to arrange points according to their significance, interest, or relevance to your main idea. Where you place the most important idea will depend on the type of writing and the audience; college essays often put the most important point last, but in other situations, such as a news story or police report, the most important points appear first.

Example Using Order of Importance

[1] Many parents today do not realize that there is a serious problem in their own home: prescription drug abuse. [2] Unfortunately, we live in a day and age where the answer for many different problems is a prescription drug of some type. [3] We are prescribed drugs for pain, illness, mental disorders, sleep disorders, and even sexual problems. [2] With so many different disorders or problems that need treatment today, it is likely that any household has at least two or three active prescriptions at any one time, but are we monitoring those pills carefully? [3] News reports have shown that adults do not typically think to take the same precautions with prescriptions as they would with other dangerous substances, namely weapons like guns or knives; however, pills are just as deadly and far more addicting. [4] If you are not keeping your prescriptions locked up, you are not keeping your home and your children safe.

Making a Plan

When you have decided how to order your primary supporting points, it is time to make a detailed plan for your paragraph or essay. One way to plan a draft is to arrange your ideas in a formal or informal outline. A formal outline uses numbers, letters, and indentations to indicate primary and secondary points:

I. Topic sentence
   A. Primary Support 1
       1. Secondary support 1
       2. Secondary support 2
   B. Primary Support 2
       1. Secondary support 1
       2. Secondary support 2

Informal outlines just list primary and secondary support in the order in which they will be presented. Both formal and informal outlines provide a map for you to follow as you write the first draft of your paragraph or essay.

Outlining Paragraphs

Look below at the outline Chelsea Wilson created using the support she developed in Chapter 4. She had already grouped similar points and put the more specific secondary details under the primary support (see p. 65). When she thought about how to order her ideas, the only way that made sense to her was by importance. If she had been telling the steps she would take to become a nurse, time order would have worked well. If she had been describing a setting where nurses work, space order would have been a good choice. However, because she was writing about why she wanted to get a college degree and become a nurse, she decided to arrange her reasons in order of importance. Notice that Chelsea also strengthened her topic sentence and expanded her primary support and secondary support. At each stage, her ideas and the way she expressed them changed as she got closer to what she wanted to say.

Chelsea Wilson's Paragraph Outline

Topic sentence: Becoming a nurse is a goal of mine because it offers so much that I value.

    Primary support 1: It is a good and practical job.

        Secondary support: Average salary of $40,000 per year, more than I make now. This salary would allow me to move to a better place and give my daughter more, including more time.

    Primary support 2: Nursing is a profession, not just a job.

        Secondary support: Job offers a chance to help people, respect, and opportunity to become a registered nurse, with more money and responsibility.

    Primary support 3: I will respect and be proud of myself for achieving my goal through hard work.

        Secondary support: Helps me be a good role model for my daughter, helps others, and helps me know that I can accomplish good things.

Conclusion: Reaching my goal is important to me and worth the work.

Chelsea's paragraph appears on pages 74–75.

Outlining Essays

The formal outline that follows is for a five-paragraph essay, in which three body paragraphs (built around three topic sentences) support a thesis statement. The thesis statement is included in an introductory paragraph; the fifth paragraph is the conclusion. However, essays may include more or fewer than five paragraphs, depending on the size and complexity of the topic.

Chelsea Wilson's Essay Outline

Thesis statement: There are many benefits to getting a college degree.

A. **Primary support 1** (topic sentence): I can work as a nurse and make more money.
   1. The average salary for a licensed practical nurse is $40,000 a year.
   2. It is hard to pay bills with salary and tips from my restaurant job.
   3. Without a degree, my finances won't get better, and I won't have time to spend with my daughter.

B. **Primary support 2** (topic sentence): I didn't get serious about getting a degree until I became a mother.
   1. I want more for my daughter than I had.
   2. I want to keep her safe and show her better ways to live.

C. **Primary support 3** (topic sentence): The most important benefit of a college degree is that it will show me I can achieve something hard.
   1. I'm going in the right direction, and I'm proud.
   2. I want to be a role model for my daughter, so she will be proud of me, too.

Concluding paragraph (paragraph 5): Because of these benefits, I want a college degree.

You can read the first draft of Chelsea's essay on page 82.

PRACTICE 5-1   Making an Outline

Reread the paragraph on pages 69–70 that illustrates time order of organization. Then make an outline for it following the model provided.

Topic sentence:

Primary support 1:

　　1. **Secondary support:**

　　2. **Secondary support:**

Primary support 2:

    1. **Secondary support:**

    2. **Secondary support:**

Primary support 3:

    1. **Secondary support:**

    2. **Secondary support:**

Writing a Draft Paragraph

To write your paragraph draft, review your draft goals (p. 69), and write with your outline in front of you. Be sure to include your topic sentence and express each point in a complete sentence. As you write, you may want to add support or change the order. It is okay to make changes from your outline as you write. Your instructor may ask you to include a title, and you will need to add a concluding sentence.

Your **concluding sentence** (or sentences) should refer back to the main idea, emphasize the importance of that idea, or make an observation based on what you have written. The concluding sentence does not just repeat the topic sentence.

In Chelsea Wilson's paragraph, the concluding sentences say, "For all of these reasons, my goal is to become a nurse. Reaching this goal is important to me and worth the work." Notice that her concluding sentences refer back to the main idea by repeating the words *these reasons, goal,* and *nurse.* They make an observation by stating that her goal is "important" and "worth the work."

Chelsea Wilson's Draft Paragraph

Chelsea Wilson

My Career Goal

1 Main idea
2 Primary
   support
3 Secondary
   support

   1 My career goal is to become a nurse because it offers so much that I value. **2** Being a nurse is a good and practical job. **3** Licensed practical nurses make an average of $40,000 per year. That amount is much more than I make now working long hours at a minimum-wage job in a restaurant. Working as a nurse, I could be a better provider for my daughter. I could also spend more time with her.

2 Also, nursing is more than just a job; it is a profession. **3** As a nurse, I will help people who are sick, and helping people is important to me. With time, I will be able to grow within the profession, like becoming a registered nurse who makes more money and has more responsibility. Because nursing is a profession, nurses are respected. When I become a nurse, I will respect myself and be proud of myself for reaching my goal, even though I know it will take a lot of hard work. **2** The most important thing about becoming a nurse is that it will be good for my young daughter. **3** I will be a good role model for her. **4** For all of these reasons, my goal is to become a nurse. Reaching this goal is important to me and worth the work.

4 **Conclusion**

Although paragraphs often begin with topic sentences, they may also begin with a quote, an example, or a surprising fact or idea. The topic sentence is then presented later in the paragraph. For examples of various introductory techniques, see pages 77–80.

> **PRACTICE 5-2**   **Writing a Concluding Sentence**

Read the following paragraph and write a concluding sentence for it:

> One of the most valuable ways parents can help children is to read to them. Reading together is a good way for parents and children to relax, and it is sometimes the only "quality" time they spend together during a busy day. Reading to children develops their vocabulary. They understand more words and are likely to learn new words more easily than children who are not read to. Hearing the words aloud helps children's pronunciation and makes them more confident with oral language. In addition, reading at home increases children's chances of success in school because reading is required in every course in every grade.

Possible concluding sentence:

Writing a Draft Essay

To write your draft essay, review your draft goals (p. 69) and keep your plan in front of you. Your draft should include the following:

- An introductory paragraph that draws readers in and includes the thesis statement

- Body paragraphs that include topic sentences stating each paragraph's primary supporting idea and secondary details supporting each topic sentence
- A concluding paragraph that draws the essay to a close

Many writers find it easier to draft the body of the essay first, so we'll start by looking at topic sentences and evidence supporting them.

Write Topic Sentences and Draft the Body of the Essay

Use your outline while drafting, writing complete sentences that state your primary supporting points. These sentences will serve as the topic sentences for the body paragraphs of your essay. (For an example, see Chelsea Wilson's outline on p. 73.)

PRACTICE 5-3   Writing Topic Sentences

Each thesis statement that follows has supporting points that could be topic sentences for the body paragraphs of an essay. For each supporting point, write a topic sentence.

Example

Thesis statement: My daughter is showing definite signs of becoming a teenager.

Primary support 1: Constantly texting friends

Topic sentence 1: She texts friends constantly, even when they are sitting in the car with her while I'm driving.

Primary support 2: Doesn't want me to know what's going on

Topic sentence 2: She used to tell me everything, but now she is secretive and private.

Primary support 3: Developing an "attitude"

Topic sentence 3: The surest and most annoying sign that she is becoming a teenager is that she has developed a definite "attitude."

Thesis statement: The Latin American influence is evident in many areas of U.S. culture.

Primary support 1: Spanish used in lots of places

Topic sentence 1:

Primary support 2: Lots of different kinds of foods

Topic sentence 2:

Primary support 3: New kinds of music and popular musicians

Topic sentence 3:

Your outline can also help you add supporting details to your paragraphs. Turn these supporting details into complete sentences and add additional support if necessary. If you get stuck, go back to the prewriting techniques in Chapter 3 to generate more ideas. If you are having trouble with a word or sentence, just keep writing. Remember that a draft is a first try; you will have time later to improve it.

Write an Introduction

The introduction to your essay should capture your audience's interest, establish the essay's topic, and present its main idea. The introduction functions like a map: It tells readers where they are and where they are going. Your introduction must make the destination clear, and it should also make readers want to accompany you there.

Basics of a Good Introduction

- A good introduction should catch readers' attention.
- It should present the thesis statement of the essay. The thesis may be the last sentence of an introduction, although it may appear in other places.
- It should give readers a clear idea of what the essay will cover.

The following sections offer some common kinds of introductions that spark readers' interest. These are not the only ways to start essays, but they should give you some useful models.

Open with a Quotation

A good, short quotation definitely gets people interested. It must lead naturally into your main idea, however, and not be there just for effect. If you start with a quotation, make sure you tell the reader who the speaker is.

In a letter to a friend, writer C. S. Lewis said, "I can't imagine a man really enjoying a book and reading it only once." In other words, one of the greatest pleasures of reading comes when we reread. Each time we reread a favorite novel, the characters become friends that we meet again in familiar settings; we can imagine their voices and faces. And we may also notice small details that escaped our attention the first time around—hints, descriptions, asides from the author. Perhaps most significantly, we may connect again with emotions and memories that may have been forgotten since the first time we picked up the book.

Give an Example or Tell a Story

People like stories, so opening an essay with a brief story or example often draws readers in.

The bank called today, and I told them my deposit was in the mail, even though I hadn't written a check yet. It'd been a rough day. The baby I'm pregnant with decided to do aerobics on my lungs for two hours, our three-year-old daughter painted the living-room couch with lipstick, the IRS put me on hold for an hour, and I was late to a business meeting because I was tired.

—*Stephanie Ericsson, "The Ways We Lie"*

Start with a Surprising Fact or Idea

Surprises capture people's interest. The more unexpected and surprising something is, the more likely people are to notice it.

Just because gyms and parks are temporarily closed doesn't mean exercise is a thing of the past. With virtual reality games, at-home workouts can be both fun and doable. Virtual reality (VR) headsets are the newest and most sought-after additions to video game consoles. While there are many immersive, beautiful and even scary games for VR, the games with the most practical use are meant for exercise. Video games as exercise may have once seemed counterintuitive, but now this is a concept of the past.

—*Margaret Troup, "Virtual Reality: Fun and Innovative Indoor Exercise"*

Offer a Strong Opinion or Position

The stronger the opinion, the more likely it is that your readers will pay attention.

Under cover of darkness early on Monday morning, workers in Louisiana took down the first of four Confederate memorials in New Orleans, which city officials had decided to remove in 2015, shortly after the Charleston shootings. Good riddance.

—Steven Thrasher, "Confederate Memorials Have No Place in
American Society. Good Riddance."

Ask a Question

A question needs an answer, so if you start your introduction with a question, your readers will need to read on to get the answer.

Why does the university need a College Assistance Migrant Program (CAMP)? The critical need for this kind of program in the North Georgia region stems from many factors.

—Christian Bello Escobar, "Grant Rationale"

PRACTICE 5-4   Marketing Your Main Idea

A good writer can make any topic sound interesting. For each of the following topics, write an introductory statement that will capture the reader's attention, using the technique indicated.

Example

Topic: Reality TV

Technique: Question

Introductory statement: *Exactly how many recent top-selling songs have been recorded by former contestants of reality TV singing contests?*

1. **Topic:** Credit cards

   Technique: Surprising fact or idea

   Introductory statement:

2. **Topic:** Role of the elderly in society

   Technique: Question

   Introductory statement:

3. **Topic:** Stress

   Technique: Quote (You can make up a good one.)

   Introductory statement:

PRACTICE 5–5   Identifying Strong Introductions

In a newspaper or magazine, an online news site, an advertising flier, or anything written, find a strong introduction. Share it with your class and explain why you chose it as an example.

Write a Conclusion

Don't stop after writing the body and the introduction; you need a conclusion as well. Remember that people usually remember best what they see, hear, or read last. Use your concluding paragraph to drive home your main idea one final time. Make sure your conclusion has the same energy as the rest of the essay, if not more.

Basics of a Good Essay Conclusion

- It refers back to the main idea or emphasizes its importance.
- It may encourage readers to take action or make a final observation about the main idea.
- It may circle back to the introductory strategy: finish the story or quote, answer the question, or revisit the surprising fact.

In general, a good conclusion creates a sense of completion. It brings readers back to where they started, but it also shows them how far they have come.

One of the best ways to end an essay is to refer directly to something in the introduction. If you asked a question, answer it. If you started a story, finish it. If you used a quote, use another one—maybe a quote by the same person or maybe one by another person on the same topic. Or use some of the same words you used in your introduction. Look again at Stephanie Ericsson's essay and notice how the writer concluded her essay. Pay special attention to the text in boldface.

Stephanie Ericsson's Introduction

> **The bank called today, and I told them my deposit was in the mail, even though I hadn't written a check yet.** It'd been a rough day. The baby I'm pregnant with decided to do aerobics on my lungs for two hours, our three-year-old daughter painted the living-room couch with lipstick, the IRS put me on hold for an hour, and I was late to a business meeting because I was tired.
>
> — *Stephanie Ericsson, "The Ways We Lie"*

Stephanie Ericsson's Conclusion

> **Maybe if I don't tell the bank the check's in the mail I'll be less tolerant of the lies told to me every day.** A country song I once heard said it all for me, "You've got to stand for something or you'll fall for anything."
>
> — *Stephanie Ericsson, "The Ways We Lie"*

PRACTICE 5-6   Writing Good Introductions and Conclusions

Find a piece of writing that has a strong introduction and conclusion. (You may want to use what you found for Practice 5-5.) Then answer the following questions:

1. What method of introduction is used?

2. What does the conclusion do? (Restate the main idea? Sum up the support? Make a further observation?)

3. How are the introduction and the conclusion linked?

Title Your Essay

Even if your **title** is the last part you write for your essay, it is the first thing readers read. Use your title to get your readers' attention and to tell them, in a brief way, what your paper is about. Use vivid, strong, specific words.

Basics of a Good Essay Title

- It makes people want to read the essay.
- It hints at the main idea (thesis statement), but it does not repeat it.

One way to find a good title is to consider the type of essay you are writing. If you are writing an argument (see Chapter 15), state your position in your title. If you are telling your readers how to do something (see Chapter 10), use the word *steps* or *how to* in the title. This way, your readers will know immediately not only what you are writing about but also how you will discuss it. Center your title at the top of the page before the first paragraph. Do not put quotation marks around it or underline it.

PRACTICE 5-7   Titling an Essay

Reread Stephanie Ericsson's introduction and conclusion on pages 80–81, and write an alternate title for the essay.

Chelsea Wilson's Draft Essay

A first draft takes time; after all, you must make several decisions as you are writing, and those decisions may leave you frustrated or uncertain. But remember the goal: A draft is one complete version, not a perfect or finished piece. Here is Chelsea Wilson's essay draft.

Chelsea Wilson

The Benefits of Getting a College Degree

My goal is to get a college degree. I have been taking college courses for two years, and it has been difficult for me. Many times I have wondered if getting a college degree is really worth the struggle. **1** However, there are many benefits of getting a college degree.
2 I can work as a nurse, something I have always wanted to do.
3 As a nurse, I can make decent money: The average salary for a licensed practical nurse is $40,000 per year. That amount is substantially more than I make now working at a restaurant job that pays minimum wage and tips. With the economy so bad, people are tipping less. It has been hard to pay my bills, even though I work more than forty hours a week. Without a degree, I don't see how that situation will change. I have almost no time to see my daughter, who is in preschool.
2 I didn't get serious about getting a degree until I became a mother. **3** Then, I realized I wanted more for my daughter than I had growing up. I also wanted to have time to raise her properly and keep her safe. She is a good girl, but she sees crime and violence around her. I want to get her away from danger, and I want to show her that there are better ways to live. Getting a college degree will help me do that.
2 The most important benefit of getting a college degree is that it will show me that I can achieve something hard. **3** My life is moving in a good direction, and I am proud of myself. My daughter will be proud of me, too. I want to be a good role model for her as she grows up.
4 Because of these benefits, I want to get a college degree. It will give me the chance to earn a better living, it will give my daughter and me a better life, and I will be proud of myself.

1 Main idea
2 Primary support

3 Secondary support

4 Conclusion

Writing Your Own Draft Paragraph or Essay

Before you begin drafting your paragraph or essay, review your assignment carefully and make sure you have prepared your draft goals and a plan for your writing. Remember that you may need to go back to prewriting to generate additional support or narrow your main idea further.

WRITING ASSIGNMENT **Paragraph**

Write a draft paragraph using the main idea and support you developed in previous chapters, or use one of the following topic sentences:

Being a good _____ requires _____.

I can find any number of ways to waste my time.

So many decisions are involved in going to college.

I thought _____ would be impossible, but it wasn't.

If you use one of these topic sentences, you may want to revise it to fit what you want to say. Before you begin writing, make sure you have worked through the steps of the writing process: narrowing your topic, generating supporting points and details, and making a plan.

WRITING ASSIGNMENT **Essay**

Write a draft essay using the main idea and support you developed in previous chapters, or use one of the following thesis statements:

Being successful at _____ requires _____.

Achieving _____ gave me a great deal of pride in myself.

Training for _____ requires a lot of discipline.

Some of the differences between men and women create misunderstandings.

If you select one of these thesis statements, you may adjust it as needed. Be sure to go back through all the steps of the process: narrow your focus, generate support, and make a plan.

After you have written your first draft paragraph or essay, review your work, using the checklist that follows. Also think about questions you may want to ask your instructor or yourself as you get ready to revise your draft (Chapter 6). Make a note of how you would complete these sentences:

1. The best thing about my draft is _____.
2. I am not certain about _____.
3. I would like help with _____.

CHECKLIST

Evaluating Your Draft Paragraph or Essay

Does the draft

☐ have a clear, confident topic sentence (paragraph) or thesis (essay) that states my main idea?

☐ offer convincing primary points supported by secondary details (evidence, facts, examples, anecdotes, observations, and so on)?

☐ arrange the paragraph's or the essay's secondary support (sentences or paragraphs) in a logical order (time, space, or order of importance)?

☐ include an introduction that conveys the main idea or purpose in a way that will grab a reader's attention?

☐ include a concluding sentence (paragraph) or paragraph (essay) that reminds readers of the main idea, emphasizes the point, or makes an observation?

☐ use complete sentences?

☐ have a title that reflects the topic and main idea?

Chapter 5 Review

1. What is a draft?

2. What are typical draft goals for the first draft of a paragraph or essay?

3. What are three ways to order ideas?

4. What is an outline and why is it helpful to writers?

5. What are five strategies for starting an essay?

6. What are three features of a strong conclusion?

7. What are two features of an essay title?

Reflect and Apply

1. Writing a draft takes time. Have you ever procrastinated on (or put off) a writing assignment? What happens if you wait until the last minute to get started?

2. What part of the drafting process challenges you the most? What strategies did you learn in this chapter that can help you overcome that challenge?

3. Interview students who have been successful in your major. What strategies have they used for successful drafting? Can they recommend strategies for writing introductions or conclusions?

6

Revising, Editing, and Proofreading

Polishing the Draft

Learning Outcomes   **In this chapter, you will learn to**

- Define revising.
- Recognize and address problems in unity, development, and coherence.
- Give and receive feedback in peer review.
- Revise a paragraph or essay.
- Define editing and proofreading.

If you have worked through Chapter 5, you have completed one full draft of your essay. That first draft is sometimes called a *rough draft*: It is not yet polished or ready for a grade. After completing your first draft, give yourself some time away from it, at least a few hours and preferably a day or two. After taking a break, you will be ready to look at the draft with fresh eyes and revise it. The strategies for revising in this chapter will help you make your draft stronger and more effective.

Understanding What Revision Is

When you finish a draft, you probably wish that you were done: You don't want to have to look at that piece of writing again. But a draft is just the first complete version—a rough cut; it is almost impossible to do your best writing on the first attempt.

Revising means making your ideas clearer, stronger, and more convincing. When revising, you are evaluating the content and organization of your writing.

Read Carefully

Before you make any changes to your paper, spend some time reading it critically and carefully. First, read your draft aloud and listen for places where the writing seems unclear. Then read it again, asking yourself questions and imagining what your readers might ask. As you ask these questions, you may make minor changes and additions directly on the draft, but for larger issues of content and organization, write notes in the margins, use the Comments tool in Google Docs or Word files, or take notes in a separate file.

Questions to Consider

- Have I addressed the requirements of the assignment?
- If readers had only my topic sentence or thesis statement, what would they think the paper is about? Would they care about the topic?
- Does each supporting point clearly relate to my main idea? How could I strengthen the support?
- Have I arranged my supporting points logically and effectively?
- Have I given enough information and context so that readers who are not familiar with my topic can understand my draft easily?
- Is the ending clear and effective? How could I make it better?

Set Revision Goals

Once you have read your draft carefully, review the notes you have taken, the assignment instructions, and any rubrics or grading criteria provided by the instructor. You may also want to talk to a friend or a tutor in your school's writing center. Then write two or three goals for the next draft of your paper. Revision goals might look like these:

- Eliminate the irrelevant details in paragraph 2.
- Add evidence to make supporting point 3 stronger.
- Move from one supporting point to another more smoothly.
- Find a stronger way to conclude the paper.

Revising for Unity, Development, and Coherence

Three of the most common issues writers address in revision are unity, development, and coherence.

Revise for Unity

Unity in writing means that all the points you make are related to your main idea; they are *unified* in support of it. As you draft a paragraph or an essay, you may detour from your main idea without even being aware of it, as the writer of the following paragraph did. The <u>main idea</u> appears in sentence 1.

[1] <u>If you want to drive like an elderly person, use a cell phone while driving.</u> [2] A group of researchers from the University of Utah tested the reaction times of two groups of people—those between the ages of sixty-five to seventy-four and those who were eighteen to twenty-five—in a variety of driving tasks. [3] All tasks were done with hands-free cell phones. [4] That part of the study surprised me because I thought the main problem was using only one hand to drive. [5] I hardly ever drive with two hands, even when I'm not talking to anyone. [6] Among other results, braking time for both groups slowed by 18 percent. [7] A related result is that the number of rear-end collisions doubled. [8] The study determined that the younger drivers were paying as much—or more—attention to their phone conversations as they were to what was going on around them on the road. [9] The elderly drivers also experienced longer reaction times and more accidents, pushing most of them into the category of dangerous driver. [10] This study makes a good case for turning off the phone when you buckle up.

Main idea

Detour

Detours, like those in sentences 4 and 5, weaken your writing because readers' focus is shifted away from your main idea. As you revise, check to make sure your paragraph or essay has unity.

PRACTICE 6–1   Revising for Unity

Each of the following paragraphs contains a sentence that detours from the main idea. Identify the main idea, and then highlight the detour sentence.

1. One way to manage time is to keep a print or electronic calendar or schedule. It should have an hour-by-hour breakdown of the day and evening, with space for you to write next to the time. As appointments or responsibilities come up, add them on the right day and time. Before the end of the day, consult your calendar to see what's going on the next day. For example, tomorrow I have to meet Kara at noon,

and if I forget, she will be furious with me. Once you are in the habit of using a calendar, you will see that it frees your mind because you are not always trying to think about what you're supposed to do, where you're supposed to be, or what you might have forgotten.

2. As you use a calendar to manage your time, think about how long certain activities will take. A common mistake is to underestimate the time needed to do something, even something simple. For example, when you are planning the time needed to get money from the cash machine, remember that a line of people may be ahead of you. Last week, in the line I met a woman I went to high school with. When you are estimating time for a more complex activity, such as reading a chapter in a textbook, block out more time than you think you will need. If you finish in less time than you have allotted, so much the better.

Revise for Development

Development in writing means that each primary supporting point contains enough secondary support—evidence, details, or examples—to be clear for readers. Ask yourself if readers have enough information to understand and be convinced by the main idea. Consider the following paragraphs. In the first one, the writer has not provided enough details for all the supporting points. In the second paragraph, however, the writer has developed the supporting ideas more fully.

Insufficient Development

1 Main idea
2 Primary support

3 Secondary support

4 Conclusion

1 Our county should start school earlier each year to benefit all the students. **2** Currently, the county postpones the start of school until after Labor Day, **3** which probably made sense years ago, when it was harder for families to send their kids to school in late August. **2** Also, it's true that the week before Labor Day is the county fair, and many of our students participate in the farming activities of the fair. **3** But we could find a way to let students start school and still attend the fair. **2** Most important, if we start earlier, our students will not be three or four weeks behind everyone else for state tests and AP exams in May. **3** Right now, our students have to cram a lot of information in a condensed amount of time, and then they are left with little to do but watch videos and play games for the last three weeks of school. **4** If we start the school year earlier, we can preserve our farming culture without putting our students at a disadvantage.

Revised to Improve Development

[1] Our county should start school earlier each year to benefit all the students. [2] Currently, the county postpones the start of school until after Labor Day even though every other county in the state starts the first or second week in August. [3] Years ago, the late start made sense. Schools did not have air conditioning, and August was the hottest month of the year. But all of our schools are air-conditioned now. Also, with farming technology today, families don't need their children to work on the farm as much. [2] Supporters of the current start date point out that the week before Labor Day is the county fair, and many of our students participate in the farming activities of the fair. [3] But those students can still do that if school starts earlier in August and students get a three-day "fair holiday" before Labor Day. [2] Most important, if we start earlier, our students will not be three or four weeks behind everyone else for state tests and AP exams in May. [3] Right now, our students have to cram a lot of information in a condensed amount of time, and then they are left with little to do but watch videos and play games for the last three weeks of school. [4] If we start the school year earlier, we can preserve our farming culture without putting our students at a disadvantage.

[1] **Main idea**
[2] **Primary support**

[3] **Secondary support**

[4] **Conclusion**

PRACTICE 6-2   Revising for Development

Read the following paragraphs, identify the main idea, and in the spaces provided under each paragraph add at least three additional supporting points (evidence, details, or examples).

1. Sports fans can turn from normal people into destructive maniacs. After big wins, a team's fans sometimes riot. Police have to be brought in. Even in school sports, parents of the players can become violent. People get so involved watching the game that they lose control of themselves and are dangerous.

   1.

   2.

   3.

2. If a friend is going through a hard time, try to be as supportive as you can. For one thing, ask if you can help out with any errands or chores. Also, find a time when you can get together in a quiet, calm place. Here, the two of you can talk about the friend's difficulties or just

spend time visiting. Let the friend decide how the time is spent. Just knowing that you are there for him or her will mean a lot.

1.

2.

3.

Revise for Coherence

Coherence in writing means that the ideas in each paragraph connect to form a whole. In other words, you have provided enough "glue" to lead readers from one point to the next. Improving coherence is a common draft goal in revision. One strategy for improving coherence is to add or improve **transitions**—words, phrases, and sentences that connect your ideas so that your writing moves smoothly from one point to the next.

Here are two paragraphs: one that does not use transitions and one that does. Read them and notice how much easier the second paragraph is to follow because of the underlined transitions.

No Transitions

It is not difficult to get organized—it takes discipline to stay organized. All you need to do is follow a few simple ideas. You must decide what your priorities are and do these tasks first. You should ask yourself every day: What is the most important task I have to accomplish? Make the time to do it. To be organized, you need a personal system for keeping track of things. Making lists, keeping records, and using a schedule help you remember what tasks you need to do. It is a good idea not to let belongings and obligations stack up. Get rid of possessions you do not need, put items away every time you are done using them, and do not take on more responsibilities than you can handle. Getting organized is not a mystery; it is just good sense.

Transitions Added

It is not difficult to get organized—<u>although</u> it takes discipline to stay organized. All you need to do is follow a few simple ideas. You must decide what your priorities are and do these tasks first. <u>For example</u>, you should ask yourself every day: What is the most important task I have to accomplish? <u>Then</u> make the time to do it. To be organized, you <u>also</u> need a personal system for keeping track of things. Making lists, keeping records, and using a schedule help you remember what tasks you need to do. <u>Finally</u>, it is a good idea not to let belongings and obligations stack up. Get rid of possessions you do not need, put items away every time you are done using them, and do not take on more responsibilities than you can handle. Getting organized is not a mystery; it is just good sense.

The table below shows some common transitions and what they are used for.

Common Transitional Words and Phrases

Indicating Space

above	below	near	to the right
across	beside	next to	to the side
at the bottom	beyond	opposite	under
at the top	farther/further	over	where
behind	inside	to the left	

Indicating Time

after	eventually	meanwhile	soon
as	finally	next	then
at last	first	now	when
before	last	second	while
during	later	since	

Indicating Importance

above all	in fact	more important	most important
best	in particular	most	worst
especially			

Signaling Examples

for example	for instance	for one thing	one reason

Signaling Additions

additionally	and	as well as	in addition
also	another	furthermore	moreover

Signaling Contrast

although	however	nevertheless	still
but	in contrast	on the other hand	yet
even though	instead		

Signaling Causes or Results

as a result	finally	so	therefore
because			

> **PRACTICE 6–3** **Adding Transitions**
>
> Read the following paragraphs. In each blank, add a transition from the list that would smoothly connect the ideas (there may be more than one correct answer). You will not need to use all the transitions listed, and you may need to use some transitions more than once.

Example

Transitions: *After, Although, Because of, First, Since, Then*

LifeGem, a Chicago company, has announced that it can turn cremated human ashes into high-quality diamonds. _After_ cremation, the ashes are heated to convert their carbon to graphite. _Then_ a lab wraps the graphite around a tiny diamond piece and again heats it and pressurizes it. _After_ about a week of crystallizing, the result is a diamond. _Because of_ the time and labor involved, this process can cost as much as $20,000. _Although_ the idea is very creative, many people will think it is also very weird.

1. **Transitions:** *Because, Before, During, Eventually, However, In contrast, Nevertheless*

   Frida Kahlo (1907–1954) is one of Mexico's most famous artists. From an early age, she had an eye for color and detail. _____ it was not until she was seriously injured in a traffic accident that she devoted herself to painting. _____ her recovery, she went to work on what would become the first of many self-portraits. _____ she married the famous muralist Diego Rivera. _____ Rivera was unfaithful to Kahlo, their marriage was difficult. _____ Kahlo continued to develop as an artist and produce great work. Rivera may have summed up Kahlo's paintings the best, describing them as "acid and tender, hard as steel and delicate and fine as a butterfly's wing, lovable as a beautiful smile, and profound and cruel as the bitterness of life."

2. **Transitions:** *Also, Although, Finally, For example, However, Therefore*

   Many fast-food restaurants are adding healthier foods to their menus. _____ several kinds of salads are now on most menus. These salads offer fresh vegetables and roasted, rather than fried, chicken. _____ be careful of the dressings, which can be very high in calories. ____ avoid the huge soft drinks that have large amounts of sugar. _____ skip the French fries. They are high in fat and calories and do not have much nutritional value.

Giving and Receiving Feedback

Even the most experienced writers need to revise their work, and they often collaborate with others in a writing community during revision, getting feedback on their drafts and commenting on the drafts of others. This exchange of feedback is called **peer review**, and in many composition courses, students participate in peer review to practice giving and receiving feedback. Peer review can help you identify and achieve your revision goals. To create a successful peer review experience, keep the following in mind:

- Tell your peers about your concerns to guide their responses:
  - → I am most concerned about _____.
  - → I need help with _____.
- Have your classmates identify your main idea and primary support first. Then ask them what sections (if any) they find unclear or where additional information might help convince them to accept the main idea.
- Don't feel shy about asking for help. If you get confused or stuck in your writing, ask about it during the peer review process. Your peers may have the same writing assignment that you do, so they may be able to explain it to you in a way that makes more sense. If not, you may feel better knowing that someone else is also confused, and the two of you can ask for clarification from the instructor.
- Read carefully and critically, following the guidelines for reading in Chapter 1.
- When responding to another person's paper, be specific and constructive:
  - → The most effective part of the paper was _____ because _____.
  - → I got confused when you said _____ because _____.
  - → Could you tell us more about _____?
  - → I don't understand how _____ relates to the thesis. Could you explain?
- Avoid being vague or overly positive. Telling other writers that "everything looks good" does not help them improve their paper.
- Most important, when you receive feedback on your paper or your ideas, try to think about the feedback objectively. It is up to you to decide how to revise your writing. Peer review is a process meant to help by giving you an additional set of eyes.

By keeping these factors in mind, you can make the peer review process beneficial for all and help create a supportive writing community within the classroom and beyond.

Revising Your Own Paragraph

In Chapter 5, you read Chelsea Wilson's draft paragraph (pp. 74–75). Reread that paragraph now as if it were your own, asking yourself the questions on page 86. Work either by yourself or with a partner or small group to answer the questions about Chelsea's draft. Then read Chelsea's revised paragraph below and compare the changes you suggested with those that she made. Sentences and ideas Chelsea added to develop her supporting points are highlighted, and transitions she added to improve coherence are underlined. She also strengthened her final sentence.

Chelsea Wilson's Revised Paragraph

Chelsea Wilson
Professor Holmes
EN 099
September 21, 2021

My Career Goal

My career goal is to become a nurse. One practical reason I want to be a nurse is that it pays well, even in starting positions. Licensed practical nurses make an average of $40,000 per year, more than I make now working long hours at a minimum-wage job in a restaurant. With that extra money, I could be a better provider for my daughter. We could move to a better place, and I would have money for the "extras" she wants. With decent pay, I would not have to work such long hours, so I could spend more time with her. In addition, nursing has great opportunities for becoming a registered nurse. Another reason I want to be a nurse is that it is more than just a job; it is a profession, and nurses are respected. When I become a nurse, I will respect myself and be proud of myself for reaching my goal, even though I know it will take a lot of hard work. The most important reason I want to become a nurse is that it will be good for my daughter, not just because of the money, but because I will be a good role model for her. She will see that hard work pays off and that having a goal—and achieving it—is important. I have always known I wanted to be a nurse: It is a goal worth working for.

PRACTICE 6-4   **Revising a Paragraph**

1. What major changes did you suggest for Chelsea's draft?

2. Did Chelsea make any of the suggested changes? Which ones?

3. Did Chelsea make any changes that were not suggested? Which ones? Were they effective changes?

WRITING ASSIGNMENT   **Paragraph**

Revise the draft paragraph you wrote in Chapter 5. As you read your draft critically, be sure to evaluate the paragraph for unity, development, and coherence. Also consider participating in peer review with your classmates or friends. After revising your draft, complete the checklist on page 97.

Revising Your Own Essay

In Chapter 5, you read Chelsea's draft essay (p. 82). Reread that now as if it were your own, asking yourself the questions on page 86. Work either by yourself or with a partner or a small group to answer the questions about Chelsea's draft. Then read Chelsea's revised essay and compare the changes you suggested with those that she made. Make notes on the similarities and differences to discuss with the rest of the class. Sentences she added are highlighted, and transitions she added are underlined. Notice also that Chelsea strengthened her conclusion with an observation.

Chelsea Wilson's Revised Essay

Chelsea Wilson
Professor Holmes
EN 099
September 28, 2021

The Benefits of Getting a College Degree

I have been taking college courses for two years, and it has been difficult for me. I have a full-time job, a young daughter, and a car that breaks down often. Many times as I have sat, late at night, struggling to stay awake to do homework or to study, I have wondered if getting a college degree is really worth the struggle. That is when I remind myself why getting a degree is so important: It will benefit every aspect of my life.

One benefit of getting a degree is that I can work as a nurse, something I have always wanted to do. Even as a child, I enjoyed helping my mother care for my grandmother or take care of my younger brothers and sisters when they were sick. I enjoy helping others, and nursing will allow me to do so while making good money. The average salary for a licensed practical nurse is $40,000 per year, substantially more than I make now working at a restaurant. Without a degree, I don't see how that situation will change. Meanwhile, I have almost no time to spend with my daughter.

Another benefit of getting a college degree is that it will allow me to be a better mother. In fact, I didn't get serious about getting a degree until I became a mother. Then I realized I wanted more for my daughter than I had had: a safer place to live, a bigger apartment, some nice clothes, and birthday presents. I also wanted to have time to raise her properly and keep her safe. She is a good girl, but she sees crime and violence around her. I want to get her away from danger, and I want to show her that there are better ways to live. The job opportunities I will have with a college degree will enable me to do those things.

The most important benefit of getting a college degree is that it will show me that I can achieve something hard. In the past, I have often given up and taken the easy way, which has led to nothing good. The easy way has led to a hard life. Now, however, working toward a goal has moved my life in a good direction. I have confidence and self-respect. I can honestly say that I am proud of myself, and my daughter will be proud of me, too. I will be a good role model as she grows up. She will go to college, just like her mother.

So why am I working so hard to get a degree? I am doing it because I see in that degree the kind of life I want to live on this earth and the kind of human being I want to be. Achieving that vision is worth all the struggles.

PRACTICE 6–5   Revising an Essay

1. What major changes did you suggest for Chelsea's draft?

2. Did Chelsea make any of the suggested changes? Which ones?

3. Did Chelsea make any changes that were not suggested? Which ones? Were they effective changes?

WRITING ASSIGNMENT   Essay

Revise the draft essay you wrote in Chapter 5. As you read your draft critically, be sure to evaluate the paragraphs for unity, detail, and coherence. Also consider participating in peer review with your classmates or friends. After revising your draft, complete the following checklist.

> **CHECKLIST**
>
> Evaluating Your Revised Paragraph or Essay
>
> Does your revision
>
> ☐ meet the requirements of the original assignment?
> ☐ achieve your draft goals?
> ☐ have a clear main idea?
> ☐ focus on a single main idea in each paragraph (unity)?
> ☐ have well-developed supporting points with enough evidence or details for your reader?
> ☐ use transitions to help readers move smoothly from one supporting point or detail to the next?

Editing and Proofreading

After you have revised your writing to make the ideas clear and strong, you need to edit and proofread it. **Editing** means evaluating the words, phrases, and sentences you have used to make sure they are clear, accurate, and easy to read. **Proofreading** means finding and correcting mistakes in punctuation, capitalization, and spelling.

Most writers find it difficult to revise, edit, and proofread well if they try to do them all at once. It is easier to solve idea-level problems first (by revising) and then to make smaller sentence and word-level adjustments (by editing) before checking the paper one final time for any remaining errors in punctuation, capitalization, or spelling (by proofreading).

Editing

When you edit your paper, you will zoom your focus to specific sentences and words to make sure that your writing is clear and accurate so that readers will understand it. The chapters in Parts 3 and 4 will help you answer the following questions as you edit:

- Are my sentences complete? (Chapter 17)
- Are my sentences joined accurately? (Chapter 18)
- Do the verbs agree with the subjects and show time clearly? (Chapters 19 and 20)
- Have I chosen the right words? (Chapters 21, 22, and 23)
- Have I varied the sentence rhythm so that sentences are easy to read? (Chapter 24)

Proofreading

When you proofread, you make sure that your writing appears correctly on the page and that you have not left out words or punctuation. You will check for correct use of capital letters, apostrophes, and spelling (Chapter 25), as well as punctuation such as commas and quotation marks (Chapters 26 and 27). When you proofread, you must slow down and pay attention to details. The following techniques may help you proofread more effectively:

- Print out your paper before proofreading. (Many writers find it easier to detect errors on paper than on a computer screen.)

- Put a piece of paper under the line that you are reading so that you can focus on that line alone.

- Proofread your paper backward (from last word to first), one word at a time.

- Print out a version of your paper that looks noticeably different: Make the words larger, make the margins larger, triple-space the lines, or make all these changes.

- Read your paper aloud. This strategy will help you if you tend to leave out words.

- Have someone else read your paper aloud. You may hear where you have made a mistake or left a word out.

Chapter 6 Review

1. What is revising?

2. What are three common issues addressed in revision?

3. What is unity?

4. What does it mean to revise for development?

5. What are two strategies for improving coherence?

6. What is peer review?

7. What are editing and proofreading?

Reflect and Apply

1. Have you ever received useful feedback on your writing before? When? What made the feedback helpful to you?

2. Have you ever procrastinated on a writing assignment? What happens if you do not leave yourself enough time to revise, edit, and proofread your work?

3. Interview students who have been successful in your major. What strategies have they used for revising, editing, and proofreading successfully?

Part 2

Writing Different Kinds of Paragraphs and Essays

FOXLINE/GETTY IMAGES

Narration

Writing That Tells Important Stories

- List the four basics of narrative paragraphs and essays.
- Identify main events for support in narratives.
- Provide sensory details and examples for main events in narratives.
- Recognize transitions commonly used in narration.
- Write a narrative paragraph or essay with a clear main idea, strong support, and chronological organization.

One of the earliest kinds of writing that children encounter is a story. Parents often read stories to children, and students hear stories in elementary school. But stories are not just for children; many kinds of practical writing require that we tell what happened, whether we are writing a history essay, filing an insurance report, or blogging about a vacation. When we tell the story of what happened, we are narrating.

Understand What Narration Is

Narration is writing that tells the story of an event or an experience; sometimes the story itself is called a **narrative**.

Four Basics of Narration

1 **Main Idea:** An effective narrative paragraph or essay reveals something of importance to the writer (the main idea).

2 **Primary Support:** It includes all the major events of the story.

3 **Secondary Support:** It brings the story to life with specific details about the major events.

4 **Organization:** It presents the events in a clear order, usually according to when they happened (logical organization).

In the following paragraph, the numbers and colors correspond to the four basics of narration.

[1] Last year, a writing assignment I hated produced the best writing I have done. [2] When my English teacher told us that our assignment would be to do a few hours of community service and write about it, I was furious. [3] I am a single mother, I work full-time, and I am going to school—isn't that enough? [4] The next day, [2] I spoke to my teacher during her office hours and told her that I was already so busy I could hardly make time for homework, never mind housework. My own life was too full to help with anyone else's life. [3] She said that she understood and that the majority of her students had lives as full as mine. [4] Then [3] she explained that the service assignment was just for four hours and that other students had enjoyed both doing the assignment and writing about their experiences. She said they were all surprised and that I would be, too. [4] After talking with her, [2] I decided to accept my fate. [4] The next week, [2] I went to the Community Service Club and was set up to spend a few hours at an adult day-care center near where I live. [4] A few weeks later, [2] I went to the Creative Care Center in Cocoa Beach, not knowing what to expect. [3] I found friendly, approachable people who had so many stories to tell about their long, full lives. [4] The next thing I knew, [2] I was taking notes because I was interested in these people: [3] their marriages, life during the Depression, the wars they fought in, their children, their joys and sorrows. I felt as if I was experiencing everything they lived while they shared their history with me. [4] When it came time to write about my experience, [2] I had more than enough to write about: [3] I wrote the stories of the many wonderful elderly people I had talked with. I got an A on the paper, and beyond that accomplishment, I made friends whom I will visit on my own, not because of an assignment but because I value them.

In college, the word *narration* may not appear in writing assignments. Instead, an assignment might ask you to *describe* the events, *report* what happened, or *retell* what happened. Words or phrases that call for an *account of events* are situations that require narration.

First Basic: Main Idea in Narration

In narration, the **main idea** is what is important about the story—to you and to your readers. To help you discover the main idea when you are reading or writing a narrative, complete the following sentence:

Main idea in narration: What is important about the experience is that _____.

In a narrative, the topic sentence (paragraph) or thesis statement (essay) usually includes the topic and the main idea the writer wants to emphasize in the story. Let's look at a topic sentence first.

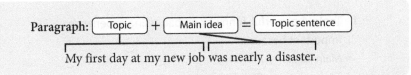

Paragraph: [Topic] + [Main idea] = [Topic sentence]

My first day at my new job was nearly a disaster.

Remember that a topic for an essay can be a little broader than one for a paragraph.

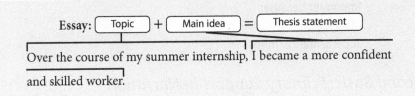

Essay: [Topic] + [Main idea] = [Thesis statement]

Over the course of my summer internship, I became a more confident and skilled worker.

Whereas the topic sentence is focused on just one workday, the thesis statement considers a season-long internship. The paragraph and essay models on pages 109–10 use the topic sentence (paragraph) and thesis statement (essay) from this main idea section. (The thesis statement has been revised slightly.)

PRACTICE 7-1   **Writing a Main Idea**

Look at the example narrative paragraph on page 102. Fill in the diagram with the paragraph's topic sentence.

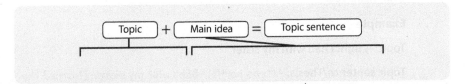

[Topic] + [Main idea] = [Topic sentence]

PRACTICE 7-2   **Deciding on a Main Idea**

For each of the following topics, write a main idea for a narration. Then write a sentence that includes your topic and your main idea. This sentence would be your topic sentence (paragraph) or thesis statement (essay).

Example:

Topic: A fight I had with my sister

Important because: It taught me something.

Main idea: I learned it is better to stay cool.

Topic sentence/Thesis: After a horrible fight with my sister, I learned the value of staying calm.

1. Topic: A powerful, funny, or embarrassing experience
   Important because:
   Main idea:
   Topic sentence/Thesis:

2. Topic: A strange or interesting incident that you witnessed
   Important because:
   Main idea:
   Topic sentence/Thesis:

Second Basic: Primary Support in Narration

In narration, support demonstrates the main idea—what's important about the story. For most narratives, the primary support includes the major events in the story. Give careful thought to the events you will include, selecting only those that most clearly demonstrate your main idea.

> **PRACTICE 7-3**   **Choosing Major Events**

Choose two items from Practice 7-2 and write down the topic sentence or thesis statement you came up with for each. Then, for each topic sentence/thesis statement, come up with three events that would help you show your main idea.

Example

Topic: A fight I had with my sister

Topic sentence/Thesis: After a horrible fight with my sister, I learned the value of staying calm.

Events: We disagreed about who was going to have the family party. She made me so mad that I started yelling at her, and I got nasty. I hung up on her, and now we're not talking.

1. Topic: A powerful, funny, or embarrassing experience
   Topic sentence/Thesis:
   Events:

2. Topic: A strange or interesting incident that you witnessed
   Topic sentence/Thesis:
   Events:

Third Basic: Secondary Support in Narration

When you write a narrative, include examples and details that will make each event easier to visualize and understand. The descriptive details that support each major event should be specific and should appeal to a reader's senses: sight, touch, taste, sound, or smell. Read the following paragraph from Amy Tan's essay, "Fish Cheeks," which appears in full on pages 117–18. The first sentence introduces the major event ("a strange menu"), and the rest of the paragraph provides supporting sensory details:

> On Christmas Eve, I saw that my mother had outdone herself in creating a strange menu. She was pulling black veins out of the backs of fleshy prawns. The kitchen was littered with appalling mounds of raw food: a slimy rock cod with bulging eyes that pleaded not to be thrown into a pan of hot oil. Tofu, which looked like stacked wedges of rubbery white sponges. A bowl soaking dried fungus back to life. A plate of squid, their backs crisscrossed with knife markings so they resembled bicycle tires.

To emphasize how different this meal is from a traditional American meal, Tan could have just listed the menu items: prawns, rock cod, tofu, fungus, and squid. But readers accustomed to turkey and dressing might not be able to imagine these Chinese foods. So Tan provides sensory details; she helps us see and feel the food. For example, the prawns are "fleshy," and there are "black veins" that must be removed from them. Even if you have never eaten prawns, you can visualize this menu item more effectively because of her description.

Another strategy for adding descriptive details in narration is to use dialogue. Dialogue occurs when you quote what a person said in a conversation, allowing readers to "hear" a speaker's voice. For example, look at what one student wrote about encouragement from a coach after a particularly difficult loss:

> Back in the locker room, Coach Ormand didn't tell us what we did wrong. Instead, he encouraged us to keep trying.

While these sentences give the reader important information, they don't provide a lot of detail. Look at this revision to the paragraph. Why is this version more effective?

> Back in the locker room, Coach Ormand didn't tell us what we did wrong. Instead, he huddled us together and said, "Gentlemen, you lost today. But you are not losers. What I saw today tells me you are winners. If you keep playing with as much heart as you did today, pretty soon the scoreboard is going to show what I already know: you are winners."
>
> "Coach," I answered, "I don't feel like a winner."
>
> "Maybe not. But it's not what you feel that makes you a winner. It's what you do when you walk out of here," he replied.

Notice the following features of dialogue:

- The dialogue is introduced by the word *said* and a comma.
- There are quotation marks at the beginning and at the end of the spoken lines.
- The quoted dialogue begins with a capital letter.
- A change in speaker is signaled by a new paragraph.

The word *said* is part of a signal phrase (a name—*Coach Ormand*—or pronoun—*he, she, they*—plus a verb), which lets the reader know a quote is coming. Other verbs, such as *ask, demand, claim, suggest, explain, yell,* or *whisper,* may also be used in signal phrases, depending on the attitude or behavior of the speaker. Writers often use signal phrases in dialogue.

> **PRACTICE 7-4**   **Giving Details about the Events**

Write down the topic sentence or thesis statement for each item from Practice 7-3. Then write the major events in the spaces provided. Give a detail about each event.

Example

Topic sentence/Thesis: After a horrible fight with my sister, I learned the value of staying calm.

Event: We disagreed about who was going to have the family party.

> **Detail:** Even though we both work, she said, "I'm just too busy—you will just have to do it." Her voice was bossy and demanding.

Event: She made me so mad, I started yelling at her, and I got nasty.

> **Detail:** I brought up times in the past when she had tried to pass responsibilities off on me, and I told her I was sick of being the one who did everything.

Event: I hung up on her, and now we are not talking.

> **Detail:** I was so mad I threw my phone into the wall, shattering my screen and putting a dent in the paint. I was mad, but I shouldn't have lost my cool. After three days of not talking to her and hearing only the sound of her voicemail instead of her quirky, high-pitched laugh, I knew it was time to apologize.

1. Topic sentence/Thesis:

   Event:

   > Detail:

   Event:

   > Detail:

Event:

    Detail:

2. Topic sentence/Thesis:

    Event:

        Detail:

    Event:

        Detail:

    Event:

        Detail:

Fourth Basic: Organization in Narration

Narration usually presents events in the order in which they happened, which is referred to as time (or *chronological*) order. As shown in the paragraph and essay models on pages 109–10, a narrative starts at the beginning of the story and describes events as they unfolded.

Using Transitions in Narration

Transitions help readers follow the chronology in a narrative, and they move readers smoothly from one main event to the next.

Common Transitions in Narration

after	eventually	meanwhile	since
as	finally	next	soon
at last	first	now	then
before	last	once	when
during	later	second	while

Using a Graphic Organizer in Narration

A **graphic organizer** is a tool that helps you organize and understand primary and secondary support in paragraphs and essays, so you can see the big picture of how a paragraph or essay is arranged. As a writer, you can use this information to make adjustments if needed. As a reader, you can use a graphic organizer to identify and understand the primary support and secondary supporting details in a text.

Graphic organizers for narration include the main idea followed by the major events and supporting details in order. You may add as many boxes as needed.

The following graphic organizer illustrates the paragraph on page 109.

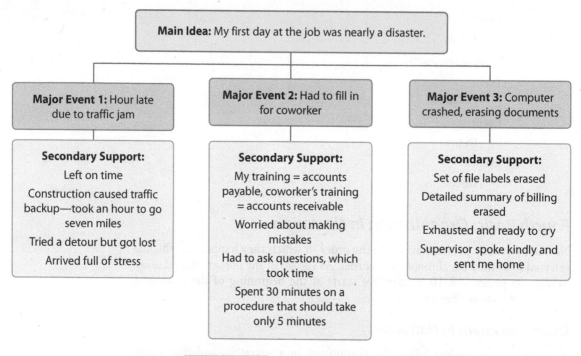

PRACTICE 7–5   Using Transitions in Narration

Read the paragraph that follows, and fill in the blanks with one of the following: *after, at, at last, before, during, earlier, eventually, once, next, then, when, while*. When you have finished, create a graphic organizer to illustrate the organization of the paragraph. (Note that more than one option may be correct.)

Some historians believe that as many as four hundred women disguised themselves as men to serve in the U.S. Civil War (1861–1865). One of the best known of these women was Sarah Emma Edmonds. _____ the beginning of the war, Edmonds, an opponent of slavery, joined the Union Army, which fought for the free states. _____ President Abraham Lincoln asked for army volunteers, she disguised herself as a man, took the name Frank Thompson, and enlisted in the infantry. _____ her military service, Edmonds worked as a male nurse and a messenger. _____ serving as a nurse, she learned that the Union general needed someone to spy on the Confederates. _____ extensive training, Edmonds took on this duty and, disguised as a slave, went behind enemy lines. Here, she learned about the Confederates' military strengths and weaknesses. _____, she returned to the Union side and went back to work as a nurse. In 1863, Edmonds left the army after developing malaria. She was worried that hospital workers would discover that she was a woman. As a result of her departure, "Frank Thompson" was listed as a deserter. In later years, Edmonds, under her real name, worked to get a veteran's pension and to get the desertion charge removed from her record. _____, in 1884, a special act of Congress granted her both of these wishes.

Paragraphs versus Essays in Narration

For more on the important features of narration, see the "Four Basics of Narration" on page 101.

Paragraph Form

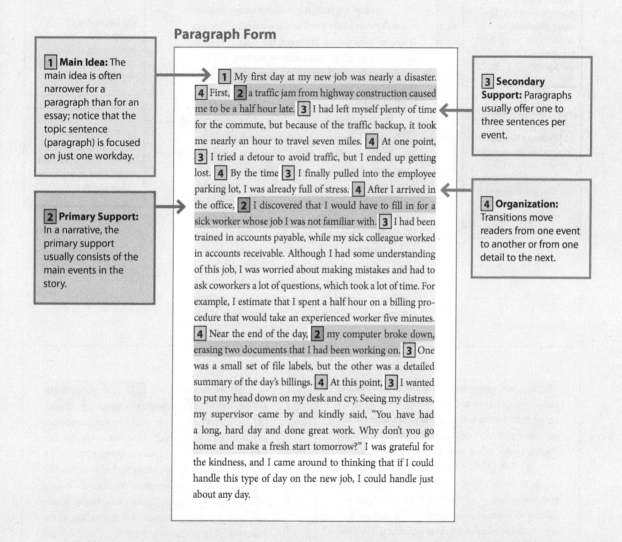

1 Main Idea: The main idea is often narrower for a paragraph than for an essay; notice that the topic sentence (paragraph) is focused on just one workday.

2 Primary Support: In a narrative, the primary support usually consists of the main events in the story.

1 My first day at my new job was nearly a disaster. **4** First, **2** a traffic jam from highway construction caused me to be a half hour late. **3** I had left myself plenty of time for the commute, but because of the traffic backup, it took me nearly an hour to travel seven miles. **4** At one point, **3** I tried a detour to avoid traffic, but I ended up getting lost. **4** By the time **3** I finally pulled into the employee parking lot, I was already full of stress. **4** After I arrived in the office, **2** I discovered that I would have to fill in for a sick worker whose job I was not familiar with. **3** I had been trained in accounts payable, while my sick colleague worked in accounts receivable. Although I had some understanding of this job, I was worried about making mistakes and had to ask coworkers a lot of questions, which took a lot of time. For example, I estimate that I spent a half hour on a billing procedure that would take an experienced worker five minutes. **4** Near the end of the day, **2** my computer broke down, erasing two documents that I had been working on. **3** One was a small set of file labels, but the other was a detailed summary of the day's billings. **4** At this point, **3** I wanted to put my head down on my desk and cry. Seeing my distress, my supervisor came by and kindly said, "You have had a long, hard day and done great work. Why don't you go home and make a fresh start tomorrow?" I was grateful for the kindness, and I came around to thinking that if I could handle this type of day on the new job, I could handle just about any day.

3 Secondary Support: Paragraphs usually offer one to three sentences per event.

4 Organization: Transitions move readers from one event to another or from one detail to the next.

Consider Readers as You Write a Narrative

Ask Yourself

- Do I have a main idea that is clear and interesting for readers?
- Have I included all the major events readers will need to know about?
- Have I provided enough detail to bring each major event to life for readers?
- Have I organized my ideas and details logically so readers can follow the story?

109

Essay Form

1

Several of my friends question whether summer internships are really worthwhile, especially if the pay is low or nonexistent. However, the right internship definitely pays off professionally in the long run even if it doesn't financially in the short run. **1** The proof is in my own summer marketing internship, which made me a far more confident and skilled worker.

4 During the first two weeks of the internship, **2** I received thorough training in every part of my job. **4** For example, **3** my immediate supervisor spent three full days going over everything I would need to do to help with email campaigns, online marketing efforts, and other promotions. She even had me draft a promotional email for a new product and gave me feedback about how to make the message clearer and more appealing. I also spent a lot of time with other staffers, who taught me everything from how to use the photocopier and printers to how to pull together marketing and sales materials for executive meetings. Most impressive, the president of the

2

company took some time out of a busy afternoon to answer my questions about how he got started in his career and what he sees as the keys to success in the marketing field. As I explained to a friend, I got a real "insider's view" of the company and its leadership.

4 Next, **2** I got hands-on experience with listening to customers and addressing their needs. **3** Specifically, I sat in on meetings with new clients and listened to them describe products and services they would like the company's help in promoting. They also discussed the message they would like to get across about their businesses. After the meetings, I sat in on brainstorming sessions with other staffers in which we came up with as many ideas as we could about campaigns to address the clients' needs. At first, I didn't think anyone would care about my ideas, but others listened to them respectfully and even ended up including some of them in the marketing plans that were sent back to the clients. I learned later that some of my ideas would be included in the actual promotional campaigns.

3

4 By summer's end, **2** I had advanced my skills so much that I was asked to return next summer. **3** My supervisor told me that she was pleased not only with all I had learned about marketing but also with the responsibility I took for every aspect of my job. I did not roll my eyes about having to make photocopies or help at the reception desk, nor did I seem intimidated by bigger, more meaningful tasks. Although I'm not guaranteed a full-time job at the company after graduation, I think my chances are good. Even if I don't end up working there long term, I am grateful for how the job has helped me grow.

4 In the end, the greatest benefit of the internship might be the confidence it gave me. I have learned that no matter how challenging the task before me—at work or in real life—I can succeed at it by getting the right information and input on anything unfamiliar, working effectively with others, and truly dedicating myself to doing my best. My time this past summer was definitely well spent.

110

Read and Analyze Narration

To become a more successful writer, it is important not only to understand the four basics of narration on page 101 but to read and analyze examples as well. In this section, you will use a rubric to evaluate the first draft of a narrative paragraph by Jelani Lynch. Then you will look at a polished student literacy narrative by Morgan Xiong. Next, you will see how Alice Adoga uses narration in her field of social work. The final example is a narration essay by Amy Tan, a professional writer.

Student Narration Paragraph

Read this first draft of a narrative paragraph. For this first draft, the instructor asked students to focus on the main idea, supporting content, and organization. Using the four basics of narration and the sample rubric that follows, decide how effective this draft of the paragraph is, and then recommend one or two goals for the student's next draft.

> **Assignment:** Write a paragraph about one moment or a decision that made a significant difference in your life. You should use clear transitions to indicate the passage of time, and you should use enough detail to bring the story to life for your reader.

Jelani Lynch

My Turnaround

Before my big turnaround, my life was headed in the wrong direction. I grew up in the city and had a typical sad story. In this world, few positive male role models are available. I played the game "Street Life." The men in my neighborhood did not have regular jobs; they got their money outside the system. No one except my mother thought school was worth much. I had a history of doing poorly in school. My pattern of failure in that area was pretty strong. When I was seventeen, though, things got really bad. I was arrested for possession of crack cocaine. I was kicked out of school for good. During this time, I realized that my life was not going the way I wanted it to be. I was headed nowhere. I knew that way of life, because I was surrounded by people who had chosen that direction. I did not want to go there anymore. When I made that decision, my life started to change. First, I met a man who had had the same kind of life I did. He got out of that life. He has a house, a wife, and children, along with great clothes. He became my role model, showing me important lessons. Since meeting him, I have turned my life around. I graduated from high school, something I thought I would never do. Working with him, I have had the opportunity to do a lot of things. Now, I am trying to help my community, and I have a bright future with goals and plans. I have turned my life around and know I will be a success.

Rubric for Narration

	1 **Falls below expectations**	2 **Nearly meets expectations**	3 **Meets expectations**	4 **Exceeds expectations**
Main idea (first basic)	No clear main idea or purpose is present.	Main idea is too broad/narrow for assignment.	Main idea is appropriate but dull, or purpose is unclear.	Main idea is engaging with a clear sense of purpose.
Support (second and third basics)	Irrelevant events and details are included; they do not convey main idea.	Some relevant events and details are present to suggest a main idea.	Main events and details are relevant, and main idea is clear but more details are needed.	Main events and details are relevant and vivid; they create a clear main idea.
Organization (fourth basic)	Organization is unclear or illogical.	Organization is inconsistent.	Organization is logical, but some transitions are missing or inappropriate.	Organization is logical, with smooth transitions throughout.

Evaluating the Paragraph

1. Does the paragraph show the four basics of narration? Explain.

2. Using the rubric as a guide, what is the strongest part of the paragraph? The weakest?

3. Write a response to this writer, using one of the following to frame your response:

   a. One thing I would like to know more about is _____.

   b. What I liked best about the paragraph is _____.

   c. In your next draft, you might consider adding _____.

Student Narration Essay

Morgan Xiong

A War for Words

Preview Xiong's essay is a **literacy narrative**, or the story of reading or writing experiences. Look at the title of the essay and skim the first paragraph. What question do you think she will answer in this essay?

From the beginning, I was always surrounded by books. You could say I had a similar upbringing to Sherman Alexie's. In the beginning of Alexie's essay "Superman and Me," he tells about his past and the influence his father had on his developing love of literature. For me, it was my mother. I remember her taking my brothers and me to the library at least once a week, and we never left without something to read. As I grew older, I discovered that people would write their own stories online, and it was free for anyone to look at! This discovery was one of the best things to ever happen in my life. Sadly, although reading came easy to me, writing was another story. Because of my experiences in theater, I am a fairly decent writer now. But before my time in drama class, writing was a never-ending war. Some battles I won, while others had me retreating, ready to wave a white flag.

2   When I first started elementary school, I used to have multiple notebooks that were supposed to be diaries. The reason why they weren't diaries was because inside each notebook were not my thoughts from day to day or gossip that my neighborhood friends had shared with me, but mostly blank pages. The few that weren't blank had random pictures that I had drawn or scribbles that I put so that it would look like I wrote something. I scribbled illegible nonsense because I was in love with the idea of being able to write stories. Then I would have been just like the authors I loved to read. However, whenever I would sit and try to write, my mind would go blank. Each and every time I wanted to create something, I would get nothing done. Time would pass, and I would give up on storytelling and just draw. So, my notebooks became sketchbooks instead. Score: Writing 1, Morgan 0.

3   Writing still wasn't easy for me later on in school, but at least then I had teachers who would give the class a basic idea and then let the children run wild with it. I remember in third grade, we had a writing assignment about an animal of our choosing going on some kind of adventure. At the time, I was obsessed with *Barbie of Swan Lake*. So, I wrote a tale about a swan whose pond was hit by a crazy storm that swept her away. Alone and homesick, she had to embark on this epic journey across foreign lands. Later, in my sixth grade earth science class, we had to write about the process of the water cycle. So, I wrote about Timmy Raindrop's travels, how he first started in a lake and then how he would soar to the sky and wait in the clouds until the time was right. He would then free fall back down to earth. Both of these writings got pretty good feedback, and they made me feel better about my writing capabilities. Score: Morgan 2, Writing 1. I was in the lead, or so I thought.

4   I may have won the first few battles, but the war was far from over. My freshman year of high school started, and I couldn't write fictional stories about humanized raindrops and talking lost swans for grades anymore. My writing had to come from resources and research and not be fabricated from my imagination. What was this blasphemy? Not only that, but it seemed that no matter how much I tried, I couldn't get anything right. I would try to make what we were working on more fun for me and throw in a twist. My teacher didn't like that too much

and my grade would suffer. So I would try my best to wrap my head around how an assignment was originally intended to be, but by then I was bored with it. The constant searching and having to make up an opinion on something did not interest me. And then having my research back up my made-up opinion was agonizing as well. Because I half-heartedly did the work, again, my grades suffered. I started to lose faith in everything I did. It came to the point where I didn't turn anything in because it was either incomplete or I didn't even start it at all. I felt like my elementary self. No matter how long I sat in front of the open notebook, nothing would come to mind. I couldn't get any ideas down. I was ready to admit defeat.

5   We moved the end of my freshman year. I kept in contact with my best friends, but it just wasn't the same. They were no longer a ten-minute walk away. I was alone and didn't know what to do with myself. So to liven my life up a bit, I decided to make theater my elective class during sophomore year. It was a great call on my part. I found where I truly belonged, my discourse, you might call it. Linguist James Paul Gee explains that a discourse is sort of "an identity kit." He describes it as a way a person speaks or writes to show they belonged to a certain group. Discourses can relate to ethnicity and even employment fields. I had found myself, my identity, through theater. Soon, my grades improved tremendously because I wanted to pursue acting. I knew I couldn't do it if I was stuck in high school. During my time in drama class, I learned so many new things, all of which assisted me academically and recreationally. For example, script analysis gave me some great habits to help me when I had research papers to do.

Thescon: a conference for actors (or *thespians*) and others involved in theater

Also, while at Thescon, a few friends and I took a writing workshop. This taught me better ways to organize my chaotic imagination so that I could connect my stories or regular writing projects to a greater degree.

6   Being a thespian has allowed me to do numerous things. Not only could I tell my own stories that I had longed to produce, but I could also be a part of someone else's. My war against writing may never end. However, with theater under my belt, all the battles I face from here on out will be downhill, and with little doubt, I will conquer them.

Write to Read: Annotate

1. Identify the main idea and underline or highlight the main events in Xiong's story.

2. Put exclamation points by the most effective descriptions in her narrative.

Read to Write: Think Critically

1. Xiong repeats the image of a battle or competition by giving a score in her essay. How do these images support her main idea?

2. Xiong refers to two writers, Sherman Alexie and James Paul Gee. Why do you think she does this? Does she give readers enough information about these

Profile of Success: Alice Adoga
Narration in the Real World

Title Family Service Specialist

Background In January 2007, I moved from West Africa, Nigeria, to the United States at the age of eighteen to live with my stepmom and three siblings. Before leaving Nigeria, I knew my life was going to change a great deal. However, I had no idea what these changes would be. In the fall of 2007, I started the twelfth grade at Franklin High School after taking many of Virginia's grade-level standardized tests. Not only did I have to deal with cultural differences, I also had to adjust to the educational system of this country. In my English classes, I was lacking in grammar, and I had difficulties writing research papers. I was always self-conscious about my writing and panicked when asked to write a paper. After graduating from high school in 2008, I decided to further my education at Paul D. Camp Community College (PDCCC). While at PDCCC, I had to take developmental English, and I struggled through most English classes during my freshman year in college. I worked very

closely with all my English teachers and professors in college. I also had several tutors assist me with my papers. Although my grammar has improved, I am still learning how to be a better writer today.

Writing at Work My writing at work is an objective narrative of reports from mandated reporters and clients' documentation during intake assessment or investigations. My job requires accurate documentation of interactions with clients during interviews and any interactions carried out with child victims and anyone involved. Reports made to our agency need to be documented in the Online Automated Structured Information System (OASIS). Part of my job is to write out accurately what has been reported to me during interviews to help give the reader a better picture of what took place during the incident. After interviews with a client, I write a descriptive narrative of what was said to me without inclusion of personal thoughts or opinions.

Alice Adoga

Family Service Specialist

writers to understand why they appear in her story? If Xiong brought this paper to your group for peer review, what suggestions (if any) would you make about these two references?

Use Reading Strategies: Summarize

Review the skills you learned in Chapter 1, pages 18–20, and then write a short summary of Xiong's essay.

Reflect and Respond

Did you struggle with reading, math, writing, or other skills in school when you were younger? How does your experience compare with Xiong's? Write a paragraph describing your difficulty and how you overcame it.

Workplace Narration

Alice Adoga

Incident Description

Preview This narrative is a report based on an interview. Skim the narrative and make a note of the names that appear. Who are the participants in the narrative?

Caller, Ms. Joyce Baton, stated that she knows that Courtney Moses is leaving her seven-year-old daughter, Lilian Moses, at home alone in the evening several nights of the week and all day during the weekends without any food. Also, the apartment has been without power for the past three weeks. Caller informed this worker that she noted several times over the past month that Lilian has come over to their house after school and near dinnertime to see their daughter, Melody Baton. Caller informed this worker that Lilian and her daughter Melody go to the same school and ride the same bus to and from school. Whenever she stops by their house, Lilian asks if she can join Melody for dinner because "Mom doesn't have anything for me to eat." Ms. Baton stated that her daughter and Lilian "hang out" after school, and sometimes Lilian stays over for dinner. Ms. Baton says she always makes Lilian call her mother to get permission, and she has even talked with Ms. Moses about Lilian's frequent dinner requests. Ms. Baton reports that Ms. Moses does not mind that Lilian stays over and profusely thanks her for letting Lilian eat dinner with them. When this first began, Ms. Baton thought Lilian just didn't like what was being offered at home. However, Ms. Baton said she recently began to notice that Lilian "wolfs her food down" when she eats and is always finished earlier than her family. Lilian has told Ms. Baton on a few occasions, "We don't have any food left."

2   Ms. Baton stated that Melody is in the same class as Lilian. Melody told her that Lilian did not have food in her lunch bag several times last week. She also told her that Lilian asks other kids for food at school and on the bus. Ms. Baton has been to the Moses's home but has not been comfortable talking with Ms. Moses about the lack of food. Ms. Baton is concerned because her daughter has come home every day this week and reported that Lilian was begging for food. She has begun putting extra sandwiches and fruit in her daughter's lunch to share with Lilian. Ms. Baton informed this worker that she saw Lilian and her daughter get on the bus this morning. They use the same bus stop. Lilian is currently at All Kings Elementary School. The address is 1539 Lakeview Drive, Lakely, Virginia 23333. Ms. Baton stated that she wants to remain anonymous because no one knows she is calling us. She believes Ms. Moses knows about Lilian's behavior.

Write to Read: Annotate

1. What is your main impression of what is happening in the Moses' home? Number the primary details that support the main impression.

2. Underline or highlight any secondary details that help tell the story.

Read to Write: Think Critically

1. Who is the intended audience for this report, and what is its purpose?

2. Sometimes Adoga uses quotation marks in the narrative, and other times she does not. What is the difference?

Use Reading Strategies: Create a Graphic Organizer

Following the model on page 108, create a graphic organizer to show the major events in Adoga's narration. Compare your chart with a classmate's. Do you have the same number of major events? If not, discuss the differences.

Reflect and Respond

How is this report different in style and tone from the narratives of Tan (p. 118) or Xiong (p. 113)? Why do you think this is the case? What are other situations in which you might be asked to write in this objective style, without adding comments?

Professional Narration Essay

Amy Tan

Fish Cheeks

MIREYA ACIERTO/GETTY IMAGES

Amy Tan was born in Oakland, California, in 1952, several years after her mother and father emigrated from China. She studied at San Jose City College and later San Jose State University, receiving a B.A. with a double major in English and linguistics. In 1973, she earned an M.A. in linguistics from San Jose State University. In 1989, Tan published her first novel, *The Joy Luck Club*, which was nominated for the National Book Award and the National Book Critics Circle Award. She has written six other novels, as well as several short stories and essays. The following essay was originally published in *Seventeen* (a magazine for girls ages 13–19).

Preview   Skim the first paragraph. What conflict do you think the narrator in this story will have to face?

I fell in love with the minister's son the winter I turned fourteen. He was not Chinese, but as white as Mary in the manger. For Christmas I prayed for this blond-haired boy, Robert, and a slim new American nose.

2   When I found out that my parents had invited the minister's family over for Christmas dinner, I cried. What would Robert think of our shabby Chinese Christmas? What would he think of our noisy Chinese relatives who lacked proper American manners? What terrible disappointment would he feel upon seeing not a roasted turkey and sweet potatoes but Chinese food?

appalling: horrifying

3   On Christmas Eve I saw that my mother had outdone herself in creating a strange menu. She was pulling black veins out of the backs of fleshy prawns. The kitchen was littered with appalling mounds of raw food: a slimy rock cod with bulging eyes that pleaded not to be thrown into a pan of hot oil. Tofu, which looked like stacked wedges of rubbery white sponges. A bowl soaking dried fungus back to life. A plate of squid, their backs crisscrossed with knife markings so they resembled bicycle tires.

clamor: noise

4   And then they arrived—the minister's family and all my relatives in a clamor of doorbells and rumpled Christmas packages. Robert grunted hello, and I pretended he was not worthy of existence.

5   Dinner threw me into despair. My relatives licked the ends of their chopsticks and reached across the table, dipping them into the dozen or so plates of food. Robert and his family waited patiently for platters to be passed to them. My relatives murmured with pleasure when my mother brought out the whole steamed fish. Robert grimaced. Then my father poked his chopsticks just below the fish eye and plucked out the soft meat. "Amy, your favorite," he said, offering me the tender fish cheek. I wanted to disappear.

6   At the end of the meal, my father leaned back and belched loudly, thanking my mother for her fine cooking. "It's a polite Chinese custom to show you are satisfied," explained my father to our astonished guests. Robert was looking down at his plate with a reddened face. The minister managed to muster up a quiet burp. I was stunned into silence for the rest of the night.

7   After everyone had gone, my mother said to me, "You want to be the same as American girls on the outside." She handed me an early gift. It was a miniskirt in beige tweed. "But inside you must always be Chinese. You must be proud you are different. Your only shame is to have shame."

8   And even though I didn't agree with her then, I knew that she understood how much I had suffered during the evening's dinner. It wasn't until many years later—long after I had gotten over my crush on Robert—that I was able to fully appreciate her lesson and the true purpose behind our particular menu. For Christmas Eve that year, she had chosen all my favorite foods.

Write to Read: Annotate

1. Identify the main idea and underline or highlight the major events in the story.

2. List all the transition words and time references that Tan uses to help readers follow the story.

Read to Write: Think Critically

1. Why is this essay called "Fish Cheeks"?

2. The essay was originally published in *Seventeen* magazine. How does this information help you understand Tan's intended audience and her choice of details?

3. Does Tan's attitude about being Chinese change during the story? Explain.

Use Reading Strategies: Paraphrase

In Chapter 1, you learned how to paraphrase, to explain a concept briefly in your own words so that others can understand it. Review the information about paraphrasing in Chapter 1, pages 14–15, and then study the following example:

> **Original:** Amy Tan says, "I fell in love with the minister's son the winter I turned fourteen. He was not Chinese, but as white as Mary in the manger. For Christmas I prayed for this blond-haired boy, Robert, and a slim new American nose."
>
> **Paraphrase:** Amy Tan suggests that she was not happy with her obvious Asian features, and at the age of fourteen, she wanted to be more American, with a blond boyfriend and an attractive nose.

In her essay, Tan describes important words her mother said to her. Read these quotes from Tan's mother and paraphrase each one. Make sure that you cover the original quote while you are writing so that you avoid a cut-and-paste paraphrase (see Chapter 1). You can begin each paraphrase this way: "Tan's mother says that _____."

1. Tan's mother says, "You want to be the same as American girls on the outside."

2. Tan's mother says, "But inside you must always be Chinese. You must be proud you are different."

3. Tan's mother says, "Your only shame is to have shame."

Reflect and Respond

1. Have you ever been embarrassed by your family or by others close to you? Write about the experience and describe what you learned from it.

2. Write about a time when you felt different from other people. How did you react at the time? Have your feelings about the situation changed since then? If so, how?

Grammar for Narration

Because narration describes events as they unfold over time, it is important to pay attention to verb tenses when you are editing a narrative paragraph or essay. Be consistent in your use of tenses, and make sure the tenses fit the order of the events in the narrative. Take a look at some of the tenses used in sentences from Amy Tan's essay:

Sentence	Tense	Explanation
I <u>fell</u> in love with the minister's son the winter I <u>turned</u> fourteen.	Simple past	Use simple past for major events in the story.
When I found out that my parents <u>had invited</u> the minister's family over for Christmas dinner, I cried.	Past perfect	Use past perfect for events that occurred before the major events in the story.
Robert <u>was looking</u> down at his plate with a reddened face.	Past progressive	Use past progressive for actions that were in progress during the major events.

For more information about verb tenses and verb endings, see Chapter 20.

Write Your Own Narrative

In this section, you will write your own narrative essay based on one of the following assignments. For help, refer to the "How to Write Narration" checklist on page 123.

Assignment Options: Writing about College, Work, and Everyday Life

Write a narration paragraph or essay on one of the following topics or on one of your own choice:

College

- Tell the story of how a teacher, coach, or other mentor made a difference in your life.
- Interview a college graduate working in your field. Tell that person's story, focusing on how he or she achieved success.

Work	•	Write about a situation/incident that made you leave a job.
	•	Write about your own work history, guided by a statement that you would like to make about this history or your work style. Here is one example: "Being a people person has helped me in every job I have ever had." You might imagine that you are interviewing with a potential employer.
Everyday Life	•	Write about an experience that triggered a strong emotion: happiness, sadness, fear, anger, regret.
	•	Find a campus community service club that offers short-term assignments. Take an assignment and write about your experience.

Assignment Options: Reading and Writing Critically

Complete one of the following assignments that asks you to apply the critical thinking, reading, and writing skills discussed in Chapter 1.

Writing Critically about Readings

Both Alice Adoga's "Incident Description" (p. 116) and James Roy's "Malicious Wounding" (p. 164) require the writer to tell a story objectively, recording only the facts. Review both of these pieces. Then follow these steps:

1. **Summarize.** Briefly summarize the works, listing the major events in each.

2. **Analyze.** Identify the intended audience for each piece and consider how the details used reflect the purpose and audience. List any types of examples or details the authors could have added to their reports. Also, write down any questions that the pieces raise for you.

3. **Synthesize.** Using examples from either Adoga's or Roy's stories and from your own experience, write about an observation in your own life. Choose an event that was significant and write about it clearly and with detail.

4. **Evaluate.** Which piece do you find more effective? Why? To write your evaluation, look back on your responses to step 2.

Writing Critically about Visuals

Study the photograph below, and complete the following steps:

DAN BANNISTER/GETTY IMAGES

1. **Read the visual.** Ask yourself: What is the setting of the photo? What details does the photographer focus on? What seems to be the photo's message? (For more information on reading visuals, see Chapter 1.)

2. **Write a narration.** Write a narration paragraph or essay about what has happened (or is happening) in the photograph. Be as creative as you like, but be sure to include details and reactions from step 1. As you write, consider a possible purpose and audience for your essay.

Writing Critically about Problems

Read or review the discussion of problem solving in Chapter 1 (pp. 26–28). Then consider the following problem:

> You have learned that a generous scholarship is available for low-income, first-generation college students. You really need the money to cover day-care expenses while you are taking classes. (In fact, you had thought you would have to stop going to college for a while.) Many people have been applying. Part of the application is to write about yourself and why you deserve the scholarship.
>
> **Assignment:** Write a paragraph or essay that tells your story and why you should be considered for the scholarship. Think about how you can make your story stand out. You might start with the following sentence:
>
> *Even though you will be reading applications from many first-generation college students, my story is a little different because . . .*

CHECKLIST

How to Write Narration

| Prewrite | Draft | Revise | Edit & Proofread |

CONSIDER THE CONTEXT AND FIND A NARROW TOPIC. (See Chapters 2 and 3.)

- ☐ Identify your audience and purpose before choosing a topic.
- ☐ Narrow the topic to fit the assigned genre and length.
- ☐ Prewrite to get ideas about the narrowed topic.

| Prewrite | **Draft** | Revise | Edit & Proofread |

DRAFT A TOPIC SENTENCE (PARAGRAPH) OR THESIS STATEMENT (ESSAY). (See Chapter 3.)

- ☐ State what is most important to you about the topic (the main idea).
- ☐ Make sure you can develop the main idea fully within the length specified for the assignment.

SUPPORT YOUR MAIN IDEA. (See Chapter 4.)

- ☐ Come up with examples to explain your main idea to readers, including all the major events in the story.
- ☐ Use concrete, sensory details to make the major events come alive.
- ☐ Consider using dialogue.

WRITE A DRAFT. (See Chapter 5.)

- ☐ Put events in time (or chronological) order.
- ☐ Include a topic sentence (paragraph) or thesis statement (essay) and all the supporting events, examples, and details.
- ☐ Add an appropriate introduction and conclusion.

| Prewrite | Draft | **Revise** | Edit & Proofread |

REVISE YOUR DRAFT. (See Chapter 6.)

- ☐ Make sure it has *all* four basics of narration (p. 101).
- ☐ Make sure each paragraph is unified (all ideas should relate to the topic sentence).
- ☐ Make sure each paragraph is fully developed (there are enough supporting details to demonstrate the point).
- ☐ Make sure you include transitions to move readers smoothly from one event or detail to the next.

| Prewrite | Draft | Revise | **Edit & Proofread** |

EDIT AND PROOFREAD YOUR REVISED DRAFT. (See Parts 3 and 4.)

- ☐ Make sure grammar, word usage, and punctuation choices are clear, accurate, and effective.
- ☐ Check spelling and capitalization.

Chapter 7 Review

1. What is narration?

2. List the four basics of narration.

3. The topic sentence in a narration paragraph or the thesis statement in a narration essay usually includes what two things?

4. What type of organization do writers of narration usually use?

5. List five common transitions for this type of organization.

Reflect and Apply

1. Have you ever written or read narration before? How does that experience confirm, contradict, or complicate what you have learned in this chapter?

2. Interview someone studying in your major or working in your career. Ask how that person uses narration at work.

3. What was most difficult about your writing for this chapter? What do you want to do differently next time?

4. What part of your writing for this chapter was most successful? What do you need to remember for next time?

Illustration

Writing That Gives Examples

Learning Outcomes   In this chapter, you will learn to

- List the four basics of illustration paragraphs and essays.
- Identify examples to support illustration paragraphs and essays.
- Support examples in illustration with specific details.
- Recognize transitions commonly used in illustration paragraphs and essays.
- Write an illustration paragraph or essay with a clear main idea, strong support, and logical organization.

One of the most effective ways to explain a concept or idea is to **illustrate** it—in other words, to give examples. Illustration occurs in almost every communication situation, whether you are answering an exam question for your psychology class or writing to complain about the lack of maintenance in your apartment building. Examples can make a point effectively and clearly.

Understand What Illustration Is

Illustration is writing that uses examples to support a point.

Four Basics of Illustration

1 **Main Idea:** An effective illustration paragraph or essay has a point to communicate to readers.

2 **Primary Support:** It gives specific examples that show, explain, or prove the point.

3 **Secondary Support:** It gives details to support the examples.

4 **Organization:** It is organized with transitions to guide readers through the examples.

In the following paragraph, the numbers and colors correspond to the four basics of illustration.

> **1** Many people would like to serve their communities or help with causes that they believe in, but they do not have much time and do not know what to do. Now, the Internet provides people with ways to help that do not take much time or money. **2** Websites now make it convenient to donate online. With a few clicks, an organization of your choice can receive your donation or money from a sponsoring advertiser. **4** For example, **2** if you are interested in helping rescue unwanted and abandoned animals, you can go to the Animal Rescue Site. **3** When you click as instructed, a sponsoring advertiser will make a donation to help provide food and care for the millions of animals in shelters. **4** Also, **3** a portion of any money you spend in the site's online store will go to providing animal care. **2** If you want to help fight world hunger, go to the Hunger Site's website **3** and click daily to have sponsor fees directed to hungry people in more than seventy countries via the Mercy Corps, Feeding America, and Millennium Promise. Each year, hundreds of millions of cups of food are distributed to one billion hungry people around the world. **2** Other examples of click-to-give sites are the Child Health Site, the Literacy Site, and the Breast Cancer Site. **4** Like the animal-rescue and hunger sites, **3** these other sites have click-to-give links, online stores that direct a percentage of sales income to charity, and links to help you learn about causes you are interested in. One hundred percent of the sponsors' donations go to the charities, and you can give with a click every single day. Since I have found out about these sites, I go to at least one of them every day. **1** I have learned a lot about various problems, and every day I feel as if I have helped a little.

In college, the words *illustration* and *illustrate* may not appear in writing assignments. Instead, you might be asked to *give examples, cases, or samples* of a topic. Regardless of an assignment's wording, to be clear and effective, most types of writing require specific examples. Include them whenever they help you make your point.

First Basic: Main Idea in Illustration

In illustration, the **main idea** is the message readers should understand from the writing. To help you discover a main idea for writing (or in reading), complete the following sentence:

Main idea in illustration: What readers need to know about this topic is that _____.

The topic sentence (in a paragraph) or thesis statement (in an essay) usually includes the topic and the main idea that the writer wants to express about the topic. Let's look at a topic sentence first.

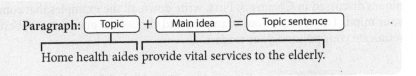

Remember that a thesis statement for an essay can be a little broader than a topic sentence for a paragraph.

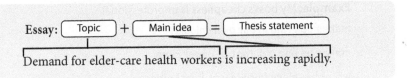

Whereas the topic sentence is focused on just home health aides, the thesis statement considers elder-care careers in general. The paragraph and essay models on pages 132–33 use the topic sentence (paragraph) and thesis statement (essay) from this section.

> **PRACTICE 8-1**   **Forming a Main Idea**
>
> Each of the items in this practice is a narrowed topic. Think about each of them and write a main idea about each topic in the space provided.
>
> **Example:** The words to songs I like *relate closely to experiences I have had.*
>
> 1. A few moments alone
>
> 2. A course I am taking
>
> 3. The busiest time at work
>
> 4. Being a parent of a newborn baby
>
> 5. Working with people from other countries

Second Basic: Primary Support in Illustration

The paragraph and essay models in "Paragraphs versus Essays in Illustration" on pages 132–33 use the topic sentence (paragraph) and thesis statement (essay) from the "First Basic: Main Idea in Illustration" section of this chapter. Both models include the support used in all illustration writing: examples backed up by details about the examples. In the essay model, however, the primary supporting points (examples) are topic sentences for individual paragraphs.

To generate good detailed examples, use one or more of the prewriting techniques discussed in Chapter 3. First, write down all the examples that come into your mind. Then review your examples, and choose the ones that will best communicate your point to your readers.

PRACTICE 8-2   **Supporting Your Main Idea with Examples**

Read the following main ideas, and give three examples you might use to support each one.

Example: My boss's cheapness is unprofessional.

makes us bring in our own calculators

makes us use old, rusted paper clips

will not replace burned-out lightbulbs

1. My (friend, sister, brother, husband, wife—choose one) has some admirable traits.
2. This weekend is particularly busy.

Third Basic: Secondary Support in Illustration

Effective examples in illustration are supported by specific details, which may include sensory details and dialogue (see Chapter 7, pp. 105–07). In addition, writers of illustration may use **proper nouns** to help readers visualize the examples. A proper noun is a name, and it is always capitalized. A proper noun is always more specific than a general noun. For example, in her essay "When Poor People Have Nice Things" (p. 140), Andrea Whitmer makes the following point:

> Now, I could understand it if I had a Lamborghini or two in my garage.

Whitmer could have said *expensive car* in this sentence. But *expensive car* means different things to different readers. Instead, Whitmer uses the proper noun *Lamborghini* to emphasize her point: a *Lamborghini* is one of the most expensive luxury vehicles in the world.

| PRACTICE 8-3 | **Giving Details about the Examples** |

In the spaces provided, copy your main ideas and examples from Practice 8-2. Then, for each example, write a detail that further shows, explains, or proves what you mean.

Example:

Main idea: *My boss's cheapness is unprofessional.*

Example: *makes us bring in our own calculators*

    Detail: *Some people do not have a calculator and must use their iPhones.*

Example: *makes us use old, rusted paper clips*

    Detail: *They leave rust marks on important documents.*

Example: *will not replace burned-out lightbulbs*

    Detail: *The dim light leads to more errors.*

1. Main idea:
    Example:

    Detail:

    Example:

    Detail:

    Example:

    Detail:

2. Main idea:
    Example:

    Detail:

    Example:

    Detail:

    Example:

    Detail:

Fourth Basic: Organization in Illustration

Illustration often uses **order of importance**, saving the most powerful example for last. This strategy is used in the paragraph and essay models on pages 132–33. If the examples are given according to when they happened, the writing might be organized by **time** (or **chronological**) **order**.

Using Transitions in Illustration

Transitions in illustration let readers know that you are introducing an example or moving from one example to another.

Common Transitions in Illustration

also	first, second, and so on	for one/another thing
another	for example	in addition
finally	for instance	one/another example

Using a Graphic Organizer in Illustration

One strategy for deciding how to organize your illustration is to use a graphic organizer.

Consider the following graphic organizer for the paragraph in "Paragraphs versus Essays in Illustration" on page 132. The center box contains the main point, while each box connected to the center lists a primary supporting example. The outermost boxes contain details that support the primary examples. If the supporting examples happen in a sequence, you might use chronological order for the paragraph. But if the supporting examples occur simultaneously, as they do in this example, you should use order of importance to organize the illustration.

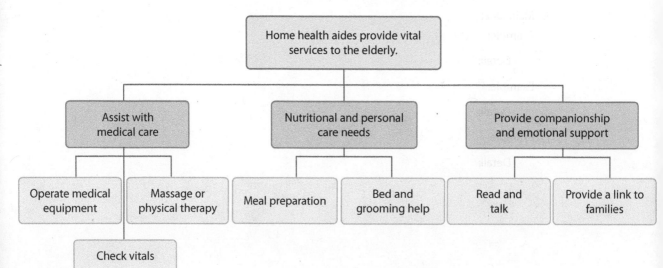

PRACTICE 8–4   Using Transitions in Illustration

Read the paragraph that follows and fill in the blanks with one of the
following: *another example, for example, in addition, in fact, one example,
second, the most.* When you have finished, create a graphic organizer to
illustrate the organization of the paragraph. (Note that more than one
option may be correct.)

Greek myths include many heroes, such as the great warriors Achilles and
Heracles. _____, the myths describe several monsters that tested the
heroes' strength. _____ of these frightening creatures was the Hydra,
a water serpent with many heads. When a warrior cut off one of these
heads, two or more would sprout up in its place. _____ of these
mythical monsters was the Gorgons, three sisters who had snakes for hair.
Any person who looked into the Gorgons' eyes would turn to stone. ____
_____ terrifying monster was Cerberus, a three-headed dog with snapping
jaws. He guarded the gates to the underworld, keeping the living from
entering and the dead from leaving. Fortunately, some heroes' cleverness
equaled the monsters' hideousness. _____, Heracles discovered that
by applying a torch to the wounds of the Hydra, he could prevent the
creature from growing more heads. ____, Orpheus, a famous mythical
musician, soothed Cerberus by plucking the strings of a lyre. In this way,
Orpheus got past the beast and entered the underworld, from which he
hoped to rescue his wife.

Paragraphs versus Essays in Illustration

For more on the important features of illustration, see the "Four Basics of Illustration" on page 125.

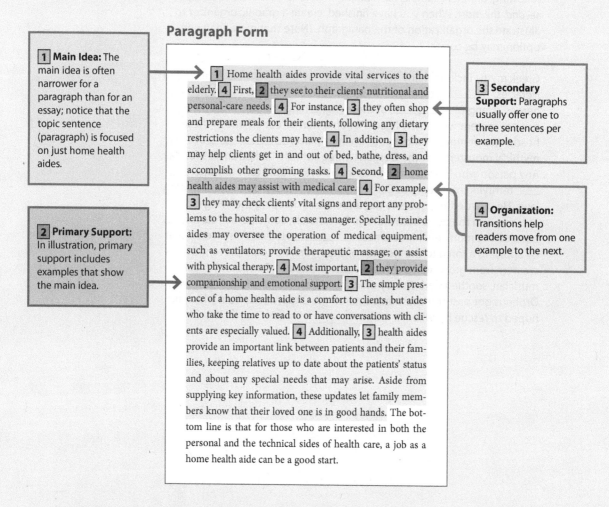

Paragraph Form

1 Main Idea: The main idea is often narrower for a paragraph than for an essay; notice that the topic sentence (paragraph) is focused on just home health aides.

2 Primary Support: In illustration, primary support includes examples that show the main idea.

1 Home health aides provide vital services to the elderly. **4** First, **2** they see to their clients' nutritional and personal-care needs. **4** For instance, **3** they often shop and prepare meals for their clients, following any dietary restrictions the clients may have. **4** In addition, **3** they may help clients get in and out of bed, bathe, dress, and accomplish other grooming tasks. **4** Second, **2** home health aides may assist with medical care. **4** For example, **3** they may check clients' vital signs and report any problems to the hospital or to a case manager. Specially trained aides may oversee the operation of medical equipment, such as ventilators; provide therapeutic massage; or assist with physical therapy. **4** Most important, **2** they provide companionship and emotional support. **3** The simple presence of a home health aide is a comfort to clients, but aides who take the time to read to or have conversations with clients are especially valued. **4** Additionally, **3** health aides provide an important link between patients and their families, keeping relatives up to date about the patients' status and about any special needs that may arise. Aside from supplying key information, these updates let family members know that their loved one is in good hands. The bottom line is that for those who are interested in both the personal and the technical sides of health care, a job as a home health aide can be a good start.

3 Secondary Support: Paragraphs usually offer one to three sentences per example.

4 Organization: Transitions help readers move from one example to the next.

Consider Readers as You Write an Illustration

Ask Yourself

- Do I have a main idea that makes a clear observation that will be interesting to readers?
- Will readers find each of my current examples clear and effective?
- Have I provided enough detail to make my examples compelling for readers?
- Have I organized my examples and supporting details logically, so readers can move easily from example to example?

Essay Form

1 **Main Idea:** The main idea is often broader for an essay than for a paragraph; notice that the thesis statement is focused on health-care workers for the elderly, not just home health aides.

2 **Primary Support:** In an illustration, the examples that illustrate the main idea are the primary support.

3 **Secondary Support:** Body paragraphs in essays usually include three to eight sentences per example.

4 **Organization:** Transitions help readers move from one example to the next.

1

During these difficult economic times, many students are looking to pursue careers in expanding fields with good long-term prospects. One field that they should seriously consider is elder care. 1 Because the U.S. population is aging, demand for workers who specialize in the health of the elderly is increasing rapidly. 4 One set of workers in great demand 2 consists of nutritionists who specialize in older people's dietary needs. 3 These professionals may plan meals and provide nutrition advice for hospitals, nursing homes, and other institutions, or they may counsel individual patients on how to eat more healthfully or on how to prepare meals that meet certain dietary restrictions. For instance, elderly patients suffering from heart disease may need to eat foods that are low in salt and saturated fat. Other patients might have to avoid foods that interfere with the absorption of certain medications. Although the market for nutritionists is not expected to grow as quickly as that

2

for others who work with the elderly, it is projected to increase steadily as the population continues to age.

4 Also in demand 2 are physical therapists, who help elderly patients improve their mobility and retain their independence. 3 Some of these therapists are based at hospitals, others at clinics or private offices. Regardless of where they work, they provide a variety of services to elderly patients, from helping stroke sufferers relearn how to walk and perform other daily activities to showing others how to live a more active life. Physical therapists can also help injured patients reduce their reliance on painkillers, which can become less effective over time and in certain cases can even become addictive. According to the U.S. Department of Labor's *Occupational Outlook Handbook* online, employment of physical therapists will grow by 18 percent over the next year, largely because of the increasing number of elderly Americans.

4 The highest-demand workers 2 are those who provide at-home health care to the elderly. 4 One subset of these workers 3 consists of home nurses, who often provide follow-up care after patients are released from a hospital or other medical facility. These nurses help patients transition from an institutional setting while making sure they continue to receive high-quality care.

3

4 For instance, 3 they track patients' vital signs, administer and monitor medications, and carry out specific tasks required to manage particular diseases. 4 Another subset of home health workers 3 is made up of home health aides, who assist nurses and other professionals with medical care, see to clients' nutritional and personal-care needs, and provide companionship and emotional support. Both home health aides and nurses provide an important link between patients and their families, keeping relatives up to date about the patients' status and about any special needs that may arise. In addition to supplying key information, these updates let family members know that their loved one is in good hands. Because of home health-care workers' vital role in serving the expanding elderly population, their employment is expected to grow significantly: on average, 30 to 40 percent over the next ten years.

Given the growing demand for elder-care workers, people pursuing these professions stand an excellent chance of getting jobs with good long-term outlooks. The best candidates are those who have a strong interest in health or medicine, a willingness to work hard to get the necessary qualifications, and, perhaps most important, an ability to connect with and truly care for others.

Read and Analyze Illustration

To become a more successful writer, it is important not only to understand the four basics of illustration but to read and analyze examples as well. In this section, you will use a rubric to evaluate an early draft of an illustration paragraph by Inez King. Next, you will see an illustration essay by Margaret Troup and an example of illustration in the workplace by Juan Gonzalez. The final example is an illustration essay by Andrea Whitmer, a professional writer.

Student Illustration Paragraph

Read this first draft of a narrative paragraph. For this first draft, the instructor asked students to focus on the main idea, supporting content, and organization. Using the four basics of illustration and the sample rubric, decide how effective this draft of the paragraph is, and then recommend one or two revision goals for the student's next draft.

> **Assignment:** Write a paragraph explaining a word that is important to you.

Inez King

Empathy

When I first learned the word *empathy*, I couldn't connect my life with the word. Now that I have studied the definition, however, I can recall times when I probably displayed "empathy." While watching the movie *The Color Purple*, without warning, I was crying my eyes out and laughing at the same time. I cried when Sophia was physically attacked and jailed for standing up for her beliefs. I rejoiced when Ms. Celie battled with Mr. Albert and rose above her past. In fact, the same emotions I experienced while viewing *The Color Purple* occur each time I read a Danielle Steel novel. Each novel draws me into the emotional lives of every character to the point where I feel their joy, anger, and pain. Not only have I experienced "empathy" vicariously through movies and novels but also through a personal experience. "Empathy" took a silent approach with me; it ignited tears of sadness and sparked my feelings.

Rubric for Illustration

	1 **Falls below expectations**	**2** **Nearly meets expectations**	**3** **Meets expectations**	**4** **Exceeds expectations**
Main idea (first basic)	No clear main idea or purpose is present.	Main idea is too broad/narrow for assignment.	Main idea is appropriate but dull, or purpose is unclear.	Main idea is engaging with a clear sense of purpose.
Support (second and third basics)	Irrelevant examples and details are included; they do not support main idea.	Some relevant examples and details are present to suggest a main idea.	Examples support main idea, but more details are needed.	Examples support main idea with vivid, well-developed details.

	1 **Falls below** **expectations**	**2** **Nearly meets** **expectations**	**3** **Meets** **expectations**	**4** **Exceeds** **expectations**
Organization (fourth basic)	Organization is unclear or illogical.	Organization is inconsistent.	Organization is logical, but some transitions are missing or inappropriate.	Organization is logical, with smooth transitions throughout.

Evaluating the Paragraph

1. Does the paragraph show the four basics of illustration? Explain.

2. Using the rubric as a guide, what is the strongest part of the paragraph? The weakest?

3. Write a response to this writer, using one of the following to frame your response:

    a. One thing I would like to know more about is _____.

    b. What I liked best about the paragraph is _____.

    c. In your next draft, you might consider adding _____.

Student Illustration Essay

Margaret Troup

Virtual Reality: Fun and Innovative Indoor Exercise

Preview Based on the title, what sorts of examples do you expect to see in this essay?

Just because gyms and parks are temporarily closed doesn't mean exercise is a thing of the past. With virtual reality games, at-home workouts can be both fun and doable. Virtual reality (VR) headsets are the newest and most sought-after additions to video game consoles. While there are many immersive, beautiful and even scary games for VR, the games with the most practical use are meant for exercise. Video games as exercise may have once seemed counterintuitive, but now this is a concept of the past.

2   Cloudhead Games' "Pistol Whip" is one example of an exercise-centered VR game. After being released on Steam in 2019, the rhythm-based shooter garnered immediate glowing reviews. This game does not have a specific plot, but instead it centers around the player being propelled through various environments while catchy music, which the player is encouraged to shoot their in-game

pistol at various targets on-beat to, plays all around them. "Pistol Whip" is not a high-intensity exercise, but is more suited for players who want to headbang while getting on their feet every once in a while.

3   A more intensive exercise game is Beat Games' "Beat Saber." This VR exclusive came to consoles in 2018. It currently holds a 10/10 score on Steam and its popularity has only seemed to rise since its release. "Beat Saber" is similar to "Pistol Whip" in that it is a rhythm-based VR game. The difference here though is the directions the player needs to follow in order to remain on-beat to the songs. Similarly to old "Dance Dance Revolution" games, players must both hit the targets on-beat as they appear to them while also striking them in the right direction with their hand controllers. Missing too many beats or directions will abruptly end the song.

4   There are additional settings to make "Beat Saber" more player-friendly, such as activating the "no fail" option where the song will continue no matter how many hits are missed. Additionally, the song difficulty level can be adjusted. Most songs that come with "Beat Saber" have "Easy," "Hard," "Expert," and "Expert+" modes, where the intensity of the rhythms and speeds vary based on player ability.

5   One man who can attest to "Beat Saber's" uses in exercise is Robert Long, a player who used the game to lose almost 140 pounds. In his original Reddit post, Long explains his workout routine. "Now, load it ["Beat Saber"] up and then set a timer for 35 minutes," Long said. "Thirty minutes for workouts and five for relax time and quick stops for 30 seconds to catch your breath and select a new song. But, do not do an hour at once. I have, and I did burn 1500+ calories in that one workout, but yeah. Recovery was [not] fun."

6   "Beat Saber," when played on the higher-intensity levels of difficulty can be a very extreme workout. For players who are just starting an exercise routine, take Long's advice and do not overdo it.

Write to Read: Annotate

1. Identify the main idea in Troup's essay.

2. Number the primary supporting examples, and then highlight or put a check mark next to the details that describe the examples.

Read to Write: Think Critically

1. Troup says, "Video games as exercise may have once seemed counterintuitive." What does she mean?

2. Why is it important for Troup to include the example of Robert Long?

Profile of Success: Juan C. Gonzalez

Illustration in the Real World

Title   Vice Chancellor for Student Affairs, University of California, San Diego (Retired)

Background   I grew up in Amarillo, Texas, in a family of ten children. For most of my life, going to college never even occurred to me. I was a marginal student, on the slow track in school. I expected to either join the military or to work with the Rock Island Railroad, as my father did for thirty-seven years.

However, my circumstances changed when I was a sophomore in high school. That year, my father lost both of his legs in a railroad accident at work. As I sat with him through his long stay in the hospital, I realized that I wanted a different future. I knew then that I had to go to college, but I didn't know how I could accomplish that seemingly impossible goal.

Timing is often miraculous. Soon after making the decision to pursue higher education, I was approached by a TRiO/ Upward Bound counselor who asked me

to consider participating in the program. I jumped at the opportunity. The TRiO/ Student Support Services program gave me the support, encouragement, and skills I needed for college work, and I will always be deeply grateful for their help.

Writing at Work   Most of the writing I did at work was in creating lectures and presentations for a variety of different audiences, reviewing and revising statements of school policy, and writing and updating various reports on student life at the school. I worked closely with graduate students, and much of our communication was oral—shared exchanges of ideas during class and meetings. However, in those meetings I took minutes of what occurred so that I had accurate records. I maintained active correspondence with students, administrators in other areas of the college, and faculty. I also spent a good amount of time writing email messages to people at the university, in the community, and to colleagues around the country.

Juan C. Gonzalez

Vice Chancellor
for Student Affairs,
University of California,
San Diego (Retired)

COURTESY OF JUAN C. GONZALEZ

minutes: notes of what is said during a meeting

Use Reading Strategies: Create a Graphic Organizer

Following the model on page 130, create a graphic organizer for Troup's illustration essay.

Reflect and Respond

Troup illustrates how to exercise when you cannot get to the gym. What are some other examples of creative exercise that might appeal to students who cannot afford gyms or VR equipment? Write a paragraph illustrating how students can work out on a budget.

Workplace Illustration

Juan C. Gonzalez

Excerpt from an Address to New Students

Preview   What follows is part of a speech Gonzalez wrote when he was Vice President of Student Affairs at the University of Texas, Austin. What can new students expect to hear when a college official (president, chancellor, vice president, or provost) welcomes them to campus?

embarking: beginning

As new students, you are embarking on an incredibly exciting and challenging time, a time of expanding knowledge, relationships, viewpoints, and achievements. In my role as vice president, I am constantly *striving* to match that energy level so that we can offer the highest level of service on this very diverse campus. I frequently marvel at college students who seem to have an unlimited amount of energy that allows them to attend classes, read and study, maintain a social life, run for political office, pursue a hobby, play an intramural sport, volunteer for a worthy cause, hold down a job. We in the Division of Student Affairs strongly encourage activities outside the classroom that enrich the academic experience, as we recognize that a university education is enhanced through involvement in our campus community.

diligently: with care, effort, and focus

2   Last November, a group of Student Affairs staff, students, and faculty began work on creating a strategic plan for the division. They have been laboring diligently on this document, and I am excited to share with you the fruit of that labor: our newly developed Student Affairs Strategic Plan, which has as its motto "Student Affairs: Where Life and Learning Intersect."

encapsulates: shows clearly in a brief way

gauge: a way of measuring something

3   This phrase encapsulates the driving force behind the Division of Student Affairs. We exist, in essence, to help students succeed and grow, and we believe that growth and success must be measured in many ways. Academic success is one gauge of how well students are performing, but there are a variety of indicators other than grades. Those who take the most from their college experience are those who recognize that learning happens both inside and outside the classroom.

collaborative: marked by groups of people who work together

integrated: linked or blended

4   In fact, I recently had our units count the services they offer that are collaborative efforts with the academic side of the family, and a rough survey yielded 140 programs. This idea of integrated learning carries through most of what we do, whether it is a program to recruit the best students from around Texas like the Honors Colloquium, the increasingly popular "Academic Community Centers" for studying and advising on site in the residence halls, Summer Orientation, or the professor-led Freshman Reading Round-Up book discussions.

Our Vision Statement

5   Our vision statement lights the path we are following to where we aspire to be:

> The Division of Student Affairs at the University of Texas at Austin seeks to become the premier organization of its kind. We envision a network of programs and services that excels in meeting students' out-of-classroom needs, complementing their academic experiences, and building community on a diverse campus. In doing so, we will contribute to developing citizens and leaders who will thrive in and enrich an increasingly complex world.

aspire: to hope or desire; to have as a goal

Our Mission

6   Our mission, or the explanation of what we do, is described this way:

> The Division of Student Affairs facilitates students' discovery of self and the world in which they live. We enhance students' educational experiences through programs and services that support academic success. We provide for fundamental needs, including shelter, nourishment, and a sense of security. We create environments that foster physical, emotional, and psychological wellness, and advance healthy lifestyles. Student Affairs builds communities, both real and virtual, that encourage inclusiveness, invite communication, and add to the cultural richness of the institution. We focus on personal development, including career decision making, problem solving, and group dynamics, challenging students to work both independently and as part of a team.

facilitate: to help

foster: to encourage or support

7   The work group that wrote the strategic plan also composed a defining phrase to encapsulate Student Affairs: "Our passion is complete learning." These, I hope you will agree, are stirring words. We take our responsibility for providing an environment that is inclusive and promotes a healthy lifestyle seriously. We are committed to supporting you as you achieve your goals at this university.

Write to Read: Annotate

1. What is Gonzalez illustrating? Underline or highlight his examples.
2. Circle or highlight all transitions that Gonzalez uses.

Read to Write: Think Critically

1. Gonzalez does not use as many transitions as other writers in this chapter. Why not? Recall that Gonzalez first wrote this as a speech. How is a speech different from an essay?

2. Who is the audience for Gonzalez's illustration? What is his purpose?

3. Carefully reread the "Four Basics of Illustration" (p. 125) and decide whether you think Gonzalez's essay is a good example of illustration. Make notes to support your opinion.

Use Reading Strategies: Summarize

Review the information about summary writing in Chapter 1, and then write a short summary of Gonzalez's illustration essay.

Reflect and Respond

1. Why does Gonzalez quote the vision statement? Does your college have a vision statement? Where can you find it?

2. What is the difference between a mission statement and a vision statement?

3. Review your college's mission or vision statement. Write a paragraph giving examples of how your college demonstrates its mission or vision for students.

Professional Illustration Essay

Andrea Whitmer

When Poor People Have Nice Things

Andrea Whitmer is a web developer and blogger. Most of her writing attempts to help others—mothers in particular—find the humor in everyday situations. She also hopes to share her hard-earned wisdom with others so that they can learn from and, possibly, not make some of the same choices she did. This essay first appeared on her blog, *So Over This*, in June 2012.

Preview What examples will you find in Whitmer's essay?

There's a graphic circulating on some of my friends' Facebook profiles that really gets on my nerves. I told myself I wouldn't write about it, but I saw it again last night, and I just can't help myself. The graphic says, "Maybe someday I'll be able to afford an iPhone like the person in front of me at the grocery store. The one paying with FOOD STAMPS!"

2   Anytime that picture (or something similar) is posted, it gets about fifty "likes" and a long string of comments from indignant people who have personally witnessed a poor person owning something of value. The rage is evident—how dare someone on food stamps have a smartphone! Why should they even be allowed to have a phone at all? Our tax dollars blah blah blah blah . . .

indignant: a feeling of extreme disgust or anger

3   Here's the thing: we can all think of at least one person who games the system. After working as a therapist for almost seven years, I can think of quite a few. But no one knows the life situation of every single person on the planet, no matter how much they think they do.

4   A good friend of mine got fired from her job just days after her husband was laid off. Both of them had iPhones on his parents' plan, which cost them $50 a month total. Now what makes the most sense—breaking that contract at hundreds of dollars, or scrounging up the $50 a month in hopes that one or both of them would find another job soon? They didn't have to sign up for assistance—they were both lucky to get jobs before their emergency fund was drained—but if they had, they would have been in the grocery checkout line with iPhones in their pockets.

scrounging: attempting to gather something by looking carefully or asking for the help of others

I Speak from Experience

5   The only assistance I've ever personally used was Medicaid for my son at two different times during his life. But I will tell you—during both of those times, I had cable television. I had Internet access at home. This last time, I had an iPhone (gasp!). I also owned several items that could have been pawned or sold for a decent amount of money.

6   Was I living it up? No. Not even close. But as someone with two college degrees and tons of ambition, I also never planned to continue collecting that assistance forever. Why should I empty my house of all the things I bought with my own money, only to have to buy them again when the crisis was over? That really doesn't make sense.

7   Now, I could understand it if I had a Lamborghini or two in my garage. But when you're used to a fairly middle-class existence and something happens to you (no matter what it is), you assume that your situation will improve at some point. It's not like the poverty police come take all your stuff in the middle of the night. You still own all the things you did before. If you had nice clothes, you'll still have nice clothes. If your cousin bought you an expensive handbag last Christmas, you'll still have that handbag. No one drops off a tattered, dirty wardrobe for you to put on before you leave your house.

I Know What You're Thinking

8   I can just hear the comments now. "Well, I know someone who did X and Y," or "I saw a lady buy Z at the mall." I know. I've seen it too. That's not the point.

9   The point is, some people are in situations that we know nothing about. Some people own nice things from a better time in their lives and choose to keep

those things during a setback. And some people make choices after becoming poor that we wouldn't personally make. Talking smack about those people on Facebook isn't doing anything to eradicate poverty or to change the fact that there is widespread abuse of our current system.

10   If you get upset when you see a poor person with nice things like smartphones, all I ask is that you consider this:

Maybe they just got laid off last month and they already owned the iPhone.

Maybe a family member pays the phone bill.

Maybe they're picking up groceries for a disabled neighbor with the neighbor's food stamp card.

Maybe the phone was a gift and it's on a prepaid plan.

Maybe you should worry less about what someone else has and more about yourself.

11   To many people, I could be considered "poor" right now (even though my bills are paid and I'm saving money). And guess what? I own several nice things. Some of you will judge me for that, and there's nothing I can do about it. But I will continue to be disgusted when people criticize another person's choices, especially when they can't possibly know the full set of circumstances.

Write to Read: Annotate

1. Underline or highlight the examples Whitmer provides to support her main idea.

2. Put a check mark by Whitmer's transitions. What sort of organization is she using?

3. Highlight each question that Whitmer asks. Why do you think she asks these questions?

Read to Write: Think Critically

1. In your own words, state Whitmer's main idea. Has she successfully supported it? Explain.

2. In paragraph 2, why does Whitmer use "blah blah blah" instead of finishing the sentence?

3. In paragraph 8, what does Whitmer suggest by using the letters X, Y, and Z here instead of specific examples?

4. In the last sentence of paragraph 9, Whitmer makes an assumption that there is "widespread abuse of our current system." What do you make of Whitmer's claim? Is there sufficient evidence to support it?

Use Reading Strategies: Paraphrase

Whitmer's essay uses both general statements and specific examples. Look at the following general statements. After reviewing the guidelines for paraphrasing in Chapter 1, write a paraphrase of each of these statements. Can you think of your own example to illustrate each one?

1. "Here's the thing: we can all think of at least one person who games the system." (para. 3)

2. "But when you're used to a fairly middle-class existence and something happens to you (no matter what it is), you assume that your situation will improve at some point." (para. 7)

3. "Talking smack about those people on Facebook isn't doing anything to eradicate poverty or to change the fact that there is widespread abuse of our current system." (para. 9)

Reflect and Respond

1. Write about a time when someone made a snap judgment about you. This could be because of where you work, how you speak, or how you dress. How did you find out about it? How did it make you feel? How close to being accurate was it? Why do you think that person made those assumptions?

2. With social networking and its primary focus on images and short text, it has become easier than ever to publicly humiliate or bully others. Do you think that social networking has created more bullying and caused more harm than there was before media like Facebook, Instagram, Twitter, and other platforms existed? Explain your answer in a paragraph.

Grammar for Illustration

Several of the illustration essays in this chapter use lists of examples. We can format a list by making each item a separate paragraph, as Whitmer does with her list of suggestions on page 142. Or we might choose to format a list with bullets or numbers. Finally, we can put the items in a list within a single sentence. In that case, we must separate each item in the list with commas, as Juan Gonzalez has done in this sentence:

> I frequently marvel at college students who seem to have an unlimited amount of energy that allows them to attend classes, read and study, maintain a social life, run for political office, pursue a hobby, play an intramural sport, volunteer for a worthy cause, hold down a job.

For more on the uses of commas, see Chapter 26.

Write Your Own Illustration

In this section, you will write your own illustration based on one of the following assignments. For help, refer to the "How to Write Illustration" checklist on pages 147–48.

Assignment Options: Writing about College, Work, and Everyday Life

Write an illustration paragraph, essay, or other document (as described below) on one of the following topics or on one of your own choice:

College	• Choose a concept from another course you are taking and illustrate it for students who have not taken the course.
	• Produce a one- or two-page newsletter for other students in your class on one of the following topics. Make sure to describe each club, opportunity, or event in enough detail for readers. Also, include contact information, as well as hours and locations for events and club meetings.
	• Student clubs
	• Volunteer opportunities
	• Upcoming campus events (such as lectures, movies, and sports events)
	• Upcoming events in the larger community
Work	• What is the best or worst job you have ever had? Give examples of what made it the best or worst job.
	• Think of the job you would most like to have after graduation. Then write a list of your skills—both current and those you will be building in college—that are relevant to the job. To identify skills you will be building through your degree program, you might refer to a course catalog. To identify relevant work skills, consider your past or present jobs as well as internships or other work experiences you would like to have before graduation. Finally, write a cover letter explaining why you are the best candidate for your ideal job. Be sure to provide several examples of your skills, referring to the list that you prepared.

Everyday Life   • Think about people who work behind the scenes at your school, workplace, or community. Write an essay that shows how jobs we don't always notice are critical for success and give examples of these jobs. Give enough details about each job to make it clear why that job is important.

• Give examples of memories that have stayed with you for a long time. For each memory, provide enough details so that readers will be able to share your experience.

Assignment Options: Reading and Writing Critically

Complete one of the following assignments that asks you to apply the critical thinking, reading, and writing skills discussed in Chapter 1.

Writing Critically about Readings

Both Andrea Whitmer's *When Poor People Have Nice Things* (pp. 140–42) and Eugene Robinson's *A Special Brand of Patriotism* in Chapter 12 (pp. 236–37) illustrate the assumptions that people make about others every day. Read or review both of these pieces, and then follow these steps:

1. **Summarize.** Briefly summarize the works, listing the primary examples.

2. **Analyze.** What questions do the essays raise for you? Are there any other issues you wish they had covered?

3. **Synthesize.** Using examples from both Whitmer's and Robinson's essays and from your own experience, discuss why we make these assumptions about others or how it feels to have others make assumptions about you.

4. **Evaluate.** Which essay, Whitmer's or Robinson's, do you think is more effective? Why? Does the writers' use of examples get their points across? Why or why not? In writing your evaluation, you might look back on your responses to step 2.

Writing Critically about Visuals

Study the infographic on the next page, and complete these steps.

1. **Read the visual.** Ask yourself: What is the main idea in this graphic? Who is the intended audience? How has the designer used both color and image size to illustrate the point? What evidence of credibility or reliability do you see in the infographic? (Look back at the section "Writing Critically

about Visuals" in Chapter 1 for information about summarizing, analyzing, synthesizing, and evaluating visuals.)

2. **Write an illustration.** This public service announcement illustrates an important point about the role government regulations play in fair housing. Explore government regulations about fair housing (or another issue, such as fair employment), and then write an essay illustrating how these regulations affect people in your community; alternatively, create your own public service announcement to illustrate what you have learned.

DIFFERENT NATIONAL ORIGINS.

SAME FAIR HOUSING RIGHTS.

It is illegal for landlords and real estate agents to deny you housing opportunities because of your ethnicity. The Fair Housing Act prohibits housing discrimination based on national origin. If you believe you have experienced a violation of your rights, file a complaint.

Go to **hud.gov/fairhousing** or call **1-800-669-9777**
Federal Relay Service **1-800-877-8339**

FAIR HOUSING: THE LAW IS ON YOUR SIDE.
A public service message from the U.S. Department of Housing and Urban Development in cooperation with the National Fair Housing Alliance. The federal Fair Housing Act prohibits discrimination because of race, color, religion, national origin, sex, familial status or disability.

Writing Critically about Problems

Read or review the section "Write Critically about Problems" in Chapter 1 (pp. 26–28). Then consider the following problem:

> Your college is increasing its tuition by $500 next year, and you do not think that you can continue. You have done well so far, and you really want to get a college degree.

Assignment: Rather than just giving up and dropping out next year, as many students do, working in a small group or on your own, make a list of resources you could consult to help you, and explain how they might help. You might want to start with the following sentence:

> Before dropping out of school for financial reasons, students should consult _____ because _____.

For a paragraph: Name your best resource, and give examples of how this person or office might help you.

For an essay: Name your three best resources, and give examples of how they might help you.

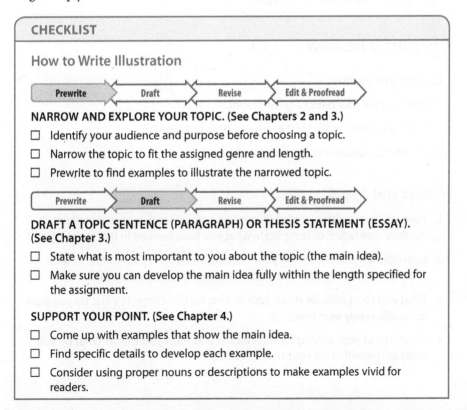

CHECKLIST

How to Write Illustration

> [Prewrite] > [Draft] > [Revise] > [Edit & Proofread]

NARROW AND EXPLORE YOUR TOPIC. (See Chapters 2 and 3.)

☐ Identify your audience and purpose before choosing a topic.

☐ Narrow the topic to fit the assigned genre and length.

☐ Prewrite to find examples to illustrate the narrowed topic.

> [Prewrite] > [**Draft**] > [Revise] > [Edit & Proofread]

DRAFT A TOPIC SENTENCE (PARAGRAPH) OR THESIS STATEMENT (ESSAY). (See Chapter 3.)

☐ State what is most important to you about the topic (the main idea).

☐ Make sure you can develop the main idea fully within the length specified for the assignment.

SUPPORT YOUR POINT. (See Chapter 4.)

☐ Come up with examples that show the main idea.

☐ Find specific details to develop each example.

☐ Consider using proper nouns or descriptions to make examples vivid for readers.

WRITE A DRAFT. (See Chapter 5.)

☐ Make an outline or graphic organizer that puts examples in a logical order.

☐ Include a topic sentence (paragraph) or thesis statement (essay) and all the supporting examples and details.

☐ Add an appropriate introduction and conclusion.

Prewrite ＞ Draft ＞ **Revise** ＞ Edit & Proofread

REVISE YOUR DRAFT. (See Chapter 6.)

☐ Make sure it has *all* four basics of illustration.

☐ Make sure each paragraph is unified (all ideas relate to the topic sentence).

☐ Make sure each paragraph is developed (there are enough supporting details to make each example clear for readers).

☐ Make sure you include transitions to move readers smoothly from one example to the next.

Prewrite ＞ Draft ＞ Revise ＞ **Edit & Proofread**

EDIT AND PROOFREAD YOUR REVISED DRAFT. (See Parts 3 and 4.)

☐ Make sure grammar, word usage, and punctuation choices are clear, accurate, and effective.

☐ Check spelling and capitalization.

Chapter 8 Review

1. What is illustration?

2. What are the four basics of illustration?

3. How can writers make their examples clear to a reader?

4. How is illustration usually organized?

Reflect and Apply

1. Have you ever written or read illustration before? How does that experience confirm, contradict, or complicate what you have learned in this chapter?

2. Interview someone studying your major or working in your career. In what situations have they used illustrations (or examples) in their work?

3. What was most difficult about your writing for this chapter? What do you want to do differently next time?

4. What part of your writing for this chapter was most successful? What do you need to remember for next time?

Description

Writing That Creates Pictures in Words

Learning Outcomes | **In this chapter, you will learn to**

- List the four basics of descriptive paragraphs and essays.
- Identify specific examples or key characteristics that support the main impression you want to convey to readers.
- Support examples or key characteristics with sensory details that appeal to the five senses.
- Recognize transitions commonly used in description.
- Write a descriptive paragraph or essay with a clear main idea, strong support, and a logical organization.

Like telling stories and giving examples, describing what you observe or imagine is a skill you can use in college, work, and everyday life. From describing specimens in a biology class to describing your backpack to the lost-and-found clerk at the store where you work, you use description to give crucial information to others. When you help others see what you see, you are using description.

Understand What Description Is

Description is writing that creates a clear and vivid impression of a person, place, or thing, often by appealing to the physical senses.

Four Basics of Description

1 **Main Idea:** An effective description paragraph or essay creates a main impression—an overall effect, feeling, or image—about the topic.

2 **Primary Support:** It uses specific examples to support the main impression.

3 **Secondary Support:** It supports those examples with details that appeal to the five senses: sight, hearing, smell, taste, and touch.

4 **Organization:** It arranges examples and details logically, by space, time, or order of importance.

In the following student paragraph, the numbers and colors correspond to the four basics of description.

[1] Nojoqui Falls is a special place to me because its beauty provides a break from human worries. [4] At the start of the trail leading to the falls, [2] the smell and sound of oak trees and pine trees help visitors feel they are up for the journey. [3] The sun hitting the trees makes the air fresh with a leafy aroma. [4] Overhead, [3] the wind blows through the leaves, making a soft noise. [4] Closer to the waterfall, [2] the shade from the trees creates a shielding blanket. [3] When the sun comes out, it fills the place with light, showing the vapor coming out of the trees and plants. [4] To the left of the trail, rocks are positioned perfectly for viewing the waterfall. [3] Water splashes as it hits the rocks. [2] The waterfall itself is beautiful, like a transparent, sparkling window of diamonds. [3] The water is so clear that objects on the other side are visible. It appears like a never-ending stream of water that splashes onto the rocks. [1] The total effect of these sights, sounds, and smells is a setting where daily cares can be set aside for a while.

—Liliana Ramirez, student

In college assignments, the word *describe* may mean *tell about* or *report*. When an assignment asks you to describe a person, place, or thing, however, you will need to use the kinds of specific details discussed later in this chapter.

First Basic: Main Idea in Description

In description, the **main idea** is the main impression you want to create for your readers. To help you discover the main idea when you are reading or writing, complete the following sentence:

Main idea in description: What is most interesting, vivid, and important about this topic is that _____.

If you do not have a main impression about your topic, think about why it is important and how it smells, sounds, looks, tastes, or feels.

> **PRACTICE 9-1** **Finding a Main Impression**
>
> For the following general topics, jot down impressions that appeal to you, and circle the one you would use as a main impression. Base your choice on what is most interesting, vivid, and important to you.

Example:

Topic: A vandalized car

Impressions: *wrecked, smashed, damaged, battered*

1. **Topic:** A fireworks display

   Impressions:

2. **Topic:** A football player

   Impressions:

3. **Topic:** The room you are in

   Impressions:

The topic sentence (paragraph) or thesis statement (essay) in description usually contains both your narrowed topic and your main impression. Here is a topic sentence for a description paragraph:

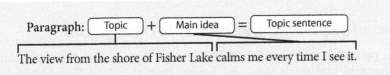

Remember that a topic for an essay can be a little broader than one for a paragraph:

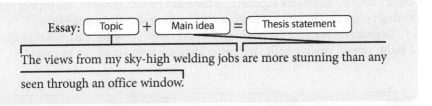

Whereas the topic sentence is focused on just one location and view, the thesis statement sets up descriptions of different views from different sites. The paragraph and essay models on pages 156–57 use the topic sentence (paragraph) and thesis statement (essay) from this section.

To be effective, your topic sentence or thesis statement should be a complete, specific sentence. You can make it specific by adding details that appeal to the senses.

PRACTICE 9-2   Writing a Statement of Your Main Impression

For two of the items from Practice 9-1, write the topic and your main impression. Then write a statement of your main impression. Finally, revise the statement to make the main impression sharper and more specific.

Example:

Topic/main impression: A vandalized car/battered

Statement: The vandalized car on the side of the highway was battered.

More specific: The shell of a car on the side of the road was dented all over, apparently from a bat or club, and surrounded by broken glass.

1. Topic/main impression:

   Statement:

   More specific:

2. Topic/main impression:

   Statement:

   More specific:

Second Basic: Primary Support in Description

The paragraph and essay models on pages 156–57 use the topic sentence (paragraph) and thesis statement (essay) from the "First Basic: Main Idea in Description" section of this chapter. Both models include the primary and secondary support used in all descriptive writing—examples that communicate the writer's main impression (primary support), backed up by specific supporting sensory details (secondary support). In the essay model, however, the primary supporting points (examples) are topic sentences for individual paragraphs.

To generate support for your main impression, consider qualities that appeal to sight, sound, smell, touch, and taste. Here are some qualities to consider:

Sight	Sound	Smell
Colors?	Loud/soft?	Sweet/sour?
Shapes?	Piercing/soothing?	Sharp/mild?
Sizes?	Continuous/off and on?	Fresh/rotten?
Patterns?	Pleasant/unpleasant?	New/old? (New/old what? Leather? Dead leaves?)
Textures?	Shrill/gentle	
Does it look like anything else?	Does it sound like anything else?	Does it smell like anything else?

Taste	Touch
Bitter? Metallic?	Hard/soft?
Burning? Spicy?	Liquid/solid?
Rich? Sweet?	Hot/cold?
Rotten? Canned?	Dry/oily?
Does it taste like anything else?	Rough/smooth?
	Does it feel like anything else?

PRACTICE 9-3   **Finding Details to Support a Main Impression**

Read the following statements, and write four sensory details you might use to support the main impression.

Example: The physical sensations of a day at the beach are as vivid as the visual ones.

a. softness of the sand

b. push and splash of waves

c. chill of the water

d. smoothness of worn stones and beach glass

1. My favorite meal smells as good as it tastes.

2. The new office building has a contemporary look.

3. A classroom during an exam echoes with the "sounds of silence."

Third Basic: Secondary Support in Description

The examples and sensory qualities you choose to support the main impression in description should be backed up with enough detail to make them come alive for your reader. You can do this by introducing additional adjectives (describing words) that appeal to the reader's senses: *rough, sweet,* or *shrill.*

You can also expand your support by adding comparisons, using words such as *like, similar to, just as,* or *as if.* The table might be *just as rough as chipped concrete,* while the shrill alarm could be *similar to the whistle of a tea kettle left far too long on the stove.* In his essay, "The Grandfather" (pp. 164–66), Gary Soto describes the fruit trees lovingly cared for by his grandfather, noting that "winter brought oranges, juicy and large as softballs." Comparing the oranges to softballs helps readers visualize more than just the color of the fruit.

Fourth Basic: Organization in Description

Description can use any of the orders of organization—**time**, **space**, or **importance**—depending on your purpose. If you are writing to create a main impression of an event (for example, a description of fireworks), you might use time order. If you are describing what someone or something looks like, you might use space order, the strategy used in the paragraph model on page 156. If one detail about your topic is stronger than the others, you could use order of importance and leave that detail for last. This approach is taken in the essay model on page 157.

Order	Sequence
Time	first to last/last to first most recent to least recent/least recent to most recent
Space	top to bottom/bottom to top right to left/left to right near to far/far to near
Importance	end with detail that will make the strongest impression

Using Transitions in Description

No matter which organization you choose, you will need to use **transitions** to move your readers from one sensory detail to the next.

Common Transitions in Description

Time			
at last	finally	next	then
before/after	first	now	when
during	last	second	while
eventually	meanwhile	since	

Space			
above	beneath	inside	over
across	beside	near	to the left/right
at the bottom/top	farther/further	next to	to the side
below	in front of	opposite	under/underneath

Importance		
especially	more/even more	most vivid
in particular	most	strongest

Using a Graphic Organizer in Description

A graphic organizer is a tool that helps you decide how to organize your description. When you are reading or writing a description organized spatially, your graphic organizer will emphasize locations, as in the paragraph on page 150.

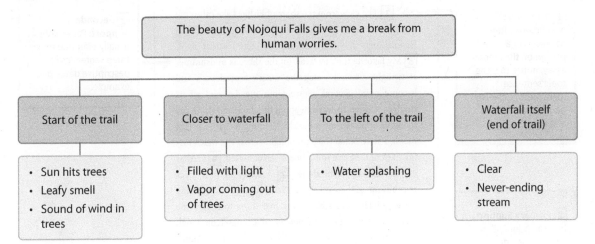

If this type of graphic organizer does not fit your description, consider using the cluster diagram in Chapter 8, page 130.

PRACTICE 9–4   **Using Transitions in Description**

Read the paragraph that follows, and fill in the blanks with one of the following transitions: *across, also, behind, especially, however, inside, last, next to, on top of, the first, when*. When you have finished, create a graphic organizer to illustrate the organization of this paragraph. (Note that more than one option may be correct.)

I saw the kitchen at Morley's Place on my first day assisting the town restaurant inspector. _____, Morley's was empty of customers, which made sense for 3 p.m. on a Tuesday. _____ my boss and I saw the kitchen, we hoped the restaurant would stay empty. _____ from the kitchen entrance was the food-prep counter that was covered with a faint layer of grime. _____ the counter were three food bins. ____, as I aimed my flashlight into one bin, numerous roaches scuttled away from the light. _____ the counter, a fan whirred loudly in an open window. _____ the stove, we discovered a mousetrap holding a shriveled, long-dead mouse. Because of the violations, the health department closed Morley's Place.

Paragraphs versus Essays in Description

For more on the important features of description, see the "Four Basics of Description" on page 149.

Paragraph Form

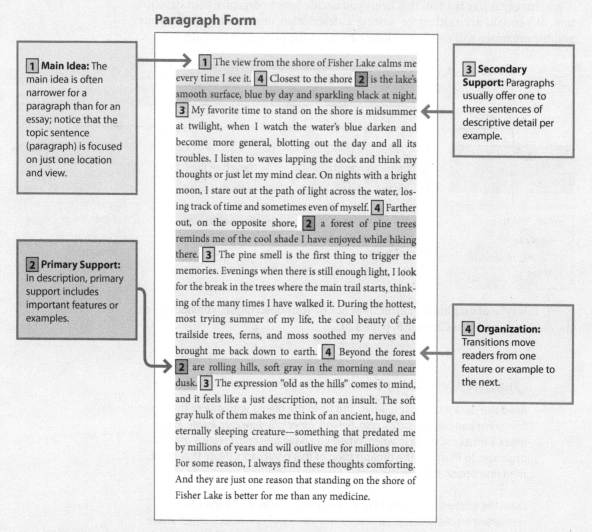

1 Main Idea: The main idea is often narrower for a paragraph than for an essay; notice that the topic sentence (paragraph) is focused on just one location and view.

2 Primary Support: In description, primary support includes important features or examples.

3 Secondary Support: Paragraphs usually offer one to three sentences of descriptive detail per example.

4 Organization: Transitions move readers from one feature or example to the next.

1 The view from the shore of Fisher Lake calms me every time I see it. 4 Closest to the shore 2 is the lake's smooth surface, blue by day and sparkling black at night. 3 My favorite time to stand on the shore is midsummer at twilight, when I watch the water's blue darken and become more general, blotting out the day and all its troubles. I listen to waves lapping the dock and think my thoughts or just let my mind clear. On nights with a bright moon, I stare out at the path of light across the water, losing track of time and sometimes even of myself. 4 Farther out, on the opposite shore, 2 a forest of pine trees reminds me of the cool shade I have enjoyed while hiking there. 3 The pine smell is the first thing to trigger the memories. Evenings when there is still enough light, I look for the break in the trees where the main trail starts, thinking of the many times I have walked it. During the hottest, most trying summer of my life, the cool beauty of the trailside trees, ferns, and moss soothed my nerves and brought me back down to earth. 4 Beyond the forest 2 are rolling hills, soft gray in the morning and near dusk. 3 The expression "old as the hills" comes to mind, and it feels like a just description, not an insult. The soft gray hulk of them makes me think of an ancient, huge, and eternally sleeping creature—something that predated me by millions of years and will outlive me for millions more. For some reason, I always find these thoughts comforting. And they are just one reason that standing on the shore of Fisher Lake is better for me than any medicine.

Consider Readers as You Write Description

Ask Yourself

- Does my essay convey to readers a single main impression about my topic?
- Will my examples and details bring my subject to life for my readers?
- Will the examples and details appeal to more than one of the readers' senses (sight, hearing, smell, taste, and touch)?
- Have I arranged my examples and details logically, with transitions that help readers follow the paragraph or essay?

Essay Form

1 Main Idea: The main idea is often broader for an essay; notice that the thesis for the essay covers several views.

2 Primary Support: In description, primary support includes important features or examples.

3 Secondary Support: Essays usually offer three to eight sentences of descriptive detail per paragraph.

4 Organization: Transitions move readers from one feature or example to the next.

1

I have worked in many places, from a basement-level machine shop to a cubicle in a tenth-floor insurance office. Now that I am in the construction industry, I want to sing the praises of one employment benefit that does not get enough attention: **1** the views from my sky-high welding jobs have been more stunning than any seen through an office window.

4 From a platform at my latest job, on a high-rise, **2** the streets below look like scenes from a miniature village. **3** The cars and trucks—even the rushing people—remind me of my nephews' motorized toys. **4** Sometimes, **3** the breeze carries up to me one of the few reminders that what I see is real: the smell of sausage or roasting chestnuts from street vendors, the honking of taxis or the scream of sirens, the dizzying clouds of diesel smoke. **4** Once, **3** the streets below me were taken over for a fair, and during my lunch break, I sat on a beam and watched the scene below. I spotted the usual things—packs of people strolling by concession stands or game tents, and

2

bands playing to crowds at different ends of the fair. **4** As I finished my lunch, **3** I saw two small flames near the edge of one band stage, nothing burning, nothing to fear. It was, I soon realized, an acrobat carrying two torches. I watched her climb high and walk a rope, juggling the torches as the crowd looked up and I looked down, fascinated.

4 Even more impressive **2** are the sights from an oil rig. **4** Two years ago, **3** I worked on a rig in Prudhoe Bay, Alaska, right at the water's edge. In the long days of summer, I loved to watch the changing light in the sky and on the water: bright to darker blue as the hours passed, and at day's end, a dying gold. **4** At the greatest heights **3** I could see white dots of ships far out at sea, and looking inland, I might spot musk ox or bears roaming in the distance. **4** In the long winter dark, **3** we worked by spotlights, which blotted the views below. But I still remember one time near nightfall when the spotlights suddenly flashed off. As my eyes adjusted, a crowd of caribou emerged below like ghosts. They snuffled the snow for food, oblivious to us.

3

4 To me, the most amazing views **2** are those from bridges high over rivers. **4** In 2020, **3** I had the privilege of briefly working on one of the tallest bridge-observatories in the world, over the Penobscot River in Maine. **4** As many tourists now do, **3** I reached the height of the observatory's top deck, 437 feet. Unlike them, however, my visits were routine and labor-intensive, giving me little time to appreciate the beauty all around me. But on clear days, during breaks and at the end of our shift, my coworkers and I would admire the wide, sapphire-colored river as it flowed to Penobscot Bay. Looking south, we would track the Maine coast winding to the Camden Hills. Looking east, we would spot Acadia National Park, the famous Mount Desert Island offshore in the mist. Each sight made up a panoramic view that I will never forget.

My line of work roots me in no one place, and it has a generous share of discomforts and dangers. But I would never trade it for another because it lets me see the world from on high. For stretches of time, I feel nearly superhuman.

Read and Analyze Description

To become a more successful writer, it is important not only to understand the four basics of description on page 149 but to read and evaluate examples as well. In this section, you will use a sample rubric to evaluate a student's draft description paragraph. After the paragraph, you will analyze a student essay. Finally, you will read a short description from college police chief James Roy and a professional description essay by Gary Soto.

Student Description Paragraph

Read the following sample description paragraph. Using the four basics of description and the sample rubric below, evaluate the paragraph, and then provide advice to the writer for the next draft.

> **Assignment:** Describe a scene that moved you to act in some way and your response to the scene.

Alessandra Cepeda

Bird Rescue

When the owner opened the storage unit, we could not believe that any living creature could have survived under such horrible conditions. Inside it was dark and smelly. A flashlight revealed three birds in the back corner. They looked sickly. Two of the birds had injured wings, obviously broken. They were exotic birds that should have had bright and colorful feathers, but their feathers were on the floor. We entered slowly and retrieved the abused birds. I cried at how such beautiful and helpless creatures had been mistreated. We adopted two of them, and our Samantha is now eight years old, with beautiful green feathers topped off with a colorful head. She talks, flies, and is a wonderful pet who is dearly loved and, I admit, very spoiled. She deserves it after such a rough start to her life.

Rubric for Description

	1 Falls below expectations	2 Nearly meets expectations	3 Meets expectations	4 Exceeds expectations
Main idea (first basic)	No clear main impression of the scene is present.	Main impression of the scene is unclear or too broad.	Main impression is clear, but its importance is not.	Main impression is clear as is its importance.

	1 **Falls below** **expectations**	**2** **Nearly meets** **expectations**	**3** **Meets** **expectations**	**4** **Exceeds** **expectations**
Support (second and third basics)	Few relevant examples or sensory details are provided.	Not enough, or not enough relevant, sensory details are provided.	Enough relevant supporting examples and sensory details are provided.	Good variety of examples and ample, well-chosen sensory details are provided.
Organization (fourth basic)	Organization is unclear or illogical.	Organization is inconsistent.	Organization is logical, but some transitions are missing or inappropriate.	Organization is logical, with smooth transitions throughout.

Evaluating the Paragraph

1. Does the paragraph show the four basics of description? Explain.

2. Using the rubric as a guide, what is the strongest part of the paragraph? The weakest?

3. Write a response to this writer, using one of the following to frame your response:

    a. One thing I would like to know more about is _____.

    b. What I liked best about the paragraph is _____.

    c. In your next draft, you might consider adding _____.

Student Description Essay

Brian Healy

First Day in Fallujah

Preview What type of experience will Healy be describing? Based on the title, how will it be organized? *Note:* Healy's descriptive essay shows readers what it is like to be in a war zone, and for this reason, some of the images he presents may be disturbing.

The year was 2004, and I was a young, 21-year-old U.S. Marine corporal on my second tour of Iraq. I had been in the country for five months and was not enjoying it any more than I had the first time. From the first time I set foot in Iraq, I perceived it as a foul-smelling wasteland where my youth and, as I would soon find out, my innocence were being squandered. I had been in a number

wasteland: an area that is uncultivated and barren or devastated by natural disasters or war

squandered: wasted; not used to good advantage

of firefights, roadside bomb attacks, and mortar and rocket attacks; therefore, I had thought I had seen it all. So when the word came down that my battalion was going to Fallujah to drive through the center of the city, I was as naïve as a child on the first day of school. The lesson of that first day would be taught with blood, sweat, and tears, learned through pain and suffering, and never forgotten.

2   At 2:00 in the morning on November 10, the voice of my commander pierced the night: "Mount up!" Upon hearing these words, I boarded the Amtrak transport. I heard a loud "clank, clank," the sound of metal hitting metal as the ramp closed and sealed us in. Sitting shoulder to shoulder, we had no more room to move than sardines in a pitch-dark can. The diesel fumes choked our lungs and burned our throats. There was a sudden jolt as the metal beast began to move, and with each bump and each turn, I was thrown from side to side inside the beast's belly with only the invisible bodies of my comrades to steady myself. I thought back to my childhood, to a time of carefree youth. I thought how my father would tell me how I was the cleanest of his sons. I chuckled as I thought, "If only he could see me now, covered in sweat and dirt and five days away from my last shower."

3   I was violently jerked back into the present with three thunderous explosions on the right side of the Amtrak vehicle. We continued to move faster and faster with more intensity and urgency than before. My heart was racing, pounding as if it were trying to escape from my chest when we came to a screeching halt.

4   With the same clank that sealed us in, the ramp dropped and released us from our can. I ran out of the Amtrak nearly tripping on the ramp. There was no moon, no streetlight, nothing to pierce the blanket of night. Therefore, seeing was almost completely out of the question. However, what was visible was a scene that I will never forget. The massive craters from our bombs made it seem as if we were running on the surface of the moon. More disturbing were the dead bodies of those enemies hit with the bombs. Their bodies were strewn about in a frenzied manner: a leg or arm here, torso there, a head severed from its body. Trying to avoid stepping on them was impossible. Amid all this and the natural "fog of war," we managed to get our bearings and move toward our objective. We were able to take the entrance to a government complex located at the center of the city, and we did so in fine style. "Not so tough," we all thought. We would not have to wait long until we would find out how insanely foolish we were.

5   As the sun began to rise, there were no morning prayers, no loudspeakers, and no noise at all. This, of course, was odd since we had become accustomed to the sounds of Iraq in the morning. However, this silence did not last long and was shattered as the enemy released hell's wrath upon us. The enemy was relentless in its initial assault but was unable to gain the advantage and was slowly pushed back.

6   As the day dragged on, the enemy fought us in an endless cycle of attack and retreat. There was no time to relax as rocket-propelled grenades whistled by our heads time and time again. Snipers' bullets skipped off the surface of the roof

fog of war: a term describing the general uncertainty that soldiers experience during military operations

relentless: steady; persistent; unyielding

we were on. While some bullets tore through packs, radios, boots, and clothing, a lucky few found their mark and ripped through flesh like a hot knife through butter.

7   Suddenly, there was a deafening crack as three 82-millimeter mortars rained upon us, throwing me to the ground. The dust blacked out the sun and choked my lungs. I began to rise only to be thrown back down by a rocket-propelled grenade whizzing just overhead, narrowly missing my face. At this point, it seemed clear to me that there was no end to this enemy. In the windows, out the doorways, through alleyways, and down streets, they would run. We would kill one and another would pop up in his stead, as if some factory just out of sight was producing more and more men to fight us.

8   As the sun fell behind the horizon, the battle, which had so suddenly started, ended just as swiftly. The enemy, like moths to light, were nowhere to be seen. The rifles of the Marines, which were so active that day, were silent now. We were puzzled as to why it was so quiet. My ears were still ringing from that day's events when the order came down to hole up for the night. There was no sleep for me that night; the events of the day made sure of that. I sat there that cold November night not really thinking of anything. I just sat in a trance, listening to small firefights of the battle that were still raging: a blast of machine gun fire, tracer rounds, and air strikes. Artillery flying through the air gave the appearance of a laser light show. Explosions rattling the earth lit my comrades' faces. As I looked over at them, I did not see my friends from earlier in the day; instead, I was looking at old men who were wondering what the next day would bring. I wondered if I would survive the next day.

tracer rounds: ammunition containing a substance that causes bullets or rounds to leave a trail

9   The battle for Fallujah would rage on for another three weeks. The Marines of the First Battalion Eighth Marine Regiment would continue to fight with courage and honor. As each day of the battle passed, I witnessed new horrors and acts of bravery, of which normal men are not capable. However, none of those days would have the impact on me that that first day did.

10   The battle is over, but for the men who were there, it will never end. It is fought every day in their heads and in voices of friends long gone, all the while listening to the screams and taunts of people who know nothing of war but would call these men terrorists.

Write to Read: Annotate

1. Underline the sensory details. Do these details appeal to sight, sound, smell, touch, or taste?

2. Highlight any transitional words or phrases Healy uses and make a note of any comparisons he makes.

Profile of Success: James Roy
Description in the Real World

James Roy

Chief of Police

Lord Fairfax
Community College

COURTESY OF JAMES ROY

Title   Chief of Police, Lord Fairfax Community College

Background   I joined the Marine Corps immediately after graduating from high school and served for four very eventful years. Since joining the Marines I had the pleasure of traveling to many parts of Europe, Africa, Asia, and South America. At the age of thirty-five I was offered a position as a deputy sheriff in my hometown, a choice I gladly accepted. My success in law enforcement led to numerous promotions from patrol supervisor to investigator, and I now serve as a chief of police at a community college.

Writing at Work   I learned very quickly how important writing is to my position as a law enforcement officer. Our reports are used in criminal and civil cases that many times have serious, long-lasting, and often life-changing outcomes for victims, suspects, and witnesses. These reports must be written accurately and articulately to convey the facts and circumstances of the case for the courts and prosecutors to do their job. Learning to write well has given me the confidence to present cases before judges, juries, and the public.

Read to Write: Think Critically

1. What is the main idea of Healy's essay?

2. Is Healy's paper organized by space, time, or importance? How do you know?

3. Who is Healy's intended audience? How does he try to create suspense for his readers?

4. Healy suggests that his friends had become "old men" in one day. How did that happen? What caused it? Explain.

5. Does this essay have the four basics of description? Explain.

Use Reading Strategies: Create a Graphic Organizer

Use the model graphic organizer on page 155 to illustrate the main idea, support, and organization of Healy's essay.

Reflect and Respond

Have you ever had an experience that made you feel frightened or overwhelmed? What did you do to work through that situation or try to deal with it? Write a paragraph describing what you saw or heard.

Workplace Description

James Roy

Malicious Wounding

Preview Read the first sentence of the report. What can you learn about Roy's tone from that sentence?

At 03:20 a.m. I responded to a call that reported a fight and gunshots. When I arrived in the area, several people in the roadway pointed across a field to a mobile home on Yancey Drive. A woman, Ginny Pyle, was walking around a car in front of the mobile home and shouting. Two men, later identified as Jerry Smythe and his father Willie Smythe, were sitting on the porch of the mobile home, and two other men were on the ground. I approached them and saw Gary Pyle Sr. on top of his son, Gary Pyle Jr., holding him down on the ground. Pyle Sr. yelled, "Arrest him! He's drunk and out of control." Pyle Jr. was bleeding from his nose and had small bloody scrapes on his arms. A strong odor of alcohol was on his breath, and he exhibited blood shot eyes, slurred speech, and unsteady balance. Deputy White arrested Pyle Jr. for being drunk in public.

2   When I walked back to the mobile home, Jerry Smythe said, "I've been shot." I noticed two bloody wounds above and below his right knee. Smythe claimed he was sleeping on his couch when Pyle Jr. shot him through the window of the front door of his mobile home. The front door window was approximately 10 inches by 10 inches and was broken, with most of the broken glass lying on the inside of the doorway. Blood was mingled with broken glass on the porch.

3   I spoke with Pyle Jr., who was handcuffed and sitting in the back of Deputy White's patrol vehicle. I read him his Miranda rights and then asked, "Where is the gun?" Pyle Jr. laughed and said, "You'll never find it." Deputy White transported Pyle Jr. to the county jail, and Jerry Smythe was transported to the hospital at 03:30 a.m. Detective Gomez arrived on location at 04:14 a.m. to process the scene.

Read to Write: Annotate

1. Underline or highlight the supporting details in this workplace description. What senses do these details appeal to?

2. Circle or highlight the transitions Roy has used. How is the piece organized?

Write to Read: Think Critically

1. What is your main impression of the scene and of the incident?

2. What is Roy's purpose? Who is the intended audience?

3. Unlike other descriptive pieces in this chapter, Roy's description does not use comparisons. Given his audience and purpose, why do you think this might be the case?

4. Roy's description is written in the first person (using "I"). Why does he choose to write this way?

Use Reading Strategies: Summarize

Review information in Chapter 1 about writing a summary (pp. 18–20). Write a short summary of Roy's report.

Reflect and Respond

Imagine this scene as it occurred from the point of view of Ginny Pyle or William Smythe. Write the report from their viewpoints. How do the details of the description change?

Professional Description Essay

Gary Soto

CHLOE AFTEL/CONTOUR/
GETTY IMAGES

Writer and poet Gary Soto earned his B.A. from California State University, Fresno, and M.F.A. (Master of Fine Arts) from the University of California, Irvine. His published work illustrates the lives of migrant workers and farmers who travel and work in California, as well as depictions of Latinx families in the barrios there. He has written poetry, novels, essays, young adult fiction, and even children's books.

The Grandfather

Preview What will be the topic of this essay? Skim the first lines of each paragraph. Do these lines suggest your prediction is accurate? Explain.

Grandfather believed a well-rooted tree was the color of money. His money he kept hidden behind portraits of sons and daughters or taped behind the calendar of an Aztec warrior. He tucked it into the sofa, his shoes and slippers, and into the tight-lipped pockets of his suits. He kept it in his soft brown wallet that was machine tooled with "MEXICO" and a campesino and donkey climbing a hill. He had climbed, too, out of Mexico, settled in Fresno and worked thirty years at Sun Maid Raisin, first as a packer and later, when he was old, as a watchman with a large clock on his belt.

campesino: a poor farmer

2   After work, he sat in the backyard under the arbor, watching the water gurgle in the rose bushes that ran along the fence. A lemon tree hovered over the clothesline. Two orange trees stood near the alley. His favorite tree, the avocado, which had started in a jam jar from a seed and three toothpicks lanced in its sides, rarely bore fruit. He said it was the wind's fault, and the mayor's, who allowed office buildings so high that the haze of pollen from the countryside could never find its way into the city. He sulked about this. He said that in Mexico buildings only grew so tall. You could see the moon at night, and the stars were clear points all the way to the horizon. And wind reached all the way from the sea, which was blue and clean, unlike the oily water sloshing against a San Francisco pier.

3   During its early years, I could leap over that tree, kick my bicycling legs over the top branch and scream my fool head off because I thought for sure I was flying. I ate fruit to keep my strength up, fuzzy peaches and branch-scuffed plums cooled in the refrigerator. From the kitchen chair he brought out in the evening, Grandpa would scold, "Hijo, what's the matta with you? You gonna break it."

hijo: Spanish word for "son"

4   By the third year, the tree was as tall as I, its branches casting a meager shadow on the ground. I sat beneath the shade, scratching words in the hard dirt with a stick. I had learned "Nile" in summer school and a dirty word from my brother who wore granny sunglasses. The red ants tumbled into my letters, and I buried them, knowing that they would dig themselves back into fresh air.

5   A tree was money. If a lemon cost seven cents at Hanoian's Market, then Grandfather saved fistfuls of change and more because in winter the branches of his lemon tree hung heavy yellow fruit. And winter brought oranges, juicy and large as softballs. Apricots he got by the bagfuls from a son, who himself was wise for planting young. Peaches he got from a neighbor, who worked the night shift at Sun Maid Raisin. The chile plants, which also saved him from giving up his hot, sweaty quarters, were propped up with sticks to support an abundance of red fruit.

6   But his favorite tree was the avocado because it offered hope and the promise of more years. After work, Grandpa sat in the backyard, shirtless, tired of flagging trucks loaded with crates of raisins, and sipped glasses of ice water. His yard was neat: five trees, seven rose bushes, whose fruit were the red and white flowers he floated in bowls, and a statue of St. Francis that stood in a circle of crushed rocks, arms spread out to welcome hungry sparrows.

7   After ten years, the first avocado hung on a branch, but the meat was flecked with black, an omen, Grandfather thought, a warning to keep an eye on the living. Five years later, another avocado hung on a branch, larger than the first

omen: a sign of something that will happen in the future; like a prophecy

and edible when crushed with a fork into a heated tortilla. Grandfather sprinkled it with salt and laced it with a river of chile.

8   "It's good," he said, and let me taste.

9   I took a big bite, waved a hand over my tongue, and ran for the garden hose gurgling in the rose bushes. I drank long and deep, and later ate the smile from an ice cold watermelon.

10   Birds nested in the tree, quarreling jays with liquid eyes and cool, pulsating throats. Wasps wove a horn-shaped hive one year, but we smoked them away with swords of rolled up newspapers lit with matches. By then, the tree was tall enough for me to climb to look into the neighbor's yard. But by then I was too old for that kind of thing and went about with my brother, hair slicked back and our shades dark as oil.

11   After twenty years, the tree began to bear. Although Grandfather complained about how much he lost because pollen never reached the poor part of town, because at the market he had to haggle over the price of avocados, he loved that tree. It grew, as did his family, and when he died, all his sons standing on each other's shoulders, oldest to youngest, could not reach the highest branches. The wind could move the branches, but the trunk, thicker than any waist, hugged the ground.

Write to Read: Annotate

1. Underline or highlight the sensory details. Do these details appeal to the readers' sight, sound, smell, touch, or taste?

2. Circle the transitions or highlight them in a different color.

3. Put a check mark by all descriptions that involve fruit. How do these references contribute to the overall impression in the essay?

Read to Write: Think Critically

1. Do we know what the grandfather looks like? Is this essay more about the grandfather or the tree? Explain your answer.

2. In paragraphs 4 and 10, the author describes his own interaction with the tree. How do these paragraphs contribute to your impression of the tree? Of the grandfather?

3. Why do you think the author includes the story of the first and second avocados in paragraphs 7 to 9?

4. How is the description organized? How can you tell?

Use Reading Strategies: Recognize Metaphorical Language

Soto's description includes proper nouns, adjectives, comparisons, and dialogue. But Soto also uses metaphorical language to make his descriptions more vivid for his readers. Metaphorical language makes a comparison without using the words *like* or *as*. Instead, the writer uses a word in a nonliteral way. For example, Soto says his grandfather put "a river of chile" on an avocado. He did not mean a real, literal river. Instead, the image of a river helps the reader imagine the chiles pouring over the avocado.

Find at least two more examples of metaphorical language in the essay. How does this language help Soto create his main impression?

Reflect and Respond

1. Describe a place that is important to you or associated with significant memories. It might be a city, a favorite park, a friend's or relative's home, or a vacation spot.

2. Describe an outdoor scene from your favorite season. You might work from a personal photograph taken during that season.

3. Describe a person who has played a major role in your life. Try to include sensory details that go beyond the person's appearance. For instance, you might describe the sound of that person's voice or the texture of a favorite piece of clothing.

Grammar for Description

One way to appeal to a reader's senses is to use descriptive adjectives. Adjectives are words that describe or modify nouns: adjectives can specify age, size, color, condition, appearance, and many other features. In addition, writers can make adjectives from the *-ing* or *-ed* forms of verbs, also called **participles**. Participles can describe nouns, just as other adjectives do. In the following sentences from Soto's essay, the participles are underlined, and the nouns they describe are italicized.

> I took a big bite, waved a hand over my tongue, and ran for the garden *hose* <u>gurgling</u> in the rose bushes.
>
> Birds nested in the tree, <u>quarreling</u> *jays* with liquid eyes and cool, <u>pulsating</u> *throats*. Wasps wove a horn-shaped hive one year, but we smoked them away with swords of <u>rolled up</u> *newspapers* <u>lit</u> with matches.
>
> But by then I was too old for that kind of thing and went about with my brother, *hair* <u>slicked</u> back and our shades dark as oil.

For more on adjectives, see Chapter 23.

Write Your Own Description

In this section, you will write your own description based on one of the following assignments. For help, refer to the "How to Write Description" checklist on pages 170–71.

Assignment Options: Writing about College, Work, and Everyday Life

Write a description paragraph or essay on one of the following topics or on one of your own choice:

| College | • Describe the sights, sounds, smells, and tastes in the cafeteria or another popular spot on campus. |
| | • Find a place where you can get a good view of your campus (for instance, a window on an upper floor of one of the buildings). Then describe the scene using space order (p. 154). |

| Work | • Describe your workplace, including as many sensory details as you can. |
| | • Describe your boss or a colleague you work with closely. First, think of the main impression you get from this person. Then choose details that would make your impression clear to readers. |

| Everyday Life | • Describe a favorite photograph, using as many details as possible. |
| | • Visit an organization that serves your community, such as an animal shelter or a food pantry. During your visit, take notes about what you see. Later, write a detailed description of the scene. |

Assignment Options: Reading and Writing Critically

Complete one of the following assignments that ask you to apply the critical thinking, reading, and writing skills discussed in Chapter 1.

Writing Critically about Readings

Both Gary Soto's "The Grandfather" (p. 164) and Amy Tan's "Fish Cheeks" (p. 117) describe scenes from the past. Read or review both of these pieces, and then follow these steps:

1. **Summarize.** Briefly summarize the works, listing major examples and details.

2. **Analyze.** Tan uses humor to make her point, whereas Soto's essay is more serious. Why do you think the authors might have chosen these different approaches?

3. **Synthesize.** Using examples from both Tan's and Soto's essays and from your own experience, discuss the types of details that make certain memories in our lives (such as an event or a place) so memorable.

4. **Evaluate.** Which essay, Tan's or Soto's, do you think is more effective? Why? In writing your evaluation, you might look back at your responses to step 2.

Writing Critically about Visuals

Study the photograph below, and complete the following steps:

VLADIMIR VLADIMIROV/GETTY IMAGES

1. **Read the image.** Ask yourself: What part of the photograph draws your attention the most, and why? What main impression does the picture create, and what details contribute to this impression? (For more information on reading images, see Chapter 1.)

2. **Write a description.** What did voting look like in 2020 and 2021? Write a paragraph or essay that describes this photograph and explains the main impression it gives, or describe what you saw as you participated in a recent election.

Writing Critically about Problems

Read or review the discussion of problem solving in Chapter 1 (pp. 26–28). Then consider the following problem:

An abandoned house on your street is a safety hazard for the children in the neighborhood. Although you and some of your neighbors have called the local board of health, nothing has been done. Finally, you and your neighbors decide to write to the mayor.

Assignment: Working in a small group or on your own, write to the mayor describing why this house is a safety hazard. Thoroughly describe the house (outside and inside). Imagine a place that is not just ugly; it must also pose safety problems to children. You might start with the following sentence:

Not only is the abandoned house at 45 Main Street an eyesore, but it is also

_____.

For a paragraph: Describe in detail one room on the first floor of the house or just the exterior you can see from the street.

For an essay: Describe in detail at least three rooms in the house or the exterior you can see if you walk entirely around the house.

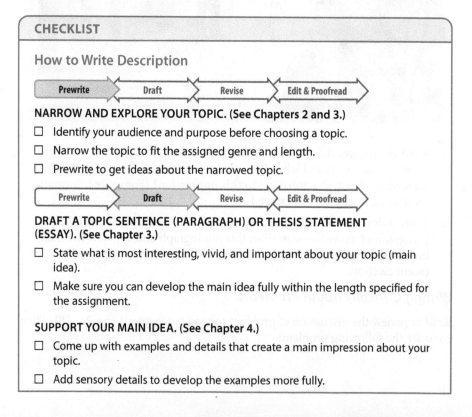

CHECKLIST

How to Write Description

| **Prewrite** | Draft | Revise | Edit & Proofread |

NARROW AND EXPLORE YOUR TOPIC. (See Chapters 2 and 3.)

☐ Identify your audience and purpose before choosing a topic.

☐ Narrow the topic to fit the assigned genre and length.

☐ Prewrite to get ideas about the narrowed topic.

| Prewrite | **Draft** | Revise | Edit & Proofread |

DRAFT A TOPIC SENTENCE (PARAGRAPH) OR THESIS STATEMENT (ESSAY). (See Chapter 3.)

☐ State what is most interesting, vivid, and important about your topic (main idea).

☐ Make sure you can develop the main idea fully within the length specified for the assignment.

SUPPORT YOUR MAIN IDEA. (See Chapter 4.)

☐ Come up with examples and details that create a main impression about your topic.

☐ Add sensory details to develop the examples more fully.

WRITE A DRAFT. (See Chapter 5.)

☐ Make a plan that puts examples in a logical order (time, space, or importance).

☐ Include a topic sentence (paragraph) or thesis statement (essay) and all the supporting examples and details.

Prewrite → Draft → **Revise** → Edit & Proofread

REVISE YOUR DRAFT. (See Chapter 6.)

☐ Make sure it has *all* the four basics of description.

☐ Make sure each paragraph is unified (all ideas should relate to the topic sentence).

☐ Make sure each paragraph is fully developed (there are enough supporting details to demonstrate the point).

☐ Make sure you include transitions to move readers smoothly from one detail to the next.

Prewrite → Draft → Revise → **Edit & Proofread**

EDIT AND PROOFREAD YOUR REVISED DRAFT. (See Parts 3 and 4.)

☐ Make sure grammar, word usage, and punctuation choices are clear, accurate, and effective.

☐ Check spelling and capitalization.

Chapter 9 Review

1. What is description?

2. What are the four basics of description?

3. The topic sentence in a description paragraph or the thesis statement in a description essay includes what two elements?

4. How can writers make a description come alive for readers?

Reflect and Apply

1. Have you ever written or read description before? How does that experience confirm, contradict, or complicate what you have learned in this chapter?

2. Interview someone studying in your major or working in your career. In what situations have they used description in their work?

3. What was most difficult about your writing for this chapter? What do you want to do differently next time?

4. What was most successful about your writing for this chapter? What do you need to remember for next time?

10

Process Analysis

Writing That Explains How Things Happen

Have you ever heard someone ask, "Did you read the instructions?" Whether we are at work, at school, or at home, we have to follow instructions for all sorts of tasks, from operating equipment and writing lab reports to setting up a new phone or baking a birthday cake. Each of these tasks is a process that requires several steps. Explaining the steps in a process is called **process analysis**.

Understand What Process Analysis Is

Process analysis either explains how to do something (so that your readers can do it) or explains how something works (so that your readers can understand it).

Four Basics of Process Analysis

1 **Main Idea:** An effective process analysis paragraph or essay tells readers what process the writer wants them to know about and makes a point about it.

2 **Primary Support:** It presents the essential steps in the process.

3 **Secondary Support:** It explains the steps in detail.

4 **Organization:** It presents the steps in a logical order (usually time order).

In the following paragraph, the numbers and colors correspond to the four basics of good process analysis.

The poet Dana Gioia once said, "Art delights, instructs, consoles. It educates our emotions." [1] Closely observing paintings, sculpture, and other forms of visual art is a great way to have the type of experience that Gioia describes, and following a few basic steps will help you get the most from the experience. [4] First, [2] choose an art exhibit that interests you. [3] You can find listings for exhibits on local museums' websites or in the arts section of a newspaper. Links on the websites or articles in a newspaper may give you more information about the exhibits, the artists featured in them, and the types of work to be displayed. [4] Second, [2] go to the museum with an open mind and, ideally, with a friend. [3] While moving through the exhibit, take time to examine each work carefully. As you do so, ask yourself questions: What is my eye most drawn to, and why? What questions does this work raise for me, and how does it make me feel? How would I describe it to someone over the phone? Ask your friend the same questions, and consider the responses. You might also consult an exhibit brochure for information about the featured artists and their works. [4] Finally, [2] keep your exploration going after you have left the museum. [3] Go out for coffee or a meal with your friend. Trade more of your thoughts and ideas about the artwork, and discuss your overall impressions. If you are especially interested in any of the artists or their works, you might look for additional information or images on the Internet, or you might consult books at the library. [4] Throughout the whole experience, [1] put aside the common belief that only artists or cultural experts "get" art. The artist Eugène Delacroix described paintings as "a bridge between the soul of the artist and that of the spectator." Trust your ability to cross that bridge and come to new understandings.

In college, a writing assignment may ask you to *describe the process of doing something*, but you might also be asked to *describe the stages of something* or *explain how something works*. Whenever you need to identify and explain the steps or stages of anything, you will use process analysis.

First Basic: Main Idea in Process Analysis

A process analysis can have two purposes: to explain or to instruct. An **explanatory process analysis** explains how something works *so that readers can understand*. For example, a text that explains the circulatory system is an explanatory process analysis. An **instructional process analysis**, on the other hand, explains how to do something *so that readers can actually try the process themselves*. For example, a nursing textbook that explains how to take and record vital signs uses instructional process analysis to teach students to perform this task.

Regardless of the purpose, the main point in a process analysis is what the writer wants readers to know about the process—its significance, expected results, or reasons to try the process for themselves. To help you discover the main idea for a process analysis, complete the following sentence:

Main idea in process analysis: What readers need to know about this process is that _____.

Here is an example of a topic sentence for a paragraph:

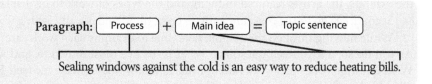

Remember that the topic for an essay can be a little broader than one for a paragraph.

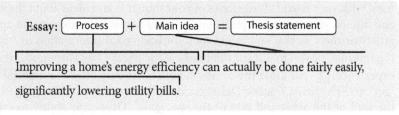

Whereas the topic sentence focuses on just one method to improve energy efficiency, the thesis statement sets up a discussion of multiple methods.

PRACTICE 10–1   Writing a Main Idea

For each of the following topics, write a main idea for a process analysis in the space below.

Example: Creating a budget *can help anyone manage money more effectively.*

1. Making (your favorite food)

2. Playing (a video game you know well)

3. Washing a car

4. Shopping for (something you buy often) online

5. Learning how to (do something)

Second Basic: Primary Support in Process Analysis

In process analysis, primary support shows the readers the steps in the process. When you are planning primary support, consider your audience and purpose to make sure you have included all the important steps. While some steps may seem too obvious to mention, readers who are not familiar with the process may not know what to do. Be careful to include all the information that a reader needs to understand or complete the process.

> **PRACTICE 10-2**   **Finding and Choosing the Essential Steps**
>
> Look at the main ideas that you wrote for Practice 10-1. For each one, write the essential steps in the order you would perform them.

Third Basic: Secondary Support in Process Analysis

The major steps in a process analysis need to be clear to the reader. Some steps may include unfamiliar terms that could cause confusion. Therefore, writers often include definitions, descriptions of tools and materials, or examples with each step so that readers can follow the process easily. For example, the second step in the paragraph on page 173 tells readers to "go to the museum with an open mind." What does it mean to have an open mind at the museum? The writer explains an open mind by giving examples of questions an open-minded person might ask:

What is my eye most drawn to, and why? What questions does this work raise for me, and how does it make me feel? How would I describe it to someone over the phone?

> **PRACTICE 10-3**   **Adding Details to Essential Steps**
>
> Choose one of the topics from Practice 10-1. In the spaces that follow, copy that topic and the steps you wrote for it in Practice 10-2. Then add a detail to each of the steps.
>
> **Example:**
>
> Topic: Creating a budget *can help anyone manage money more effectively.*
>
> Step 1: List all essential expenses for each month.
>
> > Detail: *Include rent, utilities, food, and cell phone*
>
> Step 2: Determine take-home pay for each month.
>
> > Detail: *Use the amount after taxes and insurance; add other tips or expected income.*

Step 3: Set aside enough for essential expenses.

    Detail: *Subtract essential expenses from take-home pay, and set aside some for savings.*

Step 4: Determine how to spend what is left based on priorities.

    Detail: *Make a list of priorities for the rest, including travel, entertainment, gifts, gym memberships, and clothes.*

Topic:

Step 1:

    Detail:

Step 2:

    Detail:

Step 3:

    Detail:

Step 4:

    Detail:

Fourth Basic: Organization in Process Analysis

Process analysis is usually organized by **time order** because it explains the steps of the process in the order in which they occur. This is the strategy used in the paragraph and essay models on pages 178–79.

Using Transitions in Process Analysis

Transitions move readers smoothly from one step to the next.

Common Transitions in Process Analysis				
after	during	last	now	soon
as	eventually	later	once	then
at last	finally	meanwhile	second	when
before	first	next	since	while

Using a Graphic Organizer in Process Analysis

A common graphic organizer used with process analysis is a flowchart like the following, which shows the major steps for the paragraph on page 173. The major steps are listed in the circles, while supporting details and examples are in bulleted lists on the arrows.

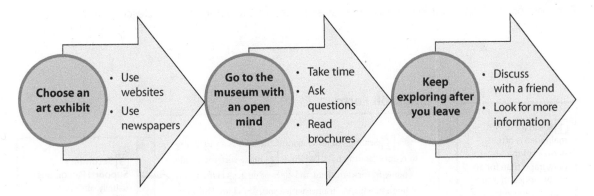

PRACTICE 10–4   **Using Transitions and Graphic Organizers in Process Analysis**

Read the paragraph that follows, and fill in the blanks with one of the following transitions: *before this, eventually, first, meanwhile, next, once, while.* When you have finished, create a graphic organizer (such as the flowchart above) to show the organization of the paragraph. (Note that more than one option may be correct.)

      Scientists have discovered that, like something from a zombie movie, a mind-controlling fungus attacks certain carpenter ants. ____, as if following the fungus's orders, the ants help their invader reproduce. The process begins when an ant is infected. ____, the ant begins to act strangely. For instance, instead of staying in its home high in the trees, it drops to the forest floor. ____ wandering, it searches for a cool, moist place. ____ the zombie-ant finds the right place, it clamps its jaws to a leaf and dies. _____, the fungus within the ant grows until it bursts from the insect's head, and more ants are infected. By studying this process, researchers may find better ways to control the spread of carpenter ants.

Read and Analyze Process Analysis

To become a more successful writer, it is important not only to understand the four basics of process analysis but to read and analyze examples as well. In this section, you will use a rubric to evaluate the first draft of a student process analysis paragraph by Ibrahim Alfaqeeh. Next, you will analyze a finished draft of a process analysis essay by Katie Horn. Then you will see how editorial assistant Paola Garcia-Muniz uses process analysis in her job with Macmillan Learning. The final essay is a process analysis by journalist Samantha Levine-Finley.

Paragraphs versus Essays in Process Analysis

For more on the important features of process analysis, see the "Four Basics of Description" on page 172.

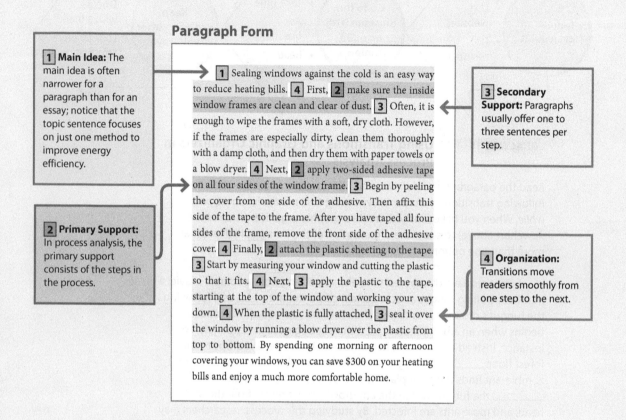

Paragraph Form

1 Main Idea: The main idea is often narrower for a paragraph than for an essay; notice that the topic sentence focuses on just one method to improve energy efficiency.

2 Primary Support: In process analysis, the primary support consists of the steps in the process.

3 Secondary Support: Paragraphs usually offer one to three sentences per step.

4 Organization: Transitions move readers smoothly from one step to the next.

1 Sealing windows against the cold is an easy way to reduce heating bills. 4 First, 2 make sure the inside window frames are clean and clear of dust. 3 Often, it is enough to wipe the frames with a soft, dry cloth. However, if the frames are especially dirty, clean them thoroughly with a damp cloth, and then dry them with paper towels or a blow dryer. 4 Next, 2 apply two-sided adhesive tape on all four sides of the window frame. 3 Begin by peeling the cover from one side of the adhesive. Then affix this side of the tape to the frame. After you have taped all four sides of the frame, remove the front side of the adhesive cover. 4 Finally, 2 attach the plastic sheeting to the tape. 3 Start by measuring your window and cutting the plastic so that it fits. 4 Next, 3 apply the plastic to the tape, starting at the top of the window and working your way down. 4 When the plastic is fully attached, 3 seal it over the window by running a blow dryer over the plastic from top to bottom. By spending one morning or afternoon covering your windows, you can save $300 on your heating bills and enjoy a much more comfortable home.

Consider Readers as You Write Process Analysis

Ask Yourself

- Will readers recognize the main idea that identifies the process and understand the point I want to make?

- Have I included all the essential steps so my readers can follow the process?

- Have I given enough details to make the steps clear and easy to understand for readers?

- Have I organized the steps in chronological order and included appropriate transitions so readers will find the process easy to follow?

Essay Form

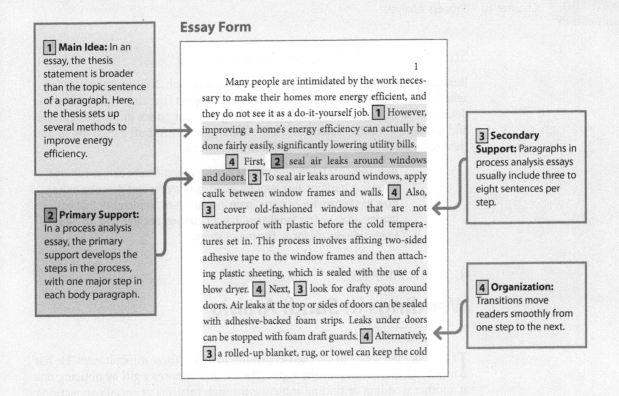

1 **Main Idea:** In an essay, the thesis statement is broader than the topic sentence of a paragraph. Here, the thesis sets up several methods to improve energy efficiency.

2 **Primary Support:** In a process analysis essay, the primary support develops the steps in the process, with one major step in each body paragraph.

3 **Secondary Support:** Paragraphs in process analysis essays usually include three to eight sentences per step.

4 **Organization:** Transitions move readers smoothly from one step to the next.

1

Many people are intimidated by the work necessary to make their homes more energy efficient, and they do not see it as a do-it-yourself job. **1** However, improving a home's energy efficiency can actually be done fairly easily, significantly lowering utility bills. **4** First, **2** seal air leaks around windows and doors. **3** To seal air leaks around windows, apply caulk between window frames and walls. **4** Also, **3** cover old-fashioned windows that are not weatherproof with plastic before the cold temperatures set in. This process involves affixing two-sided adhesive tape to the window frames and then attaching plastic sheeting, which is sealed with the use of a blow dryer. **4** Next, **3** look for drafty spots around doors. Air leaks at the top or sides of doors can be sealed with adhesive-backed foam strips. Leaks under doors can be stopped with foam draft guards. **4** Alternatively, **3** a rolled-up blanket, rug, or towel can keep the cold

2

from coming in. All of these measures can save up to $600 per season on heating bills. **4** Second, **2** install water-saving showerheads and faucet aerators. **3** These fixtures are inexpensive and are available in most hardware stores. Also, they are easy to install. **4** First, **3** unscrew the old shower or faucet head. **4** Then **3** follow the package instructions for affixing the new showerhead or aerator. In some cases, you might have to use pipe tape or a rubber washer to ensure a good seal. **4** After this step, **3** run the water to make sure there are no leaks. If you find any leaks, use pliers to tighten the seal. In time, you will discover that the new showerheads and aerators will cut your water usage and the cost of water heating by up to 50 percent. **4** Finally, **2** look for other places where energy efficiency could be increased. **3** One simple improvement is to replace traditional light bulbs with compact fluorescent bulbs, which use up to 80 percent

3

less energy. **4** Also, **3** make sure your insulation is as good as it can be. Many utilities now offer free assessments of home insulation, identifying places where it is missing or inadequate. **4** In some cases, **3** any necessary insulation improvements may be subsidized by the utilities or by government agencies. It is well worth considering such improvements, which, in the case of poorly insulated homes, can save thousands of dollars a year, quickly covering any costs. Although some people prefer to have professionals blow insulating foam into their walls, it is not difficult to add insulation to attics, where a large amount of heat can be lost during cold months.

Taking even one of these steps can make a significant financial difference in your life as well as reduce your impact on the environment. My advice is to improve your home's energy efficiency as much as possible, even if it means doing just a little at a time. The long-term payoff is too big to pass up.

179

Student Process Analysis Paragraph

Read the following first draft process analysis paragraph. Note that the instructor asked the students to focus on the main idea, support (the steps and supporting details), and organization in this draft. Using the four basics of process analysis and the sample rubric, determine how effective Ibrahim's draft paragraph is, and then recommend one or two goals for his next draft.

> **Assignment:** Traditional events can be very different across cultures. Choose a traditional ceremony, holiday, or event and describe either how to prepare for or participate in that event. Remember that your readers may not be familiar with your cultural background, so be sure to include details for all the major steps.

Ibrahim Alfaqeeh

Weddings in Saudi Arabia

If a Saudi man wants to get married, he has to follow these difficult steps. He has to ask his mother to look for a girl. The mother chooses a girl by noticing one at another wedding or finding someone through relatives or social connections. When his mother finds the perfect girl for him, he and his father go to the girl's father in order to ask for her hand. Both the fathers and the mothers agree on the price of the dowry, which can be expensive. The groom pays for many other traditional parts of the wedding, too. The groom should pay to rent the hall for the celebration and all the staff. The people celebrate the wedding from 6:00 in the evening until 4:00 in the morning. Because a traditional Saudi wedding is so difficult, I plan to get married in a casual way and choose my own wife.

dowry: the money and gifts offered by the groom to the bride's family or the money or belongings the bride brings to a marriage

Rubric for Process Analysis

	1 Falls below expectations	2 Nearly meets expectations	3 Meets expectations	4 Exceeds expectations
Main idea (first basic)	No clear main idea is present or main idea does not fit assignment.	Main idea is too broad or narrow for assignment.	Main idea is appropriate but dull, or purpose is unclear.	Main idea is engaging with a clear sense of purpose.
Support (second and third basics)	Key steps and supporting details are missing.	Most steps are included, but details are lacking.	All steps included with enough details.	All steps are clear and fully developed.
Organization (fourth basic)	Steps are unclear or not organized logically.	Steps are organized inconsistently.	Steps are organized logically, but some transitions are missing or inappropriate.	Steps are organized logically with smooth transitions throughout.

Evaluating the Paragraph

1. Does the paragraph show the four basics of process analysis? Explain.

2. Using the rubric as a guide, what is the strongest part of the paragraph? The weakest?

3. Write a response to this writer, using one of the following to frame your response:

    a. One thing I would like to know more about is _____.

    b. What I liked best about the paragraph is _____.

    c. In your next draft, you might consider adding _____.

Student Process Analysis Essay

Katie Horn

A Beginner's Guide to Movie Night

Preview Skim the title and the first paragraph of Horn's essay. What process will Horn describe? Who might be interested in this topic?

Going to the movies presents many choices, from which theater and which snacks to which seats. The possibilities can be overwhelming, but by following a few simple steps, you can enjoy the ultimate movie experience.

2 The first thing to consider is which theater to visit. Be careful to choose a location that spells its name "theater" and not "theatre." Theatres are places full of hoity-toity people in uncomfortable shoes watching foreign films (for the cultural experience, not just the nudity). Theaters, on the other hand, offer thrilling action sequences and heart-wrenching love stories on forty-foot screens. Beyond that, any establishment that is nearby, offers stadium seating, and has an Icee machine should work.

3 Next, you must select a movie from the films currently available at the theater you have chosen. Most theaters will have at least one action movie, one sappy romantic movie, and one family-friendly movie. If you are on a date, keep in mind that the potential for future dates hinges on your movie selection. For those hoping to indulge in mid-movie snuggling, a film from the romance or suspense genre is likely to encourage couples to get a little closer together—albeit for quite different reasons. If these are sold out, you may choose to view a comedy, which can be very useful in assessing if your date has a sense of humor.

4 The next step is to purchase movie munchies. Traditionally speaking, popcorn is the ultimate movie snack and, therefore, must be included in every movie menu. Popcorn can be supplemented by beverages and candies, including classics like Goobers and Junior Mints and newfangled treats such as chocolate-covered cookie dough bites and Sour Skittles. The alternative to purchasing candy at the

theater is to smuggle it in, which requires skills carefully honed over a lifetime of moviegoing. Beginners should practice their smuggling techniques during the winter, when large coats and awkward bulges arouse less suspicion. With a little practice, anyone can successfully sneak a bag of M&M's into the movies. Over time, you may develop the skills of hiding snacks in skimpier clothing or managing more impressive snacks, such as ice cream or fried mozzarella sticks.

5   Once snacks are in hand, the next step is to select a seat. Begin with a quick scan of the patrons who have already been seated. It is important to avoid small children (who are messy), people with cell phones (which will buzz during the movie), and tall people (because they block the screen). Having avoided these hazards, head toward the back of the theater, avoiding the social stigma that comes with sitting in the front. The back rows should be surveyed for spilled soda and stray candies—getting stuck in a half-chewed gumdrop ruins the movie experience. Then test the seat to determine the viewing angle. While the center seats of each row generally offer prime views, moviegoers with small bladders may prefer easier access to the bathrooms.

6   After choosing a seat, settle in and watch the previews. As other patrons trickle in and fill the remaining seats, the wise moviegoer will protect nearby seats from tall people and anyone who has an obnoxious laugh. You can accomplish this with outright lies, such as "This seat is saved," or with more subtle methods, such as balancing jackets or purses across the seats. As a last resort, you can make yourself unappealing to potential neighbors by using the seatbacks as a footrest, chewing open-mouthed, and laughing noisily—annoying behaviors that must be halted as soon as the movie begins.

aspiration: goal or hope

valiant: courageous

aficionados: experts

7   Once these skills have been mastered, anyone can be a successful moviegoer. Some may even move on to become movie buffs, which is a noble aspiration indeed. It takes hard work, dozens of movies, and gallons of popcorn, but eventually these valiant film aficionados will bask in the glow of their movie buff success. As for the rest of us, we will still be sneaking around with licorice in our shoes.

Write to Read: Annotate

1. Underline the steps in Horn's process.

2. Circle or highlight all the transition words Horn uses to move readers through the process. Pay attention to the punctuation she uses with her transition words.

3. Note any proper nouns (names with capital letters) Horn uses. How do these words help Horn develop her analysis?

Read to Write: Think Critically

1. What is Horn's tone in this essay? Is she completely serious? How do you know?

2. What does Horn's description of theaters tell you about her audience and purpose? What specific words help you answer this question?

3. Why does Horn put some comments in parentheses in paragraph 5?

Profile of Success: Paola Garcia-Muniz
Process Analysis in the Real World

Title   Editorial Assistant, Macmillan Learning

Background   My family is truly a salad bowl. I have a mother and a father, a stepmother, a brother, a stepsister, and a brilliant younger half-sister. Although we aren't perfect and not every moment has been colorful, they have pushed me, challenged me, and loved me unconditionally all the way through my life. They are a huge part of who and where I am today. Leaving them and my home island of Puerto Rico to attend Fairfield University in Connecticut was the hardest decision of my life. Regardless of the sacrifices I've made, they were there cheering me on as I completed a bachelor's degree in creative writing with a minor in psychology. I graduated with the dream of becoming a trade publishing editor or a well-known writer myself, and then I stepped foot into the Macmillan Learning offices in Boston. Having spent more than thirteen years of my life in a classroom as a student and having the teacher's perspective from my step-mother, an elementary school teacher, I wasn't surprised when I fell in love with educational publishing.

Writing at Work   My daily life in publishing is all about writing. I send and answer emails throughout the day, communicating with professors, editors, and authors about different aspects of our textbooks.

Professionalism in email writing is a key skill. I also edit manuscript pages for our titles in development, which means I have to think about how students will respond to each example, sentence, or chapter. Editing manuscripts means I make sure the writing is clear and accessible.

At the beginning, even though I am fluent in both English and Spanish, I often doubted myself and my writing because English is still my second language. However, as time went by and more emails were drafted, pages edited, corrections made, suggestions received, and compliments appreciated, I understood that my dual-language skills are a gift, not an obstacle. They allow me to look at words and interpret them for two different communities. I am working for those native English speakers and making sure that their native language lives up to its potential, as well as ensuring it is accessible to those non-English speakers who are trying to grasp the language or strengthen their understanding of it.

Once I am outside of the office walls, I text, help edit my siblings' and friends' school papers, and work on my own personal writing. In other words, the only part of my day that does not involve writing—or reading other people's writing—is when I am sound asleep; even then, I may dream about writing, too!

Paola Garcia-Muniz

Editorial Assistant

Use Reading Strategies: Paraphrase

1. What is Horn's thesis? Paraphrase it.
2. Horn says, "Some may even move on to become movie buffs, which is a noble aspiration indeed. It takes hard work, dozens of movies, and gallons of popcorn, but eventually these valiant film aficionados will bask in the glow of their movie buff success." What does she mean? Use paraphrase to explain her point.

Reflect and Respond

Do you think people really need instructions to enjoy a night at the movies? Why did Horn write this essay, and what assumptions does she make about her audience? What is an otherwise ordinary process that you could explain in a light-hearted manner, as Horn has?

Workplace Process Analysis

Paola Garcia-Muniz

Submitting Reprint Corrections

Preview Skim the first paragraph and the definitions in the margin. Who is the audience of this piece? Why did Garcia-Muniz write it?

PLEASE, submit corrections as soon as you are made aware of them. Do NOT wait until a reprint is called for your title; titles often come up for reprint with just 24-hours' notice, and then it is too late to make the corrections.

Reprints include changes to any of the following:

- Interior Text
- Covers
- Custom Titles
- Card Inserts
- Access Cards

Make sure that the following are clearly marked on every page:

- Author
- Title
- Edition
- Split/Version
- ISBN

compositor: the person who takes a book's original manuscript and converts it into the designed book that will go to the printer

development editors: the people who work from start to finish with the author(s) and their publishing colleagues to help craft the published book

The preferred method for transmitting reprints is via PDF files, which should be emailed to the Assistant Content Project Manager and the Senior Managing Editor. Ideally, these PDFs should be pulled from the PDF book files and marked up using Adobe editing tools.

2   Please DO NOT submit handwritten corrections, as the compositor (a) has trouble finding these and (b) cannot always read the handwriting. Handwritten corrections can cause delays in printing books. Although authors sometimes submit handwritten corrections, development editors should incorporate these into electronic markups.

3   Your correction MUST show the whole page where the correction occurs. It MUST be from the correct version (i.e., full versus brief). And it MUST be from the final version of the document. If there was a large reprint correction made (for example, due to an update of the MLA, *Chicago,* or APA formatting styles), please track down these final pages, because often content and reflow has drastically changed. If PDF book files cannot be located, the book pages may be scanned, but markup should be done electronically.

4   Multiple pages of corrections can be submitted as a single PDF file, but please remove any unneeded pages. (Don't submit PDFs of an entire chapter if only three pages in that chapter have corrections; send only the three corrected pages.) For special reprints like updates to the MLA, *Chicago,* or APA formatting styles, where entire chapters are being overhauled, it is okay to submit the entire chapter without removing extraneous pages.

5   The phrase "trim size" refers to the dimensions (length and width) of a printed book. Color matters if it's relevant to the correction.

6   The editorial department should retrieve updated files for authors through the Electronic File Requests spreadsheet. The most updated files (including reprint corrections) can be found in the Digital Asset Management system.

7   Email corrected PDFs to the Senior Managing Editor.

8   For corrections that apply to multiple versions that may vary in pagination, trim size, or content, please create a separate PDF for each version.

Write to Read: Annotate

1. Double-underline or highlight the main idea.

2. Underline the steps in the process (primary support), or highlight them in another color.

Read to Write: Think Critically

1. What text features (underlines, bullets, bold, capitalization) has Garcia-Muniz used? Why? Would these features be appropriate in all types of writing? Explain.

2. How are these instructions organized?

3. Does this piece demonstrate the four basics of process analysis? Explain.

Use Reading Strategies: Create a Graphic Organizer

Following the model on page 177, create a graphic organizer to show the main events in Garcia-Muniz's process analysis. Compare your chart with a classmate's. Do you have the same number of steps (primary support)? If not, discuss the differences.

Reflect and Respond

How is this process different in style and tone from the essay by Horn (p. 181)? Why do you think this is the case? In what sorts of situations will you need to write the same kind of instructions that Garcia-Muniz has written?

Professional Process Analysis Essay

Samantha Levine-Finley

Isn't It Time You Hit the Books?

COURTESY OF SAMANTHA
LEVINE-FINLEY

The author of the essay "Isn't It Time You Hit the Books?,"
Samantha Levine-Finley, has worked as a reporter for
several publications, including the *Houston Chronicle,*
where she covered topics relating to national politics, and
U.S. News & World Report, where she contributed to the
"Education" and "Nation & World" sections. This article was
originally published in *U.S. News & World Report*'s "America's
Best Colleges" in 2008.

Preview   The title of this essay is a question. Who is asking this question, and to
whom?

It was freshman year, and Angie Trevino thought she'd ace her microeconomics
class at the University of Oklahoma. An older student had told her she could skip
the lectures—the required discussion sessions would cover all the course material.
So Trevino gladly slept in on lecture days and faithfully attended the discussions.
"I was doing fairly well—I got high grades on tests and quizzes. I went in and took
the final and thought I did great," she says. When she ended up with a B, she was
shocked. "It was because my professor didn't see my face in the lecture," she says.
"It was a rude awakening."

2   Now a graduating senior, Trevino, 22, realizes she got bum advice. "In high
school, I was so monitored to go to class, it was hard to miss," she says. "In
college, you are responsible for your own actions and can't blame problems on
someone else. It doesn't work like that."

3   Disappointing grades are just one hint that the approach many students took
during high school won't work in college. The answer for new students is to step
up their academic game. So, in addition to a "things to do" list, here are a few
"things to be" that can help your transition to college.

4   *Be there.* "You will get an experience in the classroom that you will not get
from a book," says Gavin Sands, 22, a graduating senior from Elon University in
North Carolina. Skipping class may seem tempting, especially those introductory classes that can have several hundred students in them. The professors are
unlikely to take attendance or even learn most students' names. But Trevino says
class is great for meeting people, feeling connected to campus, and getting those
crucial snippets of advice that professors mete out to help with exams.

5   *Be willing to talk to teachers.* Stress, confusion, and a low grade here or there
are all part of college. Talking to a professor or adviser can keep those problems

mete: give

from spiraling. But talking up takes moxie. "If you are shy, it might be intimidating, but you have to put yourself out there," says Heath Thompson, 19, a sophomore at the University of Oklahoma. Sands thought "professors were going to be crazy, ridiculous, intense academic scholars, and I would be racing to keep up with them. But when I got here, I was amazed that they were real people and approachable."

moxie: courage, nerve

6   You won't be wasting anyone's time. Professors are usually required to maintain a certain number of office hours per week to see students, says Alice Lanning, who teaches a freshman-year experience class, also at Oklahoma. The problem is when "students don't take advantage of these office hours until the end of the semester, and the grades are scary." Her advice? Visit each professor at least once during the first month of school. "Ask what the professor is looking for and how to get the most out of class," Lanning says. That's especially critical because you'll have fewer exams and graded papers than in high school, so rebounding from a bad grade is tough.

7   Trevino recalled a time when she had a family problem and needed an extension on a project in her business communications class. She had already talked with the professor several times about career and academic issues. When the problem came up, Trevino says, the professor's reaction blew her away. "He gave me an extension because he felt that he knew me and could trust me."

8   *Be a syllabus-ologist.* The syllabus can be your salvation. Professors hand out these precious pages at the start of each semester. The syllabus outlines the material required for the class, all assignments, and the dates that papers are due and exams are held. "You have to keep track of things because there is not going to be anyone handing you a reminder note before you leave for home or writing everything on the board," says Sands. Her solution: go through each syllabus immediately, highlight all the quizzes, tests, and assignments, and put them in a day planner. "If you know you have three big projects due around the same time," she says, "you can think about it early on."

9   *Be deep.* College-level assignments require a questioning attitude, analytical abilities, and a level of organization beyond anything you came across in high school. College-level writing assignments also demand higher-order thinking. Independent and creative thinking is key. Sands says she was baffled at first in a class that focused on how to ask questions and do research. "I couldn't understand why you would ask a question you couldn't find an answer to," she says. "But that wasn't the point. It was to find something that hasn't been asked a million times before. I struggled with that for weeks." As for writing the papers themselves, Ian Brasg, 18, a sophomore at Princeton, accidentally learned many ways to annoy professors. "Random, fancy-sounding adjectives may not make a paper better," he says. And in a paper about the philosopher Descartes, Brasg's grade suffered because he inconsistently capitalized certain words. "To the professor, it showed a lack of preparation," he says.

Descartes: French philosopher and mathematician René Descartes (1596–1650), who has been called the "Father of Modern Philosophy"

10   One sure way to stay on track with college papers is to give yourself enough time to write a couple of drafts before you hand them in. Some professors require students to rewrite their papers so they can see where they're doing well and where they need to do more work. It gets ugly, but it helps. "There is a point

when the students will hate me, and I will hate them because we are handing things back and forth," says Carol Zoref, a writing instructor at Sarah Lawrence College. "And then this amazing thing happens: they all get much better at it. They have a kind of fearlessness. If they can put themselves through that, there will be a big payoff."

11   *Be a good manager.* The important thing is to manage your day and not waste time. Pay attention to how your time is spent and manage it to fit your preferences and habits and your various responsibilities. Time management methods vary according to the individual.

12   If time management methods differ among students, so do study styles. Sands stays organized using three-ring binders with dividers, loose-leaf paper, and pencil pouches in the front (high-tech approaches work, too). Trevino cheats her brain by writing due dates for assignments as earlier than they really are. Finding your own way to work, but also time for fun, is key, Thompson says. "You can't study every day of the week, and you can't play video games every day of the week," he says. "Balancing things is the most important part."

13   *Be cool.* Colleges know that students, especially those who were successful in high school, might resist seeking help, says Steven Lestition, dean of Mathey College, one of five residential colleges at Princeton. Get over it! "If nobody had that problem, the resources wouldn't be there," Trevino says. "If you are embarrassed or shy about getting help, weigh your options. Are you more worried about hurting your pride or your grade point average?"

14   Tip: all-nighters should be rare; same with end-of-semester cram sessions. Plugging away as assignments come in is the best way to get the most out of college.

Write to Read: Annotate

1. Underline or highlight the major steps in this process.

2. Circle or highlight in a different color the name of each person interviewed and quoted for this essay. Pay attention to the way that quotes are introduced and punctuated.

Read to Write: Think Critically

1. Are the steps in this process in chronological order? Why or why not?

2. What words, quotes, or examples help you understand who Levine-Finley's audience is? What strategies does Levine-Finley use to develop secondary support for her steps?

3. How does the final tip connect to the steps Levine-Finley has already presented?

Use Reading Strategies: Summarize

Review the summary skills you learned in Chapter 1, pages 18–20, and then write a short summary of Levine-Finley's essay.

Reflect and Respond

1. Interview instructors, advisers, and experienced students from your college to find out what steps they believe are essential to success. Then write an essay that describes the process of success at your school, using quotes from your interviews.

2. In paragraph 10, Levine-Finley suggests that there is a big "payoff" for working through the hard process of revising writing. What is something else that requires a lot of work but offers a big payoff? Write an essay that describes this process.

3. Levine-Finley recommends visiting professors during office hours, but many students—especially new students—are nervous about doing this. Talk to several instructors to discover tips for successfully talking with professors, and then write an essay that explains how to visit and talk to teachers in your school.

Grammar for Process Analysis

Like many other writers, Levine-Finley includes quotations from others to help support the steps in her process. Those quoted include students, professors, and a dean (an academic official who oversees a department within a college or university). Notice how Levine-Finley introduces one of the students:

> "You will get an experience in the classroom that you will not get from a book," says Gavin Sands, 22, a graduating senior from Elon University in North Carolina.

Pay attention to the commas in this sentence: there is a comma after the quotation, before the speaker's name is introduced. There are also commas after the student's name and the student's age. We use commas to mark extra information in a sentence. Specifically, we use commas to mark an appositive.

An **appositive** follows a noun and either explains or renames the noun. In this sentence, the appositive *graduating senior* explains who Gavin Sands is. When Levine-Finley uses the appositive, she is showing her readers *why* she is quoting Gavin Sands: he is a graduating senior, so he has a lot of experience with studying.

For more about appositives and commas, see pages 528–30 in Chapter 26.

Write Your Own Process Analysis

In this section, you will write your own process analysis essay based on one of the following assignments. For help, refer to the "How to Write Process Analysis" checklist on pages 192–93.

Assignment Options: Writing about College, Work, and Everyday Life

Write a process analysis paragraph or essay on one of the following topics or on one of your own choice:

College	• Interview at least two members of your class about how they study, and then describe the process of preparing for an exam.
	• Attend a tutoring session at your college's writing center. Afterward, describe the process: What specific things did the tutor do to help you? What did you learn from the process?
Work	• Describe how to make a positive impression at a job interview.
	• Think of a challenging task you had to accomplish at work. What steps did you go through to complete it?
Everyday Life	• Describe the process of making something, such as a favorite meal, a set of shelves, or a sweater.
	• Think of a challenging process that you have completed successfully, such as fixing a leak under the sink, applying for a loan, or finding a good deal on a car or an apartment. Describe the steps specifically enough so that someone else could complete the process just as successfully.

Assignment Options: Reading and Writing Critically

Complete one of the following assignments that asks you to apply the critical thinking, reading, and writing skills discussed in Chapter 1.

Writing Critically about Readings

Both Moses Maddox's email to his clients (pp. 236–38) and Samantha Levine-Finley's "Isn't It Time You Hit the Books" (pp. 186–88) suggest strategies for overcoming challenges and fears. Read or review both of these pieces, and then follow these steps:

1. **Summarize.** Briefly summarize the works, listing the primary supporting points in each one.

2. **Analyze.** What other steps or details might the authors have included?

3. **Synthesize.** Using examples from both Maddox's and Levine-Finley's writings and from your own experience, discuss what steps teachers, parents, and administrators could take to prepare graduates for college success.

4. **Evaluate.** Which piece, Maddox's or Levine-Finley's, do you think is more effective? Why?

Writing Critically about Visuals

Study this infographic, and complete the following steps:

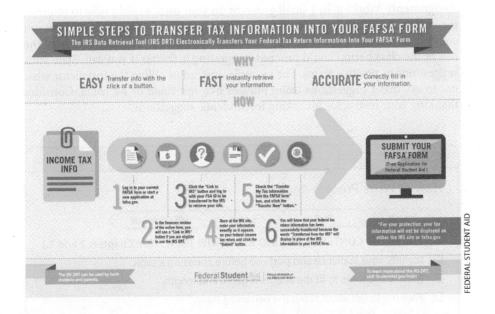

FEDERAL STUDENT AID

1. **Read the Infographic.** Ask yourself: What is the "thesis" in this infographic? How is this main idea presented to viewers? What are the major steps in the process? Do you think that the infographic successfully supports the main idea? (For more information on reading images, see "Write Critically about Visuals," pp. 23–26, in Chapter 1.) Is it as simple to read and comprehend this visual process as it would be if there were detailed written instructions? Why or why not?

2. **Write a process analysis.** Write a paragraph or essay that describes the process shown in this infographic.

Writing Critically about Problems

Read or review the discussion of problem solving in Chapter 1 (pp. 26–28). Then consider the following problem:

> Midway through a course you are taking, your instructor asks the class to suggest ways to improve the course. You have not been happy with the class because the instructor is always late, comes in seeming rushed and tense, and ends up releasing class late. During class, the instructor uses PowerPoint slides and reads to the class from them, seldom adding new information. Then, after handing out an assignment for students to work on, the instructor just sits and grades papers. You are afraid to ask questions about the lecture or assignment because the instructor does not seem overly helpful. You want to explain these problems, but you do not want to be offensive.

Assignment: Working in a small group or on your own, explain how to improve the course. Think of how the class could be structured differently so that you could learn more. Begin with how the class could start. Then describe how the rest of the class period could proceed, suggesting activities if you can. State your suggestions in positive terms. For example, instead of telling the instructor what not to do, make suggestions using phrases like *you could* or *we could*. Consider thanking your instructor for asking for students' suggestions.

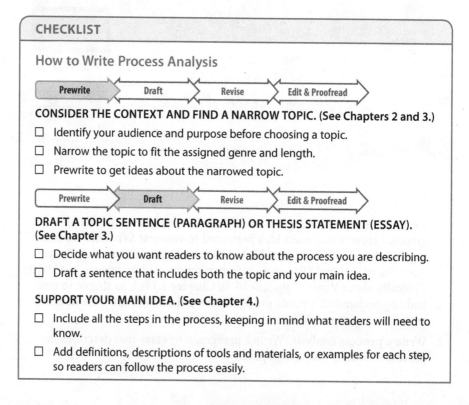

CHECKLIST

How to Write Process Analysis

| Prewrite | Draft | Revise | Edit & Proofread |

CONSIDER THE CONTEXT AND FIND A NARROW TOPIC. (See Chapters 2 and 3.)

☐ Identify your audience and purpose before choosing a topic.

☐ Narrow the topic to fit the assigned genre and length.

☐ Prewrite to get ideas about the narrowed topic.

| Prewrite | Draft | Revise | Edit & Proofread |

DRAFT A TOPIC SENTENCE (PARAGRAPH) OR THESIS STATEMENT (ESSAY). (See Chapter 3.)

☐ Decide what you want readers to know about the process you are describing.

☐ Draft a sentence that includes both the topic and your main idea.

SUPPORT YOUR MAIN IDEA. (See Chapter 4.)

☐ Include all the steps in the process, keeping in mind what readers will need to know.

☐ Add definitions, descriptions of tools and materials, or examples for each step, so readers can follow the process easily.

WRITE A DRAFT. (See Chapter 5.)

☐ Make a plan that puts the steps in a logical order (often chronological).

☐ Include a topic sentence (paragraph) or thesis statement (essay), all the essential steps, and the supporting examples and details.

☐ Add an appropriate introduction and conclusion.

Prewrite ⟩ Draft ⟩ **Revise** ⟩ Edit & Proofread

REVISE YOUR DRAFT. (See Chapter 6.)

☐ Make sure it has *all* four basics of process analysis.

☐ Make sure you have included all the steps readers will need to understand how the process works or how to complete the process.

☐ Make sure each paragraph is unified (all ideas should relate to the topic sentence).

☐ Make sure each paragraph is fully developed (there are enough supporting details to demonstrate the point).

☐ Make sure you include transitions to move readers smoothly from one step to the next.

Prewrite ⟩ Draft ⟩ Revise ⟩ **Edit & Proofread**

EDIT AND PROOFREAD YOUR REVISED DRAFT. (See Parts 3 and 4.)

☐ Make sure grammar, word usage, and punctuation choices are clear, accurate, and effective.

☐ Check spelling and capitalization.

Chapter 10 Review

1. What is process analysis?

2. What are two purposes for process analysis?

3. What are the four basics of process analysis?

4. How is process analysis usually organized?

Reflect and Apply

1. When have you written or read process analysis before? What makes reading or writing process analysis difficult?

2. Interview someone studying in your major or working in your career. Ask the person you interview how they use process analysis.

3. What challenged you the most when writing for this chapter? What do you want to do differently next time?

4. What worked well in your writing for this chapter? What do you need to remember for next time?

11

Classification

Writing That Sorts Things into Groups

> **Learning Outcomes**   In this chapter, you will learn to
>
> - List the four basics of classification paragraphs and essays.
> - Identify the principle used to group items and devise relevant categories.
> - Support the categories with definitions, descriptions, examples, and other details.
> - Recognize transitions commonly used in classification.
> - Write a classification paragraph or essay with a clear main idea, logical categories, detailed support, and logical organization.
>
> Categories help us make sense of the world around us and the work we do. When we classify—or sort things into categories—we organize information or ideas in ways that are useful, whether we are sorting expenses to make a budget or sorting assignments to make a schedule for the coming month.

Understand What Classification Is

Classification is writing that organizes, or sorts, people or items into categories. It uses an **organizing principle**: *how* the people or items are sorted. The organizing principle is directly related to the purpose for classifying. For example, you might sort clean laundry (your purpose) using one of the following organizing principles: by ownership (yours, your roommate's) or by where it goes (the closet, the dresser, or the bathroom).

> **Four Basics** of Classification
>
> **1** **Main Idea:** An effective classification paragraph or essay makes sense of a group of people or items by organizing them into categories according to a single organizing principle.
>
> **2** **Primary Support:** It sets up logical and comprehensive categories.
>
> **3** **Secondary Support:** It gives detailed explanations or examples of what fits into each category.
>
> **4** **Organization:** It organizes information by time, space, or importance, depending on its purpose.

In the following paragraph, the numbers and colors correspond to the four basics of classification.

1 In researching careers I might pursue, I have learned that there are three major types of workers, each having different strengths and preferences. **4** The first type of worker **2** is a big-picture person, who likes to look toward the future and think of new businesses, products, and services. **3** Big-picture people might also identify ways to make their workplaces more successful and productive. Often, they hold leadership positions, achieving their goals by assigning specific projects and tasks to others. Big-picture people may be drawn to starting their own businesses, or they might manage or become a consultant for an existing business. **4** The second type of worker **2** is a detail person who focuses on the smaller picture, whether it be a floor plan in a construction project, a spreadsheet showing a business's revenue and expenses, or data from a scientific experiment. **3** Detail people take pride in understanding all the ins and outs of a task and doing everything carefully and well. Some detail people prefer to work with their hands, doing such things as carpentry or electrical wiring. Others prefer office jobs, such as accounting or clerical work. Detail people may also be drawn to technical careers, such as scientific research or engineering. **4** The third type of worker **2** is a people person, who gets a lot of satisfaction from reaching out to others and helping them meet their needs. **3** A people person has good social skills and likes to get out in the world to use them. Therefore, this type of worker is unlikely to be happy sitting behind a desk. A successful people person often shares qualities of the other types of workers; for example, he or she may show leadership potential. In addition, his or her job may require careful attention to detail. Good jobs for a people person include teaching, sales, nursing, and other health-care positions. Having evaluated my own strengths and preferences, I believe that I am equal parts big-picture person and people person. I am happy to see that I have many career options.

In college, writing assignments probably will not use the word *classification*. Instead, you might be asked to *describe* or *explain the types or kinds of something*. You might also be asked, *How is something organized?* or *What are the parts of something?* These phrases signal that you need to write classification.

First Basic: Main Idea in Classification

The **main idea** in classification uses a single organizing principle to sort items in a way that serves your purpose. The organizing principle determines how you will organize (by cost, by size, by date, by function, and so on), and it is logically related to your purpose. For example, the paragraph on page 195 classifies types of workers according to their strengths and skills (the organizing principle) to help the writer choose a career focus (purpose).

To help you discover the organizing principle for your classification, complete the following sentences:

Main idea in classification: My purpose for classifying my topic is to _____.

It would make most sense to my readers if I sorted this topic by _____.

Use the purpose and organizing principle to write your main idea:

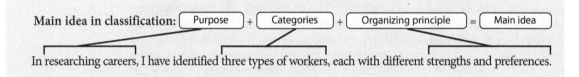

Main idea in classification: Purpose + Categories + Organizing principle = Main idea

In researching careers, I have identified three types of workers, each with different strengths and preferences.

In classification, the main idea may not state the categories or the organizing principle explicitly. Consider the following topic sentence for the paragraph on page 203:

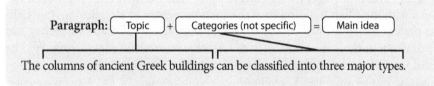

Paragraph: Topic + Categories (not specific) = Main idea

The columns of ancient Greek buildings can be classified into three major types.

In this topic sentence, *how* the columns will be classified (the organizing principle) isn't clear, but the rest of the paragraph explains that the columns will be classified by structural features.

The next example, in contrast, mentions the organizing principle (structural features) specifically:

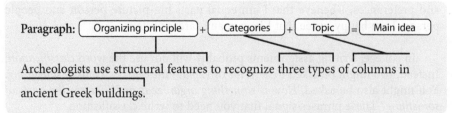

Paragraph: Organizing principle + Categories + Topic = Main idea

Archeologists use structural features to recognize three types of columns in ancient Greek buildings.

The thesis for an essay may be broader: for example, "The structures of ancient Greece may be divided into specific types according to the purpose of the structure (sports, performances, or worship)." The words *type of building* and *purpose* are not stated directly. Instead, the categories themselves—stadiums, theaters, and temples—and the details given about each one later in the paper make the organizing principle clear.

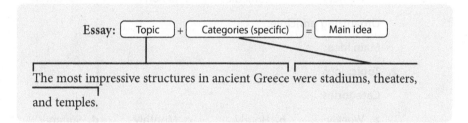

Essay: [Topic] + [Categories (specific)] = [Main idea]

The most impressive structures in ancient Greece were stadiums, theaters, and temples.

The organizing principle in classification should logically support the purpose of the paper. For example, it makes sense to classify Greek structures according to their function in ancient Greek society if the purpose of the paper is to show the cultural accomplishments of that civilization. Similarly, a writer organizing a restaurant guide for newcomers to the city might either use cost or type of cuisine as a logical organizing principle. There are many other ways to classify restaurants—by the pay that kitchen staff receive, for example—but those principles would not logically support the purpose of the paper. When you are writing or reading classification, ask yourself if there are other ways of classifying the topic and, if so, whether the organizing principle selected makes sense for the purpose of the text.

PRACTICE 11–1   Using a Single Organizing Principle to Write a Main Idea

For each topic that follows, one of the categories does not fit the same organizing principle as the rest. Circle or highlight the letter of the category that does not fit. Then write down the organizing principle, and use that organizing principle to come up with a main idea.

Example:

Topic: *Sports*

Categories:

a. Sports played on fields   **b.** Sports played on courts   **(c.)** Sports played by both men and women   **d.** Sports played on ice

Organizing principle: *location/playing surface*

Main idea: We can classify sports into three categories based on the facilities required to play them.

1. **Topic:** Movies

   Categories:

   a. Oscar winners   **b.** Romantic comedies   **c.** Science fiction   **d.** Action/Adventure

   Organizing principle:

   Main idea:

2. **Topic:** Jobs

   Categories:

   a. Weekly   **b.** Hourly   **c.** Monthly   **d.** Summer

   Organizing principle:

   Main idea:

3. **Topic:** Classes

   Categories:

   a. Face-to-face   **b.** Science   **c.** Online   **d.** Hybrid

   Organizing principle:

   Main idea:

Second Basic: Primary Support in Classification

The primary support in classification are the categories that the writer sets up, and as you learned in the first basic, the categories must follow an organizing principle that logically supports the purpose of the paper. As you select your categories, make sure you can answer these questions:

- *Do all of the categories match the organizing principle logically?* Make sure all of your categories relate to the same organizing principle. If, for example, you plan to classify types of devices according to size, you might include desktop, laptop, tablet, handheld devices, and wearable devices, but you would not also include cheap imitations, which is a category logically related to quality or cost, not size.

- *Have you included all the categories that could be covered by your organizing principle?* Returning to the classification of electronic devices by size, if you stop at just three categories (desktop, laptop, and tablet), you have left out a significant number of other members of the group. Your classification should cover all or nearly all of the possible examples of the topic.

- *Do you have enough information to develop each category equally?* When you select your organizing principle and set up your categories, make sure that you have enough information to address all categories with the same level of detail. If you have never used wearable electronics, for example, you might want to reconsider your classification of devices or plan to do some research before you begin writing.

PRACTICE 11–2 **Choosing Categories**

In the items that follow, you are given a topic and a purpose for sorting. For each item, list at least three categories that serve your purpose.

Example:

Topic: Pieces of paper in my wallet

Purpose for sorting: To get rid of what I do not need

Categories:

a.   Things I need to keep in my wallet

b.   Things I can throw away

c.   Things I need to keep, but not in my wallet

1.   **Topic:** College courses

    Purpose for sorting: To decide what I will register for

    Categories:

2.   **Topic:** Stuff in my notebook

    Purpose for sorting: To organize my schoolwork

    Categories:

3.   **Topic:** Wedding guests

    Purpose for sorting: To arrange seating at tables

    Categories:

4.   **Topic:** Tools for home repair

    Purpose for sorting: To make them easy to find when needed

    Categories:

Third Basic: Secondary Support in Classification

Within each category, a writer may choose different ways to provide supporting details. For example, a writer may choose to *define* each category. A **definition** explains what something is or what it means. The writer of the sample paragraph on page 195, for example, gives a definition for each type of worker:

- *Big-picture people* are those who like to look to the future and think of new businesses, products, and services.

- *Detail people* are those who focus on the smaller picture.
- *People people* are those who get satisfaction from reaching out to others and meeting their needs.

A writer may also choose to *describe* each category. In the essay on page 204, for example, the primary support are stadiums, theaters, and temples, and the writer has provided details describing each type of structure.

Writers may also *illustrate* each category with examples. Most classification essays use some form of illustration. For example, Stephanie Ericsson offers several examples in her essay, "The Ways We Lie" (pp. 211–14).

Fourth Basic: Organization in Classification

Classification can be organized in different ways (time order, space order, or order of importance or emphasis), depending on its purpose:

Purpose	Likely Organization
To explain categories that show changes over time	Time
To describe the arrangement of groups in space	Space
To discuss groups in relation to a specific purpose (cost, size, appeal, usefulness, value, etc.)	Importance or emphasis

The essay on page 203 uses emphasis order to highlight the beauty of the structures.

Using Transitions in Classification

As you write your classification, use **transitions** to move your readers smoothly from one category to another.

Common Transitions in Classification

General Classification Transitions

for example	for instance	one/another example	one/another kind

Time

at first	finally	later	second
before/after	first	next	soon
eventually	last	now	then

(continued)

Space			
at the bottom/top	beside	inside	to the side
behind	beyond	next to	under/underneath
beneath	farther/further	on top of	where
Importance			
especially	more/even more	most important	

Using a Graphic Organizer in Classification

A common graphic organizer used with classification is a diagram like the one below, which shows the categories for the paragraph on page 195.

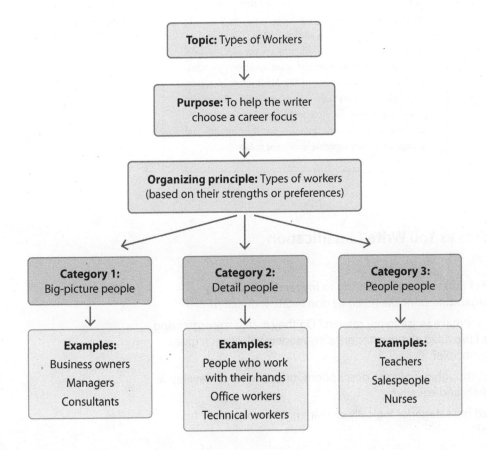

Paragraphs versus Essays in Classification

For more on the important features of classification, see the "Four Basics of Classification" on page 195.

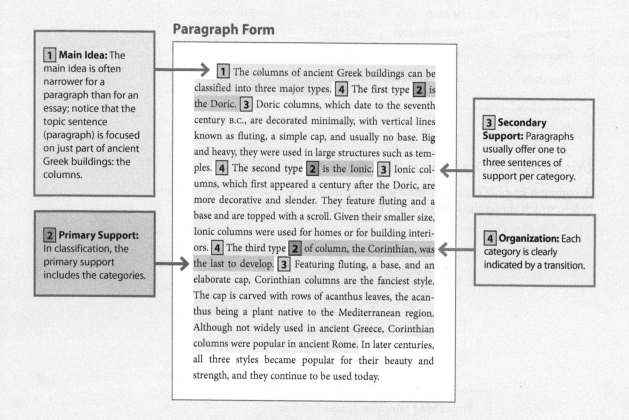

Paragraph Form

1 Main Idea: The main idea is often narrower for a paragraph than for an essay; notice that the topic sentence (paragraph) is focused on just part of ancient Greek buildings: the columns.

2 Primary Support: In classification, the primary support includes the categories.

1 The columns of ancient Greek buildings can be classified into three major types. **4** The first type **2** is the Doric. **3** Doric columns, which date to the seventh century B.C., are decorated minimally, with vertical lines known as fluting, a simple cap, and usually no base. Big and heavy, they were used in large structures such as temples. **4** The second type **2** is the Ionic. **3** Ionic columns, which first appeared a century after the Doric, are more decorative and slender. They feature fluting and a base and are topped with a scroll. Given their smaller size, Ionic columns were used for homes or for building interiors. **4** The third type **2** of column, the Corinthian, was the last to develop. **3** Featuring fluting, a base, and an elaborate cap, Corinthian columns are the fanciest style. The cap is carved with rows of acanthus leaves, the acanthus being a plant native to the Mediterranean region. Although not widely used in ancient Greece, Corinthian columns were popular in ancient Rome. In later centuries, all three styles became popular for their beauty and strength, and they continue to be used today.

3 Secondary Support: Paragraphs usually offer one to three sentences of support per category.

4 Organization: Each category is clearly indicated by a transition.

Consider Readers as You Write Classification

Ask Yourself

- Will my main idea and topic be interesting to my readers? Will they recognize my organizing principle (even if I don't state it directly)?
- Will my categories make sense to my readers? Do they match my organizing principle? Have I provided all the categories my readers will expect, given my organizing principle?
- Have I provided enough definitions, descriptions, or examples to develop all my categories fully and equally?
- Have I organized my categories logically so readers can move easily from one to the next?

Essay Form

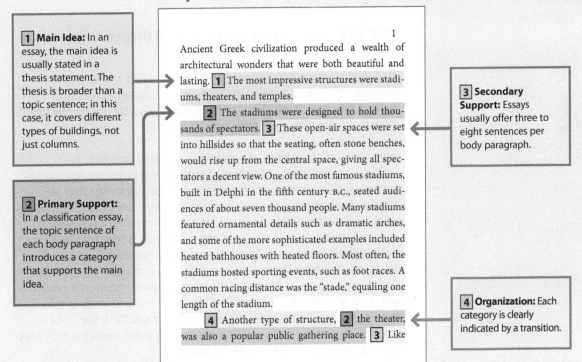

1 Main Idea: In an essay, the main idea is usually stated in a thesis statement. The thesis is broader than a topic sentence; in this case, it covers different types of buildings, not just columns.

2 Primary Support: In a classification essay, the topic sentence of each body paragraph introduces a category that supports the main idea.

3 Secondary Support: Essays usually offer three to eight sentences per body paragraph.

4 Organization: Each category is clearly indicated by a transition.

1

Ancient Greek civilization produced a wealth of architectural wonders that were both beautiful and lasting. **1** The most impressive structures were stadiums, theaters, and temples.

2 The stadiums were designed to hold thousands of spectators. **3** These open-air spaces were set into hillsides so that the seating, often stone benches, would rise up from the central space, giving all spectators a decent view. One of the most famous stadiums, built in Delphi in the fifth century B.C., seated audiences of about seven thousand people. Many stadiums featured ornamental details such as dramatic arches, and some of the more sophisticated examples included heated bathhouses with heated floors. Most often, the stadiums hosted sporting events, such as foot races. A common racing distance was the "stade," equaling one length of the stadium.

4 Another type of structure, **2** the theater, was also a popular public gathering place. **3** Like

2

stadiums, the theaters were open-air sites that were set into hillsides. But instead of sports, they featured plays, musical performances, poetry readings, and other cultural events. In the typical Greek theater, a central performance area was surrounded by semicircular seating, which was often broken into different sections. Wooden, and later stone, stages were set up in the central area, and in front of the stage was a space used for singing and dancing. This space was known as the "orchestra." Among the most famous ancient Greek theaters is the one at Epidaurus, built in the fourth century B.C. and seating up to fourteen thousand people. Performances still take place there.

4 The most beautiful structures **2** were the temples, with their grand entrances and large open spaces. **3** Temples were rectangular in shape, and their outer walls as well as some interior spaces were supported by columns. Their main structures were typically made of limestone or marble, while their

3

roofs might be constructed of terra-cotta or marble tiles. Temples were created to serve as "homes" for particular gods or goddesses, who were represented by statues. People left food or other offerings to these gods or goddesses to stay in their good graces, and communities often held festivals and other celebrations in their honor. Temples tended to be built in either the Doric or Ionic style, with Doric temples featuring simple, heavy columns and Ionic temples featuring slightly more ornate columns. The most famous temple, in the Doric style, is the Parthenon in Athens.

Turning to the present day, many modern stadiums, theaters, and columned civic buildings show the influence of ancient Greek buildings. Recognizing the lasting strength and beauty of these old structures, architects and designers continue to return to them for inspiration. I predict that this inspiration will last at least a thousand more years.

| PRACTICE 11-3 | Using Transitions and Graphic Organizers in Classification |

Read the paragraph that follows, and fill in the blanks with one of the following transitions: *first kind, for example, in addition, most important, the last kind, the second type.* Then create a graphic organizer for the paragraph. (Note that more than one option may be correct.)

Every day, I get three kinds of email: work, personal, and junk. The _____ of email, work, I have to read carefully and promptly. Sometimes the messages are important ones directed to me, but mostly they are group messages about meetings, policies, or procedures. _____, it seems as if the procedure for leaving the building during a fire alarm is always changing. _____ of email, personal, is from friends or my mother. These I read when I get a chance, but I read them quickly and delete any that are jokes or messages that have to be sent to ten friends for good luck. _____ of email is the most common and most annoying: junk. I get at least thirty junk emails a day, advertising all kinds of things that I do not want, such as life insurance or baby products. Even when I reply asking that the company stop sending me these messages, they keep coming. Sometimes, I wish email did not exist.

Read and Analyze Classification

To become a more successful writer, it is important to understand the four basics of classification; reading and analyzing samples of classification can help you see these basics at work. In this section, you will use a rubric to evaluate the first draft of Tiffany Montgomery's classification paragraph. Then you will analyze a classification essay published by Maria Olloqui in her university's newspaper. You will also learn how Lisa Currie uses classification in her job as mayor of Toms Brook, Virginia. Finally, you will read a professional classification essay by Stephanie Ericsson.

Student Classification Paragraph

Read the following first draft of a classification paragraph. Note that the instructor asked the students to focus on the main idea (topic, purpose, and organizing principle), support (categories and supporting details), and organization in this draft. Using the four basics of classification and the sample rubric, decide how effective this draft of Tiffany's paragraph is, and then recommend one or two goals for her next draft.

Assignment: Write a paragraph that will help new students understand how college works. Use classification to explain one of the following: types of classes, types of activities, types of students, or types of professors. Make sure your paragraph has a topic sentence, categories that support the topic sentence, details to develop the categories, and transitions to help readers move from category to category.

Tiffany Montgomery
University Classes

A typical university offers three different course types to choose from: regular session classes, hybrid session classes, and online classes. Regular session classes are the most common. You attend class two to three days a week on campus at a set time. Classes usually meet on Mondays, Wednesdays, and Fridays, or Tuesdays and Thursdays. Hybrid classes contain both in-class and online learning. You typically attend class once a week, and the rest of your work is completed online. These classes require a little more self-discipline to make sure your online work is completed. Online classes are taken completely in an online setting. They take a lot of self-discipline, and you are responsible for learning the material and turning your assignments in on time. Most classes have deadlines at the end of each week. No matter which combination of classes you take, as long as you put effort in and do the work, you should succeed.

Rubric for Classification

	1 **Falls below expectations**	2 **Nearly meets expectations**	3 **Meets expectations**	4 **Exceeds expectations**
Main idea (first basic)	No clear main idea or purpose is present.	Main idea does not show topic, purpose, or categories clearly.	Main idea is appropriate, but purpose or categories are unclear.	Main idea is engaging with clear sense of purpose and categories.
Support (second and third basics)	Categories are missing or inappropriate; few details are provided.	Some clear categories and details are present.	Clear categories are included but may lack detail.	Clear and well-developed categories support main idea.
Organization (fourth basic)	Organization is not clear or logical.	Organization is inconsistent.	Organization is logical, but some transitions are missing or inappropriate.	Organization is logical, with smooth transitions throughout.

Evaluating the Paragraph

1. Does the paragraph show the four basics of classification? Explain.

2. Using the rubric as a guide, what is the strongest part of the paragraph? The weakest?

3. Write a response to this writer, using one of the following to frame your response:

   a. One thing I would like to know more about is _____.

   b. What I liked best about the paragraph is _____.

   c. To develop your categories more, I think you could add _____.

Student Classification Essay

Maria Olloqui

The Five Main Types of Texters

Preview This article was published in the *Washington Square News,* a publication for students at New York University. Scan the title and the bold headings. What do you think Olloqui's organizing principle is?

Texting is undoubtedly the comfort zone of communication. Being able to hide behind screens and plan out messages allows for crafted conversations with perfectly timed jokes and thought-out emojis. However, among the sea of smiley faces, acronyms, and lingo, it can be hard to decipher the meaning behind an iMessage. Luckily, there are patterns that can easily categorize us into the type of texters we are. Here are some of the most dominant:

The Emoji Texter

2   Last year, over 900 million emojis were sent every day without text—you can thank the emoji texter for this surplus of emoticons. "I always make sure to include emojis in my texts, because I think it's a great tool to express yourself beyond words," CAS first-year Karen San Agustin Ruiz said. "It depends who I am texting and why, though." These texters often have an arsenal of emojis ready at their fingertips. Some iconic choices beyond the typical laughing face include the smiling cowboy, black heart, and peering eyes. CAS senior Tiffany Zhang has a go-to emoji that comes in handy when words fail her. "My most frequently used emoji is the 'slightly smiling face,'" Zhang said. "Probably because most of the time my tone is sarcastic—but not in a bad way."

CAS: College of Arts and Sciences

The One-Word Texter

3   Efficiency. Brevity. Clarity. Some find that peppering texts with single words is the most productive way of communicating. The typical one-word texter is probably on the run or too busy to flesh out their ideas in full-fledged sentences.

"I like being direct with messages—quick and to the point," Stern first-year Josh Williams said. "It's just more convenient in my day-to-day life." While it may be hard at first to communicate with this kind of texter, we could all learn something from removing the nonsense and getting down to business.

Stern: Stern School of Business at New York University

The Paragraph Texter

4   On the opposite side of the spectrum, there are those who take several sentences per text to convey their thoughts. Call it free-form poetry or ranting—these texts might bury yours in a sea of words. "The length of my response depends on the topic," Zhang said. "I personally always prefer to elaborate on things as much as possible. This is probably because I'm a Virgo, so I feel compelled to do that."

The Lowercase Texter

5   Others believe importance lies in how the text looks rather than what it says. The lowercase trend includes using breaks, limited punctuation, and few capitals. Some students like CAS first-year Jean Park argue this type of texting is more appealing to the eye. "I like the uniform aesthetic of typing in lowercase," Park said. "It's cute, youthful and matches my personal aesthetic of being minimalist." As for punctuation, she feels that less is more. "A period can sometimes overdo it," Park said.

The Multilingual Texter

6   Changing languages mid-text may seem like a flex to those who only have one mother tongue, but it is out of comfort that some students tend to switch back and forth. Stern first-year Carlos Figueroa said it's easier not only for himself but for others that he typically texts. "I normally go back and forth with English and Spanish when I'm talking to people who are fluent in both languages," Figueroa said. "It allows people to express themselves better."

Write to Read: Annotate

1. Identify the thesis statement and underline or highlight the categories in Olloqui's essay.
2. Circle the transitions or highlight them in a different color.

Read to Write: Think Critically

1. What is Olloqui's organizing principle? Is there another way of categorizing texters?
2. What kind of support does Olloqui provide for each category? What else could she have included?
3. What kind of organization does Olloqui use? Would you recommend a different arrangement? Why or why not?

Use Reading Strategies: Summarize

Review the skills you learned in Chapter 1, pages 18–20, and then write a short summary of Olloqui's essay.

Reflect and Respond

What kind of texter are you? Talk to several friends about their texting styles. Following Olloqui's model, write a short essay classifying the most common texting styles among your friends.

Workplace Classification

Lisa Currie

Letter to the State Budget Officials

Preview This classification essay is a letter from the mayor to a state board that helps local communities pay for renovations and improvements. Skim the first sentence of each paragraph. What sorts of projects does the town want to accomplish?

Thank you for taking the time to meet with the town planner and myself. We learned a great deal about the types of funding available. After careful consideration of resources and project immediacy, we have classified the town's proposals into three types of projects: soil and water erosion projects, town wall and sidewalks, and curb and guttering projects.

2   The first project that requires attention is the problem with water runoff and soil erosion. Currently, the town's storm water overflow, or dry bed, allows rainwater to move from west to east and flow into the town's creek, which feeds into the Shenandoah River and then the Chesapeake Bay, a protected water source. Over the years, the dry gully that cuts under Main Street and across several properties on the eastern side of town has filled with soil and sediment. This soil and sediment, combined with debris from careless property owners, has changed the depth and shape of the gully, distorting the storm water flow to the creek. Now, shifted from its normal path, rainwater overflows the bed, crosses the creek bank, and threatens homeowners' properties while eroding the bank of the creek, altering the natural flow of the creek. This erosion, in turn, threatens the creek bank's stability as well as property on both sides of the creek. Besides engineering and legal expertise, this project requires input from soil and water erosion professionals. The erosion issue needs attention before the sidewalk and town wall renovations.

Profile of Success: Lisa Currie

Classification in the Real World

Title   Mayor of Toms Brook, Virginia; ESL and International Student Advisor, Lord Fairfax Community College

Background   Reading and writing have been and are the bedrock of my life. With a B.A. in English/writing from George Mason University, I became a journalist, writing about local government, health, and education, as well as writing feature stories for several different newspapers in western Virginia. While serving as both an editor and reporter, I learned the importance of background reading prior to writing, the value of concise writing under deadlines, and the magnitude of editing. I left the newspaper when I was elected to the local school board, and later I earned an M.S. in education from Shenandoah University. I currently teach English as Another Language courses at Lord Fairfax Community College and work as the adviser for international students. In this position, I must communicate with students, colleagues, and even foreign governments that have sent students to study in the United States.

I am an active member of local government. I was first elected to the Toms Brook town council in 1992 and served on the council until my election to the school board in 2002. As a member of the town council, and later as a member of the school board, I read volumes of information on a weekly basis—local, state, and national documents. This comprehensive reading prepared me for weekly meetings and reports.

Writing at Work   Now, as mayor, I communicate in writing with various county and state elected officials, service agencies, and local businesses. I also produce the town's bimonthly newsletter. Writing is a daily aspect of the job. My writing must be concise and comprehensive at the same time. Background reading—approached carefully—is also critical now because social media inundates us daily with a deluge of reading materials. Finally, editing skills play as great a role in my current position as mayor as they did in my role as journalist.

Lisa Currie
Mayor of Toms Brook, Virginia

COURTESY OF LISA CURRIE

3   Another type of project concerns the maintenance and repair of the town wall. The blue stone town wall dates back to the late 1930s, a Civilian Conservation Corp (CCC) project. Today, only remnants of the wall remain. When the main thoroughfare was widened in the early 1950s, much of the wall was either removed or replaced with concrete; over the last seventy years, the concrete has weakened and been damaged. The deteriorating wall is no longer secure, and if the wall collapses, the sidewalk that extends the length of the eastern side, from the northern to the southern end, would follow. Considering the eastern wall's proximity to the sidewalk, any repairs made to the wall impact the sidewalk's condition. Because the wall ranges in height from several inches to several feet above the ground, the restorations require engineering expertise.

4   The final project requiring our attention is the replacement of the curb and guttering that run the length of Main Street. The pockmarked guttering remains a byproduct of years of weather and daily abuse by vehicles. Debris and refuse collect in these areas creating unsafe conditions. The broken and damaged curbs are the result of a lack of maintenance; again, the unsightly decay creates unsafe conditions. In our meeting, we discussed these repairs as part of the overall maintenance of the road, which is budgeted and planned for the future. After the new asphalt is laid down, the town will again be bordered by the brightly painted curbs.

5   We need funding for these projects to provide for the safety and well-being of the town's citizens. Considering the town's limited budget, the town welcomes the assistance of your grants and expertise. The town has multiple projects to address, which must be completed in a systematic method for best results.

Write to Read: Annotate

1. Identify the main idea of Currie's letter.
2. Highlight the names of the categories Currie has set up.
3. Circle (or underline) the transitions she uses to signal a shift from category to category.

Read to Write: Think Critically

1. What is Currie's purpose? Who is her audience?
2. Why does Currie provide information about her town's history within her categories?
3. Does the letter demonstrate the four basics of classification? Explain.

Use Reading Strategies: Create a Graphic Organizer

Following the model on page 201, create a graphic organizer to show how Currie's classification is organized.

Reflect and Respond

How would you describe the level of formality and the tone in this essay? Why do you think Currie wrote the letter this way? Imagine that the town gets funding to accomplish all the projects, and Currie wishes to talk about this success in her reelection campaign. How might her discussion of the projects be different in a campaign newsletter or ad? Explain.

Professional Classification Essay

Stephanie Ericsson

The Ways We Lie

Stephanie Ericsson's life took a major turn when her husband died suddenly; she was two months pregnant at the time. She began a journal to help her cope with her grief, and she later used her writing to help others with similar struggles. An excerpt from her journal appeared in the *Utne Reader*, and her writings were later published in a book titled *Companion through the Darkness: Inner Dialogues on Grief* (1993). In "The Ways We Lie," which also appeared in the *Utne Reader* and is taken from her follow-up work, *Companion into the Dawn: Inner Dialogues on Loving* (1994), Ericsson continues her search for truth by examining and classifying lies.

COPYRIGHT © 2009 BY
STEPHANIE ERICSSON.
REPRINTED BY THE PERMISSION
OF DUNHAM LITERARY INC. AS
AGENTS FOR THE AUTHOR.

Preview   Skim the subtitles in this essay. What are Ericsson's categories? What do you think her organizing principle is?

The bank called today, and I told them my deposit was in the mail, even though I hadn't written a check yet. It'd been a rough day. The baby I'm pregnant with decided to do aerobics on my lungs for two hours, our three-year-old daughter painted the living-room couch with lipstick, the IRS put me on hold for an hour, and I was late to a business meeting because I was tired.

2   I told my client that the traffic had been bad. When my partner came home, his haggard face told me his day hadn't gone any better than mine, so when he asked, "How was your day?" I said, "Oh, fine," knowing that one more straw might break his back. A friend called and wanted to take me to lunch. I said I was busy. Four lies in the course of a day, none of which I felt the least bit guilty about.

haggard: drawn, worn out

3   We lie. We all do. We exaggerate, we minimize, we avoid confrontation, we spare people's feelings, we conveniently forget, we keep secrets, we justify lying to the big-guy institutions. Like most people, I indulge in small falsehoods and still think of myself as an honest person. Sure I lie, but it doesn't hurt anything. Or does it?

indulge: to allow ourselves to do something or have something we do not ordinarily do or have

travails: painful efforts, tribulations

4   I once tried going a whole week without telling a lie, and it was paralyzing. I discovered that telling the truth all the time is nearly impossible. It means living with some serious consequences: the bank charges me $60 in overdraft fees, my partner keels over when I tell him about my travails, my client fires me for telling her I didn't feel like being on time, and my friend takes it personally when I say I'm not hungry. There must be some merit to lying.

5   But if I justify lying, what makes me any different from slick politicians or the corporate robbers who raided the S&L industry? Saying it's OK to lie one way and not another is hedging. I cannot seem to escape the voice deep inside me that tells me: when someone lies, someone loses.

S&L industry: an S&L is a "savings and loan" company, a type of financial institution. In the 1980s and early 1990s, almost a third of these institutions went bankrupt, some as a result of their managers' corrupt practices.

hedging: avoiding the question

6   What far-reaching consequences will I, or others, pay as a result of my lie? Will someone's trust be destroyed? Will someone else pay *my* penance because I ducked out? We must consider the *meaning of our actions.* Deception, lies, capital crimes, and misdemeanors all carry meanings. *Webster's* definition of *lie* is specific:

1. a false statement or action especially made with the intent to deceive;

2. anything that gives or is meant to give a false impression.

7   A definition like this implies that there are many, many ways to tell a lie. Here are just a few.

The White Lie

8   The white lie assumes that the truth will cause more damage than a simple, harmless untruth. Telling a friend he looks great when he looks like hell can be based on a decision that the friend needs a compliment more than a frank opinion. But, in effect, it is the liar deciding what is best for the lied to. Ultimately, it is a vote of no confidence. It is an act of subtle arrogance for anyone to decide what is best for someone else.

9   Yet not all circumstances are quite so cut and dried. Take, for instance, the sergeant in Vietnam who knew one of his men was killed in action but listed him as missing so that the man's family would receive indefinite compensation instead of the lump-sum pittance the military gives widows and children. His intent was honorable. Yet for twenty years this family kept their hopes alive, unable to move on to a new life.

pittance: a small amount

Facades

facades: masks

10   We all put up facades to one degree or another. When I put on a suit to go to see a client, I feel as though I am putting on another face, obeying the expectation that serious businesspeople wear suits rather than sweatpants. But I'm a writer. Normally, I get up, get the kid off to school, and sit at my computer in my pajamas until four in the afternoon. When I answer the phone, the caller thinks I'm wearing a suit (although the UPS man knows better).

11   But facades can be destructive because they are used to seduce others into an illusion. For instance, I recently realized that a former friend was a liar. He presented himself with all the right looks and the right words and offered lots of new consciousness theories, fabulous books to read, and fascinating insights. Then I did some business with him, and the time came for him to pay me. He turned out to be all talk and no walk. I heard a plethora of reasonable excuses, including in-depth descriptions of the big break around the corner. In six months of work, I saw less than a hundred bucks. When I confronted him, he raised both eyebrows and tried to convince me that I'd heard him wrong, that he'd made no commitment to me. A simple investigation into his past revealed a crowded graveyard of disenchanted former friends.

plethora: excess

Ignoring the Plain Facts

12   In the sixties, the Catholic Church in Massachusetts began hearing complaints that Father James Porter was sexually molesting children. Rather than relieving him of his duties, the ecclesiastical authorities simply moved him from one parish to another between 1960 and 1967, actually providing him with a fresh supply of unsuspecting families and innocent children to abuse. After treatment in 1967 for pedophilia, he went back to work, this time in Minnesota. The new diocese was aware of Father Porter's obsession with children, but they needed priests and recklessly believed treatment had cured him. More children were abused until he was relieved of his duties a year later. By his own admission, Porter may have abused as many as a hundred children.

ecclesiastical: relating to a church

pedophilia: sexual abuse of children

diocese: a district or churches under the guidance of a bishop

13   Ignoring the facts may not in and of itself be a form of lying, but consider the context of this situation. If a lie is *a false action done with the intent to deceive*, then the Catholic Church's conscious covering for Porter created irreparable consequences. The church became a coperpetrator with Porter.

Stereotypes and Clichés

14   Stereotype and cliché serve a purpose as a form of shorthand. Our need for vast amounts of information in nanoseconds has made the stereotype vital to modern communication. Unfortunately, it often shuts down original thinking, giving those hungry for truth a candy bar of misinformation instead of a balanced meal. The stereotype explains a situation with just enough truth to seem unquestionable.

15   All the *isms*—racism, sexism, ageism, et al.—are founded on and fueled by the stereotype and the cliché, which are lies of exaggeration, omission, and ignorance. They are always dangerous. They take a single tree and make it a landscape. They destroy curiosity. They close minds and separate people. The single mother on welfare is assumed to be cheating. Any black male could tell you how much of his identity is obliterated daily by stereotypes. Fat people, ugly people, beautiful people, old people, large-breasted women, short men, the mentally ill,

and the homeless all could tell you how much more they are like us than we want to think. I once admitted to a group of people that I had a mouth like a truck driver. Much to my surprise, a man stood up and said, "I'm a truck driver, and I never cuss." Needless to say, I was humbled.

Out-and-Out Lies

16   Of all the ways to lie, I like this one the best, probably because I get tired of trying to figure out the real meanings behind things. At least I can trust the bald-faced lie. I once asked my five-year-old nephew, "Who broke the fence?" (I had seen him do it.) He answered, "The murderers." Who could argue?

17   At least when this sort of lie is told it can be easily confronted. As the person who is lied to, I know where I stand. The bald-faced lie doesn't toy with my perceptions—it argues with them. It doesn't try to refashion reality; it tries to refute it. *Read my lips*. . . No sleight of hand. No guessing. If this were the only form of lying, there would be no such thing as floating anxiety or the adult-children of alcoholics movement.

18   These are only a few of the ways we lie. Or are lied to. As I said earlier, it's not easy to entirely eliminate lies from our lives. No matter how pious we may try to be, we will still embellish, hedge, and omit to lubricate the daily machinery of living. But there is a world of difference between telling functional lies and living a lie. Martin Buber once said, "The lie is the spirit committing treason against itself." Our acceptance of lies becomes a cultural cancer that eventually shrouds and reorders reality until moral garbage becomes as invisible to us as water is to a fish.

19   How much do we tolerate before we become sick and tired of being sick and tired? When will we stand up and declare our *right* to trust? When do we stop accepting that the real truth is in the fine print? Whose lips do we read this year when we vote for president? When will we stop being so reticent about making judgments? When do we stop turning over our personal power and responsibility to liars?

20   Maybe if I don't tell the bank the check's in the mail I'll be less tolerant of the lies told to me every day. A country song I once heard said it all for me: "You've got to stand for something or you'll fall for anything."

refute: to deny

Read my lips: part of a slogan used by George H. W. Bush in his 1988 presidential campaign. The full slogan was "Read my lips: no new taxes."

sleight: a skillful trick

pious: religious

embellish: to decorate

shrouds: covers, conceals

reticent: reserved, silent, reluctant

Write to Read: Annotate

1. Underline or highlight the thesis statement, and then paraphrase it (put it into your own words).

2. Identify Ericsson's categories. Has she included all possible categories?

3. Make a note of all the places Ericsson asks questions. What is the purpose of her questions?

Read to Write: Think Critically

1. Do you agree that all of her categories are types of lies? If not, which would you delete or change?

2. What is the purpose of the word *but* in the middle of paragraph 8?

3. How does Ericsson organize her essay?

4. What is Ericsson's attitude toward lying? What examples in the essay support your answer?

Use Reading Strategies: Paraphrase

Review the information about paraphrasing in Chapter 1, page 14, and then paraphrase each of the following sentences, making sure that you are explaining Ericsson's idea clearly and accurately:

1. "It is an act of subtle arrogance for anyone to decide what is best for someone else" (para. 8).

2. "All the *isms*—racism, sexism, ageism, et al.—are founded on and fueled by the stereotype and the cliché, which are lies of exaggeration, omission, and ignorance. They are always dangerous. They take a single tree and make it a landscape" (para. 15).

3. "No matter how pious we may try to be, we will still embellish, hedge, and omit to lubricate the daily machinery of living" (para. 18).

Reflect and Respond

1. Do you think social media makes it easier for people to lie? What types of lies occur most often on social media? Do these lies fit into Ericsson's categories, or do you think new categories are needed to cover the lies of social media?

2. Is there a difference between lying and being wrong? If so, would that difference change any of Ericsson's categories? Explain.

Grammar for Classification

Study this sentence from the third paragraph of Ericsson's essay.

"We exaggerate, we minimize, we avoid confrontation, we spare people's feelings, we conveniently forget, we keep secrets, we justify lying to the big-guy institutions."

What do the underlined phrases have in common? In a list, all the words or phrases must have the same grammatical structure. This is called **parallelism**. In this case, each item in the list contains the subject *we* and a verb in the present tense. For more information on parallel structure, see the section "Create Balance with Parallel Structures" in Chapter 24, pages 475–80.

Write Your Own Classification

In this section, you will write your own classification based on one of the following assignments. For help, refer to the "How to Write Classification" checklist on pages 218–19.

Assignment Options: Writing about College, Work, and Everyday Life

Write a classification paragraph or essay on one of the following topics or on one of your own choice:

College
- Classify the types of resources available in your college's library, giving examples of things in each category. If you can't visit the library, spend time looking at its website. (Some library websites include virtual tours.)

- Working with your classmates, study different types of assignments given by instructors in different classes. What organizing principle (other than the classes themselves) could you use to classify the types of assignments students may be given in college? Write a classification essay that categorizes the types of assignments to help students understand how to be successful with each type.

Work
- Classify the different types of bosses or employees, giving explanations and examples for each category.

- Classify the types of skills you need in your current job or a job you have held in the past. Give explanations and examples for each category of skill.

Everyday Life
- Write about the types of challenges you face in your everyday life, giving explanations and examples for each category.

- Write about the types of social-service volunteer opportunities in your community.

Assignment Options: Reading and Writing Critically

Complete one of the following assignments and apply the critical thinking, reading, and writing skills discussed in Chapter 1.

Writing Critically about Readings

Both Stephanie Ericsson's "The Ways We Lie" (pp. 211–14) and Maria Olloqui's "The Five Main Types of Texters" (pp. 206–07) describe behaviors that can easily become habits. Read or review both of these essays, and then follow these steps:

1. **Summarize.** Briefly summarize both essays, listing the categories they include.

2. **Analyze.** Are there any other categories or supporting examples that the authors might have provided? Are their classifications complete? Do they achieve their purposes?

3. **Synthesize.** Using examples from both Ericsson's and Olloqui's essays and from your own experience, discuss habits that can lead to miscommunication or misunderstandings in relationships.

4. **Evaluate.** Which piece, Ericsson's or Olloqui's, do you think is more effective? Why? In writing your evaluation, you might look back on your responses to step 2.

Writing Critically about Visuals

Study the image below, and complete the following steps:

FLASHPOP/GETTY IMAGES

1. **Read the visual.** Ask yourself: What purpose does the visual serve? What do the expressions and gestures in each frame tell us about our emotions? (For more information on reading visuals, see the section "Write Critically about Visuals" in Chapter 1, pp. 23–26.)

2. **Write a classification.** Write a paragraph or essay classifying the emotions we can express with body language, especially in class or at work. You might include or expand on the expressions and gestures shown in the visual.

Writing Critically about Problems

Read or review the discussion of problem solving in Chapter 1 (pp. 26–28). Then consider the following problem:

> You are planning to buy a new car soon, but you know you will need to adjust your spending to cover the monthly payments on the car loan. You decide to make a monthly budget that categorizes the kinds of expenses you have.

Assignment: Working with a group or on your own, break your monthly expenses into categories, including everything that you spend money on. Then review the expenses carefully to see which ones might be reduced. Next, write a classification paragraph or essay that classifies your monthly expenses, gives examples, and ends with one or two suggestions about how you might reduce your monthly spending.

CHECKLIST

How to Write Classification

Prewrite > Draft > Revise > Edit & Proofread

CONSIDER THE CONTEXT AND FIND A NARROW TOPIC. (See Chapters 2 and 3.)

☐ Identify your audience and purpose before choosing a topic.

☐ Narrow the topic to fit the assigned genre and length.

☐ Prewrite to get ideas about the narrowed topic.

Prewrite > **Draft** > Revise > Edit & Proofread

DRAFT A TOPIC SENTENCE (PARAGRAPH) OR THESIS STATEMENT (ESSAY). (See Chapter 3.)

☐ Identify the purpose and main idea for your classification.

☐ Determine your categories and organizing principle.

SUPPORT YOUR MAIN IDEA. (See Chapter 4.)

☐ List all the categories needed to support your classification.

☐ Find examples, definitions, and details to illustrate each category.

WRITE A DRAFT. (See Chapter 5.)

☐ Put the categories in a logical order, usually order of importance or emphasis.

☐ Include a topic sentence (paragraph) or thesis statement (essay); all the categories; and supporting descriptions, definitions, or examples.

☐ Add an appropriate introduction and conclusion.

Prewrite ⟩ Draft ⟩ **Revise** ⟩ Edit & Proofread ⟩

REVISE YOUR DRAFT. (See Chapter 6.)

☐ Make sure it has *all* the four basics of classification.

☐ Make sure each paragraph is unified (all ideas should relate to the topic sentence).

☐ Make sure each paragraph is fully developed (there are enough supporting details to demonstrate the point).

☐ Make sure you include transitions to move readers smoothly from one category to the next.

Prewrite ⟩ Draft ⟩ Revise ⟩ **Edit & Proofread** ⟩

EDIT AND PROOFREAD YOUR REVISED DRAFT. (See Parts 3 and 4.)

☐ Make sure grammar, word usage, and punctuation choices are clear, accurate, and effective.

☐ Check spelling and capitalization.

Chapter 11 Review

1. What is classification?

2. What are the four basics of classification?

3. What information may be included in the main idea of a classification paragraph or essay?

4. What are three ways to develop secondary support for the categories of classification?

5. What transitions are commonly used in classification?

Reflect and Apply

1. When have you written or read classification before? What makes reading or writing classification difficult?

2. Interview someone studying in your major or working in your career. Ask the person you interviewed what kinds of classification he or she has written.

3. What challenged you the most when writing for this chapter? What do you want to do differently next time?

4. What worked well in your writing for this chapter? What do you need to remember for next time?

12

Definition

Writing That Tells What Something Means

- List the four basics of definition paragraphs and essays.
- Identify the term to be defined and what sets it apart from other, similar terms.
- Support the definition with examples or other details.
- Recognize transitions commonly used in definition.
- Write a definition paragraph or essay with a clear main idea, detailed support, and logical organization.

When you hear the word *definition*, you might think of a dictionary. The definitions in a dictionary provide short, basic meanings of words, but in some situations, you may need more extensive and detailed definitions. Imagine, for example, you are working as a sales associate at a local market, and your boss tells you to be polite at all times. What does politeness look like when you see a customer shoplifting? Or think about your instructor's policy of punishing all forms of cheating. How does the instructor define *cheating*? Is it cheating to do homework with a friend? Clear and precise definitions give you guidance for work, college, and everyday life.

Understand What Definition Is

Definition is writing that gives the essential features or characteristics of a concept so that readers understand what it means and why it is important.

> **Four Basics** of Definition
>
> **1** **Main Idea:** An effective definition paragraph or essay makes a point by defining a concept.
>
> **2** **Primary Support:** It presents characteristics or key features of the concept.
>
> **3** **Secondary Support:** It uses examples and details to illustrate the key characteristics.
>
> **4** **Organization:** It arranges key characteristics and examples in a logical order.

In the following paragraph, the numbers and colors correspond to the four basics of definition.

1 A stereotype is a conventional idea or image that is simplistic—and often wrong, particularly when it is applied to people or groups of people. **2** Stereotypes can prevent us from seeing people as they really are because stereotypes blind us with preconceived notions about what a certain type of person is like. **4** For example, **3** I had a stereotyped notion of Native Americans until I met my friend Daniel, a Chippewa Indian. I thought all Indians wore feathers and beads, had long black hair, and avoided all contact with non-Native Americans because they resented their land being taken away. Daniel, however, wears jeans and T-shirts, and we talk about everything—even our different ancestries. After meeting him, I understood that my stereotype of Native Americans was completely wrong. **4** Not only was it wrong, but **2** it set up an us–them concept in my mind that made me feel that I, as a non-Native American, would never have anything in common with Native Americans. **3** My stereotype would not have allowed me to see Native Americans as individuals: I would have seen them only as part of a group that I thought was all alike and all different from me. **4** From now on, I won't assume that any individual fits my stereotype; I will try to see that person as I would like them to see me: as myself, not a stereotyped image.

In college, writing assignments may include the word *define,* but they might also use phrases such as *explain the meaning of a concept* and *discuss the meaning of a term.* You might also be asked to determine *important characteristics* or *essential features* of a concept. In these cases, use the strategies discussed in this chapter to complete the assignment.

First Basic: Main Idea in Definition

In definition, the **main idea** usually defines a term or concept. The main idea is related to your purpose: to help your readers understand the term or concept and why it is important.

When you write your definition, do not just copy the dictionary definition; write it in your own words as you want your readers to understand it. To help you, you might first complete the following sentence:

Main idea in definition: I want readers to understand that this term
                                 means _____ because _____.

Then, based on your response, write a topic sentence (paragraph) or thesis statement (essay) using the **term** (or word) you are defining. The main idea statement may take several different forms.

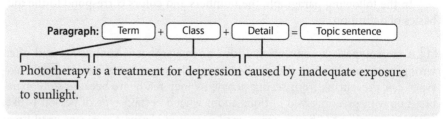

In this topic sentence, the *class* is the larger group the term belongs to. Main idea statements do not have to include a class, however, as in the following topic sentence:

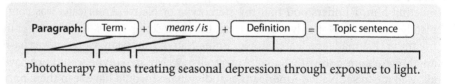

The following thesis statement is broader in scope than the topic sentences because it sets up a discussion of the larger subject of seasonal affective disorder. In contrast, the topic sentences consider one particular treatment for this disorder (phototherapy).

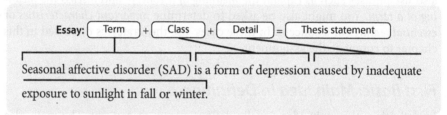

PRACTICE 12–1   **Writing a Statement of Your Definition**

For each of the following terms, write a definition statement using the pattern indicated in brackets, and identify a possible purpose for defining each term. Remember not to copy the definition from a dictionary.

Example:

Internet troll [term + class + detail]:

An Internet troll is a person who posts rude, divisive, or harassing messages on social media.

Purpose: *To set clear guidelines for a private GroupMe, Discord, or Slack group*

1. Stress [term + class + detail]:

2. Vacation [term + *means / is* + definition]:

3. Confidence [term + class + detail]:

4. Conservation [term + *means / is* + definition]:

5. Patriotism [term + *means /is* + definition]:

Second Basic: Primary Support in Definition

Primary support in a *definition* includes the important characteristics that explain what a term or concept means. For example, a person might define *science fiction* as a type of writing that imagines how a scientific concept could affect humanity. The following are three essential characteristics of science fiction that support this definition:

1. Reference to a scientific concept
2. A setting or technology that is not part of the world now
3. A description of how humans react to the concept

The following example illustrates a thesis and primary support for an essay defining the term *introvert*:

Thesis:	Any prospective roommate needs to know that I am an introvert.
Support:	I need time alone with privacy.
	I am not comfortable with loud social events like parties; I will need a place to get away.
	I disconnect from social media every now and then.

PRACTICE 12-2   **Selecting Key Features for the Definition**

List three key features you could use to support the following thesis statements.

Example:

Insomnia means sleeplessness.

    a. hard to fall asleep

    b. wake up in the middle of the night

    c. wake up without feeling rested in the morning

1. A good workout is essential to self-care.

2. A real friend is not just someone for the fun times.

3. Time management is a skill all college students need to acquire.

4. Beauty can be found anywhere, even in the most unlikely places, if we are willing to look for it.

Third Basic: Secondary Support in Definition

A strong definition provides detailed examples to explain and illustrate the key characteristics of the concept or term you are defining. For an essay defining *science fiction* (see p. 223), for example, a writer could use the novel *Out of the Silent Planet* by C. S. Lewis as an example to illustrate the three primary supporting points:

Primary Support	Secondary Support
Involves a scientific concept	*Out of the Silent Planet* focuses on space travel.
Includes unusual setting or technology	The story is set on Mars, with different creatures and social structures.
Explores human reaction	The novel examines the effects of human conquest of other planets, painting a pessimistic picture of the result.

Notice how the following details support each of the major supporting points that define *introvert*:

Primary Support	Secondary Support
I need time alone with privacy.	I have to have a bedroom with a lock on it. I study alone for hours at a time, such as the 7-hour marathon before my history final.
I am not comfortable with loud social events like parties; I will need a place to get away.	At parties, I may leave for 15 minutes or so in order to let my brain calm down. Long stretches of loud music and talk give me a migraine. I always take my own car in case I need to leave early.
I disconnect from social media every now and then.	I do not answer or look at texts, emails, snapchats, or messages while I am talking with someone face-to-face. Last week, I stayed off social media for five days so that I could focus on a project for work.

> **PRACTICE 12–3**   **Selecting Examples and Details for the Definition**
>
> Choose one of the thesis statements and defining features from Practice 12-2. Give one or two examples or details to explain or illustrate each characteristic.

Fourth Basic: Organization in Definition

The characteristics and examples in definition are often organized by **order of importance**, meaning that the example that will have the most effect on readers is saved for last.

Using Transitions in Definition

Transitions in definition move readers from one characteristic or example to the next. Here are some transitions you might use in definition, although many others are possible, too:

Common Transitions in Definition

alternately	another kind	for instance
another; one/another	for example	first, second, third, and so on

Paragraphs versus Essays in Definition

For more on the important features of definition, see the "Four Basics of Definition" on page 221.

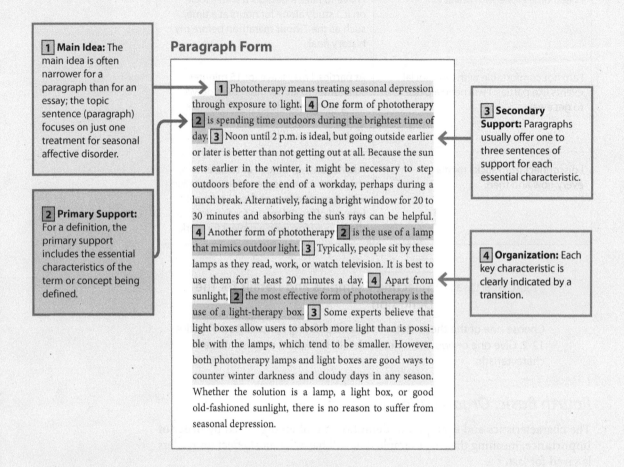

1 Main Idea: The main idea is often narrower for a paragraph than for an essay; the topic sentence (paragraph) focuses on just one treatment for seasonal affective disorder.

2 Primary Support: For a definition, the primary support includes the essential characteristics of the term or concept being defined.

Paragraph Form

1 Phototherapy means treating seasonal depression through exposure to light. **4** One form of phototherapy **2** is spending time outdoors during the brightest time of day. **3** Noon until 2 p.m. is ideal, but going outside earlier or later is better than not getting out at all. Because the sun sets earlier in the winter, it might be necessary to step outdoors before the end of a workday, perhaps during a lunch break. Alternatively, facing a bright window for 20 to 30 minutes and absorbing the sun's rays can be helpful. **4** Another form of phototherapy **2** is the use of a lamp that mimics outdoor light. **3** Typically, people sit by these lamps as they read, work, or watch television. It is best to use them for at least 20 minutes a day. **4** Apart from sunlight, **2** the most effective form of phototherapy is the use of a light-therapy box. **3** Some experts believe that light boxes allow users to absorb more light than is possible with the lamps, which tend to be smaller. However, both phototherapy lamps and light boxes are good ways to counter winter darkness and cloudy days in any season. Whether the solution is a lamp, a light box, or good old-fashioned sunlight, there is no reason to suffer from seasonal depression.

3 Secondary Support: Paragraphs usually offer one to three sentences of support for each essential characteristic.

4 Organization: Each key characteristic is clearly indicated by a transition.

Consider Readers as You Write Definition

Ask Yourself

- Will readers find my main idea and definition clear and interesting?
- Will readers think I have included the most important characteristics and examples to define the term?
- Have I added specific details for each characteristic so that readers who are not familiar with the term can understand it?
- Have I organized my definition so readers can move easily from one characteristic to the next?

Essay Form

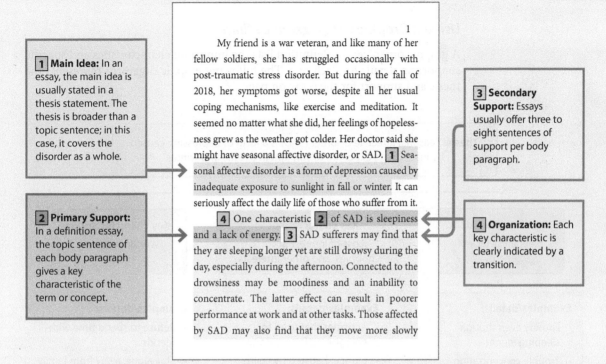

1 Main Idea: In an essay, the main idea is usually stated in a thesis statement. The thesis is broader than a topic sentence; in this case, it covers the disorder as a whole.

2 Primary Support: In a definition essay, the topic sentence of each body paragraph gives a key characteristic of the term or concept.

3 Secondary Support: Essays usually offer three to eight sentences of support per body paragraph.

4 Organization: Each key characteristic is clearly indicated by a transition.

1

My friend is a war veteran, and like many of her fellow soldiers, she has struggled occasionally with post-traumatic stress disorder. But during the fall of 2018, her symptoms got worse, despite all her usual coping mechanisms, like exercise and meditation. It seemed no matter what she did, her feelings of hopelessness grew as the weather got colder. Her doctor said she might have seasonal affective disorder, or SAD. **1** Seasonal affective disorder is a form of depression caused by inadequate exposure to sunlight in fall or winter. It can seriously affect the daily life of those who suffer from it.

4 One characteristic **2** of SAD is sleepiness and a lack of energy. **3** SAD sufferers may find that they are sleeping longer yet are still drowsy during the day, especially during the afternoon. Connected to the drowsiness may be moodiness and an inability to concentrate. The latter effect can result in poorer performance at work and at other tasks. Those affected by SAD may also find that they move more slowly

2

than usual and that all types of physical activity are more challenging than they used to be. All these difficulties can be a source of frustration, sometimes worsening the depression.

4 Another characteristic **2** of SAD is loss of interest in work, hobbies, and other activities. **3** To some extent, these symptoms may be connected to a lack of energy. Often, however, the feelings run deeper than that. Activities that once lifted one's spirits may have the opposite effect. For instance, a mother who at one time never missed her child's soccer games might now see attending them as a burden. Someone who was once a top performer at work may find that it is all he or she can do to show up in the morning. Such changes in one's outlook can contribute to a feeling of hopelessness.

4 The most serious **2** symptom of SAD is withdrawal from interactions with others. **3** SAD sufferers may find that they are no longer interested in going out with friends, and they may turn down requests to get together for movies, meals, or social

3

events. They may even withdraw from family members, engaging less frequently in conversations or even spending time alone in their room. Furthermore, they may postpone or cancel activities, such as vacation trips, that might require them to interact with family for hours at a time. Withdrawal symptoms may also extend to the workplace, with SAD sufferers becoming less vocal at meetings or avoiding lunches or conversations with colleagues. Concern that family members or coworkers may be noticing such personality changes can cause or worsen anxiety in those with SAD.

Because the symptoms and effects of SAD can be so significant, it is important to address them as soon as possible. Fortunately, as my friend learned, there are many good therapies for the condition, from drug treatment to greater exposure to sunlight, whether real or simulated through special lamps or light boxes. In my friend's case, using the light boxes and scheduling regular time outside—along with exercise and time with friends—helped her feel like herself again.

Using a Graphic Organizer in Definition

A graphic organizer for definition lists the important characteristics and specific supporting details for each one. The following graphic organizer represents the thesis and support for the essay on page 227.

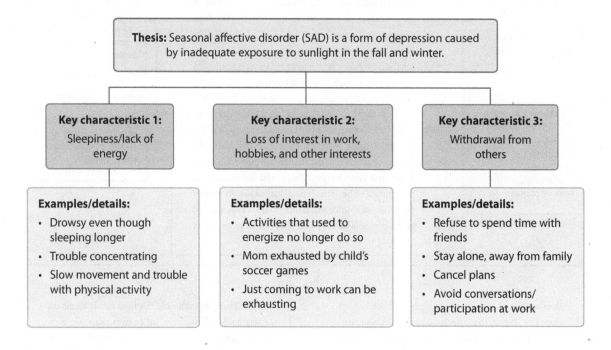

Thesis: Seasonal affective disorder (SAD) is a form of depression caused by inadequate exposure to sunlight in the fall and winter.

Key characteristic 1:
Sleepiness/lack of energy

Key characteristic 2:
Loss of interest in work, hobbies, and other interests

Key characteristic 3:
Withdrawal from others

Examples/details:
- Drowsy even though sleeping longer
- Trouble concentrating
- Slow movement and trouble with physical activity

Examples/details:
- Activities that used to energize no longer do so
- Mom exhausted by child's soccer games
- Just coming to work can be exhausting

Examples/details:
- Refuse to spend time with friends
- Stay alone, away from family
- Cancel plans
- Avoid conversations/ participation at work

PRACTICE 12–4 **Using Transitions in Definition**

Read the paragraph that follows, and fill in the blanks with one of the following transitions (some words will not be used): *alternately, although, another, for example, the other, on the other hand, one.* When you have finished, create a graphic organizer for this paragraph.

Each year, *Business Week* publishes a list of the most family-friendly companies to work for. The magazine uses several factors to define the organizations as family-friendly. _____ factor is whether the company has flextime, allowing employees to schedule work hours that better fit family needs. _____, a parent might choose to work from 6:30 a.m. to 2:30 p.m. to be able to spend time with children. _____, a parent might split his or her job with a colleague, so each person has more time for child care. _____ factor is whether family leave programs are encouraged. _____ to maternity leaves, for example, does the company encourage paternity leaves and leaves for care of elderly parents? Increasingly, companies are trying to become more family-friendly to attract and keep good employees.

Read and Analyze Definition

To write successfully in college and at work, it is important to understand the four basics of definition; reading and analyzing samples of definition can help you see these basics at work and write your own definition. In this section, you will use a rubric to evaluate the first draft of Corin Costas's definition paragraph. You will also review a student essay by Amanda Martinez. In the Profile of Success, Moses Maddox describes how he uses definition in his career. Finally, a professional essay by Eugene Robinson defines the notion of black patriotism.

Student Definition Paragraph

Read this draft of a definition paragraph. Note that the instructor asked the students to focus on the main idea, support (examples and supporting details), and organization in this draft. Using the four basics of definition and the sample rubric (p. 230), decide how effective this draft of the paragraph is, and then recommend one or two goals for the student's next draft.

> **Assignment:** Students who have just arrived at our college do not always understand the different groups and opportunities available to them through our Student Activities Office. Write a paragraph that defines a student group you know well: What are its essential features and activities? How has it affected you? Consider a new student as your audience for this paragraph, and make sure you edit it carefully so that it could be published in our online student activities brochure.

Corin Costas

What Community Involvement Means to Me

S.H.O.C.W.A.V.E.S. is a student organization at Bunker Hill Community College. S.H.O.C.W.A.V.E.S. stands for Students Helping Our Community with Active Volunteer Experiences. Its mission is to get students involved with the community—to become part of it by actively working in it in positive ways. Each year, S.H.O.C.W.A.V.E.S. is assigned a budget by the Student Activities Office. It spends that budget in activities that help the community in a variety of ways. Some of the money is spent in fund-raising events for community causes. We have money to plan and launch a fund-raiser, which raises far more than we spend. In the process, other students and members of the community also become involved in the helping effort. We get to know lots of people. We usually have a lot of fun. We are helping others at the same time. We have worked as part of the Charles River Cleanup, the Walk for Hunger, collecting toys for sick and needy children, and Light One Little Candle. S.H.O.C.W.A.V.E.S. benefits its members. I have learned so many valuable skills. I always have something I care about to write about for my classes. I have learned about budgeting, advertising, organizing, and managing. I have also developed my creativity by coming up with new ways to do things. I have networked with many people, including people who are important in the business world. S.H.O.C.W.A.V.E.S. has greatly improved my life and my chances for future success.

Rubric for Definition

	1 Falls below expectations	2 Nearly meets expectations	3 Meets expectations	4 Exceeds expectations
Main idea (first basic)	Main idea is missing.	Main idea is unclear and lacks a sense of purpose.	Main idea identifies term to be defined, but without a clear purpose.	Main idea shows clearly what is being defined and why.
Support (second and third basics)	Features and details do not support the main idea effectively.	Some defining features and details are present.	Defining features are clear but lack development.	Defining features are clear and well-developed.
Organization (fourth basic)	Organization is not clear or logical.	Organization is inconsistent.	Organization is logical, but some transitions are missing or inappropriate.	Organization is logical, with smooth transitions throughout.

Evaluating the Paragraph

1. Does the paragraph show the four basics of definition? Explain.

2. Using the rubric as a guide, what is the strongest part of the paragraph? The weakest?

3. Write a response to this writer, using one of the following to frame your response:

   a. One thing I would like to know more about is _____.

   b. What I liked best about the paragraph is _____.

   c. In your next draft, you could consider _____.

Student Definition Essay

Amanda Martinez

To All the Boys I've Ghosted Before

Preview This piece appeared in the *Independent Florida Alligator*, a student newspaper for the University of Florida. Skim the first paragraph. What can the publication information and the first paragraph tell you about Martinez's audience?

Picture this: You're going through your dating apps for the third time today hoping to find something real. After swiping left on every guy with "here for a good time, not a long time" in his bio, you find him. He has no bad tattoos, no sleazy pick-up line and, most important of all, he's not holding a fish in any of his photos.

2   As Farmer Hoggett says to his pet in the movie "Babe," "That'll do pig; that'll do." You swipe right. It's an instant match.

3   After going on a few dates, the lack-of-fish charm begins to wear off. Things start to get boring with him, and you find yourself missing that sweet, melodic sound of matching with someone on Tinder. It's time to end things. You decide to screen his calls, ignore his texts, and move on with your life feeling free and relieved.

4   For those who don't know the term, *ghosting* refers to the act of terminating a romantic relationship by cutting off contact with the other person completely, almost as if the relationship never existed. In a study by *Psychology Today*, 20 percent of participants admitted to ghosting someone. By those stats, one of every five people has ghosted someone at some point in their lifetime.

5   So why do people ghost? Because it's easy, and millennialism is all about working smarter, not harder. At an age where it seems everyone is anxiety-prone with self-esteem issues, formal breakups can be soul-crushing even at a casual level. Ghosting lets the relationship end in a neutral place where things aren't positive, but they're not necessarily negative either. It's the purgatory of romance.

6   While it might be the least energy-consuming way to end a relationship, is it entirely guilt-free? It depends on the situation. In this case, and in other short-term relationships, ghosting provides a way to send a message (metaphorically, of course) without making things too emotional. Sometimes people just don't click. If the relationship was not formally defined as an exclusive relationship by both parties, disappearing with no notice is a fine choice. If they're not your girlfriend/boyfriend/partner, then their title won't change when you decide to leave them.

7   On a more serious note, ghosting your partner from a long-term relationship is unacceptable. If a person has spent the time getting to know your favorite movies, most embarrassing stories from childhood, and your preferred place to grab Boba tea, you should spend the time to give them an explanation. Face-to-face interactions are not just highly recommended but mandatory. It might be uncomfortable, but it shows the other person that, although you no longer wish to be with them, they are still deserving of your respect.

millennialism: the lifestyle of the millennial generation, born between 1981 and 1996. The term is also often applied to later generations as well.

purgatory: in Catholic Christianity, purgatory is a place where a soul may go after death. Neither heaven nor hell, purgatory is a place for purification.

Boba tea: a drink made from tea, milk, and small balls of tapioca

8   To quote Neil Sedaka's hit song from the '60s, "Breakin' up is hard to do." It's pretty awkward most of the time, and someone always ends up crying. But it doesn't have to be terrible. If you're breaking up with someone, plan what you're going to say beforehand. No one likes breakup conversations, especially impromptu ones. If you are being broken up with (or once you realize it) take your time in responding. Think up any burning questions you might have for that person, because you might not have a chance to ask them in the future. That relationship, failed as it may be, is just a chapter in your book of life.

impromptu:
unplanned

9   Being a "ghost" doesn't make someone a bad person just like being ghosted doesn't mean someone is not worthy of being loved. Whether you're ghosting someone or getting ghosted yourself, the healthiest thing to do is not dwell on the situation but think of the good times that have happened with that person instead.

10   In other, more dated words, keep calm and swipe on.

Write to Read: Annotate

1. Identify the main idea of the essay and the important characteristics of ghosting.

2. Circle or highlight the transitions used by the author.

Read to Write: Think Critically

1. The first three paragraphs of the essay describe a dating scenario. Why does the writer begin this way?

2. How is this essay organized?

3. What does the writer do in paragraph 8? How does this paragraph connect to the overall definition of ghosting?

Use Reading Strategies: Create a Graphic Organizer

Following the model on page 228, create a graphic organizer for Martinez's definition essay.

Reflect and Respond

1. Have you ever ghosted someone or been ghosted by someone? How does your experience confirm or complicate Martinez's definition?

2. Ghosting is closely connected to our use of technology. Choose another technology-related behavior (creeping, flaming, sadfishing, trolling, etc.) and define it, using Martinez's essay as a model.

Profile of Success: Moses Maddox
Definition in the Real World

Title Fellowship Specialist, The Mission Continues

Background When I was pursuing my degree, I struggled with writing. It wasn't that I didn't enjoy writing, but I had concentrations in sociology, political science, and history, as well as a minor in philosophy. The struggle was that all four subjects had different needs in writing. When writing a paper in history, I had to present facts and analysis of those facts. In philosophy, I had to be careful that I didn't commit any logical fallacies; it would also take me four pages to write something because I had to make sure the reader understood my premise before I got to my point. It was a tough learning experience to get a "C" on a history paper because I "didn't write a history paper."

What I learned through experiences like that was to understand my audience. Sometimes people just want the facts; however, in my current position, if I just presented facts, people might not take this program seriously. I have also learned how to find my voice: My professors encouraged me to experiment, to look at writing as my true expression of self. I was taught to write so that if someone one hundred years from now were to read something I've written, they would get a sense of who I am, as though I am able to communicate with a person in the future. Writing is that powerful.

Writing at Work What I do at The Mission Continues is manage returning veterans as they navigate through their six-month fellowships. A fellowship with The Mission Continues resembles an executive internship where fellows pick a nonprofit organization to serve, and also fulfill a goal (professional, continuing education, or service), and generate data. What fellows accomplish throughout their fellowships serves as résumé fodder; many of them have a ton of leadership experience from the military but do not necessarily have the relevant work experience to be marketable in the civilian job market.

Veterans are really good at the "how" part of life. If you give military members a job to do, they will do it and do it well. However, many don't know why they are doing the job. Our organization focuses on personal and professional development through goal setting, finding allies, identifying role models, identifying driving force, and creating personal mission statements. The overarching goal is for our veterans to be in a place where they can go out into the world, understand what they are looking for in a career, and understand how their military experience applies to the nonmilitary world. We feel that service is a vehicle through a successful transition, and my job is to hold the fellows accountable for the goals that they set and push them to explore their inner selves so that they can move on and find joy in their lives.

Thus, writing is a huge part of my job. Although the writing is mainly conversational in tone, creating the correct message is important. Things like punctuation are important because there is a difference between "You're doing a great job." and "You're doing a great job!" I must remain positive as well as approachable in all of my interactions. In deep philosophical conversations, if I approach the topic in a completely academic tone, then people will check out. If I approach it in a conversational tone, people are more receptive. One email—in fact, one sentence—can mean the difference between a successful fellowship and someone giving up. So writing well is one of my key competencies.

Moses Maddox

Fellowship Specialist at The Mission Continues

COURTESY OF MOSES MADDOX

résumé fodder: content to make a résumé more impressive

233

Workplace Definition

Moses Maddox

Email to Clients

The following is an email Moses sent out to his clients at The Mission Continues.

1   Hello Fellows,

2   First: amazing work! Thanks to each and every single one of you for getting me your written assignments on time. Your candid responses have let me know that you are taking this seriously and have given me a look into the impact you all want to make. All of your goals are achievable, and all of your fears can be overcome!

candid: truthful and straightforward

3   In Month 2, we talk more about overcoming fear and identifying allies. In a few minutes, I will share some tips and tricks to get the most out of Month 2. First, I want to recap the two main terms I went over with all of you in Month 1:

4   **Eudaimonia:** Gotta love the work that goes into "well-being" or "being well." My goal for all of you is to find your joy and be well.

5   **10,000 Hours:** Malcolm Gladwell stated that it takes 10,000 hours of deliberate practice to become an expert at something. The actual research suggests that it takes ten years. I think most of us have agreed that achieving 10,000 hours of deliberate practice helps you master the basics. We have also agreed that for many of you, due to your time in the military, you have devoted more than 10,000 hours of your life to service, and your fellowships add to your tally.

6   **Month 2:** Month 2 is less intimidating, but just as deep. Here are the terms that I enjoyed researching and the stuff we will talk about over the month.

7   **Mental Rehearsal:** The best way to face your fears is to think about them, visualize the worst-case scenario, and then in your visualization, come up with a way to solve your worst-case scenario. In philosophy, we call this a thought experiment. Einstein famously used thought experimentation during his development of the theory of special relativity. Long story short, with enough practice, mental rehearsal can be a great tool.

8   **Finding Allies:** You will read (or have already read) an excerpt from Reid Hoffman's book *The Start-Up of You*. The summary I attached is basically a CliffsNotes version of the book. Also, *How to Win Friends and Influence People* was mentioned, and I included the entire book mainly because it is such an amazing and enlightening read.

9   Remember that no person is an island, so when you are thinking about your allies, the reading states that "allies can be friends, spouses, colleagues, family, supervisors, mentors," which I agree with. However, don't pick your spouse as an ally just because he or she is there. Choose allies that share your goals, offer something of their own, and are willing to be helped. Also remember that an ally is:

- Someone you consult regularly for advice.
- Someone with whom you share opportunities and collaborate.

Cheers,
Mo

no person is an island: people need others to live well; no one should be isolated

Write to Read: Annotate

1. Identify the purpose of the email.
2. Underline or highlight the terms Maddox defines in his email.

Read to Write: Think Critically

1. Maddox notes that "allies can be friends, spouses, colleagues, family, supervisors, mentors"; however, he also warns his readers about choosing someone just because they are nearby. Why do you think he does this? What does he want his readers to do as they choose an ally?
2. Maddox notes that he is always aware of his audience and how they will perceive his work. What sort of relationship does Maddox have with the audience of this email? What words or phrases make this relationship clear?

Use Reading Strategies: Paraphrase

Maddox defines several terms in his email, including *eudaimonia, mental rehearsal,* and *allies.* Review the information about paraphrase in Chapter 1 (p. 14). Then choose two of these terms and paraphrase the definitions provided by Maddox.

Reflect and Respond

Maddox gives his readers advice in this email. What piece of advice can you apply to your life right now? Write a paragraph in which you explain his advice and connect it to your own situation.

Professional Definition Essay

Eugene Robinson

A Special Brand of Patriotism

Eugene Robinson is a Pulitzer prize–winning journalist. For decades he has worked at the *Washington Post*, moving from city hall reporter to foreign editor to assistant managing editor (with many jobs in between), but he is best known for his opinion columns focusing on race and politics. In addition to writing for the *Post*, he has published three nonfiction books and serves as a political analyst for MSNBC. The following column was published on July 4, 2008, as Barack Obama was running for his first term as president of the United States. Although other politicians (including the Republican nominee, John McCain) did not wear flag lapel pins every day, a brief controversy arose about whether Obama would or would not wear such a lapel pin.

Buffalo soldiers: Black soldiers who worked the Western frontier protecting settlers following the Civil War

Tuskegee Airmen: the first Black pilots in the U.S. military, they flew more than 15,000 missions during World War II and won over 150 Distinguished Flying Crosses. They got their name by training at the Tuskegee Army Air Field in Alabama.

Colin Powell: four-star general and U.S. secretary of state, 2001–2005

Rev. Jeremiah Wright: minister of the church Obama attended in Chicago. Wright made some anti-Semitic comments that Obama was asked to condemn.

Anyone who took U.S. history in high school ought to know that one of the five men killed in the Boston Massacre, the atrocity that helped ignite the American Revolution, was a runaway slave named Crispus Attucks. The question the history books rarely consider is: Why?

2   Think about it for a moment. For well over a century, British colonists in North America had practiced a particularly cruel brand of slavery, a system of bondage intended not just to exploit the labor of Africans but to crush their spirit as well. Backs were whipped and broken, families systematically separated, traditions erased, ancient languages silenced. Yet a black man—to many, nothing more than a piece of property—chose to stand and die with the patriots of Boston.

3   Now think about the Buffalo Soldiers and the Tuskegee Airmen. Think about Dorie Miller, who, like so many black sailors in the segregated U.S. Navy of the 1940s, was relegated to kitchen duty—until Pearl Harbor, when Miller rushed up to the deck of the sinking USS *West Virginia*, carried wounded sailors to safety, and then raked Japanese planes with fire from a heavy machine gun until he ran out of ammunition.

4   Think about Colin Powell— but also think about the Rev. Jeremiah Wright, a former Marine. And consider, as we celebrate Independence Day, how steadfast and complicated black patriotism has always been.

5   The subject is particularly relevant now that the first African American with a realistic chance of becoming president, Barack Obama, has felt compelled to

give a lengthy speech explaining his own patriotism. It is not common, in my experience, for sitting U.S. senators to be questioned on their love of country—to be grilled about a flag pin, for example, or critiqued on the posture they assume when the national anthem is played. For an American who attains such high office, patriotism is generally assumed.

6   It seems that some people don't want to give Obama the benefit of that assumption, however, and I have to wonder whether that's because he's black. And then I have to wonder why.

7   The fact that African American patriotism is never simple doesn't mean it's in any way halfhearted; to the contrary, complicated relationships tend to be the deepest and strongest. It's a historical fact that black soldiers and sailors who fought overseas in World War II came home to Southern cities where they had to ride in the back of the bus—and that they were angry that the nation for which they had sacrificed would treat them this way. To some whites, I guess, it may seem logical to be suspicious of black patriotism—to believe that anger must somehow temper love of country.

8   It doesn't, of course. It never has. Black Americans are just more intimately and acutely aware of some of our nation's flaws than many white Americans might be. This generalization is less true of my sons than of my parents, and I hope that someday it won't be true at all. But only in the past half-century has the United States begun to fully extend the rights of citizenship to African Americans—and only in the past year has the idea that a black man might actually be elected president been more than a plot device for movies and television shows. We're someplace we've never been.

9   Michelle Obama was sharply attacked for saying that she felt proud of her country for the first time in her adult life. Her phrasing may have been impolitic, but I know exactly what she meant.

impolitic: unwise

10   This isn't about whether or not Barack Obama wins. Just the fact that he might win is an incredible change for this country—and recognizing the importance of that change is, to me, the very essence of patriotism.

11   What's unpatriotic is pretending that the past never happened. What's unpatriotic is failing to acknowledge that we've struggled with race for nearly 400 years. What's unpatriotic is relegating "black history" to the month of February when, really, it's American history, without which this nation could never be what it is today.

12   My father, Harold I. Robinson, served in the Army during World War II and has lived to witness this transformative moment of possibility. My father-in-law, the late Edward R. Collins, was a sailor who saw action in the South Pacific; he rests at Arlington National Cemetery. I have no patience with anyone who thinks that patriots don't have brown skin.

Write to Read: Annotate

1. What is Robinson's thesis? Highlight it.

2. Make a note of the names of people Robinson uses to illustrate his definition.

Read to Write: Think Critically

1. What is the writer's purpose in this essay? Does he achieve it? Explain.

2. In paragraph 11, Robinson defines patriotism by stating what it is not. Why does he do this? Do you think his strategy is effective?

3. Look at the last sentence of the essay. What is the writer's tone? How does his tone support his purpose?

Use Reading Strategies: Summarize

Review what you learned in Chapter 1 about writing a summary (pp. 18–20), and then summarize Robinson's essay.

Reflect and Respond

1. How would you define *patriotism*? What experiences in your past or in history have shaped your understanding of that word?

2. Robinson says, "Complicated relationships tend to be the deepest and strongest." Do you agree with him? Explain.

Grammar for Definition

Because definitions describe situations or concepts that are true all the time, we often use simple present tense to write them. It is important to pay attention to subject-verb agreement in the simple present tense. Look at the following examples from Robinson's essay. The subjects are underlined once, and the verbs are underlined twice.

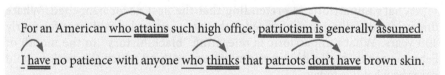

For an American who attains such high office, patriotism is generally assumed.

I have no patience with anyone who thinks that patriots don't have brown skin.

A singular subject requires a singular verb, and a plural subject requires a plural verb. For more on subject-verb agreement, see Chapter 19.

Write Your Own Definition

In this section, you will write your own definition based on one of the following assignments. For help, refer to the "How to Write Definition" checklist on page 241.

Assignment Options: Writing about College, Work, and Everyday Life

Write a definition paragraph, essay, or other document (as described below) on one of the following topics or on one of your own choice:

College	• How would you define effective and ineffective study habits? List the important characteristics of each, and give examples to support your definitions.
	• Identify a difficult or technical term from a class you are taking. Then define the term, and give examples of different ways in which it might be used.
Work	• If you have ever held a job that used unusual or interesting terminology, write about some of the terms used, what they meant, and their function on the job.
	• How do members of your profession refer to themselves or to outsiders? Write an essay that defines one of these terms, identifying the most important characteristics of the term and providing examples as needed.
Everyday Life	• What does it mean to be a good friend or parent? Provide a definition, giving the key characteristics as well as explanations and examples.
	• Write an essay defining a term that describes a problem in your community, such as *addiction, road rage, poverty, discrimination,* or *xenophobia*. Identify the key characteristics and provide explanations and examples.

Assignment Options: Reading and Writing Critically

Complete one of the following assignments that asks you to apply the critical thinking, reading, and writing skills discussed in Chapter 1.

Writing Critically about Readings

Both Margaret Troup's essay, "Virtual Reality: Fun and Innovative Indoor Exercise" (p. 135) and Stephanie Alaimo and Mark Koester's "The Backdraft of Technology" (p. 282) define potential benefits and abuses of technology in society. While these essays are primarily illustration and cause-and-effect, both define concepts through evidence and examples. Read or review both of these essays, and then follow these steps:

1. **Summarize.** Briefly summarize the works, listing examples they include.
2. **Analyze.** What questions do the essays raise for you?
3. **Synthesize.** Using examples from the essays and your own experience, describe how you draw the line between benefits and abuses of technology.
4. **Evaluate.** Which essay do you think is more effective? Why? In writing your evaluation, look back on your responses to step 2.

FATCAMERA/GETTY IMAGES

Writing Critically about Visuals

Study the photograph, and complete these steps:

1. **Read the visual.** Describe the setting and participants in this photo. What draws your attention? Why?

2. **Write a definition.** Many companies and organizations promote *workplace wellness* or *work/life balance* programs. Using your reflections in number 1 above as a starting point, write a definition of one of these two terms. List the key features of the term, as well as examples and details.

Writing Critically about Problems

Read or review the discussion of problem solving in Chapter 1 (pp. 26–28). Then consider the following problem:

A recent survey asked business managers what skills or traits they value most in employees. The top five responses were (1) motivation, (2) interpersonal skills, (3) initiative, (4) communication skills, and (5) maturity. You have a job interview next week, and you want to be able to present yourself well. Think about the five skills and traits noted above and what examples you might be able to give to demonstrate that you have them.

Assignment: Working in a group or on your own, come up with definitions of three of the five terms, and think of some examples of how the skills or traits could be used at work. Then do one of the following assignments:

For a paragraph: Choose one of the terms, and give examples of how you have demonstrated the trait.

For an essay: Write about how you have demonstrated the three traits.

CHECKLIST

How to Write a Definition

Prewrite ▷ Draft ▷ Revise ▷ Edit & Proofread

CONSIDER THE CONTEXT AND FIND A NARROW TOPIC. (See Chapters 2 and 3.)

☐ Identify your audience and purpose before choosing a topic.

☐ Narrow the topic by choosing a specific term.

☐ Prewrite to get ideas about the narrowed topic.

Prewrite ▷ Draft ▷ Revise ▷ Edit & Proofread

DRAFT A TOPIC SENTENCE (PARAGRAPH) OR THESIS STATEMENT (ESSAY). (See Chapter 3.)

☐ Decide what you want your readers to understand about the term.

☐ State the term and provide a definition for it. Your definition may include the general class of the term as well as details.

SUPPORT YOUR MAIN IDEA. (See Chapter 4.)

☐ Come up with essential characteristics of the term you are defining.

☐ Find examples and details to illustrate these characteristics.

WRITE A DRAFT. (See Chapter 5.)

☐ Put essential features and your examples and details in a logical order, usually order of importance.

☐ Include a topic sentence (paragraph) or thesis statement (essay) and all the supporting characteristics, examples, and details.

☐ Add an appropriate introduction and conclusion.

Prewrite ▷ Draft ▷ Revise ▷ Edit & Proofread

REVISE YOUR DRAFT. (See Chapter 6.)

☐ Make sure it has *all* four basics of definition.

☐ Make sure each paragraph is unified (all ideas should relate to the topic sentence).

☐ Make sure each paragraph is fully developed (there are enough supporting details to demonstrate the point).

☐ Make sure you include transitions to move readers smoothly from one event or example to the next.

Prewrite ▷ Draft ▷ Revise ▷ Edit & Proofread

EDIT AND PROOFREAD YOUR REVISED DRAFT. (See Parts 3 and 4.)

☐ Make sure grammar, word usage, and punctuation choices are clear, accurate, and effective.

☐ Check spelling and capitalization.

Chapter 12 Review

1. What is a definition?

2. What are the four basics of definition?

3. How do writers support a definition?

4. How is a definition usually organized?

Reflect and Apply

1. How is a definition essay different from a dictionary definition? How is it similar?

2. Interview someone studying in your major or working in your career. Ask the person how they have used definitions in their work.

3. What would happen if someone read or wrote a definition carelessly?

4. What was most successful about your writing for this chapter? What will you do differently the next time you read or write a definition?

Comparison and Contrast
Writing That Shows Similarities and Differences

Learning Outcomes | In this chapter, you will learn to

- List the four basics of comparison and contrast paragraphs and essays.
- Identify the subjects and the points on which you will compare and contrast them.
- Support the points of comparison and contrast with relevant and specific details.
- Recognize transitions commonly used in comparison and contrast.
- Write a comparison and contrast paragraph or essay with a clear main idea, detailed support, and logical point-by-point or subject-by-subject organization.

Every day we make choices: where to go, what to buy, what to eat, or how to spend our time. When a choice is difficult, we often put our options side by side to understand how they are alike and different so that we can choose wisely. When we look for similarities and differences in this way, we are comparing and contrasting. We compare and contrast at home, school, and work, paying attention to the side effects of two medications, this year's budget versus last year's budget, hybrid versus online classes, or the benefits of two job offers, among other examples.

Understand What Comparison and Contrast Are

Comparison is writing that shows the similarities among subjects—people, ideas, situations, or items; **contrast** shows the differences. In conversation, people may use the word *compare* to mean either compare or contrast, but this chapter distinguishes between the terms. Thus, you will be asked to *compare and contrast*, not just *compare*.

Four Basics of Comparison and Contrast

1 **Main Idea:** An effective comparison and contrast paragraph or essay has a main idea that reveals its purpose—to help readers make a decision or to help them understand the subjects.

2 **Primary Support:** It supports the main idea with parallel points of comparison/contrast.

3 **Secondary Support:** It develops points of comparison/contrast fairly, with supporting details for both subjects.

4 **Organization:** It arranges points in a logical order, either point by point or subject by subject.

In the following paragraph, written for a biology course, the numbers and colors correspond to the four basics of comparison and contrast.

1 Although frogs and toads are closely related, they differ in appearance, habitat, and behavior. 4 The first major difference 2 is in the creatures' physical characteristics. 4 Whereas 3 most frogs have smooth, slimy skin that helps them move through water, toads tend to have rough, bumpy skin suited to drier surroundings. 4 Also, whereas 3 frogs have long, muscular hind legs that help them leap away from predators or toward food, most toads have shorter legs and, therefore, less ability to move quickly. 4 Another 3 physical characteristic of frogs and toads is their bulging eyes, which help them see in different directions. This ability is important because neither creature can turn its head to look for food or spot a predator. However, frogs' eyes may protrude more than toads'. 4 The second major difference between frogs and toads 2 is their choice of habitat. 3 Frogs tend to live in or near ponds, lakes, or other sources of water. 4 In contrast, 3 toads live mostly in drier areas, such as gardens, forests, and fields. 4 But, like frogs, 3 they lay their eggs in water. 4 The third major difference between frogs and toads 2 concerns their behavior. 4 Whereas 3 frogs may be active during the day or night, most toads keep a low profile until nighttime. Some biologists believe that it is nature's way of making up for toads' inability to escape from danger as quickly as frogs can. At night, toads are less likely to be spotted by predators. 4 Finally, 3 although both frogs and toads tend to live by themselves, toads may form groups while they are hibernating. Both creatures can teach us a lot about how animals adapt to their environments, and studying them is a lot of fun.

In college, writing assignments may include the words *compare and contrast*, but they might also use phrases such as *discuss similarities and differences, how is X like (or unlike) Y?*, or *what do X and Y have in common?* Also, assignments may use only the word *compare*.

First Basic: Main Idea in Comparison and Contrast

The **main idea** should state the subjects you want to compare or contrast and help you achieve your purpose. To help you discover your main idea, complete the following sentence:

Main idea in comparison and contrast: I am comparing/contrasting subject X and subject Y to show that _____.

Then write a topic sentence (paragraph) or thesis statement (essay) that identifies the subjects and states the main idea you want to make about them. Here is an example of a topic sentence for a paragraph:

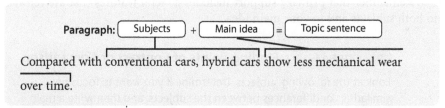

Paragraph: Subjects + Main idea = Topic sentence

Compared with conventional cars, hybrid cars show less mechanical wear over time.

[Purpose: To help readers understand mechanical differences between conventional cars and hybrids]

Remember that the topic for an essay can be a little broader than one for a paragraph:

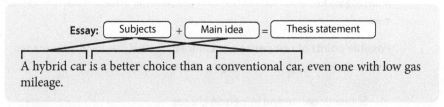

Essay: Subjects + Main idea = Thesis statement

A hybrid car is a better choice than a conventional car, even one with low gas mileage.

[Purpose: To help readers decide which type of car to buy]

Whereas the topic sentence focuses on the mechanical advantages of hybrid cars, the thesis statement sets up a broader discussion of these cars' benefits.

Second Basic: Primary Support in Comparison and Contrast

To create primary support for a comparison and contrast essay, you will list general points of comparison or contrast. A **point of comparison or contrast** is an aspect or feature that is relevant to both subjects. For example, if you are comparing two automobiles, points of comparison or contrast could include gas mileage, speed capabilities, and interior comfort. In the paragraph contrasting frogs and toads (p. 244), the points of comparison or contrast are *appearance*, *habitat*, and *behavior*.

The points of comparison or contrast that you choose should relate directly to the purpose of the essay. For example, if your purpose in contrasting two automobiles is to recommend one over the other, you should not include the companies' celebrity spokespersons as a point of contrast; while the companies may have different approaches to advertising, those differences are not relevant to the quality or value of the car.

Remember that primary support includes general features that are relevant to both subjects and to your main idea.

PRACTICE 13–1   Finding Points of Contrast or Comparison

Look at the following subjects. Determine if you want to focus on similarities or differences between the subjects, and then write a main idea statement. Finally, list at least three possible points of comparison or contrast related to the thesis.

Example:

Subjects: two credit cards

Main idea: The two credit cards I am considering offer different financial terms.

Possible points of comparison or contrast: Annual fee, cash advance fee, time before interest rate changes, finance charges

1. Subjects: online and in-person classes

    Main idea:

    Possible points of comparison or contrast:

2. Subjects: two social media platforms (TikTok, Discord, GroupMe, Facebook, Instagram, Twitter, etc.)

    Main idea:

    Possible points of comparison or contrast:

3. Subjects: Staycation and vacation

    Main idea:

    Possible points of comparison or contrast:

4. Subjects: Print book or ebook

    Main idea:

    Possible points of comparison or contrast:

Third Basic: Secondary Support in Comparison and Contrast

Secondary support in comparison and contrast gives evidence—details, descriptions, and facts—about each subject related to each point of comparison or contrast. In the sample essay on page 252, the writer mentions three points of contrast (primary support) between hybrid and conventional cars (subjects): financial benefits, long-term savings, and environment impacts. For each of these points, the writer gives details and examples (secondary support) about both hybrid and conventional cars.

The writer should also be careful to provide details fairly about both subjects. Giving extensive information about the gas mileage in a hybrid vehicle, for example, without providing similar data about the conventional car does not help the reader assess the importance of these numbers.

When developing secondary support for a comparison and contrast essay, some writers use a chart like the one below.

Main Idea: The two credit cards I am considering offer different financial terms.

Primary Support	Secondary Support	
Points of Contrast	Big Card	Mega Card
Annual fee	None	$35
Cash advance fee	$1 per advance	$1.50 per advance
Length of time before interest is charged	30 days	25 days
Finance charges	15.5%	17.9%

PRACTICE 13–2   **Finding Secondary Support**

Add a main idea, subjects, and points of comparison or contrast from Practice 13-1 to the following chart. Then list secondary support (specific details, facts, or examples) to complete the chart, using the chart above as an example.

Main Idea:

Primary Support	Secondary Support	
Points of Comparison or Contrast	**Subject 1:**	**Subject 2:**

Fourth Basic: Organization in Comparison and Contrast

Comparison and contrast can be organized in one of two ways:

1. A **point-by-point** organization presents one point of comparison or contrast between the subjects and then moves to the next point. (See the essay model on p. 252.)

2. A **subject-by-subject** organization presents all the points of comparison or contrast for one subject and then all the points for the next subject. (See the paragraph model on p. 251.)

When you are writing, consider which organization will best explain the similarities or differences to your readers. Whichever organization you choose, stay with it throughout your writing.

Using Transitions in Comparison and Contrast

Transitions in comparison and contrast move readers from one subject to another and from one point of comparison or contrast to the next.

Common Transitions in Comparison and Contrast

	Adjective + Noun	Conjunctive Adverbials	Subordinating Conjunctions	Prepositions
Comparison	one similarity	similarly	just as	like
	another similarity	likewise		similar to
	both subjects	in the same way		
Contrast	one difference	on the other hand	while	unlike
	another difference	in contrast	although	different from
	the most important difference	however	whereas	

Using a Graphic Organizer in Comparison and Contrast

A graphic organizer can help you see the difference between the two organizational patterns and plan for your own writing.

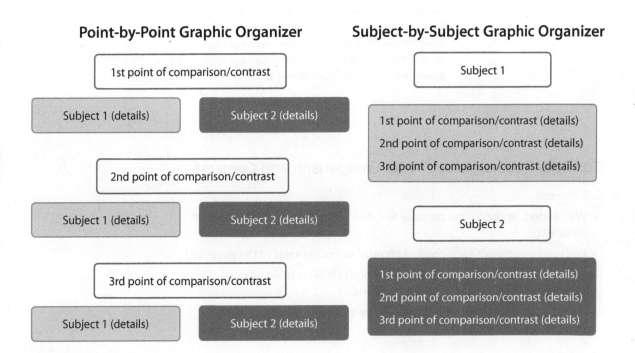

Point-by-Point Graphic Organizer

1st point of comparison/contrast

Subject 1 (details)   Subject 2 (details)

2nd point of comparison/contrast

Subject 1 (details)   Subject 2 (details)

3rd point of comparison/contrast

Subject 1 (details)   Subject 2 (details)

Subject-by-Subject Graphic Organizer

Subject 1

1st point of comparison/contrast (details)
2nd point of comparison/contrast (details)
3rd point of comparison/contrast (details)

Subject 2

1st point of comparison/contrast (details)
2nd point of comparison/contrast (details)
3rd point of comparison/contrast (details)

Paragraphs versus Essays in Comparison and Contrast

For more on the important features of comparison and contrast, see the "Four Basics of Comparison and Contrast" on page 244.

Paragraph Form

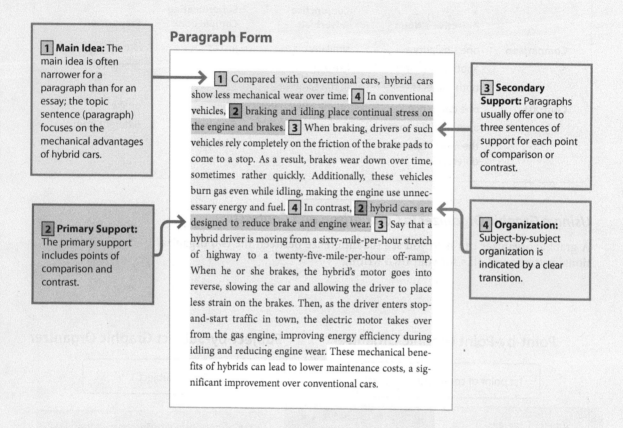

1 Main Idea: The main idea is often narrower for a paragraph than for an essay; the topic sentence (paragraph) focuses on the mechanical advantages of hybrid cars.

2 Primary Support: The primary support includes points of comparison and contrast.

3 Secondary Support: Paragraphs usually offer one to three sentences of support for each point of comparison or contrast.

4 Organization: Subject-by-subject organization is indicated by a clear transition.

[1] Compared with conventional cars, hybrid cars show less mechanical wear over time. **[4]** In conventional vehicles, **[2]** braking and idling place continual stress on the engine and brakes. **[3]** When braking, drivers of such vehicles rely completely on the friction of the brake pads to come to a stop. As a result, brakes wear down over time, sometimes rather quickly. Additionally, these vehicles burn gas even while idling, making the engine use unnecessary energy and fuel. **[4]** In contrast, **[2]** hybrid cars are designed to reduce brake and engine wear. **[3]** Say that a hybrid driver is moving from a sixty-mile-per-hour stretch of highway to a twenty-five-mile-per-hour off-ramp. When he or she brakes, the hybrid's motor goes into reverse, slowing the car and allowing the driver to place less strain on the brakes. Then, as the driver enters stop-and-start traffic in town, the electric motor takes over from the gas engine, improving energy efficiency during idling and reducing engine wear. These mechanical benefits of hybrids can lead to lower maintenance costs, a significant improvement over conventional cars.

Consider Readers as You Write Comparison and Contrast

Ask Yourself

- Will readers recognize the purpose and main idea of my comparison and contrast?
- Will readers connect each point of comparison or contrast to the purpose?
- Have I provided adequate details about both subjects to make the comparison and contrast clear for my readers?
- Have I used a point-by-point or subject-by-subject organization that readers can follow easily?

Essay Form

1

1 Main Idea: The main idea is broader than a topic sentence; the thesis (essay) in this case covers many benefits of hybrid cars.

2 Primary Support: Primary support lists the points of comparison or contrast.

3 Secondary Support: Essays usually offer three to eight sentences per body paragraph.

4 Organization: Point-by-point arrangement is clearly indicated by transitions.

They are too expensive. For the past two years, while trying to keep my dying 2009 Chevy on the road, these words have popped into my head every time I have thought about purchasing a hybrid car. But now that I have done some research, I am finally convinced: **1** a hybrid car is a better choice than a conventional car, even one with low gas mileage.

4 The first advantage of hybrid cars over conventional cars **2** is that buyers can get tax breaks and other hybrid-specific benefits. **3** Although federal tax credits for hybrid purchasers expired in 2010, several states, including Colorado, Louisiana, Maryland, and New Mexico, continue to offer such credits. Also, in Arizona, Florida, and several other states, hybrid drivers are allowed to use the less congested high-occupancy vehicle (HOV) lanes even if the driver is the only person on board. Additional benefits for hybrid drivers include longer warranties than those offered for conventional cars and, in some states and cities, rebates, reduced

licensing fees, and free parking. None of these benefits are offered to drivers of conventional cars.

4 The second advantage of hybrid cars over conventional cars **2** is that they save money over the long term. **3** In addition to using less fuel, hybrids show less mechanical wear over time, reducing maintenance costs. When braking, drivers of conventional cars rely completely on the friction of the brake pads to come to a stop. As a result, brakes wear down over time, sometimes rather quickly. Additionally, these vehicles burn gas even while idling, making the engine use unnecessary energy and fuel. In contrast, when hybrid drivers hit the brakes, the car's motor goes into reverse, slowing the car and allowing the driver to place less strain on the brakes. Then, as the driver enters stop-and-start traffic in town, the electric motor takes over from the gas engine, improving energy efficiency during idling and reducing engine wear.

4 The most important benefit of hybrid cars over conventional cars **2** is that they have a lower

impact on the environment. **3** Experts estimate that each gallon of gas burned by conventional motor vehicles produces 28 pounds of carbon dioxide (CO_2), a greenhouse gas that is a major contributor to global warming. Because hybrid cars use about half as much gas as conventional vehicles, they reduce pollution and greenhouse gases by at least 50 percent. Some experts estimate that they reduce such emissions by as much as 80 percent. The National Resources Defense Council says that if hybrid vehicles are widely adopted, annual reductions in emissions could reach 450 million metric tons by the year 2050. This reduction would be equal to taking 82.5 million cars off the road.

Although hybrid cars are more expensive than conventional cars, they are well worth it. From an economic standpoint, they save on fuel and maintenance costs. But, to me, the best reason for buying a hybrid is ethical: by switching to such a vehicle, I will help reduce my toll on the environment. So goodbye, 2009 Chevy, and hello, Toyota Prius!

> **PRACTICE 13-3**   **Organizing a Comparison and Contrast**
>
> Create both a point-by-point graphic organizer and a subject-by-subject graphic organizer for the main idea, primary support, and secondary support from Practice 13-2.

In a point-by-point comparison and contrast essay, writers may choose to organize points by **order of importance**, meaning that the most important point is saved for last. This strategy is used in the essay model on page 251. The order of the points will depend on the type of writing, the audience, and the purpose.

> **PRACTICE 13-4**   **Using Transitions in Comparison and Contrast**
>
> Read the paragraph that follows, and fill in the blanks with one of the following transitions: *also, another, however, like, one, the most important, similarly, unlike*. (Note that some answers will not be used.) When you have finished, create a graphic organizer to illustrate the organization of the paragraph.

>   Modern coffee shops share many similarities with the coffeehouses that opened hundreds of years ago in the Middle East and Europe. ____ similarity is that the coffeehouses of history, like modern cafés, were popular places to socialize. In sixteenth-century Constantinople (now Istanbul, Turkey) and in seventeenth- and eighteenth-century London, customers shared stories, information, and opinions about current events, politics, and personal matters. The knowledge shared at London coffeehouses led customers to call these places "Penny Universities," a penny being the price of admission. _____ similarity is that the old coffeehouses, like today's coffee shops, were often places of business. However, although most of today's coffee-shop customers work quietly on their laptops, customers of the old shops openly, and sometimes loudly, discussed business and sealed deals. In fact, for more than seventy years, traders for the London Stock Exchange operated out of coffeehouses. _____ similarity between the old coffeehouses and modern coffee shops is that they both increased the demand for coffee and places to drink it. In 1652, a former servant from western Turkey opened the first coffeehouse in London. As a result of its popularity, many more coffeehouses soon sprouted up all over the city, and within a hundred years there were more than five hundred coffeehouses in London. _____, in recent years the popularity of Starbucks and its shops, spread rapidly throughout the United States.

Read and Analyze Comparison and Contrast

To become a more successful writer, it is important not only to understand the four basics of comparison and contrast but to read and analyze examples as well. In this section, you will use a rubric to evaluate a draft paragraph written by student Devonta Allen. You will also review a student essay by Rita Rantung. In the Profile of Success, physician Garth Vaz uses comparison and contrast to explain the differences between dyslexia and ADHD. Finally, food and travel writer Nneka Okona contrasts stuffing and dressing.

Student Comparison and Contrast Paragraph

Read this draft of a comparison and contrast paragraph. For this first draft, the instructor asked the students to focus on the main idea, supporting content, and organization. Using the four basics of comparison and contrast and the sample rubric, decide how effective this draft of the paragraph is, and then recommend one or two goals for the student's next draft.

> **Assignment:** Write a paragraph in which you compare or contrast two kinds (or genres) of books, movies, or streaming programs. Think specifically about writing for readers who are younger than you are, and make sure you organize your paragraph according to one of the patterns we talked about: point-by-point or subject-by-subject. Leave yourself enough time to edit and proofread your paragraph.

Devonta Allen

Fiction versus Nonfiction

While there are many genres of books to read, most fall into two main categories, fiction and nonfiction. Fiction tells stories that are made up. They contain people, places, and ideas straight from the author's imagination. Some may have settings that are real places, but the people in it and the plot are the author's imagination. Fiction has many subgenres such as science, horror/mystery, historical, and romance fiction. Nonfiction tells about real people, places, and events. It is factual and informative to the audience, much like a documentary would be for movie viewers. There is some crossover when reading creative nonfiction, which is a story that really happened, but the author adds creative elements or fills in missing parts of the story. Both genres are great to read and have aspects that make them unique.

Rubric for Comparison and Contrast

	1 Falls below expectations	2 Nearly meets expectations	3 Meets expectations	4 Exceeds expectations
Main idea (first basic)	Main idea is missing.	Main idea identifies subjects to be compared but does not state main point.	Main idea identifies subjects to be compared but may not state main point or indicate a clear purpose.	Main idea identifies subjects to be compared and makes the purpose and main point clear and interesting.
Support (second and third basics)	Main points are unclear or missing; supporting detail is absent.	Main points may be unclear or lack supporting detail.	Main points are clear, but more specific details needed.	Main points are clear and well developed, with specific and relevant details.
Organization (fourth basic)	Organization is unclear or illogical, or points are missing.	Organization— point-by-point or subject-by-subject— is inconsistent, and transitions are missing or inappropriate.	Organization—point- by-point or subject-by- subject—is consistent, but transitions may sometimes be missing or inappropriate.	Organization— point-by-point or subject-by-subject— is consistent with smooth transitions throughout.

Evaluating the Paragraph

1. Does the paragraph show the four basics of comparison and contrast? Explain.

2. Using the rubric as a guide, determine the strongest and weakest parts of the paragraph.

3. Write a response to this writer, using one of the following to frame your response:

    a. One thing I would like to know more about is _____.

    b. What I liked best about the paragraph is _____.

    c. In your next draft, you might consider adding _____.

Student Comparison and Contrast Essay

Rita Rantung

Indonesian and U.S. School Systems

Preview Skim the first paragraph. What subjects and points of comparison will Rantung address?

Indonesia is not as famous as the United States; in fact, for many, it is non-existent. Nevertheless, it is still a great country to live in, and definitely, it is worth visiting. There you will find Borobudur, the largest Buddhist temple in the world, which was once considered as one of the world's seven wonders and is still a popular tourist site today. Indonesia is also the largest archipelago in the world, consisting of more than 13,000 big and small islands, bringing about the richness and diversity of its culture and language. Like America, Indonesia has been shaped by trials and triumphs that lead the nation to its distinct cultural and ideological foundation. Simply put, America's culture and dominant ideology give its citizens a lot more freedom of expression compared to Indonesia's. The distinct ideological foundation of each country inevitably affects the course of actions, goals, and objectives of each national education system.

archipelago: a group of islands

ideology: a system of values and beliefs

2   In Indonesia, starting with grade 4, a classroom appoints a student chairman and a vice chairman to manage the class responsibilities, including keeping the room clean and reporting to teachers. Students will remain in the same classroom with the same classmates during school hours for the entire school year, and the teachers rotate from classroom to classroom. Each classroom has its own class master, a teacher, who is assigned to put together the end of semester grading. School is in session six days a week, Monday to Saturday, and the school year starts sometime in mid-July and ends in the first week of June the year after. This gives students about a month of school break in addition to national and religious holidays.

3   In Indonesia, schools receive only some government support. In fact, Indonesia provides its students with only necessary things to facilitate their education. Transportation to elementary, secondary, and high school, for example, is up to the students. In cities, private cars or paid public transportation such as bus, taxi, becak (cycle rickshaw), or ojek (motorcycle taxi) may be used, but students in villages are left with almost no choice for their transportation. Cars and motorcycles are rare commodities in a lot of villages, so a bendy (buggy and horse pulling), the most economical option available for transport, is the favorite choice of transportation to and from school. Still, even the economical option requires a fee, and for that reason, students are likely to walk miles and miles, sometimes 8 to 10 miles one way, to school. In schools, the classrooms are furnished only with essential furniture, such as long benches paired with long desks for students, a small wooden desk and a chair for the teacher, and a blackboard.

A classroom usually has about twenty students, and two or three students will share a bench and a desk.

4   The relationship aspect between students and teachers in Indonesia is based on its hierarchical culture. Although there are some relaxed and easygoing teachers, for the most part, students are expected to respect the teachers and to submit without question. To some degree, teachers are allowed to give physical disciplinary actions when students misbehave, arrive late for school, or miss homework (at least that's what happened about twenty-five years ago, when I was in school). Conversations between students and teachers are limited to school subjects and almost never personal matters. Students are very intimidated by a teacher's presence; in fact, it is a common practice to hide and avoid being seen when students see teachers outside of school.

5   Finally, the curriculum in Indonesia is centralized and headed by the Ministry of Education and Culture. All over the country, students in the same grade level study the same materials. By the time students are in high school, they cover up to fourteen subjects in a week, including religion, national moral education, economics, and English, among other things. The compulsory attendance is from seven to fifteen years of age, yet this rule has never been enforced, for there is no such thing as a truancy officer in Indonesia. According to UNESCO's International Bureau of Education, Indonesia has two objectives for the national educational system. First, the nation wants to develop its citizens, whose values are based on the five principles of the state ideology: belief in one God, just and civilized humanity, the unity of Indonesia, democracy, and social justice for all. Second, it points out that the education system aims to support the Indonesian society, people, and state. Furthermore, it says that the Indonesian educational system maintains its cultural background, but at the same time, it strives to generate knowledge, skills, and scientific progress for the nation to move along with the development of the twenty-first century.

truancy officer: a school official who investigates students who do not attend school regularly

6   In the United States, on the other hand, students move from room to room to attend their classes while teachers remain in the same classroom; as a result, the responsibility to maintain the cleanliness of classrooms falls to the teachers and janitor, not students. The school day is five days a week, Monday to Friday. The school year starts sometime in the first week of September and ends in the middle of June, giving students about two-and-a-half months of long summer break along with winter and spring breaks.

7   U.S. schools are filled with conveniences that can help students soar in their education if they are willing to put in the work. Besides free public education through twelfth grade and school bus transportation, cheap but healthy cafeteria foods are also available. In almost all schools, students have their own desk and chair, and in some schools, especially at the high school level, they even have lockers. Gym rooms, computer and technology rooms, and labs with modern equipment are all within reach for most school districts. Perhaps these facilities show that the United States realizes how important it is to invest in the educational field, as it is one of the pillars of a great nation.

8   According to Thomas Lee, a graduate of the U.S. public school system, the relationship between students and teachers in the U.S. public schools is

somewhat relaxed; unfortunately, he adds, this relaxed relationship can be abused and taken advantage of by students who in turn communicate disrespectfully toward their teachers. Moreover, Lee says that the consequences toward student misconduct are generally minimal; teachers can assign after-school detention or send students to the principal's office, but no serious and physical disciplinary actions are allowed.

9   In America, although the national Common Core has been implemented, the educational system is still decentralized. To a large extent, each state is given the right to determine its own curriculum. For example, the Virginia Department of Education expected K–12 students in Virginia to cover at least nine subjects, including English, mathematics, science, history/social science, technology, fine arts, foreign language, health and physical education, and driver education. But in Pennsylvania, the code indicates that K–12 students have to cover six core subjects (English, mathematics, science, social studies, art or humanities or both, and health and physical education) plus five more approved additional courses, including foreign languages, vocational education, and industrial arts, computer science, and consumer education, among other things (Pennsylvania State Board). The United States also gives parents permission to home educate their children if they choose to do so; however, the homeschooling regulations can be different from one state to another. Another thing that varies from state to state is the compulsory attendance, but overall, it ranges from five to eighteen years of age. Unlike Indonesia, religious education is viewed as a personal subject in the United States; it is up to parents to attend to their children's spiritual education if they choose to do so.

10   Naturally, being a developing country, Indonesia looks up to America's great educational system, yet it does not forget—nor does it want to forget—its roots and identity as a nation. The educational systems of these two nations can be likened to two parenting styles: authoritarian and permissive. Indonesia leans toward the authoritarian style, while America tends toward the permissive. But in reality, implementing either style is easier said than done. Both the Indonesian and American governments consistently look for ways to improve their educational systems to first suit the needs of the nations and, at the same time, to engage in this competitive and ever-changing world.

Works Cited

International Bureau of Education. "Indonesia Goals and Objectives of Education." *UNESCO*, www.ibe.unesco.org/curriculum/Asia%20Networkpdf/ndrepid.pdf. Accessed 4 Mar. 2018.

Pennsylvania State Board of Education. "State Academic Standards." www.stateboard.education.pa.gov/Regulations/AcademicStandards/Pages /default.aspx. Accessed 4 Mar. 2018.

Virginia Department of Education. "Standards of Learning (SOL) & Testing." www.doe.virginia.gov/testing/sol/standards_docs/. Accessed 4 Mar. 2018.

Write to Read: Annotate

1. Identify the thesis statement.
2. Label and number the points of contrast.
3. Circle or highlight transition words.

Read to Write: Think Critically

1. What organization does Rantung use? Is it effective? Why or why not?
2. Does Rantung provide sufficient details to support her point? Explain.
3. What is the purpose of the contrast? Do all the details included reflect this purpose? Explain.

Use Reading Strategies: Create a Graphic Organizer

Following the model on page 249, create a graphic organizer for Rantung's comparison and contrast essay.

Reflect and Respond

1. How does Rantung's description of Indonesian classrooms compare with classrooms you have experienced?
2. Rantung suggests that a country's education system reflects important cultural values from that country. Do you agree? What values do you see reflected in the school systems you attended?

Workplace Comparison and Contrast

Dr. Garth Vaz

Dyslexia and ADHD

The following is excerpted from an article that Dr. Vaz published on the subject of dyslexia.

Preview Skim the first paragraph. Who is the intended audience for this essay? How do you know?

For decades, dyslexics have been one of the most misunderstood groups in our society. Misconceptions and misdiagnoses abound, as when dyslexics are

Profile of Success: Garth Vaz

Comparison and Contrast in the Real World

Title Physician, Community Health Centers of South Central Texas

Background I was born in Jamaica, and at school, everyone thought I was lazy because I couldn't read. I knew I worked hard but didn't understand why I had such trouble reading. When it came time to go to high school, I dropped out and moved to Brooklyn, New York. Shortly thereafter, I was drafted and served as a medic in the military, where I got my GED. After completing my service, I went to Central Florida Community College and transferred to the University of Florida. I dropped out eventually and worked for a few years as an orderly.

I was accepted at the University of Florida Medical School but flunked out, at which point I finally discovered that my reading and writing problems were caused not by laziness but by dyslexia. I petitioned the school to return and passed my courses with the help of a note-taking service. But I failed the medical boards twice before I was allowed accommodation for dyslexia.

Today I am a doctor working at a community health clinic that, in addition to other medical services, provides care for migrant workers and their families. I also travel and speak extensively on learning behaviors, especially dyslexia and attention deficit/hyperactivity disorder (ADHD).

Writing at Work For work, I write patient reports, speeches, and papers for publication. As a dyslexic, writing is still very difficult for me, though I have learned how to compensate for the difficulty. Because I still make lots of spelling errors, I have to read very carefully and reread anything I write to correct the mistakes.

Garth Vaz

Physician Community Health Centers of South Central Texas

COURTESY OF GARTH VAZ

mislabeled stupid, retarded, or lazy and placed among the mentally deficient. Many dyslexics have been placed in special education programs along with the slow learners. Later, after appropriate remediation, these same students have gone on to become educators, lawyers, and doctors. It is therefore of great importance that we be aware of the sensitive nature of dealing with these prize products of our society, our dyslexic students. We must be diligent in our efforts to help them in their struggle for success.

2   Such misdiagnoses are due to the lack of understanding of dyslexia and conditions such as attention deficit/hyperactivity disorder (ADHD), childhood depressive disorder (CDD), central auditory processing deficit (CAPD), and many others that share some similarities with common symptoms of dyslexia. I will now list, in brief, some of the differences in behaviors that characterize ADHD and dyslexia in children, particularly children in the elementary school classroom.

diligent: being careful, with effort and focus

3   A young person with ADHD cannot easily sit still, certainly a problem in the classroom. He often leaves his assigned seat, running around and attempting to climb on shelves, desks, and the like. When told firmly to remain in his seat, the child will try to obey but will squirm and fidget almost constantly, clearly in a state of agitation. He acts as if he is driven by a motor.

4   A child with ADHD often talks excessively and is unable to wait to be called on: instead, he blurts out answers and responses. He seems to just butt into games and conversations, not observing social norms that require a give-and-take among group members. Such behavior often alienates other children and frustrates teachers and others who try to maintain control. Other children may shun the child with ADHD. This ostracism, in turn, results in further negative effects, such as low self-esteem and greater isolation.

5   In contrast, a young person with dyslexia can sit still but has trouble organizing objects, belongings, and letters. She may mix up sounds, saying, for example, "plain" for "plan" or "seal" for "soul." She may have a stutter, furthering the frustration and embarrassment she already feels.

6   A dyslexic child typically reads poorly, confusing the order of letters, for example, in words such as "saw" and "was." Also, she may confuse words that have similar shapes or start and end with the same letters, as in "form" and "from" or the words cited in the last paragraph. While a dyslexic's reading is labored, her handwriting and spelling are usually worse. All of these symptoms of dyslexia, while quite different, often result in the same ostracism and loss of self-esteem. These problems then cause other behavior problems that are similar to those shown in children with ADHD and a number of other conditions. This explains why certain conditions are often confused. In addition, many children indeed have more than one condition. For example, over 40 percent of children with dyslexia have ADHD as well.

7   Unfortunately, because of budgeting restrictions, dyslexics are sometimes placed among the wrong group for remediation. In order for any intervention to succeed, it must be tailored specifically for the dyslexic. There are many improved techniques now being used successfully in reading remediation that are based on the Orton-Gillingham method. Arlene Sonday and the Scottish Rite Hospital have such programs on the market, and many other good ones can be located on the Internet.

8   There are many successful dyslexics in our society, some contemporary and others in the past. Albert Einstein, Benjamin Franklin, and General George Patton are a few who have made history. Athletes Caitlyn Jenner and Nolan Ryan and entertainers Whoopi Goldberg, Tom Cruise, and Steven Spielberg are among our contemporaries. Identifying with the successful dyslexic offers some hope to parents and children alike. The book *Succeeding with LD* is a collection of stories of successful dyslexics. The book was authored by Jill Lauren and published by Free Spirit Publishers. Each of these stories could make a book by itself but is short enough for the dyslexic to enjoy reading.

norms: standards or expectations

alienates: separates or causes to be isolated

shun: avoid

ostracism: being excluded from a group

Write to Read: Annotate

1. Identify Vaz's thesis.

2. Circle or highlight the transition words that he includes.

Read to Write: Think Critically

1. Why doesn't Vaz discuss ADHD in the first or final paragraph?

2. What is Vaz's tone in the final paragraph? How does his tone reflect his purpose?

3. Why does the author here use the pronoun *she* in paragraph 5?

4. What organization does Vaz use, point-by-point or subject-by-subject?

Use Reading Strategies: Analyze Word Parts

Many English words include a **prefix**, one or more letters added to the beginning of a word that change its meaning. Recognizing common prefixes, such as *pre-* ("before") or *re-* ("again"), can help you understand new vocabulary. Look at the following sentence from the essay, which includes four words with the prefix *mis-*. What do you think *mis-* means? Why do you think Vaz uses this prefix so many times in one sentence?

> For decades, dyslexics have been one of the most **mis**understood groups in our society. **Mis**conceptions and **mis**diagnoses abound, as when dyslexics are **mis**labeled stupid, retarded, or lazy and placed among the mentally deficient.

Reflect and Respond

1. What details does the author provide to describe ADHD? Does this describe you or someone you know? Explain.

2. Dr. Vaz suggests that both dyslexia and ADHD can lead to social challenges and a loss of self-esteem. How might the information in this article help teachers, parents, and students conquer these challenges?

Professional Comparison and Contrast Essay

Nneka M. Okona

Stuffing vs. Dressing: What You Call It Can Reveal Where You're From

Nneka Okona is a freelance writer from Atlanta, Georgia, who focuses on writing about travel and food. Her articles have appeared in the *Wall Street Journal, Food and Wine,* and the *Huffington Post,* where this essay first appeared in 2018.

Preview   This article first appeared in an online newspaper, and the writer uses subtitles to mark sections of her article. Skim these subtitles. How do they help her audience read more effectively? Do you think subtitles work equally well in print?

As a Georgia peach with roots in Huntsville, Alabama, I knew dressing to be a particular bundle of characteristics: day-old cornbread crumbled into a pile that looked as high as a mini-mountain in a mixing bowl, drippings from a turkey roasted in a Reynolds oven bag, with coarsely chopped green peppers, onions and celery showered into the mixture of bread and broth. And it was always perfectly browned and crispy at the edges once removed hot from the oven.

2   But ask someone else and you might hear about stuffing (as opposed to dressing), the different types of bread used to make it, or whether it's cooked inside the cavity of the turkey. Through the years, the differences between versions of this side dish have become an annual source of contention in November.

3   Which is the ultimate version—and whether it's called stuffing or dressing—is a subjective question at best, and limiting at worst. Differences seem to straddle geographic regions and, in some instances, racial lines.

4   When thinking of Thanksgiving, most Americans rely on the fable of European pilgrims and indigenous people gathered in an amicable setting to break bread. Today, we know it was not like that. But we don't know exactly what was served on that supposed first Thanksgiving. What we can definitively conclude is that whether dressing or stuffing was involved, the dish's bread base plays to the strengths and culinary traditions of the region where this side dish is being served.

subjective: related to personal tastes or preferences

amicable: friendly

culinary: related to cooking

Southern Living: a magazine covering travel, food, and culture in the southern part of the United States

Dressing Is for Southerners

5   As a black woman from the South, dressing is the only name I've ever known for the hallowed Thanksgiving side dish. This is the solid truth for most Southerners, whether black or white. *Southern Living* suggests that going to the map illustrates

this point succinctly. A quick scan of Google Correlate using the term "dressing" as a query shows that this time of year, finding just the right recipe and technique for making it is on the minds of those residing in Southern states, including Georgia, Florida, Mississippi, Alabama, Tennessee, South Carolina, and Arkansas.

6   The term *dressing*, per the History Channel, originated around the 1850s, when the Victorians deemed stuffing too crude for the dish to be named. This happened around the same time that the term "dark meat" began to refer to chicken legs and thighs. Just like today, cornbread was used in dressing because it was a staple in the typical Southern diet. Old, stale cornbread was repurposed instead of being thrown away, and was mixed with aromatic herbs, broth, salt, and pepper. Then it was baked until it had the consistency of a casserole, and eaten alongside turkey, collard greens, and sweet potatoes.

7   This is something that Kia Damon, sous chef of New York's Lalito who's originally from Orlando, Florida, knows to be true about the dressing she grew up eating. "Now, much older and wiser, I have so much love for dressing and watching my mother make it every time I'm home for Thanksgiving," Damon told HuffPost. Damon's mother's special dressing combines her own turkey broth with giblets and bits of the neck and boiled egg, and is served with a dish of cranberry sauce.

Stuffing Is for Northerners (and the Pacific Northwest)

8   Those outside the Deep South historically veered toward using breads for stuffing—sourdough, challah, leftover crusty baguette, even regular white sandwich bread no longer soft enough for sandwiches. Depending on which region you live in, stuffing can include seafood—mussels, oysters, clams—especially in New England or the Pacific Northwest.

9   Naomi Tomky, a food and travel writer based in Seattle, grew up eating stuffing her mother made with assistance from store-bought Stove Top mix. "For me, Thanksgiving is all about the butter-soaked stale bread that is stuffing. That means preparing it exactly as the Stove Top directions say on the box—I'm not fancy at all," she said. Tomky added that her mother made their family stuffing inside their turkey, but often there wasn't enough of it, so they made an additional pan of it on the side.

10   Layla Schlack, senior editor of *Wine Enthusiast*, said bread choice is crucial for the flavor outcome. "I like to use a combo of rye, wheat and maybe sourdough, so there's some tartness and nuttiness," she said. "It's a good foil for gravy."

Stuffing Is for Midwesterners

11   Prepare to have everything turned on its head. In the Midwest, things get a little muddled. Lacey Muszynski, a food and drink writer based in Milwaukee, said she's always called the Thanksgiving side dish *stuffing*, as do other Midwesterners. Generally, in the Midwestern states, it's called stuffing regardless of the ingredients or whether it's cooked inside a turkey. Depending on the family or cook, other ingredients can be tossed in—sauerkraut in the northern Midwest, wild rice in Minnesota, even dried cranberries or cherries, Muszynski said.

succinctly: briefly and clearly

Google Correlate: a tool that can show how people are searching for something on Google

sous chef: a chef who ranks second after the executive chef in a restaurant

12   A stuffing basic, however, cannot be missed. "In my family, the stuffing is the favorite item at Thanksgiving, and we use about a 50-50 mix of generic French bread and cornbread," Muszynski said. "My mom started making stuffing that way before I came around, and she got the recipe from one of the local newspapers, probably in the '70s or early '80s. We still have the clipping somewhere."

When Traditions Change

13   A few years ago, as I started to explore what Thanksgiving would look like as I created my own holiday traditions as an adult, I attempted to mimic the dressing I saw being prepared by my mother, maternal grandmother, and aunts.

14   It did not go so well.

15   I added fresh sage and other herbs in addition to roasted mushrooms for something a little different. But the cornbread and broth mixture felt watery instead of thick and homogenous like I'd always seen. After many trials and fails, my mother told me what I'd been missing: a box of Stove Top mix. Guess there are still surprises to the dressing I've come to know, love, and eagerly anticipate each year.

Write to Read: Annotate

1. Identify the thesis statement.

2. Number or note the points of contrast in this essay.

3. Circle or highlight the transitions.

Read to Write: Think Critically

1. What type of organization does this essay use—point-by-point or subject-by-subject?

2. Why does Okona say, "Prepare to have everything turned on its head" in paragraph 11?

3. Why does Okona include the comments of other writers throughout her essay? (As you think about this question, consider where Okona is from.)

Use Reading Strategies: Summarize

Review the skills you learned in Chapter 1 about writing a summary (pp. 18–20), and then summarize Okona's essay.

Reflect and Respond

1. Can you think of another dish or tradition that differs across regional or ethnic lines? What might you learn by contrasting different versions of the dish or tradition? Explain.

2. Does Okona suggest that there is a "right" name or recipe for a bread-based Thanksgiving side dish? Why or why not?

Grammar for Comparison and Contrast

In a sentence in the active voice, the subject acts on the direct object. The sentence below, for example, is in the active voice.

subject verb direct object

People used cornbread to make dressing.

In some cases, however, the person doing the action is either unknown or unimportant. In such cases, the writer may decide to use the **passive voice**. To form the passive voice, move the object into the subject position in the sentence and make sure the verb has a form of the verb *be* and a past participle. In the passive voice, the object receives the action of the verb, and the person or thing doing the action may not be mentioned at all. The passive voice in this example helps Okona keep the focus of the paragraph on cornbread:

Just like today, cornbread was used in dressing because it was a staple in the typical Southern diet. Old, stale cornbread was repurposed instead of being thrown away, and was mixed with aromatic herbs, broth, salt, and pepper. Then it was baked until it had the consistency of a casserole, and eaten alongside turkey, collard greens, and sweet potatoes.

For more information on past participles and the passive voice, see the section "Use Verbs Correctly: Passive Voice" in Chapter 20, pages 414–15.

Write Your Own Comparison and Contrast

In this section, you will write your own comparison and contrast based on one of the following assignments. For help, refer to the "How to Write Comparison and Contrast" checklist on page 268.

Assignment Options: Writing about College, Work, and Everyday Life

Write a comparison and contrast paragraph or essay on one of the following topics or on one of your own choice:

College	• Describe similarities and differences between high school and college (or two colleges you have attended), and give examples.
	• If you are still deciding on a major area of study, see if you can sit in on a class or two in programs that interest you. Then compare and contrast the classes. If this process helped you decide on a program, explain the reasons for your choice.
Work	• Compare a job you liked with one you did not like, and give reasons for your views.
	• Have you had experience working for both a bad supervisor and a good one? If so, compare and contrast their behaviors, and explain why you preferred one supervisor to the other.
Everyday Life	• Compare your life now with the way you would like it to be in five years (or with the way it was five years ago).
	• Participate in a cleanup effort in your community, and then compare and contrast how the area looked before the cleanup with how it looked afterward.

Assignment Options: Reading and Writing Critically

Complete one of the following assignments that asks you to apply the critical thinking, reading, and writing skills discussed in Chapter 1.

Writing Critically about Readings

Both Amy Tan's "Fish Cheeks" (p. 117) and Nneka Okona's "Stuffing vs. Dressing: What You Call It Can Reveal Where You're From" (p. 262) describe cultural traditions and the reality of change. Read or review both of these pieces, and then follow these steps:

1. **Summarize.** Briefly summarize the works, listing the points of comparison or contrast.

2. **Analyze.** How does each writer use contrast to develop the point? What questions does each piece raise for you?

3. **Synthesize.** Sometimes we are embarrassed by our cultural traditions, as Tan was, and sometimes we realize we still have more to learn about these traditions, as Okona did. Using examples from these writings and from your own experience, discuss traditions that both confirm and occasionally challenge our identities and connection to culture.

4. **Evaluate.** Which piece did you connect with more, and why? In writing your evaluation, you might look back on your responses to step 2.

Writing Critically about Visuals

Study the photographs below, and complete the following steps:

1. **Read the visuals.** Ask yourself: What details are you drawn to in each photograph? What differences do you notice as you move from the outdoor scene to the gym? (For more on reading visuals, see Chapter 1.)

2. **Write a comparison and contrast.** Write a paragraph or essay about exercising in a gym versus exercising outside. As you think about differences and similarities between the two exercise choices, consider how each might appeal to a student like you. What factors are most important as students decide how to exercise? In writing your comparison and contrast, include the details and differences you identified in step 1. You might also talk to friends who exercise regularly.

Writing Critically about Problems

Read or review the discussion of problem solving in Chapter 1 (pp. 26–28). Then consider the following problem:

> You need a new smartphone, and you want the best one for your money. Before ordering, you do some research.

Assignment: Consult a website that rates smartphones, such as www.pcworld .com. Identify three features covered by the ratings, and make notes about why each feature is important to you. Then choose a model based on these features. Finally, write a contrast paragraph or essay that explains your decision and contrasts your choice versus another model. Make sure to support your choice based on the three features you considered.

CHECKLIST

How to Write Comparison and Contrast

| Prewrite > | Draft > | Revise > | Edit & Proofread > |

NARROW AND EXPLORE YOUR TOPIC. (See Chapter 3.)

☐ Narrow the topic by choosing the subjects for comparison and contrast.

☐ Prewrite to get ideas about your two subjects.

☐ Consider your audience and purpose: Do you want to help readers understand the subjects or show that one subject is better than the other?

| Prewrite > | Draft > | Revise > | Edit & Proofread > |

DRAFT A TOPIC SENTENCE (PARAGRAPH) OR THESIS STATEMENT (ESSAY). (See Chapter 3.)

☐ Consider your audience and purpose to draft a main idea.

☐ Make sure your main idea mentions both subjects and the point of the comparison and contrast.

SUPPORT YOUR MAIN IDEA. (See Chapter 4.)

☐ Identify points of comparison and contrast.

☐ Use prewriting techniques to discover examples, details, and descriptions to support each point of comparison and contrast.

☐ Make sure you have supporting details for both subjects and for all points of comparison and contrast.

WRITE A DRAFT. (See Chapter 5.)

☐ Choose a strategy to organize your essay: point-by-point or subject-by-subject.

☐ Include a topic sentence (paragraph) or thesis statement (essay), the points of comparison and contrast, and all the supporting details.

☐ Add an appropriate introduction and conclusion.

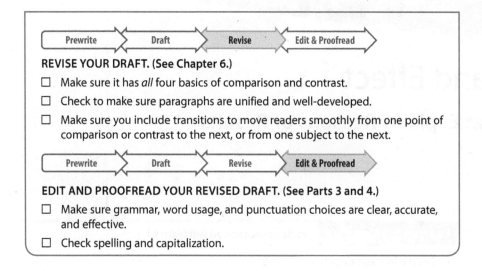

REVISE YOUR DRAFT. (See Chapter 6.)

☐ Make sure it has *all* four basics of comparison and contrast.

☐ Check to make sure paragraphs are unified and well-developed.

☐ Make sure you include transitions to move readers smoothly from one point of comparison or contrast to the next, or from one subject to the next.

EDIT AND PROOFREAD YOUR REVISED DRAFT. (See Parts 3 and 4.)

☐ Make sure grammar, word usage, and punctuation choices are clear, accurate, and effective.

☐ Check spelling and capitalization.

Chapter 13 Review

1. What is the difference between comparison and contrast?
2. What are the four basics of comparison and contrast?
3. The topic sentence (paragraph) or thesis statement (essay) in a comparison and contrast should include what two parts?
4. What is primary support in comparison and contrast called?
5. What are the two ways to organize comparison and contrast?

Reflect and Apply

1. Have you written a comparison and contrast essay before this class? If so, how was your experience in this class similar? What was new or different?

2. Interview someone studying in your major or working in your career. Ask the person whether they have used comparison or contrast in their work.

3. Did you get feedback on your writing for this chapter? If so, what parts of the feedback were most helpful?

4. What was most successful about your writing for this chapter? What will you do differently the next time you read or write a comparison and contrast essay?

14

Cause and Effect

Writing That Explains Reasons or Results

| Learning Outcomes | In this chapter, you will learn to |

- List the four basics of cause and effect.
- Identify two logical fallacies to avoid when developing support for cause and effect: post hoc and slippery slope.
- Recognize common transitions used in cause and effect paragraphs and essays.
- Write a cause and effect paragraph or essay with a main idea, clear and detailed support, and logical organization.

When we encounter events that affect our daily lives—traffic jams, an unexpected illness, or a change in salary—we ask questions: Why did this happen? What caused it? How will it impact the rest of the day, week, or year? In asking these questions, we are thinking about cause and effect.

Understand What Cause and Effect Are

A **cause** is what made an event happen. An **effect** is what happens as a result of the event.

Four Basics of Cause and Effect

1 **Main Idea:** An effective cause and effect paragraph or essay makes a point that reflects the writer's purpose: to explain causes, effects, or both.

2 **Primary Support:** It uses causes and/or effects to explain the main idea.

3 **Secondary Support:** It uses examples and details to support and explain the causes and/or effects.

4 **Organization:** It arranges the causes and/or effects in a logical order—by order of importance, space order, or time order—depending on its purpose.

In the following paragraph, the numbers and colors correspond to the four basics of cause and effect.

Followers of college football recognize several outstanding programs, including Notre Dame, Michigan, Ohio State, and Florida State. Recently, however, one school in particular has dominated the college football rankings, with championships in 2009, 2011, 2012, 2015, 2017, and 2020: the University of Alabama, known as the Crimson Tide. **[1]** What has led to Alabama's dominance? **[4]** First, **[2]** there is a tradition of winning at Alabama, **[3]** which has had eighteen national titles in its history, six under Paul "Bear" Bryant in the 1960s and 1970s, and six under current coach Nick Saban. **[2]** That tradition of winning has led to outstanding recruiting: Alabama has brought some of the best talent in the country to the university. **[3]** The 2017 and 2019 recruiting classes were ranked first in the country by 247Sports. Also, the ability to recruit well means that Alabama's teams have depth: they can substitute outstanding players throughout the game, bringing fresh energy to the field. **[4]** Another reason for Alabama's success **[2]** is the financial investment they have made in the team. **[3]** In recent years, the university has spent over $2 million annually on recruiting, and coach Nick Saban is one of the highest paid coaches in college football, earning over $9 million annually. Coach Saban does not coach alone: the university employs up to eleven assistant coaches as well. **[4]** But perhaps more important than the tradition and the money spent, **[2]** Alabama has a winning philosophy embraced by all the coaches: develop a solid defense and treat every opponent with respect. **[3]** Former Alabama quarterback Greg McElroy once noted that Coach Saban and his staff expect the same preparation each week, both for the lowest-ranked opponent and for the championship game. **[1]** With tradition, financial support, strong coaching, and a solid team philosophy, Alabama should continue winning for years to come.

In college, writing assignments might include the words *discuss the causes (or effects) of,* but they might also use phrases such as *explain the results of, discuss the impact of,* and *how did X affect Y?* In all these cases, use the strategies discussed in this chapter.

First Basic: Main Idea in Cause and Effect

The **main idea** introduces causes, effects, or both. To help you discover your main idea, complete the following sentences:

Main idea in cause and effect:	(This topic) causes (or caused) _____.
	(This topic) resulted in (or results in) _____.

Here is an example of a topic sentence for a paragraph:

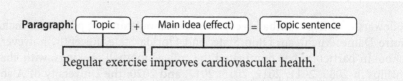

Remember that the main idea for an essay can be a little broader than one for a paragraph:

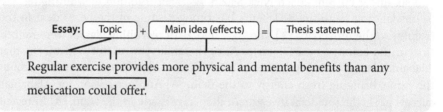

Whereas the topic sentence focuses on just one major benefit of regular exercise, the thesis statement considers multiple benefits. The paragraph and essay models on pages 278–79 use the topic sentence (paragraph) and thesis statement (essay) from this section.

PRACTICE 14–1   Stating Your Main Idea

Before starting this exercise, brainstorm possible causes and effects for the following topics. Then for each topic, write two main ideas: one that emphasizes causes and one that emphasizes effects.

Example:

Topic: Wildfires

Main idea (causes): Devastating wildfires arise from both natural events and human carelessness.

Main idea (effects): Years after a wildfire has been put out, communities may experience physical, social, and financial consequences.

1. Topic: A compromised credit card number
   Main idea (causes):
   Main idea (effects):

2. Topic: An A in this course
   Main idea (causes):
   Main idea (effects):

3. Topic: Waking up late in the morning

Main idea (causes):

Main idea (effects):

Second Basic: Primary Support in Cause and Effect

Major support in a cause and effect essay includes a list of causes or effects. It is important to think carefully when you are determining causes and effects; events, conditions, and problems often have multiple causes or effects, as the following chart illustrates.

One cause → one effect	Thunderstorm → game was cancelled
One cause → multiple effects	Finished degree → got a new job with a better schedule, able to spend time with family, have opportunities to advance in the company, etc.
Multiple causes → one effect	Lack of exercise, consumption of junk food and sweets, stress, sleeplessness → weight gain
Multiple causes → multiple effects	Joined gym, started shopping at farmers' market, got new regular hours at work, cut back on caffeine → started sleeping better, lost 10 pounds, found new friendships, have energy to finish writing projects
Cause → effect → effect → effect	Lost cell phone → missed a key business call → didn't get a contract → didn't get the promotion

As you choose causes or effects, make sure you avoid two common **logical fallacies**, or mistakes in reasoning: the post hoc fallacy and the slippery slope fallacy. The **post hoc fallacy** comes from a Latin phrase, *post hoc ergo propter hoc*, which literally means "after this, therefore because of this." We make this mistake when we look at two events and assume that the one that occurred first caused the second one. Superstitions, for example, illustrate the post hoc fallacy. Imagine a student whose teacher asks why she did not pass a test. The student responds, "Well, a black cat crossed in front of me on the way to school—and I just had bad luck." While the student may have seen a black cat crossing on the way to school, there is no logical reason to believe that the cat caused the student's problems on the test.

> **PRACTICE 14-2   Identifying Post Hoc Mistakes**
>
> Evaluate each of the following statements of cause, and identify any that are examples of the post hoc fallacy. If a statement is logical, write, "OK." Be prepared to explain why some statements are problematic.

1. John spent the past two weeks partying and getting in shape for football tryouts; he didn't even open his books. That's why he failed the test today.

2. John forgot to wear his lucky shirt to class. That's why he failed the test.

3. The professor forgot to return John's homework last week. That's why he failed the test today.

4. John injured his knees during a workout a few weeks ago. That's why he failed the test.

5. John's doctor switched his medication, and he has struggled to stay awake or concentrate for more than 10 or 15 minutes at a time. That's why he failed the test.

The **slippery slope fallacy** occurs when someone claims that a relatively small first step will lead to a disastrous chain of events. For example, a student who receives an F on a daily homework assignment might plead with her instructor this way: "If I get an F on this assignment, I will never be able to transfer to the university, graduate, or get a good job." The student is guilty of the slippery slope fallacy: A single homework assignment cannot lead to all the negative outcomes she suggested. *Post hoc thinking* leads to illogical cause statements; *slippery slope thinking* leads to illogical effect statements.

PRACTICE 14-3   Recognizing Slippery Slope Statements

Evaluate each of the statements below, and identify any that are examples of the slippery slope fallacy. If a statement is logical, write, "OK." Be prepared to explain why some statements are problematic.

1. I cannot believe I just ate that slice of pizza. There is no way I will be able to fit into my prom dress.

2. I should not have eaten that slice of pizza; I will probably have heartburn later tonight.

3. I should not have eaten that slice of pizza; it had mushrooms on it, and they always give me a headache.

4. I should not have eaten that slice of pizza. Who knows what kinds of preservatives it has? I'm going to get cancer.

5. I should not have eaten that slice of pizza. It was way too expensive; it will ruin my credit score.

Third Basic: Secondary Support in Cause and Effect

Once you have identified the causes or effects of an event or action, provide secondary support: details that will help your reader understand these causes or effects. Details may include facts, examples, descriptions, statistics, definitions, or expert opinions. The model paragraph on page 271, for example, illustrates key causes of Alabama's football success with specific facts: the number of national championships, the school's recruiting rank, and the amount of money spent on recruiting and on the head coach's salary.

> **PRACTICE 14-4** **Giving Examples and Details**
>
> List two causes or two effects for each of the topics in Practice 14-1. Then give an example or detail that explains each cause or effect.

Example:

Topic: Wildfires

Cause/Effect 1: Natural events/climate change

Example/Detail: Santa Ana winds and an unusual heat wave sparked major fires in California in August 2020.

Cause/Effect 2: Human activity

Example/Detail: The 2018 Carr fire was started by sparks from a trailer's tire rim.

1. Topic: A compromised credit card number

    Cause/Effect 1:

        Example/Detail:

    Cause/Effect 2:

        Example/Detail:

2. Topic: An A in this course

    Cause/Effect 1:

        Example/Detail:

    Cause/Effect 2:

        Example/Detail:

3. Topic: Waking up late in the morning

    Cause/Effect 1:

        Example/Detail:

    Cause/Effect 2:

        Example/Detail:

Fourth Basic: Organization in Cause and Effect

Cause and effect can be organized in a variety of ways, depending on your purpose. For more on the different types of organization, see "Arranging Your Ideas" in Chapter 5.

Main Idea	Purpose	Organization
The Black Lives Matter Protests in 2020 led to changes in police policies and review boards in several American cities.	To explain the effects of the protests	Order of importance, saving the most important effect for last
Although most protests were peaceful, a few ended in violence, as in Atlanta, Georgia.	To show that protests could have a negative impact on some cities	Space order
Each nationally publicized police killing in 2020 led to new and more intense protests.	To describe the spread of the protest movement over time	Time order

When you are writing, consider which organization will best explain the causes or effects to your readers. Whichever organization you choose, stay with it throughout your writing.

Using Transitions in Cause and Effect

Use transitions to move readers smoothly from one cause to another, from one effect to another, or from causes to effects. Because cause and effect can use any method of organization depending on your purpose, the following list shows just a few of the transitions you might use.

Common Transitions in Cause and Effect

	Conjunctive Adverbials	Subordinating Conjunctions	Adjective + Noun	Prepositions
Cause		because since	a primary cause a serious cause one cause the most important cause	as a result of because of due to
Effect	as a result consequently therefore		a long-term or short-term effect a primary effect a serious effect one effect the most important effect	

For more information on using and punctuating these transitions, see Chapter 18.

Using a Graphic Organizer in Cause and Effect

A graphic organizer such as the one below can help you plan your own cause and effect essay. Remember that you can add boxes for additional causes or effects as needed.

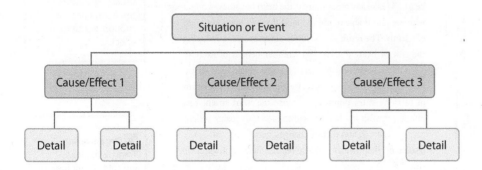

PRACTICE 14–5   **Using Transitions in Cause and Effect**

Read the paragraph that follows, and fill in the blanks with one of the following transitions: *as a result, also, a second, however, one, the final*. Not all transitions will be used. Then create a graphic organizer for the paragraph, following the model above.

Recently, neuroscientists, who have long been skeptical about meditation, confirm that it has numerous positive outcomes. ____ is that people who meditate can maintain their focus and attention longer than people who do not. This ability to stay "on task" was demonstrated among students who had been practicing meditation for several weeks. They reported more effective studying and learning because they were able to pay attention. _____ positive outcome was the ability to relax on command. Many people lead busy, stressful lives with multiple pressures on them—family responsibilities, work duties, financial worries, and uncertainties about the future. While meditating, people learned how to reduce their heart rates and blood pressure so that they could relax more easily in all kinds of situations. _____ outcome was a thickening of the brain's cortex. Meditators' cortexes were uniformly thicker than non-meditators'. Because the cortex enables memorization and the production of new ideas, this last outcome is especially exciting, particularly in fighting Alzheimer's disease and other dementias.

Paragraphs versus Essays in Cause and Effect

For more on the important features of cause and effect, see the "Four Basics of Cause and Effect" on page 270.

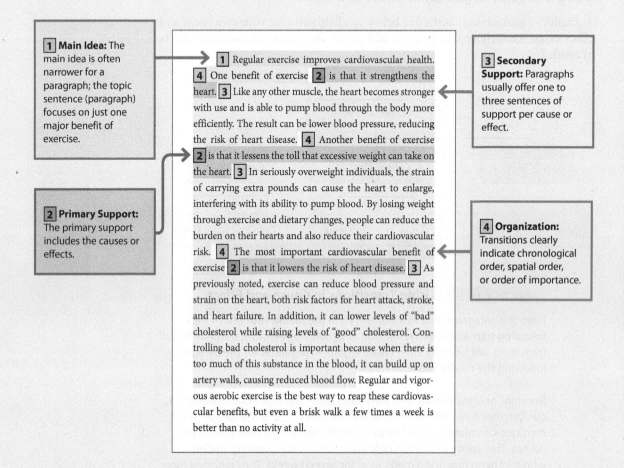

1 Main Idea: The main idea is often narrower for a paragraph; the topic sentence (paragraph) focuses on just one major benefit of exercise.

2 Primary Support: The primary support includes the causes or effects.

1 Regular exercise improves cardiovascular health. 4 One benefit of exercise 2 is that it strengthens the heart. 3 Like any other muscle, the heart becomes stronger with use and is able to pump blood through the body more efficiently. The result can be lower blood pressure, reducing the risk of heart disease. 4 Another benefit of exercise 2 is that it lessens the toll that excessive weight can take on the heart. 3 In seriously overweight individuals, the strain of carrying extra pounds can cause the heart to enlarge, interfering with its ability to pump blood. By losing weight through exercise and dietary changes, people can reduce the burden on their hearts and also reduce their cardiovascular risk. 4 The most important cardiovascular benefit of exercise 2 is that it lowers the risk of heart disease. 3 As previously noted, exercise can reduce blood pressure and strain on the heart, both risk factors for heart attack, stroke, and heart failure. In addition, it can lower levels of "bad" cholesterol while raising levels of "good" cholesterol. Controlling bad cholesterol is important because when there is too much of this substance in the blood, it can build up on artery walls, causing reduced blood flow. Regular and vigorous aerobic exercise is the best way to reap these cardiovascular benefits, but even a brisk walk a few times a week is better than no activity at all.

3 Secondary Support: Paragraphs usually offer one to three sentences of support per cause or effect.

4 Organization: Transitions clearly indicate chronological order, spatial order, or order of importance.

Consider Readers as You Write Cause and Effect

Ask Yourself

- Do I have a main idea that clearly indicates a focus on causes, effects, or both?
- Have I chosen causes and effects that are real, so readers can have confidence in what I'm telling them?
- Have I provided enough supporting evidence to convince readers about my causes or effects?
- Have I organized my causes or effects and the details that support them logically, so that readers can follow my writing?

Essay Form

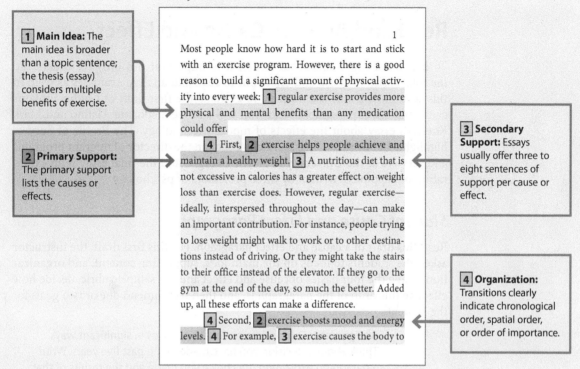

1 Main Idea: The main idea is broader than a topic sentence; the thesis (essay) considers multiple benefits of exercise.

2 Primary Support: The primary support lists the causes or effects.

3 Secondary Support: Essays usually offer three to eight sentences of support per cause or effect.

4 Organization: Transitions clearly indicate chronological order, spatial order, or order of importance.

1

Most people know how hard it is to start and stick with an exercise program. However, there is a good reason to build a significant amount of physical activity into every week: **1** regular exercise provides more physical and mental benefits than any medication could offer.

4 First, **2** exercise helps people achieve and maintain a healthy weight. **3** A nutritious diet that is not excessive in calories has a greater effect on weight loss than exercise does. However, regular exercise—ideally, interspersed throughout the day—can make an important contribution. For instance, people trying to lose weight might walk to work or to other destinations instead of driving. Or they might take the stairs to their office instead of the elevator. If they go to the gym at the end of the day, so much the better. Added up, all these efforts can make a difference.

4 Second, **2** exercise boosts mood and energy levels. **4** For example, **3** exercise causes the body to

2

release endorphins, chemicals that give us a sense of well-being, even happiness. **4** Accordingly, **3** exercise can help reduce stress and combat depression. **4** In addition, **3** because exercise can make people look and feel more fit, it can improve their self-esteem. **4** Finally, **3** by improving strength and endurance, exercise gives individuals more energy to go about their lives.

4 The most important benefit of exercise **2** is that it can help prevent disease. **4** For example, **3** exercise can improve the body's use of insulin and, as noted earlier, help people maintain a healthy weight. **4** Therefore, **3** it can help prevent or control diabetes. **4** Additionally, **3** exercise can lower the risk of heart attacks, strokes, and heart failure. **4** For instance, **3** exercise strengthens the heart muscle, helping it pump blood more efficiently and reducing high blood pressure, a heart disease risk factor.

3

4 Also, **3** exercise can lower levels of "bad" cholesterol while raising levels of "good" cholesterol. Controlling levels of bad cholesterol is important because when there is too much of this substance in the blood, it can build up in the walls of arteries, possibly blocking blood flow. **4** Finally, some research suggests that regular exercise can reduce the risk of certain cancers, including breast, colon, and lung cancer.

In my own life, exercise has made a huge difference. **4** Before starting a regular exercise program, I was close to needing prescription medications to lower my blood pressure and cholesterol. **4** Thanks to regular physical activity, however, both my blood pressure and cholesterol levels are now in the normal range, and I have never felt better. Every bit of time spent at the gym or exchanging a ride in an elevator for a walk up the stairs has been well worth it.

279

Read and Analyze Cause and Effect

To become a more successful writer, it is important not only to understand the four basics of cause and effect but to read and analyze examples as well. In this section, you will use a rubric to evaluate the first draft of Caitlin Prokop's cause and effect paragraph. Next, you will analyze Stephanie Alaimo and Mark Koester's essay about the effects of modern technology. The Profile of Success highlights the work of Christian Bello Escobar, the director of migrant programs and services at the University of North Georgia, and the final essay is an exploration of happiness, written by three professors of psychology.

Student Cause and Effect Paragraph

Read this draft of a cause and effect paragraph. For this first draft, the instructor asked the students to focus on the main idea, supporting content, and organization. Using the four basics of cause and effect and the sample rubric, decide how effective this draft of the paragraph is, and then recommend one or two goals for the student's next draft.

> **Assignment:** Our choices can affect our lives in significant ways. Think about a decision you have made in the past five years. Write a paragraph explaining the choice you made and the results of that choice. For your first draft, make sure you have a topic sentence with a clear focus on effects, along with supporting details. Also make sure your paragraph is arranged logically.

Caitlin Prokop

A Difficult Decision with a Positive Outcome

When my mother made the decision to move back to New York, I made the choice to move in with my dad so that I could finish high school. This decision affected me in a positive way. I got to graduate with my friends. Graduating with my friends was important to me because I have known most of them since we were in kindergarten. We shared a journey through childhood, and I wanted to finish it with them. Accomplishing the goal of graduating from high school with my close friends, those who accompanied me through school, made me a stronger and more confident person. Another good outcome of my difficult decision was the relationship I built with my dad. We never saw eye to eye when I lived with both of my parents. Living together for the past five years has made us closer, and I cherish that closeness we have developed. Living with my dad, I can go to Brevard Community College, which is right down the street.

In high school, I had thought that I would want to go away to college, but then I realized that I would miss my home. By staying here, I have the opportunity to attend a wonderful college that is preparing me to transfer to a four-year college and find a good career. I have done some research and believe I would like to become a police officer, a nurse, or a teacher. Through the school, I can do volunteer work in each of these areas. Right now, I am leaning toward becoming a teacher, based on my volunteer work in a kindergarten class. There, I can explore what grades I want to teach. In every way, I believe that my difficult decision was the right one, giving me many opportunities that I would not have had if I had moved to a new and unfamiliar place.

Rubric for Cause and Effect

	1 **Falls below expectations**	2 **Nearly meets expectations**	3 **Meets expectations**	4 **Exceeds expectations**
Main idea (first basic)	Main idea is missing.	Main idea does not suggest purpose, and focus on causes/effects is unclear.	Main idea suggests purpose, and focus on causes/effects is clear.	Main idea clearly indicates purpose and focus on causes/effects.
Support (second and third basics)	Causes/effects are illogical or support is missing.	Some causes/effects are logical but detail is lacking.	Causes/effects are logical, but more specific details are needed.	Causes/effects are logical with ample specific and relevant details.
Organization (fourth basic)	Organization is unclear or illogical.	Organization is inconsistent, with abrupt shifts from one cause or effect to the next.	Organization is logical, with some effective transitions from one cause or effect to the next.	Organization is logical with consistently clear transitions from one cause or effect to the next.

Evaluating the Paragraph

1. Does the paragraph show the four basics of cause and effect? Explain.

2. Using the rubric as a guide, determine the strongest and weakest parts of the paragraph.

3. Write a response to this writer, using one of the following to frame your response:

   a. One thing I would like to know more about is _____.

   b. What I liked best about the paragraph is _____.

   c. In your next draft, you might consider adding _____.

Student Cause and Effect Essay

Stephanie Alaimo and Mark Koester

The Backdraft of Technology

Preview What is a backdraft? Look the word up if you do not know the definition. Based on what you find, do you think the authors will examine positive or negative effects of technology?

You have picked up the bread and the milk and the day's miscellaneous food-stuffs at your local grocery store. The lines at the traditional, human-operated checkouts are a shocking two customers deep. Who wants to wait? Who would wait when we have society's newest upgrade in not having to wait: the self-checkout?

2   Welcome to the automated grocery store. "Please scan your next item," a repetitively chilling, mechanical voice orders you.

3   If you have yet to see it at your nearest grocer, a new technological advance has been reached. Instead of waiting for some minimally waged, minimally educated, and, most likely, immigrant cashier to scan and bag your groceries for you, you can now do it yourself. In a consumer-driven, hyperactive, "I want" world, an increase in speed is easily accepted thoughtlessly. We're too busy. But in gaining efficiency and ease, a number of jobs have been lost, particularly at the entry level, and a moment of personal, human engagement with actual people has vanished.

4   It seems easy enough to forget about the consequences when you are rushed and your belly is grumbling. The previously utilized checkout lanes at local grocery stores and super, mega, we-have-everything stores are now routinely left unattended during the peak hours. In these moments, your options are using the self-checkout or waiting for a real human being. Often in a hurried moment we choose the easiest, fastest, and least mentally involved option without much consideration.

5   We forget to consider that with the aid of the self-checkout, at least two jobs have been lost. As a result, a human cashier and grocery bagger are now waiting in the unemployment line. Furthermore, self-checkout machines are probably not manufactured in the United States, thus shipping more jobs overseas. And sadly, the job openings are now shrinking by putting consumers to work. The wages from these jobs are stockpiled by those least in need—corporations and those who own them.

6   The mechanization of the service industry has been occurring throughout our lifetimes. Gas stations were once full-service. Human bank tellers, instead of ATMs, handled simple cash withdrawals. And did you know that you can now order a pizza for delivery online without even talking to a person?

7   Sure, these new robots and computers reduce work, which could potentially be a really good thing. But these mechanizations have only increased profit

mechanization: changing from work done by hand to work done by machines

margins for large corporations and have reduced the need to hire employees. Jobs are lost along with the means of providing for one's self and family.

8   For those who find the loss of grocery store labor to be meaningless and, quite frankly, beyond impacting their future lives as accountants or lawyers, it does not seem to be entirely implausible that almost any job or task could become entirely technologically mechanized and your elitist job market nuked.

9   We are a society trapped in a precarious fork in the road. We can either eliminate the time and toil of the human workload and still allow people to have jobs and maintain the same standard of living, though working less, or we can eliminate human work in terms of actual human jobs and make the situation of the lower classes more tenuous. Is it our goal to reduce the overall time that individuals spend laboring? Or is it our goal to increase corporate profits at the loss of many livelihoods?

10   At present, corporations and their executives put consumers to work, cut the cost of labor through the use of technology such as self-checkouts and ATMs, and profit tremendously. But a host of workers are now scrambling to find a way to subsist. To choose the self-checkout simply as a convenience cannot be morally justified unless these jobs remain.

subsist: to exist or survive at a basic level

11   The choices we make on a daily basis affect the whole of our society. Choosing convenience often translates to eliminating actual jobs that provide livelihoods and opportunities to many. Think before you simply follow the next technological innovation. Maybe it could be you in their soon-to-be-jobless shoes. Say "No!" to self-checkout.

Write to Read: Annotate

1. Identify the thesis of the essay.

2. Highlight the effects introduced by the writers.

3. The writers ask several questions throughout the essay. Mark these questions, and then consider why the writers included them. Do they expect readers to answer them?

Read to Write: Think Critically

1. Do the authors use enough examples and detail to demonstrate the causes and effects in the essay?

2. Are the effects mentioned real and reasonable? Explain.

3. Notice the pronouns that the writers use in paragraphs 4 and 5. Why do you think they chose these pronouns? How do their choices affect a reader?

4. If you were reviewing this essay for class, what suggestions would you make for improving it?

Profile of Success: Christian Bello Escobar
Cause and Effect in the Real World

Christian Bello Escobar

Director of Migrant Programs and Services, University of North Georgia

COURTESY OF DIANA BELLO-ALVARADO

Title Director of Migrant Programs and Services, University of North Georgia (UNG)

Background Leaving everything behind to start something new is not easy, especially for a ten-year-old. My family emigrated from Mexico to the United States in 1998, and we have lived in the Atlanta metropolitan area ever since. Working hard at a young age showed me that education was one of the great equalizers. I earned a college degree in psychology from Georgia State University and was heavily involved in various academic and student activities, which led me to pursue a career in higher education. I earned a masters of education in professional counseling with a concentration in college student affairs from the University of West Georgia. As I finalize my doctor of education degree, I also write grants to the U.S. Department of Education to continue the work I do at UNG. The programs I lead help migrant and temporary/seasonal farmworkers and members of their immediate family to obtain a GED or start their college careers. I believe these programs empower others to break the cycle of poverty, and helping others to break this cycle has become my passion.

Writing at Work I write every day on the job. I write emails to students, faculty, or staff from the morning to the end of the workday. I've also been known to email during off-hours as I sometimes have my best ideas in the evening or at night. I stay in constant communication with my program staff. Once a week, I write down their overarching tasks and email the list to them to ensure we're on the same page. I write emails to students to ensure they complete their assignments, register for classes, complete study hours, or complete their financial aid applications. Furthermore, to ensure my students and staff have the tools to be successful, I am in constant email communication with various university departments, and all of this happens via writing. I also write grant applications so that our programs can receive federal funds; in these applications, I have to show why we need the program funding at our school. Lastly, at the end of the year, I complete annual reports that go to the federal government for the programs I lead.

Use Reading Strategies: Recognize Tone and Diction

The authors use emotional language throughout the essay. An author's choice of words conveys the tone, or attitude, expressed by the author. Identify five words that help you understand the essay's tone. Then consider what other choices the writers could have made. (For more on tone, see Chapter 2.)

Reflect and Respond

Consider a response to these writers: What are the positive effects of the technologies that concern them? Write a paragraph or essay in which you explain the benefits of technology and suggest solutions for the problems raised in the essay.

Workplace Cause and Effect

Christian Bello Escobar

Grant Application (Excerpt)

Preview In this application, Bello Escobar explains why (the causes) his university needs funding for a migrant support program (the effect). Skim the first paragraph of the grant application and the tables. What can you learn about the needs in North Georgia?

Why does the university need a College Assistance Migrant Program (CAMP)? The critical need for this kind of program in the North Georgia region stems from many factors:

The Presence of Migrant and Seasonal Farmworker (MSFW) Population with a High Number of Potential CAMP Students

2 Georgia (GA) experienced a 380% increase in migrant population growth between 1990 and 2012. A high MSFW population in North GA has existed since 1990; it has the second fastest growth rate among the 50 states, with 25.3% of foreign-born workers in GA employed in agriculture (Hooker, Fix & McHugh, 2014; Migration Policy Institute, 2017). According to a study conducted by Larson in 2008, GA ranked 8th highest among the 50 states in the number of MSFWs, with 117,119 MSFWs and family members residing in GA at any given time; with population growth, these numbers are likely higher today. Of all farmworkers in GA, 50.9% are classified as migrant, while 49.2% are seasonal. Table 1 indicates the number of active K–12 migrant students as reported by GA Department of Education's (GaDOE) Migrant Education Program (GaMEP).

3 There are an additional 5,042 current K–12 CAMP qualifying students who were at one time active in the GaMEP program, as the Gainesville, Georgia, area has become a settlement for migrant farmworkers over the years.

TABLE 1 Active K–12 Migrant Student Population in Georgia

	North Georgia	Georgia
Total Students	3,137	8,883
Percentage of Total Students	35%	100%

Source: Georgia Department of Education, Migrant Education Program, 2019

Low College Enrollment Rate and College Success

4 MSFWs and their family members experience low college enrollment rates in Georgia. The most recent GaMEP Statewide Comprehensive Needs Assessment (CNA) reported that this population is primarily of Hispanic heritage (96%),

low-income (77% of students of Hispanic heritage students are eligible to participate in the Free and Reduced Price Lunch program, an indicator of poverty), and first-generation college students (only 6% of migrant workers have a postsecondary education). In Georgia, only 27% of Hispanic students enroll in postsecondary education, compared to 63% of non-Hispanic students (Ga DOE, 2016). The CNA reported that of the Hispanic students who enter college in Georgia, only 9% earn a degree, compared to 31% of non-Hispanic students. In addition, the CNA stated that migrant students are perhaps the most educationally disenfranchised group of students in the educational system. They are highly mobile and have diverse linguistic backgrounds, which pose challenges that our educational system is minimally prepared to address. The report found a serious discrepancy in the performance of migrant and non-migrant students in Georgia high schools. Table 2 depicts the performance gap between migrant and non-migrant high school students.

disenfranchised: without a particular right or access to a privilege

discrepancy: a mismatch or difference between two things that should be similar

TABLE 2 State of Georgia High School End-of-Course Assessments by Subject

Subject	Migrant students scoring proficient or higher	Non-migrant students scoring proficient or higher	Performance gap
9th Grade Lit & Comp	18.3%	37.9%	19.6%
American Lit & Comp	17.9%	35.8%	17.9%
Coordinate Algebra	19.1%	30.0%	10.9%
Analytic Geometry	17.4%	32.8%	15.4%

Source: Georgia Department of Education Migrant Education Program, 2016

Economic Needs

5   The University of North Georgia (UNG) serves a 30-county area that experiences a higher poverty rate and lower median household income compared to state and national data, as shown in Table 3.

TABLE 3 Poverty Rates and Median Income Levels for Target Area

	Target area	Georgia	United States
Population	4,114,387	10,429,379	325,719,178
Median Household Income	$51,770	$56,183	$60,336
Living Below Poverty	16.2%	14.9%	13.4%

Source: U.S. Census Bureau, 2017 American Community Survey 1-year estimates

indispensable: essential, necessary

6   However, for migrant families in the target area, these indicators of economic need are even greater. Although MSFWs are an indispensable segment

of Georgia agriculture (U. S. Department of Agriculture, 2018; Flatt, 2019), they are among the most economically depressed workers. The incomes of about 23% of Georgia MSFW families are below poverty level (Georgia Department of Community Health, 2018). The national average annual income for agricultural workers is between $15,000 and $24,999 (U. S. Department of Labor, 2019). Annual attendance cost at a University System of Georgia (USG) 4-year institution is $22,000—more than the average MSFW family's annual income.

A Region Otherwise Unserved by CAMP

7   Currently, the only CAMP program serving the North Georgia region is the one at the University of North Georgia, which was established in 2015. There are no other CAMP programs between Georgia and Pennsylvania. UNG is deeply committed to serving the educational needs of MSFW families through its mission to provide broad access to comprehensive academic and co-curricular programs that develop students into leaders for a diverse and global society. UNG is a public institution that serves North Georgia by offering 120 academic programs on 5 campuses. UNG has been recognized on *Forbes'* Best Colleges list for four consecutive years (2016-2019), and *U.S. News & World Report* named UNG the 16th top public regional university in the south (2020). UNG's Gainesville campus houses the current UNG CAMP and High School Equivalency programs, and enrolls over 8,000 students, of whom 36% are of minority heritage, including a 22% Hispanic population (UNG, 2019). UNG-Gainesville is located in Hall County, which holds two out of the five GaMEP fully funded school districts: Hall County and Gainesville City.

8   With this application, UNG proposes to continue providing MSFWs in this high-need, underserved area the opportunity to break the cycle of poverty through UNG CAMP.

References

Flatt, W. P. (2019). Agriculture in Georgia: Overview. In *New Georgia Encyclopedia*. Georgia Humanities Council and University of Georgia Press. http://www.georgiaencyclopedia.org/articles/business-economy/agriculture-georgia-overview

Georgia Department of Community Health, State Office of Rural Health. (2018). *Georgia Farmworker Health Program — Policies and Procedures Manual.* https://dch.georgia.gov/divisionsoffices/state-office-rural-health/farmworker-health-program

Georgia Department of Education, Migrant Education Program. (2019). Personal communication.

Georgia Department of Education, Migrant Education Program. (2016). *2016 Statewide Comprehensive Needs Assessment & Service Delivery Plan Report.* https://www.gadoe.org/School-Improvement/FederalPrograms/Documents/MigrantEducationProgram/2016GeorgiaMEPStatewideCNASDPReportFINALJune302016.pdf

Hooker, S., Fix, M. & McHugh, M. (2014). *Education Reform in a Changing Georgia: Promoting High School and College Success for Immigrant Youth.* GA Migration Policy Institute. https://www.migrationpolicy.org/sites /default/files/publications/Georgia-EducationReform-FINAL.pdf

Migration Policy Institute. (2017). *State Immigration Data Profiles: Georgia* http://www.migrationpolicy.org/data/state-profiles/state/workforce/GA

University of North Georgia (2019). *Institutional report on minority students.*

United States Census Bureau. (2017). "Educational Attainment." *American Fact Finder.* http://factfinder2.census.gov/faces/tableservices

United States Department of Agriculture (2018). *Georgia Agricultural Facts.* Athens, GA. https://www.nass.usda.gov/Statistics_by_State/Georgia /Publications/More_Features/GA2018.pdf

United States Department of Labor (2019). *National Agricultural Workers Survey.* https://www.doleta.gov/agworker/pdf/NAWS_Research_Report _12_Final_508_Compliant.pdf

Write to Read: Annotate

1. Underline or highlight the main idea of the grant application.

2. Number each reason UNG is requesting money for the CAMP program.

Read to Write: Think Critically

1. This grant application explains the need for the CAMP program at UNG. How does Bello Escobar's use of sources and tables support his purpose?

2. Bello Escobar's application includes a number of abbreviations. How does Bello Escobar make sure his readers know what each abbreviation means?

3. Does this piece demonstrate the four basics of cause and effect (p. 270)? Explain.

Use Reading Strategies: Summarize

Review the skills you learned in Chapter 1 about writing a summary (pp. 18–20), and then summarize Bello Escobar's application essay.

Reflect and Respond

Bello Escobar's essay uses statistics to show why his university needs to fund the CAMP program. Which statistic was most powerful to you? Why? Do you think a similar situation exists where you live? Write a paragraph explaining your response to these questions.

Professional Cause and Effect Essay

Lisa Walsh, Julia Boehm, and Sonja Lyubomirski

COURTESY OF LISA C. WALSH   COURTESY OF DR. JULIA K. BOEHM   COURTESY OF DR. SONJA LYUBOMIRSKY

Happiness Doesn't Follow Success: It's the Other Way Round

Lisa Walsh is earning a Ph.D. in social/personality psychology from the University of California, Riverside. Julia Boehm is an assistant professor of psychology at Chapman University. Sonja Lyubomirski is a professor of psychology at the University of California, Riverside.

Preview Look quickly at the title and the first paragraph. What is the thesis of this essay?

Work hard, become successful, then you'll be happy. At least, that's what many of us were taught by our parents, teachers, and peers. The idea that we must pursue success in order to experience happiness is enshrined in the United States' most treasured institutions (the Declaration of Independence), beliefs (the American dream), and stories (Rocky and Cinderella). Most people want to be happy, so we chase success like a proverbial carrot on a stick—thinking that contentment lurks just the other side of getting into college, landing a dream job, being promoted, or making six figures. But for many chasers, both success and happiness remain perpetually out of reach. The problem is that the equation might be backwards.

perpetually: continually or constantly

2   Our hypothesis is that happiness precedes and leads to career success—not the other way around. In psychological science, "happiness" relates to "subjective wellbeing" and "positive emotions" (we use the terms interchangeably). Those with greater wellbeing tend to be more satisfied with their lives, and also to experience more positive emotions and fewer negative ones. Research suggests that it's these positive emotions—such as excitement, joy, and serenity—that promote success in the workplace.

3   Let's look first at the cross-sectional studies that examine people at a single point. This allows researchers to determine whether happiness and success are correlated. Relative to their glummer peers, happier people are more satisfied with their jobs; they also receive greater social support from co-workers and better performance evaluations from supervisors. Notably, it might be that bosses give happy employees higher performance evaluations due to a halo effect, where a favorable impression in one area (such as happiness) influences opinion in another area (such as work ability): e.g., "Tim is happy, so he must be great at his job too." However, there's also some evidence that people with higher wellbeing perform better on a range of work-related tasks: one pivotal study found that sales agents with a more positive outlook sold 37 percent more life-insurance policies than their less positive colleagues.

4   Happiness is associated with excellent work performance in other areas as well. People who frequently experience positive emotions tend to go above and beyond for their organizations; they're also less likely to be absent from work or quit their jobs. People with better wellbeing also tend to earn bigger salaries than those with lower wellbeing.

5   However, such cross-sectional research has its limits, since it can't establish which comes first—happiness or success. Longitudinal studies can help here, as they follow people over days, weeks, months, or years to see how they've changed over time. According to the longitudinal literature, people who start out happy eventually become successful, too. The more content a person is at an earlier point in time, the more likely she is to be clear later on about what kind of job she wants, as well as to fill out more job applications, and find employment. A key study found that young people who reported higher wellbeing than their peers just before graduating from college were more likely to receive follow-up job interviews three months later.

6   Positive emotions are also predictors of later achievement and earnings. In one study, happy 18-year-olds were more likely to be working in prestigious, satisfying jobs and to feel financially secure by age 26. In another, people who were more cheerful when starting college went on to have higher incomes.

7   But it's not enough to establish that happiness comes before success; we want to know, does one cause the other? After all, there could be some unmeasured variable, such as intelligence or extraversion, that's driving both wellbeing and work performance. Indeed, extraverts are more likely both to be happy and to earn greater incomes.

8   Well-designed experiments can control for these variables. For example, studies have randomly assigned people to situations that make them feel neutral,

cross-sectional: a type of research study that looks at a number of people at a single point in time, like a snapshot

e.g.: for example; from the Latin *exempli gratia*

longitudinal: over time

extraversion: a personality trait that inclines a person to find energy and enjoyment primarily from being with others

negative, or positive emotional states, and then measured their subsequent performance on work-related tasks. These experiments showed that people who are made to feel positive emotions set more ambitious goals, persist at challenging tasks for longer, view themselves and others more favorably, and believe they will succeed. Happy people's optimistic expectations appear to be realistic, too: on both clerical-coding assignments and digit-substitution tasks, people with positive emotions tend to do better and be more productive than those in the grip of neutral or negative emotions. The weight of experimental evidence suggests that happier people outperform less happy people, and that their positive demeanor is probably the cause.

> **clerical-coding:** a task requiring someone to convert information into a numerical code
>
> **digit-substitution tasks:** tasks requiring participants to replace numbers with simple symbols

9   From our review of more than 170 cross-sectional, longitudinal, and experimental studies, it's clear that wellbeing promotes career success in many ways. That's not to say that unhappy people can't succeed—which is just as well, as a sad person reading this and telling herself she must cheer up to be successful is unlikely to help matters! To the contrary, history demonstrates that depressed individuals such as Abraham Lincoln and Winston Churchill can accomplish incredible feats. Both negative and positive emotions are adaptive to situations—there's a time to be sad, just like there's a time to be happy.

10   So for any business leaders or managers reading this, we'd caution against hiring only overtly happy people or pressuring your employees to be more upbeat. Such strategies have backfired in the past—as in the case of the mandatory jollity imposed on staff at the U.S. supermarket chain Trader Joe's, where the policy ironically made workers more miserable. People and companies hoping to boost happiness in a healthier way would have better luck if they introduced positive activities, like performing acts of kindness and expressing gratitude.

11   The philosopher Bertrand Russell in 1951 said that "The good life, as I conceive it, is a happy life." But he went on: "I do not mean that if you are good you will be happy; I mean that if you are happy you will be good." When it comes to making your mark at work, we agree. If you want to be successful, don't hang around and wait to find happiness: start there instead.

Write to Read: Annotate

1. Underline or highlight the thesis statement.

2. What are the three kinds of studies that show that happiness can promote success?

Read to Write: Think Critically

1. What is the cause-effect relationship that the authors want to explain?

2. How is the essay organized? Point to the transition words that specifically show this organization.

3. Where do the authors caution readers about the way they interpret and apply their findings about happiness and success? What do these warnings tell you about the intended audience for this essay?

Use Reading Strategies: Vocabulary in Context

When professors write for a general audience, they may need to explain terms. Walsh, Boehm, and Lyubomirski, for example, refer to both cross-sectional and longitudinal studies. Did you notice that they also suggest what each term means later in the sentence, as underlined in the sentences below?

> Let's look first at the cross-sectional studies that examine people at a single point. (para. 3) Longitudinal studies can help here, as they follow people over days, weeks, months or years to see how they've changed over time. (para. 5)

In paragraph 3, the authors introduce the term *halo effect*. Use the sentences in that paragraph to find and paraphrase the definition of this term.

Reflect and Respond

1. Have you gotten the message that success makes someone happy? Choose one of the following, and describe how it promotes the idea that success leads to happiness: high school, social media, advertising, a movie, a television or streaming series, a civic organization, a religious organization.

2. Read the final sentence of the essay. Do you find this advice practical? Why or why not?

3. What causes happiness for you? How does your experience confirm, contradict, or complicate the findings described by Walsh, Boehm, and Lyubomirski?

Grammar for Cause and Effect

Look at the following sentence from the essay by Walsh, Boehm, and Lyubomirski. The subjects are underlined, and the verbs are double underlined:

> Relative to their glummer peers, happier people are more satisfied with their jobs; they also receive greater social support from co-workers and better performance evaluations from supervisors.

Did you notice the semicolon in the middle of the sentence? The authors are explaining two effects of being happy, and they have used independent clauses to introduce each effect. An **independent clause** is a group of words with a subject and verb that could be a sentence by itself. Writers can connect independent clauses using semicolons. For more information on clauses and how to join them, see Chapter 18.

Write Your Own Cause and Effect

In this section, you will write your own cause and effect paragraph or essay based on one of the following assignments. For help, refer to the "How to Write Cause and Effect" checklist on page 295.

Assignment Options: Writing about College, Work, and Everyday Life

Write a cause and effect paragraph or essay on one of the following topics or on one of your own choice:

College
- Write about the causes, effects, or both of not studying for an exam.
- If you have chosen a major or program of study, explain the factors behind your decision. How do you think this choice will shape your future?

Work
- Write about the causes, effects, or both of workplaces that treat employees like family.
- Write about the causes, effects, or both of miscommunication in the workplace.

Everyday Life
- Think of a possession that has great personal meaning for you. Then write about why you value the possession, and give examples of its importance in your life.
- Try to fill in this blank: "_____ changed my life." Your response can be an event, an interaction with a particular person, or anything significant to you. It can be something positive or negative. After you fill in the blank, explain how and why this event, interaction, or time had so much significance.

Assignment Options: Reading and Writing Critically

Complete one of the following assignments that asks you to apply the critical thinking, reading, and writing skills discussed in Chapter 1.

Writing Critically about Readings

Jelani Lynch's "My Turnaround" (p. 111); Caitlin Prokop's "A Difficult Decision with a Positive Outcome" (p. 280); and Lisa Walsh, Julia Boehm, and Sonja Lyubomirski's "Happiness Doesn't Follow Success: It's the Other Way Round" (p. 289) talk about taking control of one's life. Read or review these pieces, and then follow these steps:

1. **Summarize.** Briefly summarize the works, listing major examples.

2. **Analyze.** What questions do these pieces raise for you? Are there any other issues you wish they had covered?

3. **Synthesize.** Using examples from these writings and from your own experience, discuss different ways—big and small—in which people can take control of their lives.

4. **Evaluate.** Which of the pieces had the deepest effect on you? Why? In writing your evaluation, you might look back on your responses to step 2.

Writing Critically about Visuals

Study the following image, and then answer the following questions:

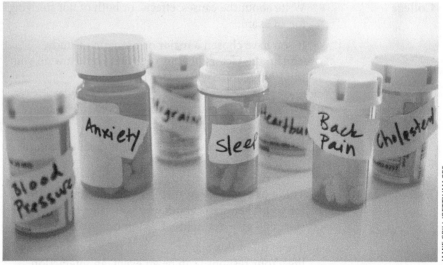

JAMIE GRILL/GETTY IMAGES

1. **Read the visuals.** What strikes you as important about this image? What situations might cause someone to have these medications on hand? What might the results of long-term use of these medications be? (For more on reading visuals, see Chapter 1.)

2. **Write a cause and effect paragraph or essay.** Using your notes from question 1 above as well as your own experience, write a paragraph or essay describing causes or effects of a highly stressful life.

Writing Critically about Problems

Read or review the discussion of problem solving in Chapter 1 (pp. 26–28). Then consider the following problem:

> You have learned of a cheating ring at school that uses cell phones to give test answers to students taking the test. A few students in your math class, who are also friends of yours, think that this scheme is a great idea and are planning to cheat on a test you will be taking next week. You decide not to participate, partly because you fear getting caught, but also because you think that cheating is wrong. Now you want to convince your friends not to cheat, because you don't want them to get caught and possibly kicked out of school. How do you make your case?

Assignment: Working in a group or on your own, list the various effects of cheating—both immediate and long term—you could use to convince your friends. Then write a cause and effect paragraph or essay that identifies and explains some possible effects of cheating.

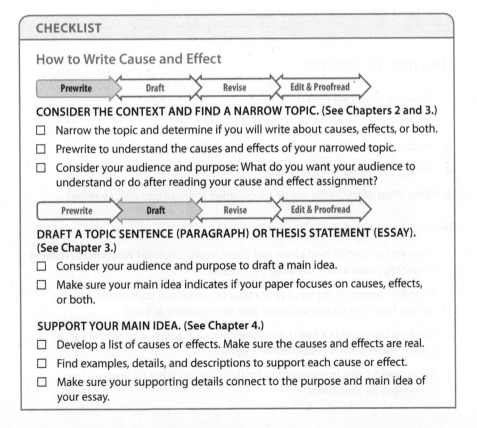

CHECKLIST

How to Write Cause and Effect

| Prewrite | Draft | Revise | Edit & Proofread |

CONSIDER THE CONTEXT AND FIND A NARROW TOPIC. (See Chapters 2 and 3.)

☐ Narrow the topic and determine if you will write about causes, effects, or both.

☐ Prewrite to understand the causes and effects of your narrowed topic.

☐ Consider your audience and purpose: What do you want your audience to understand or do after reading your cause and effect assignment?

| Prewrite | Draft | Revise | Edit & Proofread |

DRAFT A TOPIC SENTENCE (PARAGRAPH) OR THESIS STATEMENT (ESSAY). (See Chapter 3.)

☐ Consider your audience and purpose to draft a main idea.

☐ Make sure your main idea indicates if your paper focuses on causes, effects, or both.

SUPPORT YOUR MAIN IDEA. (See Chapter 4.)

☐ Develop a list of causes or effects. Make sure the causes and effects are real.

☐ Find examples, details, and descriptions to support each cause or effect.

☐ Make sure your supporting details connect to the purpose and main idea of your essay.

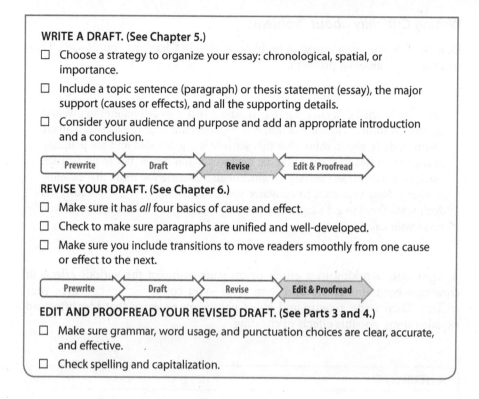

WRITE A DRAFT. (See Chapter 5.)

- ☐ Choose a strategy to organize your essay: chronological, spatial, or importance.
- ☐ Include a topic sentence (paragraph) or thesis statement (essay), the major support (causes or effects), and all the supporting details.
- ☐ Consider your audience and purpose and add an appropriate introduction and a conclusion.

Prewrite ⟩ Draft ⟩ **Revise** ⟩ Edit & Proofread

REVISE YOUR DRAFT. (See Chapter 6.)

- ☐ Make sure it has *all* four basics of cause and effect.
- ☐ Check to make sure paragraphs are unified and well-developed.
- ☐ Make sure you include transitions to move readers smoothly from one cause or effect to the next.

Prewrite ⟩ Draft ⟩ Revise ⟩ **Edit & Proofread**

EDIT AND PROOFREAD YOUR REVISED DRAFT. (See Parts 3 and 4.)

- ☐ Make sure grammar, word usage, and punctuation choices are clear, accurate, and effective.
- ☐ Check spelling and capitalization.

Chapter 14 Review

1. What is a cause? An effect?

2. What are the four basics of cause and effect?

3. What is the post hoc fallacy?

4. What is the slippery slope fallacy?

5. What kinds of transition words are common in cause and effect writing?

Reflect and Apply

1. Have you written or read cause and effect analysis before? What makes reading or writing cause and effect analysis difficult?

2. Interview someone studying your major or working in your career. Ask the person how they have used cause and effect writing at work.

3. Have you ever seen or heard someone commit a post hoc or slippery slope fallacy? When? What happened as a result?

4. What worked well in your writing for this chapter? What do you need to remember for next time?

Argument
Writing That Persuades

In this chapter, you will learn to

- List the four basics of argument paragraphs and essays.
- Take a position on an issue or topic and identify reasons to support it.
- Support the reasons with credible, specific, and accurate evidence.
- Recognize opposing viewpoints and respond with concessions and rebuttals.
- Recognize transitions commonly used in arguments.
- Write an argument paragraph or essay with a clear main idea, detailed support, and logical organization.

Have you ever tried to persuade someone else to agree with you or do something for you? Perhaps you wanted your instructor to extend a deadline, and you used the syllabus and course outcomes to make your case. Or maybe you supported one candidate for mayor, and you explained to some friends why they should vote for your candidate. In both cases, you were constructing an argument.

Understand What Argument Is

Argument is writing that takes a position on an issue and gives supporting evidence to persuade someone else to accept, or at least consider, the position. Argument is also used to convince someone to take (or not take) an action.

Four Basics of Argument

1 **Main Idea:** The argument takes a strong and definite position.

2 **Primary Support:** It defends the position with strong reasons while considering opposing views.

3 **Secondary Support:** It provides details and evidence to support each reason.

4 **Organization:** It organizes support (reasons and evidence) logically.

In the following paragraph, the numbers and colors correspond to the four basics of argument.

1 Even though I write this blog post on an 88-degree day, I am truly glad that I stopped using my air conditioner, and I urge you to follow my lead. 4 For one thing, 2 going without air conditioning can save a significant amount of money. 3 Last summer, this strategy cut my electricity costs by nearly $2,000, and I am on my way to achieving even higher savings this summer. 4 For another thing, 2 living without air conditioning reduces humans' effect on the environment. 3 Agricultural researcher Stan Cox estimates that air conditioning creates 300 million tons of carbon dioxide (CO_2) emissions each year. This amount, he says, is the equivalent of every U.S. household buying an additional car and driving it 7,000 miles annually. Because CO_2 is one of the greenhouse gases responsible for trapping heat in our atmosphere, reducing CO_2 emissions is essential to curbing climate change. 4 The final reason for going without air conditioning 2 is that it is actually pretty comfortable. 3 The key to staying cool is keeping the blinds down on south-facing windows during the day. It is also a good idea to open windows throughout the home for cross-ventilation while turning on ceiling fans to improve air circulation. Although some people argue that using fans is just as bad as switching on the air conditioner, fans use far less electricity. In closing, let me make you a promise: the sooner you give up air conditioning, the sooner you will get comfortable with the change — and the sooner you and the planet will reap the rewards.

In college, writing assignments might include questions or statements such as the following: *Do you agree or disagree with this point? Defend or refute this idea or proposal. Is this idea or proposal fair and just?* In all these cases, use the strategies discussed in this chapter.

First Basic: Main Idea in Argument

Your **main idea** in argument is the position you take on the issue (or topic) about which you are writing. In formal discussions of argument, the main idea is called a **claim.** When you are free to choose an issue, choose something that matters to you. When you are assigned an issue, try to find some part of it that matters to you. You might try starting with a "should" or "should not" sentence:

Main idea in argument: College football players should/should not be paid.

If you have trouble seeing how an issue matters or finding a claim, talk about it with a partner or write down ideas about it using the following tips:

- Talk to others to understand what different positions on the issue might be.
- Imagine yourself arguing your position with someone who disagrees.
- Imagine that your whole grade rests on persuading your instructor to agree with your position.
- Imagine how this issue could affect you or your family personally.
- Imagine that you are representing a large group of people who care about the issue very much and whose lives will be forever changed by it. It is up to you to win their case.

In argument, the topic sentence (in a paragraph) or thesis statement (in an essay) usually includes the issue/topic and states the writer's position on it. Here is an example of a topic sentence for a paragraph:

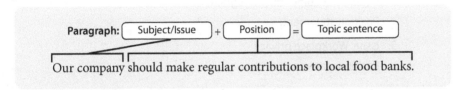

Paragraph: Subject/Issue + Position = Topic sentence

Our company should make regular contributions to local food banks.

Remember that the main idea for an essay can be a little broader than one for a paragraph:

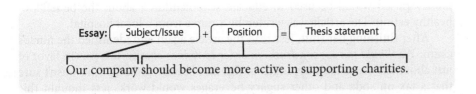

Essay: Subject/Issue + Position = Thesis statement

Our company should become more active in supporting charities.

Whereas the topic sentence focuses on just one type of charitable organization, the thesis statement sets up a discussion of different ways to help different charities. The paragraph and essay models on pages 310–11 use the topic sentence (paragraph) and thesis statement (essay) from this section.

Writing a Statement of Your Position

Write a statement of your position for each item.

Example:

Issue: Cost of college education

Position statement: Students who maintain a steady GPA should receive free tuition at state colleges.

1. Issue: Lab testing on animals

   Position statement:

2. Issue: Political advertisements

   Position statement:

3. Issue: Athletes' salaries

   Position statement:

4. Issue: Undocumented immigrants

   Position statement:

5. Issue: Workplace privacy

   Position statement:

   Jess, a college student working on sharpening her reading and writing skills, used these skills while working on an argument paper for her English class. She got an idea for the paper while waiting to start her shift at a local restaurant. Scrolling through the newsfeed on her phone, she saw a link to an article about the city's plan to tax soda and other sugary drinks to help reduce obesity. The money raised would be used to educate schoolchildren about the benefits of healthy eating. The article was written by a nurse from a local hospital.

   After finishing her shift, Jess read the article again and identified the nurse's claim: *We should tax sugary drinks in order to reduce obesity.* Jess was in favor of just about any reasonable approach to fighting obesity, although she wasn't sure that a tax on soda and other sugary beverages would work. Jess thought this would be a good topic for a paper, but she needed to do some careful thinking before writing. Jess made a note of her preliminary claim, and she set aside some time to think about the issue more carefully later.

Preliminary main idea: Taxing sugary drinks might be a good way to reduce obesity.

Second Basic: Primary Support in Argument

Primary support in an argument includes the reasons for your position as well as attention to the views of those who disagree with you. An opposing view is called a **counterclaim**; reasons that support counterclaims are called **counterarguments**.

In order to write about the issue of a soda tax, Jess had to identify her reasons and consider any possible counterarguments. She decided to record her thinking in a notebook, so she made a chart with three columns. Jess read the article again, and she identified two main reasons for the author's claim. She wrote those in the first column. Next, she tried to identify some of the **assumptions** (unquestioned ideas or opinions) behind the author's point. She put those assumptions in the second column. Finally, she questioned each of the writer's assumptions, trying to put herself in the shoes of someone opposed to beverage taxes. She noted her questions in the third column.

The Author's Reasons and Evidence	The Author's Assumptions	Questions the Other Side Might Ask about the Assumptions
"We have a problem with obesity. Since 2010, obesity in our city has risen from 26 percent to 33 percent. At the same time, sales of soda and sweet tea in 16-ounce containers and higher have increased by 10 percent."	Sugary drinks, like soda, energy drinks, and sweetened tea, are making people fat.	Soft drinks may not be the only cause of obesity. Why target sugary drinks instead of other junk food? Aren't French fries just as bad for the waistline as soda is?
"We need to discourage people from drinking so much soda. A tax of 20 to 25 cents per drink would reduce consumption of these beverages."	People won't buy as many sodas if they cost more and will therefore gain less weight.	Really? It's easy for me to say that this tax would work because I'm not a big fan of these drinks. But if they taxed coffee, the taxes would have to be pretty big to break my four-cup-a-day habit. And what if people are eating food that causes them to gain weight; how much difference would cutting out sugary drinks really make?
"The tax revenues would benefit the public through an education program."	Children are more likely to make healthy eating choices if they are provided with information on good nutrition.	Why not promote health information anyway, without taxing the drinks? And is there evidence that providing this kind of information makes a difference?

After considering the author's ideas, Jess decided to explore her own reasons for supporting the tax. Once again, Jess made a chart with three columns. She listed her reasons, the assumptions behind them, and questions that opponents might ask about the assumptions.

My Reasons	My Assumptions	Questions Opponents Might Ask about These Assumptions
"If we reduce obesity, medical expenses will go down."	Taxing beverages will reduce obesity. Obesity causes medical problems that cost a lot of money.	Do we know that taxing beverages will reduce obesity? Is there evidence that obesity increases medical costs? What kinds of costs?
"The tax will also help reduce obesity by paying for education in our schools."	If we teach children about healthy eating, they will develop good habits.	Sometimes I do things even when I know they aren't healthy. How do I know an education program will make a difference?

Creating charts like these helped Jess identify three things: reasons (column 1), assumptions that need supporting evidence (column 2), and possible questions and counterarguments to consider (column 3).

Third Basic: Secondary Support in Argument

Secondary support in argument includes the evidence that backs up reasons or addresses counterarguments. Jess, for example, started with the assumptions and questions from columns 2 and 3 of her charts as she looked for evidence. She knew her own **opinions**, which are beliefs that cannot be proved or disproved, would not convince her readers. In order to support her position on the sugar tax, she would need to gather the following types of evidence, which are used most often to support arguments:

- **Facts:** *Statements or observations that can be proved.* One type of fact is statistics, or real numbers taken from carefully designed studies of an issue. The article Jess read included statistics, such as the increased percentage of obesity in the city.

    CAUTION: Be sure to check the context and source of any statistical data. For example, if a source says that 75 percent of college students surveyed do not support a tax on soda, you need to know how many students were surveyed and where those students came from. If seven out of ten students, all identified as above-average soda drinkers, said they did not support the tax, how useful is this information? How representative is this sample? Ask who paid for the study. If a group of companies that sell sugary drinks provided this statistic, you should look for information from other sources that do not invest in the soft drink market.

- **Examples:** *Specific information or experiences that support a position.* Examples can come from a writer's reading and research, or they may be drawn from the writer's own life. Jess had a high school friend who loved to get 32-ounce sodas after school every day, and he had a problem with weight. She considered using her friend as an example in the paper.

    > **CAUTION:** Do not overgeneralize based on one or two examples. **Overgeneralizing** means drawing a conclusion based on only a few examples. Jess cannot conclude that sodas cause obesity based on one example.

- **Expert Opinions:** *The opinions of people considered knowledgeable about a topic because of their credentials (education, work, experience, or research).*

    > **CAUTION:** It is important to investigate expert opinions carefully. For example, economics professors might be very knowledgeable about the possible benefits and drawbacks of beverage taxes. They probably would not be the best source of information on the health effects of soda.

- **Predictions:** *Forecasts of the possible outcomes of events or actions.* These forecasts should be the informed or educated views of experts, not the best guesses of nonexperts.

PRACTICE 15–2 Identifying Types of Evidence

Jess talked to a librarian who helped her find sources that could provide evidence about her topic. The following chart shows the evidence that Jess pulled together to address her assumptions and her questions about them. Determine which kind of evidence Jess found: fact, example, expert opinion, or prediction. (Answers may include more than one type of evidence.) The first one has been done for you.

Assumptions/Questions to Investigate	Evidence in Response to Assumptions and Questions
To what degree do sugary drinks contribute to obesity?	**Example:** According to the Centers for Disease Control and Prevention, about half of all Americans get a major portion of their daily calories from sweetened beverages. Type of evidence: _____Fact_____ 1. In the *Journal of Pediatrics,* Robert Murray reported that one-fourth of U.S. teenagers drink as many as four cans of soda or fruit drinks a day, each one containing about 150 calories. That translates to a total of 600 calories a day, the equivalent of an additional meal. Type of evidence: _____ 2. Kerry Neville, a registered dietician, says, "Sugary foods and beverages do not cause obesity—no single food does. Although it sounds simplistic, obesity is a consequence of eating too many calories and expending too few." Type of evidence: _____

Do sugary drinks deserve to be targeted more than other dietary factors that can contribute to obesity?	3. My brother, his wife, and their three kids are all big soda drinkers, and they are all overweight. They also eat lots of junk food, however, so it is hard to tell how much the soda is to blame for their weight. Type of evidence: _____
	4. The Center for Science in the Public Interest says that sugary beverages are more likely to cause weight gain than solid foods are. After eating solid food, people tend to reduce their consumption of other calorie sources. Unlike solid foods, however, sugary beverages do not make people feel full. Therefore, they may add on calories to satisfy their hunger. Type of evidence: _____
To what degree would taxes on sugary drinks discourage people from buying these beverages and reduce obesity?	5. A panel of tax experts says that the taxes would have to be pretty significant to affect consumer behavior. The average national tax on a 12-ounce bottle of soda is 5 cents, and that has not provided enough discouragement. Type of evidence: _____
	6. In the *New England Journal of Medicine*, Kelly D. Brownell, director of the World Food Policy Center, says that a penny-per-ounce tax on sugary beverages could reduce consumption of these beverages by more than 10 percent. Type of evidence: _____
Would the taxes have any other benefits?	7. Brownell says that taxing sugary beverages could not only reduce the consumption of sugary beverages, but also reduce public expenditures on obesity. Each year, about $79 billion goes toward the health-care costs of overweight and obese individuals. Approximately half of these costs are paid by taxpayers. Type of evidence: _____
	8. Brownell also believes that the tax revenues from sugary beverages should be used for programs to prevent childhood obesity. Type of evidence: _____

PRACTICE 15-3   **Deepening the Search for Evidence**

Come up with at least one other question that could be raised about the sugary drinks tax issue. Then list the type(s) of evidence (such as personal examples, expert opinions, or predictions) that could help answer the question.

Question(s):

Type(s) of evidence:

Evaluating the Evidence

As Jess reviewed her sources, she thought critically about the evidence. According to her instructor, strong supporting evidence is accurate, **relevant** (closely related to the subject), and **credible** (trustworthy); also, whenever possible, it should come from an unbiased source. A source that is **biased** does not consider both sides fairly. For example, a referee who calls penalties on only one team (even though both are committing the same fouls) might be accused of bias; she did not treat both teams fairly and equally.

To test the strength of her evidence, Jess asked these questions:

- Are my facts and examples accurate? How do I know?
- Are my facts, examples, expert opinions, and predictions relevant, or do they distract my reader?
- Is the evidence from a credible source? Is it a recognized organization? Does the author have relevant credentials? Does anything about it seem suspicious? Does the evidence include vague sources ("Everyone knows" or "People say")?
- Does the source present evidence fairly, or does it appear to be biased toward one side or the other?

PRACTICE 15-4   **Reviewing the Evidence**

Review each position and supporting reason that follows. One piece of evidence is weak because it does not support the stated reason effectively. Select the letter of the weak evidence, and be prepared to state why it is weak.

Example:

Position: Advertisements should not use skinny models.

Reason: Advertising should not promote an unhealthy and unrealistic ideal.

a. Models including Katie Willcox, Crystal Renn, and Kylie Bisutti report pressure to be skinny — resulting in extreme and unhealthy diets.

b. Everyone knows that most people are not that thin.

c. A survey of girls shows that they think that they should be as thin as models.

d. A study from researchers in London showed that seeing very skinny models in advertisements raised body-image anxiety for women.

Not strong evidence because *"Everyone" is not a credible source*

1. **Position:** People who own guns should not be allowed to keep them at home.

   Reason: It is dangerous to keep a gun in the house.

   a. Guns can go off by accident.

   b. Keeping guns at home has been found to increase the risk of home suicides and adolescent suicides.

   c. Just last week, a story in the newspaper told about a man who, in a fit of rage, took his gun out of a drawer and shot his wife.

   d. Guns can be purchased easily.

   Not strong evidence because _____

   _____

2. **Position:** Schoolchildren in the United States should go to school all year.

   Reason: Year-round schooling promotes better learning.

   a. All my friends have agreed that we would like to end the long summer break.

   b. A survey of teachers across the country showed that children's learning improved when they had multiple shorter vacations rather than entire summers off.

   c. Research from the Northwest Evaluation Association suggests that summer learning loss is real: Seventh graders can lose as much as 50 percent of math progress during the summer before eighth grade.

   d. Test scores improved when a school system in Colorado went to year-round school sessions.

   Not strong evidence because _____

   _____

3. **Position:** The "three strikes and you're out" law that forces judges to send people to jail after three convictions should be overturned.

   Reason: Basing decisions about sentencing on numbers alone is neither reasonable nor fair.

a. A week ago, a man who stole a slice of pizza was sentenced to eight to ten years in prison because it was his third conviction.

b. The law makes prison overcrowding even worse.

c. Judges always give the longest sentence possible anyway.

d. The law may result in people getting major prison sentences for minor crimes.

Not strong evidence because _____

_____

Considering and Responding to Different Points of View

In addition to evidence, secondary support in an argument can include responses to counterarguments. Critical thinkers consider counterarguments carefully and respectfully. If they believe that a counterargument makes sense, they will make a **concession**: they will agree that some of the evidence presented by the other side is accurate or important. A concession often includes one of the following expressions:

It is true that_____.

Granted, _____.

A concession shows that a writer has thought carefully about both sides of the issue.

Another way writers show they have considered both sides of the issue is to offer a response to a counterargument, which is called a **rebuttal**. A rebuttal points out problems with the arguments of the other side. A rebuttal always responds to a counterargument, and it often begins with a word like *but, however,* or *nevertheless.*

While looking for evidence to support her claim, Jess found an opposing view from Dr. Richard Adamson of the American Beverage Association. When Jess reviewed his evidence, she thought he might be biased because he represented the interests of the beverage industry. Jess decided that as long as she mentioned his affiliation with the beverage industry, she should include his counterargument in her paper. In the following example, you will see how Jess introduced Adamson's counterargument (underlined), offered a concession (bold), and then provided a rebuttal (italics).

Some people who are opposed to taxing sugary beverages, such as Dr. Richard Adamson of the American Beverage Association, argue that it is unfair to blame one product for our expanding waistlines. **It is true that overconsumption of soda and other sweetened beverages is just one cause of obesity.** *Nevertheless, targeting this one cause could play a vital, lasting role in a larger campaign to bring this major health crisis under control.*

Jess discovered some counterarguments by reading what others had written on her topic. Another way to find counterarguments is to consider your audience. For this assignment, Jess needed to identify a specific audience for the paper and then consider what questions her readers would ask, what objections they might have, and what evidence they would find convincing. For example, if Jess's audience is the parents of teens, her first piece of evidence (a quarter of U.S. teens get 600 calories a day from sugary drinks) might be most effective, while her seventh piece of evidence (health-care costs of obesity) might be less important.

PRACTICE 15-5 **Consider the Audience**

Select one of the following target audiences. Identify one concern that the audience might have with a tax on sodas, and then review the evidence Jess collected. (See Practice 15-2.) Which piece of evidence will best address their concerns?

1. Soda company employees

2. College students

3. Restaurant owners

After reviewing your reasons, counterarguments, and evidence (the second and third basics), you may need to refine your initial topic sentence or thesis. Here is how Jess revised her preliminary main idea:

> **Revised main idea:** To help address the obesity crisis, states should place significant taxes on sugary beverages.

Notice the removal of the word *might* that was part of the original main idea. Having done some research, Jess now believes strongly that the taxes are a good idea — as long as they are high enough to make a significant dent in consumption.

Integrating Support from Sources

If you use supporting evidence from a source, you need to integrate that evidence into your writing. When you integrate facts, summaries, quotations, or paraphrases, make sure the source is identified, and connect the source information clearly to the point you are making. One strategy for integrating source material is to introduce support from sources with a **signal phrase,** the name of the author whose work you are citing plus an appropriate verb. The signal phrase helps you make clear where your words and ideas stop and the words and ideas you are borrowing from sources begin. Jess used the signal phrase "Brownell notes" (underlined below) to integrate part of her supporting evidence:

I think one reason to tax sugary drinks is that the money from such taxes could be used to prevent future cases of obesity. As Brownell notes, the taxes could fund anti-obesity programs aimed at educating children about healthy diets and encouraging them to exercise.

Fourth Basic: Organization in Argument

Arguments can be organized in a variety of ways, depending on your purpose. Many writers choose to use order of importance. For more on the different orders of organization, see "Arranging Your Ideas" (p. 69) in Chapter 5.

As you decide how to organize your reasons, also consider where to introduce counterarguments. If you are responding to someone else's argument, you may decide to introduce counterarguments first, before turning to your own reasons and evidence. On the other hand, if you are not responding to another argument, you may decide to include counterarguments after related reasons, as Jess did. (See the graphic organizer on page 312.)

Using Transitions in Argument

Use **transitions** to move your readers smoothly from one supporting reason to another. Here are some of the transitions you might use in your argument:

Common Transitions in Argument

above all	in the first (second, third) place
also	more/most important
best of all	one fact/another fact
especially	one reason/another reason
for example	one thing/another thing
in addition	remember
in fact	the first (second, third) point
in particular	worst of all

Using a Graphic Organizer in Argument

A graphic organizer such as the one Jess designed below can help you plan for your argument essay. Remember that you can add boxes for additional reasons or counterarguments.

Paragraphs versus Essays in Argument

For more on the important features of argument, see the "Four Basics of Argument" on page 297.

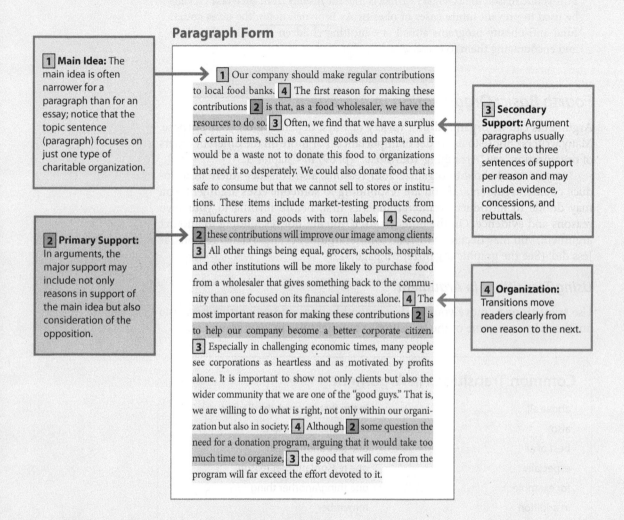

Paragraph Form

1 Main Idea: The main idea is often narrower for a paragraph than for an essay; notice that the topic sentence (paragraph) focuses on just one type of charitable organization.

2 Primary Support: In arguments, the major support may include not only reasons in support of the main idea but also consideration of the opposition.

1 Our company should make regular contributions to local food banks. **4** The first reason for making these contributions **2** is that, as a food wholesaler, we have the resources to do so. **3** Often, we find that we have a surplus of certain items, such as canned goods and pasta, and it would be a waste not to donate this food to organizations that need it so desperately. We could also donate food that is safe to consume but that we cannot sell to stores or institutions. These items include market-testing products from manufacturers and goods with torn labels. **4** Second, **2** these contributions will improve our image among clients. **3** All other things being equal, grocers, schools, hospitals, and other institutions will be more likely to purchase food from a wholesaler that gives something back to the community than one focused on its financial interests alone. **4** The most important reason for making these contributions **2** is to help our company become a better corporate citizen. **3** Especially in challenging economic times, many people see corporations as heartless and as motivated by profits alone. It is important to show not only clients but also the wider community that we are one of the "good guys." That is, we are willing to do what is right, not only within our organization but also in society. **4** Although **2** some question the need for a donation program, arguing that it would take too much time to organize, **3** the good that will come from the program will far exceed the effort devoted to it.

3 Secondary Support: Argument paragraphs usually offer one to three sentences of support per reason and may include evidence, concessions, and rebuttals.

4 Organization: Transitions move readers clearly from one reason to the next.

Consider Readers as You Write Argument

Ask Yourself

- Will my readers find my position or claim clear and direct?
- Have I questioned my assumptions, developed strong reasons, and considered opposing points of view that readers might hold?
- Will my audience find the evidence I offer relevant and convincing?
- Is my argument logically organized, so my audience can follow my reasoning?

310

Essay Form

1 Main Idea: In an essay, the main idea is usually stated in a thesis statement. The thesis is broader than a topic sentence; in this case, it sets up a discussion of ways to help different charities.

2 Primary Support: In an argument essay, the topic sentence of each body paragraph introduces a supporting reason and counterargument.

3 Secondary Support: Essays usually offer three to eight sentences per paragraph, detailing evidence, concessions, and rebuttals.

4 Organization: Transitions move readers clearly from one reason to the next.

1

At the last executive meeting, we discussed several possible ways to improve our company's marketing and advertising and to increase employee morale. Since attending the meeting, I have become convinced that one effort would help in those areas and more: **1** Our company should become more active in supporting charities.

4 First, **2** giving time and money to community organizations is a good way to promote our organization. **3** This approach has worked well for several of our competitors. For example, Lanse Industries is well known for sponsoring Little League teams throughout the city. Its name is on the back of each uniform, and banners promoting Lanse's new products appear on the ballfields. Lanse gets free promotion of these efforts through articles in the local papers, and according to one company source quoted in the *Hillsburg Gazette*, Lanse's good works in the community have boosted its sales by 5 to 10 percent. Another competitor, Great Deals, has employees serve meals at soup kitchens over the holidays and at least once

2

during the spring or summer. It, too, has gotten great publicity from these efforts, including a spot on a local television news show. It is time for our company to start reaping these kinds of benefits.

4 Second, **2** activities like group volunteering will help employees feel more connected to one another and to their community. **3** Kay Rodriguez, a manager at Great Deals' and a good friend of mine, organized the company's group volunteering efforts at the soup kitchens, and she cannot say enough good things about the results. Aside from providing meals to the needy, the volunteering has boosted the morale of Great Deals employees because they understand that they are supporting an important cause in their community. Kay has also noticed that as employees work together at the soup kitchens, they form closer bonds. She says, "Some of these people work on different floors and rarely get to see each other during the work week. Or they just do not have time to talk. But while they work together on the volunteering, I see real connections forming." I know that some members of our executive committee might think it would be too time-consuming to organize companywide volunteering efforts. Kay assures

3

me, however, that this is not the case and that the rewards of such efforts far exceed the costs in time.

4 The most important reason for supporting charities **2** is that it is the right thing to do. **3** As a successful business that depends on the local community for a large share of revenue and employees, I believe we owe that community something in return. If our home city does not thrive, how can we? By giving time and money to local organizations, we provide a real service to people, and we present our company as a good and caring neighbor instead of a faceless corporation that could not care less if local citizens went hungry, had trash and graffiti in their parks, or couldn't afford sports teams for their kids. We could make our community proud to have us around.

2 I realize that our main goal is to run a profitable and growing business. **3** I do not believe, however, that this aim must exclude doing good in the community. In fact, I see these two goals moving side by side and hand in hand. When companies give back to local citizens, their businesses benefit, the community benefits, and everyone is pleased by the results.

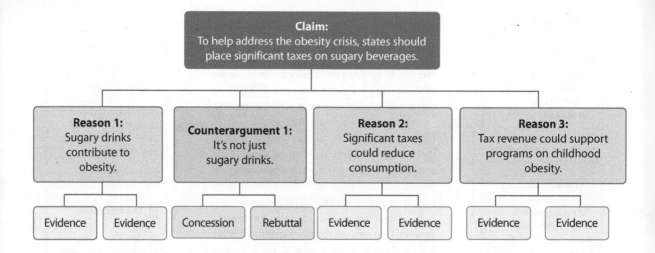

PRACTICE 15–6   **Using Transitions in Argument**

Jess used order of importance to organize her argument in favor of taxes on sugary drinks. Notice that she did not incorporate all the evidence from the chart on pages 303–04. Instead, she chose the evidence she believed offered the strongest support for her main point. She also included an opposing view. As you read the first draft of her essay below, choose from the following transitions to fill in the blanks: *another, finally, granted, however, in addition, in conclusion, on the one hand, on the other hand, the first, the most important.* (You may use a transition more than once, and you may have transitions left over.)

To help address the obesity crisis, states should place significant taxes on sugary beverages, such as soda, sweetened tea and fruit juices, and energy drinks. These drinks are a good target for taxation because they are a major contributor to obesity. According to the Centers for Disease Control and Prevention, about half of all Americans get a major portion of their daily calories from sweetened beverages. _____, the *Journal of Pediatrics* reports that one-fourth of U.S. teenagers get as many as 600 calories a day from soda or fruit drinks. This consumption is the equivalent of an additional meal.

_____, some people who are opposed to taxing sugary beverages, such as Dr. Richard Adamson of the American Beverage Association, argue that it is unfair to blame one product for our expanding waistlines. _____, overconsumption of soda and other sweetened beverages is just one cause of obesity. But it's a cause that is everywhere: sugary beverages are sold in convenience stores, grocery stores, restaurants, vending machines, schools, malls, and theaters. If we need to start somewhere, why not start by looking at one of the most common and widely available contributors to obesity in our society?

_____ reason to tax sugary drinks is that such taxation could reduce consumption. However, it is important that these taxes be significant, because taxes of just a few additional pennies per can or bottle probably wouldn't deter consumers. According to Kelly D. Brownell, director of the Rudd Center for Food Policy and Obesity, a penny-per-ounce tax on sugary beverages could cut consumption of these beverages by more than 10 percent. It could also reduce the estimated $79 billion of taxpayer money spent each year on health care for overweight and obese individuals.

_____ reason to tax sugary drinks is that the money from such taxes could be used to prevent future cases of obesity. As Brownell notes, the taxes could fund anti-obesity programs aimed at educating children about healthy diets and encouraging them to exercise. _____, since we currently spend $79 million on obesity-related health care, according to Brownell, using tax revenues to educate and promote healthy eating would ultimately help society reduce health-care costs. _____, targeting this one cause could play a vital, lasting role in a larger campaign to bring this major health crisis under control.

PRACTICE 15–7   **Creating a Graphic Organizer in Argument**

Using the graphic organizer above as a model, create a graphic organizer that illustrates the structure of the argument in Jess's first draft essay in Practice 15-6.

Read and Analyze Argument

To become a more successful writer, it is important to understand the four basics of argument; reading and analyzing examples of arguments will help you write your own. In this section, you will first read and evaluate the first draft of Jamila Dennison's argument paragraph. Next, in the Profile of Success, you will see how Stacie Brown uses argument in her job in a legal office. Finally, two professional articles present different positions in the debate surrounding the removal of statues and monuments to confederate leaders or others who supported slavery in the past.

Student Argument Paragraph

Read the following first draft of an argument paragraph. Note that the instructor asked the students to focus on the main idea (topic and position), support (reasons and evidence), and organization in this draft. Using the four basics of argument and the sample rubric, decide how effective this draft of the paragraph is, and then recommend one or two goals for the student's next draft.

Assignment: Concealed carry laws are becoming increasingly controversial, especially when people feel as though their rights are being restricted or that they are in danger. Write a paragraph that takes a position on the question: Should students be allowed to carry a concealed weapon on a college campus? Support your argument with specific examples and evidence.

Jamila Dennison

Allow Concealed Carry Permits on Campus

College students should be allowed to carry concealed weapons on campus if they are legally permitted to do so. To have a firearm legally, people are required to apply for a FOID card (Firearms Owner Identification) and subject themselves to a background check. This process is meant to ensure that the people who are allowed to carry these weapons have no history of violence or mental illness that may create future problems. Although there has not been a security issue at my own campus, I would like to know that I have the option to protect myself if a situation like this occurred. In addition, the legal age for owning specific firearms is eighteen or twenty-one, depending on what type of gun a person chooses to carry. I am safer with a weapon than without.

Rubric for Argument

	1 **Falls below expectations**	2 **Nearly meets expectations**	3 **Meets expectations**	4 **Exceeds expectations**
Main idea (first basic)	No clear main idea is present or no position is taken.	Main idea does not show position clearly.	Main idea suggests position but may be dull or inappropriate given audience.	Main idea makes a clear, strong claim or position.
Support (second and third basics)	Reasons and evidence are missing.	Some reasons are offered but they lack detail or consideration of opposing views.	Reasons, some evidence, and some consideration of opposing views are offered.	Good reasons; relevant, credible evidence; and fair consideration of opposing views are offered.
Organization (fourth basic)	Organization is unclear or illogical.	Organization is inconsistent, with abrupt shifts from reason to reason.	Organization is logical, but some transitions from reason to reason are missing or inappropriate.	Organization is logical, with smooth transitions between reasons.

Profile of Success: Stacie Brown
Argument in the Real World

Title   Legal Assistant

Background   I grew up in an exceptionally small town (population 99) where it was easy for me to excel in high school—and I did—because all the teachers would know why I didn't do well if I didn't. After my dad died during my senior year of high school, though, school was just something I had to finish.

After high school, I couldn't settle on anything because everything seemed useless or pointless. Hoping to find my way, I enrolled in Blinn College for the first time. I ended up dropping two classes and failing the other two, one of which was English 1301. A few years later, I enrolled in a veterinary technician course, but I soon decided that also wasn't for me.

I started dating my husband a while after that and soon became pregnant. Twenty-five years old, no career plan, no college degree, baby on the way—I knew I had to get my act together. With support from family and friends, I enrolled in college for the third time.

While at Blinn College, a few encouraging teachers helped me to realize my

potential, and I started writing again. (I had put the pen down after my dad died.) Indeed, I graduated Blinn College with honors, earning an associate of applied science degree. My long-term goal is to become a novelist.

After getting my associate's degree, I started my career in the administrative field as a legal assistant, and I get to use my writing and editing skills every day to communicate with clients, attorneys, courts, and other business entities. I am now situated to pursue my passion. My career has taught me that everyone has at least one remarkable story. It's up to me to write it.

Writing at Work   I write business emails, letters, memos, legal pleadings, and other legal documents. Working with clients often involves discussing uncomfortable or difficult topics. Addressing issues related to billing is necessary not only for a business to succeed but also for building a strong, successful attorney-client relationship. Many times, an attorney needs to communicate with not only a client but also the client's family members—and family members can be quite inexorable. One must respond in a firm but tactful manner.

Stacie Brown
Legal Assistant
STACIE BROWN

inexorable: hard to stop or manage

Evaluating the Paragraph

1. Does the paragraph show the four basics of argument? Explain.
2. Using the rubric as a guide, determine the strongest part of the paragraph and the weakest parts of the paragraph.
3. Write a response to this writer, using one of the following to frame your response:
   a. One thing I would like to know more about is _____.
   b. What I liked best about the paragraph is _____.
   c. In your next draft, you might consider adding _____.

Workplace Argument

Stacie Brown

Billing Email (Example)

Preview   What is the problem that this email will address?

Dear John Doe:

We recently sent your most recent invoice (November 2017) to the address we have in our file: 555 No Name Street, Anywhere, Texas 55555. It was returned to us as "not deliverable as addressed, unable to forward." As a result, I am emailing your November 2017 invoice, which is attached. If the mailing address we have on file is incorrect, please notify our office immediately of your correct mailing address.

2   Additionally, when we last spoke about payment arrangements, you agreed to send a money order once you received your tax return, which you indicated would be in ten to twelve days. It has been six months since that phone conversation, and our office has yet to receive payment of any kind. As you are aware, our office policy dictates that attorneys may not continue work for a client for which there is no money left in the Trust account. This means that any pending or future issues related to your case will not be considered until your balance is paid in full.

3   If you believe there has been an error in receiving payment, please contact our office to discuss. Otherwise, please consider this email a formal demand for payment in full. If your payment is not received within fifteen days from the date of this email, our office will have no choice but to begin formal collection actions. These actions will, of course, increase the amount owed to this office. I sincerely hope this will not be necessary.

Thank you,

Stacie

Stacie Brown
Legal Assistant
Law Firm
555 No Name Street
Anywhere, Texas 55555
Phone: 555.555.5555
Fax: 555.555.5556
Email: emailaddress@domain.net

Write to Read: Annotate

1. Identify the thesis statement.

2. Circle or number the transitions that introduce the reasons supporting the argument.

3. Highlight the parts of the email that present each supporting reason for the argument.

Read to Write: Think Critically

1. Does this workplace sample follow the four basics of argument? Why or why not?
2. What is the tone of the email? What words help you identify the tone?

Use Reading Strategies: Paraphrase

Legal language can be difficult to understand. Review the paraphrasing skills you learned in Chapter 1, page 14, and then paraphrase the following sentences from the email, putting them into everyday language: "As you are aware, our office policy dictates that attorneys may not continue work for a client for which there is no money left in the Trust account. This means that any pending or future issues related to your case will not be considered until your balance is paid in full."

Reflect and Respond

Have you ever received a phone call, email, or letter regarding a late payment on a bill or credit card? How did you determine that the information was legitimate? How did you respond?

Professional Argument Essay 1: Remove Confederate Monuments

Steven Thrasher

Confederate Memorials Have No Place in American Society. Good Riddance.

Steven Thrasher is a journalist whose articles have appeared in the *New York Times,* the *Guardian,* and the *Village Voice.* He is currently teaching journalism at Northwestern University. The following piece appeared in the *Guardian* in 2017.

Preview Skim the title and the first paragraph. Note that Thrasher uses the expression *good riddance* in both. What does this tell you about his claim and his tone?

ADELA LOCONTE/
SHUTTERSTOCK

Under the cover of darkness early on Monday morning, workers in Louisiana took down the first of four Confederate memorials in New Orleans, which city officials had decided to remove in 2015, shortly after the Charleston shootings. Good riddance.

2   It was fitting that the workers wore black, bulletproof clothing, donned masks which hid their identities, and were protected by police snipers. Their

evoke: bring to mind
propagated: spread

outfits speak to the history of racial violence these monuments evoke and idealize, a history propagated by Ku Klux Klan members who wore white clothing and masks to hide their identities (often in collusion with the police).

3   The Confederacy was an attempt to hold on to a way of life made possible by chattel slavery — and that violent way of life was soaked in the blood from the enslavement, murder, and rape of African Americans. Removing these monuments raises no issue of "erasing history," as some have charged. The monument taken down this week, originally inscribed in dedication to "white supremacy in the South," was built in 1891. It was a monument to how, as W. E. B. Du Bois wrote in *Black Reconstruction in America*, "the slave went free; stood a brief moment in the sun; then moved back into slavery."

W. E. B. Du Bois: American writer, scholar, and civil rights activist

4   For too long, U.S. society has stood for monuments erected on government property to the Confederacy, its losing war, and its genocidal values because the Confederacy battled for white supremacy and its hagiography is meant to intimidate black people. Now, after a mass murder in Charleston, we as a nation are finally confronting this.

hagiography: writing that idealizes a person or people

mass murder: In June 2015, white supremacist Dylann Roof opened fire during a Bible study class at an African American church in Charleston, killing nine church members.

5   But we're still treating these relics of the Confederacy with an absurd amount of care. When the Confederate flag was taken down in South Carolina, it was done with such pomp and circumstance it was like the thing was being given a state funeral. It ought to have been taken down without ceremony in the middle of the night as the New Orleans monument was. And the monument is not being destroyed, but will reportedly be taken to "a place where [it] can be put in historical context."

6   As a historian myself, I am mindful of preserving the history of the country, no matter how awful, violent, and racist it is. But I am also mindful that the performance of preserving remnants of the Confederacy in such a showy manner highlights a painful gap in our society. This country will lovingly care for symbols of racial violence in a way it has never cared for the bodies of raped black women, of whipped black men, of black families bred and torn apart under enslavement.

reparations: payments or other support for victims of crime or mistreatment

7   U.S. governments will spend money preserving these Confederate monuments, demonstrating the kind of care that we never showed to the bodies consumed by the Confederacy (and their descendants). And America won't find money to even talk about reparations for black people — a project which would really keep us from erasing our economic and cultural history — but we will easily find money to preserve Confederate monuments.

Mason-Dixon line: boundary between states; slavery was legal below the line

8   These monuments are coming down just as a kind of cold–civil war 2.0 is unfolding in the nation. The geographic boundaries of our present civil war are not as explicit as when the Mason-Dixon line demarcated freedom or bondage for enslaved black people. But as states take such different stances on matters of freedom — as "blue" states like California affirm their commitment to protecting our climate and retain former attorney general Eric Holder to defend its interests against the Trump administration, and as "red" states like Texas and North Carolina try to deny LGBT rights and make it ever harder for women to obtain abortions — it's like a slow-moving civil war, as different states regulate race, sexuality, and citizenship so differently.

9   And in federal matters, the union's position has perhaps flipped. Consider that as some cities take on "sanctuary status" to protect immigrants, coming down hard on them is Attorney General Jefferson Beauregard Sessions III — a man who is named for Confederate President Jefferson Davis (whose statue is one of the three still to come down in New Orleans).

10   The moment of this monument coming down is not a call for collective amnesia. Rather, it marks how we need to critically study American history more — by reading more Du Bois, and studying more books like Michelle Alexander's *The New Jim Crow*, more *Teen Vogue* articles on Andrew Jackson, and studying more films like Ava DuVernay's *The 13th*.

11   But let's not, in a misguided fashion, think that becoming most educated about our history is contingent upon monuments built to an illegitimate government decades after the civil war — and that glorify the most violently racist aspects of our American story.

Sessions: Jeff Sessions, former Alabama senator and attorney general 2017–2018

Jim Crow: laws enacted in the South that mandated racial segregation and legalized racial discrimination

Andrew Jackson: American president 1829–1837, known for signing the Indian Removal Act, which forced Native Americans to leave ancestral lands

The 13th: a documentary film by director Ava DuVernay that explores the history of racial injustice in the prison system

contingent: dependent on; happens under certain conditions

Read to Write: Annotate

1. Identify the thesis statement.

2. Note the reasons and evidence that the writer provides.

Write to Read: Think Critically

1. This writer contrasts those who removed the statue in New Orleans to members of the KKK. Why does he make this contrast?

2. The writer also contrasts treatment of the Confederate monuments with treatment of Black Americans, both before and after the abolition of slavery (paras. 5–7). How do these paragraphs support his argument?

3. In paragraphs 10–11, the author addresses a counterargument without stating it directly. What is the counterargument he addresses? Is his response effective?

4. What is the author's tone? Give an example to support your answer.

5. Who is the author's intended audience? How do you know?

Use Reading Strategies: Summarize

Review the information about summary writing in Chapter 1, pp. 18–20, and then write a short summary of Thrasher's argument essay.

Reflect and Respond

1. In paragraphs 8 and 9, the writer suggests that the removal of monuments fits into a larger national context, something he calls "cold–civil war 2.0." What does he mean? What evidence do you see that the United States is in such a "civil war"? Do you think Thrasher's description of the tensions is appropriate or exaggerated? Explain.

2. Thrasher claims that we can learn more about history without keeping statues up in public spaces. Do you agree with his claim? Explain.

Professional Argument Essay 2: Do Not Remove Confederate Monuments

Alfred Brophy

Why the Case for the Removal of Confederate Memorials Isn't So Clear-cut

---

Alfred Brophy is a professor of law at the University of Alabama. He earned an undergraduate degree from the University of Pennsylvania, a law degree from Columbia University, and a Ph.D. from Harvard University. As an expert in property law and legal history, he has written several books, including *Reparations Pro and Con* (2006) and *University, Court, and Slave: Proslavery Thought in Southern Colleges and Courts and the Coming of Civil War* (2016). Before teaching at the University of Alabama, he taught at the University of North Carolina School of Law.

Preview Skim the title and the first paragraph of Brophy's essay. What is his claim and his primary reason?

On April 24, New Orleans city employees began the process of removing four Confederate monuments. But there are pitfalls in eliminating memorials to the Confederacy — statues and monuments, along with the buildings, parks, schools and military bases named after Confederate soldiers. Primarily, we risk forgetting the connections of past racial crimes to current racial inequality.

Confederate Memorials Abound

2   Statues of Confederate soldiers are common in the South in a number of courthouse squares, while streets and parks bear the names of people or events associated with the Confederacy. In Southampton, Virginia, Black Head Signpost Road is named for the head of a slave executed during the Nat Turner Rebellion. (His head was put on a post along the road as a warning.) Jefferson Davis Memorial Highway, which runs from Florida to California, was named in the 1920s. The Virginia legislature even continues to pay US$5 per year to cemeteries in the state for every Confederate soldier buried in them. (The money is supposed to help preserve the cemeteries.)

3   In prior years, some cities and institutions have responded to the concerns of those who view these monuments as distasteful symbols of discrimination and oppression. In little towns throughout the South, from Reidsville, North Carolina, to Southampton County, Virginia (scene of the Nat Turner Rebellion), Confederate statues have been moved from courthouse squares and town centers to less prominent places, like cemeteries.

Nat Turner Rebellion: an 1831 uprising of enslaved people in Virginia. Nat Turner led the revolt, in which over fifty white people were killed.

Davis: Jefferson Davis (1801–1889), the president of the Confederate states, 1861–1865

4   Meanwhile, buildings named after Confederate officers (such as Saunders Hall at the University of North Carolina), Klansmen (Simkins Hall at the University of Texas–Austin) and politicians supporting Jim Crow (Governor Charles Aycock at Duke and East Carolina) have been renamed.

5   In recent years, the call to remove or rename is getting even louder. In 2015, Senator Mitch McConnell said Kentucky should consider ridding the Kentucky State House of its Jefferson Davis statue; in Memphis, one City Council member drew up an ordinance to remove the statue of Confederate cavalry officer and Klansman Nathan Bedford Forrest from a public park; and Tennessee's governor has suggested that a bust of Forrest be removed from State Capitol grounds.

Legal Obstacles

6   Some monuments may be so offensive to the local community that they'll need to be removed. And certainly, they can serve as rallying points for contemporary white supremacists. Others are particularly poignant reminders of the days of slavery and Jim Crow. Nathan Bedford Forrest Park, in an African American section of Memphis, was renamed because the City Council thought it was an affront to the local population. In such cases, the redistribution of cultural capital may serve to stop a continuing harm.

7   This is a decision that should largely be made at the local level. However, the legislatures of four states—South Carolina, Georgia, Mississippi and Tennessee—have passed Heritage Protection Acts that prohibit the removal of Confederate monuments from public property (or renaming of public buildings). This movement started in South Carolina in 2000, and the statutes were pushed by supporters of Confederate heritage.

A Case for Preservation

8   Clearly, there's a lot of work to be done if we're going to completely wipe out all traces of names and structures that honor the Confederacy. However, while I'm no supporter of the Confederacy, there are several reasons not to remove monuments or rename buildings.

9   As an aside: Confederate flags are entirely different. New flags have to be put up constantly, because they can wear out quickly. Thus, flying a Confederate flag reflects a continuing commitment to maintaining a symbol of white supremacy. Confederate monuments, on the other hand, were almost all erected decades ago.

10   For this reason, they're part of our landscape. Yes, they're reminders of the days of slavery and secession. But they teach important lessons: they point to a Southern political system that, from the 1870s to the 1930s (the period of most frequent commemoration), continued to support the ideals of the Confederacy. They're graphic reminders of Jim Crow, and the ways white supremacy was codified in statutes, social practices and stone. And they reveal the psychology (however misguided) of an era and people: the fact that white Southerners and their elected leaders believed in the righteousness of their society.

Saunders: William Laurence Saunders (1835–1891), colonel in the Confederate Army and leader in the Ku Klux Klan

Simkins: William Stewart Simkins (1842–1929), Confederate soldier, lawyer, and cofounder of the Florida Ku Klux Klan

Jim Crow: laws enacted in the South that mandated racial segregation and legalized racial discrimination

Aycock: Charles Aycock (1859–1912), governor of North Carolina (1901–1905) and proponent of white supremacy

McConnell: Mitch McConnell (1942–), Republican senator from Kentucky

Forrest: Nathan Bedford Forrest (1821–1877), general in the Confederate army and first Grand Wizard of the Ku Klux Klan

cultural capital: habits or cultural institutions that society recognizes as valuable

11   Ultimately, removal of the monuments will, quite literally, erase an unsavory — but important — part of our nation's history.

In Present-Day Poverty, the Echoes of a Racist Past

12   There's a second reason to go slow on renaming. It's important (for individuals, as well as communities) to understand how our past is connected to the present. The legacy of violence and limited educational and vocational opportunities during the eras of slavery and Jim Crow are undeniably connected to the fact that one-third of African American children today live in poverty.

13   Those who argue for expanded social welfare spending to alleviate the ravages of poverty make the plea that poverty is related not to personal culpability, but to legacies of racism that have lasted for generations. Confederate statues are tangible symbols of this legacy of oppression.

14   They're another reminder of the need for nuance in the telling of our nation's history; in understanding how we get to where we are today, we need to acknowledge the good along with the bad — which means not tearing it down.

culpability: guilt or responsibility

nuance: small differences in meaning or emphasis

Read to Write: Annotate

1. Identify the writer's claim, and then paraphrase it.

2. Highlight the key examples used as evidence in the article.

Write to Read: Think Critically

1. What are the writer's two reasons for opposing the removal of statues? What questions do you have about his reasons?

2. In paragraph 9, Brophy discusses the Confederate flag. Why does he introduce this issue? Does it distract readers from his argument, or does it support his argument? Explain.

3. Why does Brophy cite statistics about poverty among Black Americans today? What point is he making?

4. What is the writer's tone? List examples of words or phrases that support your answer.

Use Reading Strategies: Summarize

Review the information about summary writing in Chapter 1, pages 18–20, and then write a short summary of Brophy's argument essay.

Reflect and Respond

1. Look at the arguments by Thrasher and Brophy again, and review your summaries. Which author makes a stronger argument? Why? Do you see any points at which the authors might find agreement? Explain.

2. In paragraphs 6 and 7, Brophy discusses legal obstacles to removing statues. What are the specific challenges he mentions? How do you think Thrasher might respond to these challenges? Explain your answer. Are there solutions to these challenges that might be acceptable to both authors?

Grammar for Argument

Study the following sentences from the professional argument essays. Pay attention to the underlined parts of the sentences.

> **When** the Confederate flag was taken down in South Carolina, it was done with such pomp and circumstance it was like the thing was being given a state funeral. (Thrasher)
>
> However, **while** I'm no supporter of the Confederacy, there are several reasons not to remove monuments or rename buildings. (Brophy)

The underlined parts of these sentences are called *subordinate clauses*; they are clauses that contain a subject and a verb and begin with a subordinating conjunction — words like *when, while, after, because,* and *although.* (The subordinating conjunctions are bolded in the example passage above.) In arguments, a subordinate clause can help a writer make a point more specific. In these sentences, for example, the writers use subordinate clauses to show a specific time. A writer may also use subordinate clauses to specify a cause, a condition, or a contrasting situation.

Notice that when a subordinate clause appears at the beginning of a sentence, it is usually followed by a comma. But when the subordinate clause comes at the end of the sentence, it is usually not marked by a comma. For more information about subordinate clauses, see the section "Joining Ideas: Subordination" in Chapter 24, p. 483.

Write Your Own Argument

In this section, you will write your own argument based on one of the following assignments. For help, see the "How to Write Argument" checklist on pages 326–27.

Assignment Options: Writing about College, Work, and Everyday Life

Write an argument paragraph or essay on one of the following topics or on one of your own choice:

College	• Take a position on a controversial issue on your campus. If you need help coming up with topics, consult the campus newspaper.
	• Within the past few years, the media have started to discuss how student loans often cause college students to enter the workforce deeply in debt. Does it cost too much to attend college? Is there a way, other than student loans, for a potential student to be able to afford a college education? Take one clear position on the issue and support that position with evidence.
Work	• Argue for something that you would like to get at work, such as a promotion, a raise, or a flexible schedule. Explain why you deserve what you are asking for, and give specific examples.
	• Argue for an improvement in your workplace, such as the addition of a bike rack, new chairs in the break room, or a place to swap books or magazines. Make sure your request is reasonable in cost and will be beneficial to a significant number of employees.
Everyday Life	• Take a position on a controversial issue in your community.
	• Oscar Wilde (1854–1900), a famous Irish writer, once commented, "Most people are other people. Their thoughts are someone else's opinions, their lives a mimicry, their passions a quotation." Write an argument that supports or opposes Wilde's views, giving reasons and examples for your position.

mimicry: an imitation of something else

Assignment Options: Reading and Writing Critically

Complete one of the following assignments that asks you to apply the critical thinking, reading, and writing skills discussed in Chapter 1.

Writing Critically about Readings

Stephanie Ericsson's article titled "The Ways We Lie" (p. 211) and Eugene Robinson's essay "A Special Brand of Patriotism" (p. 236) both take a strong position on an issue. That position can be expressed either implicitly (you have to use clues in the writing to determine the position) or explicitly (the position is stated directly). Read or review these pieces, and then follow these steps:

1. **Summarize.** Briefly summarize the two essays, listing major examples and details.

2. **Analyze.** What features of argument do you see in each essay?

3. **Synthesize.** Using examples from one or both of the two essays and from your own experience, describe the features that make an argument successful and convincing. Think of features beyond those in the four basics of good argument.

4. **Evaluate.** In your opinion, is it better to state a strong claim explicitly or to show it implicitly? Are there times when one strategy is better than another? Explain your answer.

Writing Critically about Visuals

The following images illustrate two sides of the debate over monuments. Study the photographs, and complete the following steps:

CRUSH RUSH/ALAMY

TOM PUMPHRET/MEGA/NEWSCOM

1. **Read the visuals.** Ask yourself: What details are you drawn to, and why? What emotions or reactions arise when you see the person dressed as a Confederate soldier by the statue or the statue being removed? (Look back at the section "Writing Critically about Visuals" in Chapter 1 for information about summarizing, analyzing, synthesizing, and evaluating visuals.)

2. **Write an argument.** Write a paragraph or essay in which you respond to these images and discuss the arguments you think each is making. How effective do you find the visual argument? Is it a good way to convey the discussion about monuments? Why or why not? Include details and reactions from step 1.

Writing Critically about Problems

Read or review the "Write Critically about Problems" in Chapter 1 (pp. 26–28). Then consider the following problem:

> You've been asked to talk to a group of students who are planning to drop out of high school. These students are struggling in school, and if they drop out, they can each earn more money by increasing their hours from after-school and weekends to full time. As a current college student, you think this is a bad idea, and you'd like to encourage these students to think differently about their educations.

Assignment: In a group or on your own, come up with reasons in support of your opinion. Consider, too, possible objections to your argument, and account for them. Then write an argument paragraph or essay to persuade the students to complete high school. Give at least three solid reasons, and support your reasons with good evidence or examples.

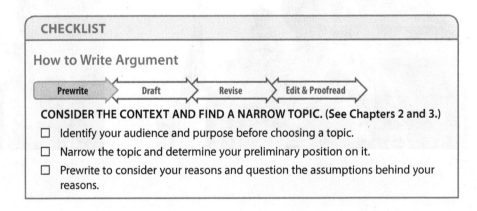

CHECKLIST

How to Write Argument

Prewrite ▷ Draft ▷ Revise ▷ Edit & Proofread

CONSIDER THE CONTEXT AND FIND A NARROW TOPIC. (See Chapters 2 and 3.)

☐ Identify your audience and purpose before choosing a topic.

☐ Narrow the topic and determine your preliminary position on it.

☐ Prewrite to consider your reasons and question the assumptions behind your reasons.

| Prewrite | Draft | Revise | Edit & Proofread |

DRAFT A TOPIC SENTENCE (PARAGRAPH) OR THESIS STATEMENT (ESSAY). (See Chapter 3.)

☐ Identify your purpose and draft a main idea.

☐ Make sure your main idea clearly shows your position on the topic.

SUPPORT YOUR MAIN IDEA. (See Chapter 4.)

☐ Use prewriting to develop a list of reasons and possible counterarguments.

☐ Find evidence (examples, facts, statistics, or expert opinions) to support each reason.

☐ Find concessions or rebuttals to address counterarguments.

☐ Evaluate your evidence: Is it credible, relevant, and unbiased?

WRITE A DRAFT. (See Chapter 5.)

☐ Use a graphic organizer or outline to plan your argument.

☐ Include a topic sentence (paragraph) or thesis statement (essay), the major support (reasons and counterarguments), and all the supporting details (evidence, concessions, and rebuttals).

☐ Consider your audience and purpose to add an introduction and a conclusion.

| Prewrite | Draft | Revise | Edit & Proofread |

REVISE YOUR DRAFT. (See Chapter 6.)

☐ Make sure it has *all* four basics of argument.

☐ Make sure paragraphs are unified and well-developed. Find additional reasons or evidence if needed.

☐ Make sure you include transitions to move readers smoothly from one reason to the next.

| Prewrite | Draft | Revise | Edit & Proofread |

EDIT AND PROOFREAD YOUR REVISED DRAFT. (See Parts 3 and 4.)

☐ Make sure grammar, word usage, and punctuation choices are clear, accurate, and effective.

☐ Check spelling and capitalization.

Chapter 15 Review

1. What is an argument?

2. What are the four basics of good argument?

3. Define *claim*, and list three types of evidence used to support a claim.

4. Why do you need to be aware of opposing views (counterarguments), and how can you respond to them?

5. What are some common transitions used in argument?

Reflect and Apply

1. When have you written or read argument in the past? What happened?

2. Why do you need to consider your audience when you are preparing to write an argument? What can happen if you don't consider the audience?

3. Interview someone who has taken advanced courses in your major or who is working in your chosen profession. Ask the person you interviewed what kinds of arguments they have read or written.

4. Review your writing from this chapter, including the feedback you received on your drafts. What worked well? What do you need to improve?

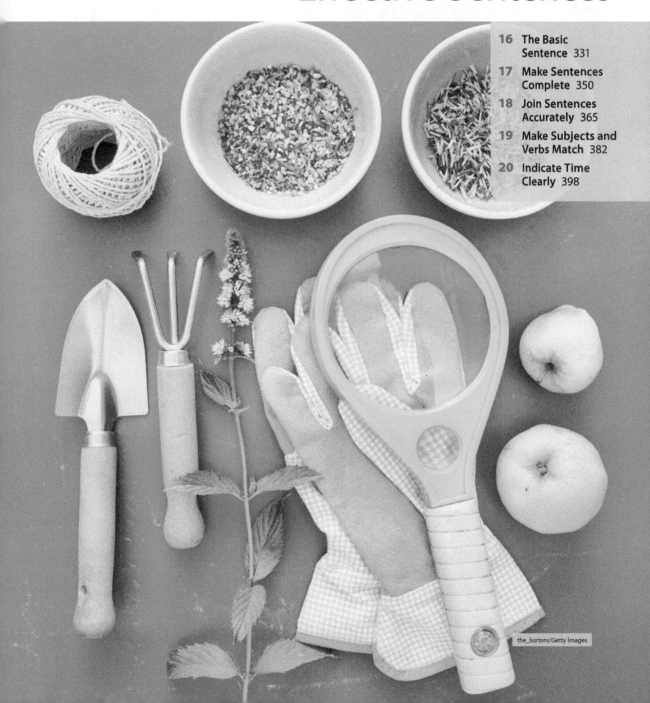

Part 3

Four Building Blocks of Effective Sentences

The Basic Sentence:

An Overview

In this chapter, you will learn to

- Recognize the parts of speech.
- Identify the main parts of a basic sentence.
- Identify six basic sentence patterns.

This chapter reviews the basic sentence elements that you will need to understand in order to build effective sentences. The terms in this chapter will help you to determine if your sentences are complete, clearly indicating the actors, actions, and times of the events you are describing. The concepts in this chapter will also help you understand how to punctuate sentences and join ideas together to create longer sentences. In short, this chapter provides you with the vocabulary you need to analyze and evaluate sentence structure — both the sentences you read and those you write.

Recognize the Parts of Speech

There are seven basic parts of speech:

1. **Nouns.** Nouns name a person, place, thing, or idea. Nouns are often preceded by articles (*a, an, the*) or adjectives, and we can replace a noun with a pronoun (see the next page). A **noun phrase** is a group of words that includes a noun (or a word that functions as a noun) and all the words modifying the noun.

> For **Christmas,** I prayed for this blond-haired **boy, Robert**, and a slim new American **nose**. (Tan 118)

The noun phrases are underlined in this example.

Language note: *The, a,* and *an* are articles, and they function as noun markers; they always introduce nouns or noun phrases. But it can be difficult knowing which article to use with nouns. For more information on using articles, see Chapter 21, pp. 431–34.

2. **Pronouns.** Pronouns replace a noun in a sentence. *He, she, it, we,* and *they* are pronouns.

> **He** was not Chinese, but as white as Mary in the manger. (Tan 118)

3. **Verbs.** Verbs tell what action the subject does or links a subject to another word that describes it. All sentences have a verb, and the verb has information about the time of the sentence, also known as *tense.*

> For Christmas, I **prayed** for this blond-haired boy, Robert, and a slim new American nose. (Tan 118)

[The verb *prayed* tells us what the subject — *I* — did.]

> He **was** not Chinese, but as white as Mary in the manger. (Tan 118)

[The verb *was* links the subject, *he,* to the describing word *Chinese.* In this case, the link is negative.]

4. **Adjectives.** Adjectives describe a noun or a pronoun.

> For Christmas, I prayed for this **blond-haired** boy, Robert, and a **slim new American** nose. (Tan 118)

[The adjective *blond-haired* describes the noun *boy,* while the adjectives *slim, new,* and *American* describe the noun *nose.*]

5. **Adverbs.** Adverbs describe an adjective, a verb, or another adverb. Adverbs often end in *-ly.*

I discovered that telling the truth all the time is **nearly** impossible. (Ericsson 214)

[The adverb *nearly* describes the adjective *impossible*.]

. . . they needed priests and **recklessly** believed treatment had cured him. (Ericsson 215)

[The adverb *recklessly* describes the verb *believed*.]

6. **Prepositions.** Prepositions connect a noun, pronoun, or verb with information about it. *Across, around, at, in, of, on,* and *out* are examples of common prepositions. See the chart below for a list of additional prepositions.

He was not Chinese, but as white as Mary **in** the manger. (Tan 118)

[The preposition *in* connects a noun, *Mary*, with a place, *the manger*.]

Language note: *In* and *on* can be tricky prepositions for people whose native language is not English. Keep these definitions and examples in mind:

- *in* = **inside of** (*in* the box, *in* the classroom); on a nonspecific day in a month, season, or year (*in* September, *in* spring, *in* 2014); for any time within a limited period of time (*in* three weeks, *in* two years, *in* six days); indicating a general location (*in* the United States, *in* London)
- *on* = **resting on top of something** (*on* the table, *on* my head); indicating a more specific location (*on* this side of the street, *on* the next page, *on* Elm Avenue); on a specific day (*on* December 25, *on* Thursday)

Common Prepositions

about	before	for	on	until
above	behind	from	out	up
across	below	in	outside	upon
after	beneath	inside	over	with
against	beside	into	past	within
along	between	like	since	without
among	by	near	through	
around	down	next to	to	
at	during	of	toward	
because of	except	off	under	

7. **Conjunctions.** Conjunctions connect words to each other. The most common conjunctions are the seven coordinating conjunctions. You can memorize these easily using the word **FANBOYS**: *for, and, nor, but, or, yet, so.*

> →
> . . . they needed priests **and** recklessly believed treatment had cured him. (Ericsson 215)
>
> [The coordinating conjunction *and* connects the two parts of this sentence: "needed priests" and "recklessly believed."]

PRACTICE 16–1 Using the Parts of Speech

Read through this paragraph, identify what kind of word — noun, verb, adjective, adverb, preposition, or conjunction — is needed for each blank, and provide an appropriate example. Be prepared to explain your choice. You may compare your choices with those of Samantha Levine-Finley, who wrote the original paragraph (see Chapter 10, p. 186).

Example: You won't be wasting anyone's <u>noun</u> (time). *We need a noun here; the blank comes after a possessive word.*

Professors are _____ required to maintain a certain number _____ office hours per week to _____ students, says Alice Lanning, who _____ a freshman-year experience class, also _____ Oklahoma. The _____ is when "students don't take advantage of these office hours _____ the end of the _____, and the grades _____ scary." Her advice? _____ each professor at least once during the _____ month of school. "Ask what the professor _____ and how to get the most out of _____," Lanning says. That's _____ critical because you'll have fewer exams _____ graded papers than in high school, so rebounding from a _____ grade is _____.

Identify Parts of Basic Sentences

A sentence is the basic unit of written communication. A sentence must contain at least one independent clause. A **clause** is a group of words with a subject and a verb. A clause is **independent** if it is complete; in other words, it expresses a thought by itself and does not need to be connected to another clause in order to make sense. To make sure that each sentence contains an independent clause, readers and writers look for three required elements: a verb, a subject, and completeness. Let's look at each of these elements separately.

Verbs

Every sentence has a **main verb**, the word or words that tell what the subject does or that link the subject to another word or group of words that describes it. The main verb of a sentence indicates the time of the events or descriptions in the sentence (past, present, future) and the nature of the events or descriptions (in progress or completed). In addition, the main verb can help readers and writers find the subject of the sentence. Thus, when analyzing a sentence, readers and writers often look for the main verb first. There are three types of verbs: *action verbs, linking verbs,* and *auxiliary (helping) verbs.*

Action Verbs

An **action verb** tells what action occurs in the sentence. To find the main action verb(s) in a sentence, ask yourself: *What action occurs in this sentence?* Or *What happened?*

Subject   Action verb

A child with ADHD often talks excessively. . . . (Vaz 263)

Linking Verbs

A **linking verb** connects (links) the subject to another word or group of words that describes the subject. Linking verbs show no action; they are used to describe. The most common linking verb is *be* (*am, is, are,* and so on). Other linking verbs, such as *seem* and *become,* can usually be replaced by a form of the verb *be,* and the sentence will still make sense. To find linking verbs, ask yourself this question: *What word joins the subject and the words that describe it?* You can also ask yourself about time in the sentence: *Which word shows if the description was true in the past, present, or future?*

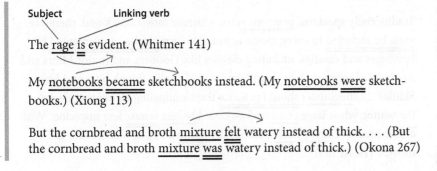

Subject   Linking verb

The rage is evident. (Whitmer 141)

My notebooks became sketchbooks instead. (My notebooks were sketchbooks.) (Xiong 113)

But the cornbread and broth mixture felt watery instead of thick. . . . (But the cornbread and broth mixture was watery instead of thick.) (Okona 267)

Some words can be either action verbs or linking verbs, depending on how the verb is used in a particular sentence.

Action verb Justine smelled the flowers.

Linking verb The flowers smelled wonderful.

Common Linking Verbs

Forms of *be*: am, are, is, was, were

Forms of *seem* and *become*: seem, seems, seemed; become, becomes, became

Forms of sense verbs: look, looks, looked; appear, appears, appeared; smell, smells, smelled; taste, tastes, tasted; feel, feels, felt

---

 Language note: The linking verb *be* and its other forms cannot be left out of sentences in English.

Incorrect Sergio not here today.

Correct Sergio is not here today.

Auxiliary (Helping) Verbs

An auxiliary verb or helping verb joins the main verb in a sentence to form a complete verb. The helping verb is often a form of the verb *be*, *have*, or *do*. A sentence may have more than one helping verb along with the main verb.

$$\boxed{\text{Helping verb}} + \boxed{\text{Main verb}} = \boxed{\text{Complete verb}}$$

The complete verbs in the following sentences have been double-underlined:

Traditionally speaking, popcorn is the ultimate movie snack and, therefore, must be included in every movie menu. Popcorn can be supplemented by beverages and candies, including classics like Goobers and Junior Mints and newfangled treats such as chocolate-covered cookie dough bites and Sour Skittles. . . . Beginners should practice their smuggling techniques during the winter, when large coats and awkward bulges arouse less suspicion. With a little practice, anyone can successfully sneak a bag of M&M's into the movies. (Horn 183)

> ## Common Helping Verbs
>
> **Forms of *be*:** am, are, been, being, us, was, were
> **Forms of *have*:** have has, had
> **Forms of *do*:** do does, did
> **Other:** can, could, may, might, must, should, will, would

Before you begin Practice 16-2, look at these examples to see how action, linking, and helping verbs are different:

Action verb   Jahleel <u>graduated</u> last year.

[The verb *graduated* is an action that the subject Jahleel performed.]

Linking verb   <u>Jahleel</u> <u>is</u> a graduate.

[The verb *is* links Jahleel to the word that describes him: *graduate*. No action is performed.]

Helping verb   <u>Jahleel</u> <u>is graduating</u> next spring.

[The helping verb *is* joins the main verb *graduating* to make the complete verb *is graduating*, which tells what action the subject (Jahleel) is taking.]

PRACTICE 16–2   ## Identifying the Verb (Action, Linking, or Helping Verb + Main Verb)

The following sentences are adapted from the essay "Happiness Doesn't Follow Success: It's the Other Way Round" by Lisa Walsh, Julia Boehm, and Sonja Lyubomirski (pp. 289–91). Read each sentence and highlight the complete verb in each. Then identify each verb as an action verb, a linking verb, or a helping verb + a main verb.

Linking verb

Example: Positive emotions <u>are</u> also predictors of later achievement and earnings.

1. Longitudinal studies can help here . . .

2. . . . as they follow people over days, weeks, months, or years.

3. Well-designed experiments can control for these variables.

4. Happier people outperform less happy people . . .

5. ... and their positive demeanor is probably the cause.

6. Depressed individuals such as Abraham Lincoln and Winston Churchill can accomplish incredible feats.

> **PRACTICE 16-3** **Identifying the Verb (Linking or Helping Verb + Main Verb)**
>
> Read paragraphs 3 and 4 in Brian Healy's essay, "First Day in Fallujah" (p. 160). Make a note of each time he uses *was* or *were* in the paragraphs and determine if it is a linking verb or a helping verb (occurring with another verb form).

Subjects

The **subject** of a sentence (or of a clause) is the person, place, or thing that does the action of the sentence or that is described in the sentence. The subject of a sentence is usually a noun or a pronoun. For a list of common pronouns, see page 437.

To find the subject, first identify the verb. Then create a question, using the verb to fill in the blank: Who or what _____?

Person as subject   Grandfather saved fistfuls of change and more. (Soto 166)

[The verb is *saved*. *Who* saved? *Grandfather*]

Thing as subject   The kitchen was littered with appalling mounds of raw food. (Tan 118)

[The verb is *was*. *What* was littered? *The kitchen*].

A **compound subject** consists of two or more subjects joined by *and, or,* or *nor.*

Two subjects   Alana and Sh'Nai love animals of all kinds.

Several subjects   The baby, the cats, and the dog play well together.

The subject of a sentence is *never* in a **prepositional phrase**, a word group that begins with a preposition and ends with a noun or pronoun called the **object of a preposition**.

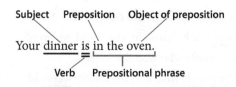

Subject   Preposition   Object of preposition

Your dinner is in the oven.

Verb   Prepositional phrase

Preposition	Object	Prepositional Phrase
from	the bakery	from the bakery
to	the next corner	to the next corner
under	the table	under the table

Can you identify the subject of the following sentence?

One of my best friends races cars.

Although you might think that the word *friends* is the subject, it isn't. *One* is the subject. The word *friends* cannot be the subject because it is in the prepositional phrase *of my best friends*. It is only *one* person who races cars, not all of the speaker's best friends. When you are looking for the subject of a sentence, cross out the prepositional phrase.

Prepositional phrase crossed out   One ~~of the students~~ won the science prize.

The rules ~~about the dress code~~ are specific.

PRACTICE 16–4   Identifying Subjects

Look back at the verbs you identified in Practice 16-2. Find the subject for each verb and underline it once.

Completeness

A sentence (or an independent clause) is complete when it expresses an entire thought. It does not need additional words, nor does it need to be connected to another clause. Imagine you hear someone answer a question, but you don't hear the original question. As a result, the answer doesn't quite make sense. That's what an incomplete sentence does: It provides only part of the information that a reader needs.

Incomplete thought	because my alarm did not go off
Complete thought	I was late because my alarm did not go off.
Incomplete thought	the people who won the lottery
Complete thought	The people who won the lottery were old.

To determine whether a thought is complete, ask yourself: *Do I need to ask a question for this thought to make sense?*

Incomplete thought   Once snacks are in hand.

[We need to ask, "What happens once the snacks are in hand?" so it is not a complete thought.]

Complete thought   Once snacks are in hand, the next step is to select a seat. (Horn 183)

Recognize Six Basic English Sentence Patterns

In English, there are six basic sentence patterns, some of which you have just worked through in this chapter. Although there are other patterns, they build on these six. The following examples show statements in each pattern:

1. **Subject-Verb (S-V).** This pattern is the most basic one.

   Musicians practice.

2. **Subject-Linking Verb-Noun (S-LV-N)**

   My students are musicians.

3. **Subject-Linking Verb-Adjective (S-LV-ADJ)**

   My students are talented.

4. **Subject-Verb-Adverb (S-V-ADV)**

> They <u>practice</u> regularly.

5. **Subject-Verb-Direct Object (S-V-DO).** A direct object directly receives the action of the verb.

> <u>Students</u> <u>write</u> essays. [essays = direct object]

6. **Subject-Verb-Direct Object-Indirect Object (S-V-DO-IO).** An indirect object does not directly receive the action of the verb.

> <u>Students</u> <u>give</u> essays to the instructor. [essays = direct object; instructor = indirect object]

This pattern can also have the indirect object before the direct object.

> <u>Students</u> <u>give</u> the instructor essays.

Language note: Some verbs occur only in specific patterns in English. For example, the verb *eat* can occur in patterns 1, 4, and 5:

> The <u>athletes</u> <u>ate</u>.
> The <u>athletes</u> <u>ate</u> quickly.
> The <u>athletes</u> <u>ate</u> their postgame steak dinner quickly.

The verb *devour*, however, occurs only in pattern 5:

Incorrect	The <u>athletes</u> <u>devoured</u>.
Incorrect	The <u>athletes</u> <u>devoured</u> quickly.
Correct	The <u>athletes</u> <u>devoured</u> their postgame steak dinner quickly.

PRACTICE 16–5   **Identifying Basic Sentence Patterns**

Underline the subject, double underline (or highlight) the complete verb, and indicate the sentence pattern for each of the following sentences, adapted from Alfred Brophy's essay "Why the Case for the Removal of Confederate Memorials Isn't So Clear-cut" (p. 320). Sentence pattern options include the following:

S-V   S-LV-N   S-LV-ADJ   S-V-ADV   S-V-DO   S-V-DO-IO

Remember to cross out any prepositional phrases before you identify the subject.

**Example: George W. Bush signed the legislation
to authorize the museum.** S-V-DO

1. Statues of Confederate soldiers are common in the South in a number of courthouse squares.

2. The Virginia legislature even pays US$5 per year to cemeteries in the state for every Confederate soldier buried in them.

3. But they teach important lessons.

4. Confederate statues are tangible symbols of this legacy of oppression.

5. Ultimately, removal of the monuments will, quite literally, erase an unsavory—but important—part of our nation's history.

6. We can have a constructive dialogue at places like Montpelier.

7. South Carolinians taught us all a profound lesson of love, compassion and reconciliation.

8. It was an unforgettable experience.

PRACTICE 16–6   **Recognizing Sentence Patterns**

Study the sentences in the essays by Morgan Xiong and Amy Tan in Chapter 7. See if you can find one example of each sentence pattern.

Negatives

No matter which sentence pattern you use, you can form a **negative** by adding the word *not* after the auxiliary (helping) verb. If a sentence does not have a helping verb, make the verb negative by adding a form of the helping verb *do* and the word *not*. (For a list of common helping verbs, see p. 337.)

Statement	Negative
Dina can sing.	Dina cannot sing. (can't sing)
The store sells cigarettes.	The store does not sell cigarettes. (doesn't)
Nestor will call.	Nestor will not call. (won't)
Caroline walked.	Caroline did not walk. (didn't)

Make sure you pay attention to the following when you write a negative sentence:

1. You must include an auxiliary verb with the negative *not*.

Incorrect	The store not *sell* cigarettes.
Correct	The store *does not sell* cigarettes.

   [*Does*, a form of the helping verb *do*, must come before *not*.]

2. Use only one negative word per sentence; double negatives are not used in standard English.

Incorrect (negative subject and negative verb)	No students aren't finished with the tests.
Correct	No students are finished with the tests.
	The students are not finished with the tests.

Incorrect (negative object and negative verb)	Najee does not have no ride.
Correct	Najee does not have a ride.
	Najee has no ride.
Incorrect (two negatives in a verb)	Eun has not never seen a snowstorm.
Correct	Eun has never seen a snowstorm.
	Eun has not ever seen a snowstorm.

Common Negative Words

never	nobody	no one
no	none	nowhere

---

3. Use the helping verb *did* for a past tense negative; do not add *-ed* to the main verb.

Incorrect	I did not talked to Jairo last night.
	I do not talked to Jairo last night.
Correct	I did not talk to Jairo last night.

PRACTICE 16–7   **Making Negative Sentences**

Read the statements in Practice 16-5. Make each statement negative. If the statement is already negative, make the verb positive.

Questions

To turn a statement into a **question**, also called an **interrogative**, move the helping verb so that it comes before the subject. Add a question mark (?) in place of the period at the end of the statement.

| Statement | Johan can go tonight. |
| Question | Can Johan go tonight? |

If the only verb in the statement is a form of *be*, it should be moved before the subject.

> **Statement**   Jamie is at work.
>
> **Question**   Is Jamie at work?

If the statement does not contain a helping verb or a form of *be*, add a form of *do* and put it before the subject.

> **Statements**   Norah sings in the choir.   Tyrone goes to college.
>
>   The building burned.   The plate broke.
>
> **Questions**   Does Norah sing in the choir?   Does Tyrone go to college?
>
>   Did the building burn?   Did the plate break?

Notice that the verb changed once the helping verb *do* (*do, does, did*) was added. The main verb does not have the past tense (*-ed*) or third-person present tense (*-s*) ending when you add the helping verb.

> **PRACTICE 16-8**   **Making Interrogative Sentences**
>
> Read the statements in Practice 16-5. Turn each statement into a question.

Gerunds and Infinitives

All of the sentence patterns on pages 340–41 include a subject slot. The subject slot is generally filled by a noun or pronoun. In the same way, the direct object slot is usually filled by a noun or pronoun.

A **gerund** is a verb form that ends in *-ing* and acts as a noun; a gerund can fill a noun slot (subject or direct object) in a sentence. An **infinitive** is a verb form that is preceded by the word *to*. An infinitive can be used as an adverb (to show a purpose for an action), or it can be used as a noun. As a noun, it can fill a subject or direct object slot.

> **Gerund**   Keyara loves swimming.
>
> [*Loves* is the main verb, and *swimming* is a gerund, the direct object of *loves*.]
>
> **Infinitive**   Keyara loves to run.
>
> [*Loves* is the main verb, and *to run* is an infinitive, the direct object of *loves*.]

Language note: How do you decide whether to use a gerund or an infinitive after the main verb in a sentence? The decision depends on the main verb. A good ESL dictionary will include information about using gerunds and infinitives, or you may refer to the following charts.

Verbs That Can Be Followed by Either a Gerund or an Infinitive Direct Object

begin	hate	remember	try
continue	like	start	
forget	love	stop	

Sometimes, using a gerund or an infinitive after one of these verbs results in the same meaning:

Gerund	Janelle likes **playing** the piano.
Infinitive	Janelle likes **to play** the piano.

Other times, however, the meaning changes depending on whether you use a gerund or an infinitive:

Gerund   Carla stopped **helping** me.

[This wording means Carla no longer helps me.]

Infinitive   Carla stopped **to help** me.

[This wording means Carla stopped what she was doing and helped me.]

Verbs That Are Followed by a Gerund

admit	discuss	keep	risk
avoid	enjoy	miss	suggest
consider	finish	practice	
deny	imagine	quit	

The politician risked **losing** her supporters.

Sophia considered **quitting** her job.

Verbs That Are Followed by an Infinitive

agree	decide	need	refuse
ask	expect	offer	want
beg	fail	plan	
choose	hope	pretend	
claim	manage	promise	

Aunt Sally wants **to help**.

Miguel hopes **to become** a millionaire.

Do not use the base form of a verb when you need a gerund or an infinitive.

      base form (used as subject)

Incorrect   Swim is my favorite activity.

      gerund form (used as subject)

Correct   Swimming is my favorite activity.

      base form (used as direct object)

Incorrect   I need stop at the store.

      infinitive form (used as direct object)

Correct   I need to stop at the store.

      base form (used as direct object)

Incorrect   My instructor enjoys tell jokes.

      gerund form (used as direct object)

Correct   My instructor enjoys telling jokes.

PRACTICE 16-9   **Using Gerunds and Infinitives**

Read the paragraphs, and fill in the blanks with either a gerund or an infinitive as appropriate.

> **Example:**   If you want _to be_ (be) an actor, be aware that the profession is not all fun and glamour.

When you were a child, did you pretend _____ (be) famous people? Did you imagine _____ (play) roles in movies or on television? Do you like _____ (take) part in plays? If so, you might want _____ (make) a career out of acting.

Be aware of some drawbacks, however. If you hate _____ (work) with others, acting may not be the career for you. Also, if you do not enjoy _____ (repeat) the same lines over and over, you will find acting dull. You must practice _____ (speak) lines to memorize them. Despite these drawbacks, you will gain nothing if you refuse _____ (try). Anyone who hopes _____ (become) an actor has a chance at succeeding through hard work and determination.

Chapter 16 Review

1. List the seven parts of speech, and give an example of each one.

2. What are three things that a sentence must have?

3. What is a prepositional phrase?

4. What is the difference between action verbs, linking verbs, and auxiliary verbs?

5. What are gerunds and infinitives?

Chapter 16 Quiz

In Exercises 1–4, identify the part of speech or verb type for the underlined word.

___ 1. The syllabus <u>outlines</u> the material required for the class. (Levine-Finley 118)

   a. Noun   b. Verb   c. Preposition   d. Adjective

___ 2. Professors hand out these <u>precious</u> pages at the start of each semester. (Levine-Finley 118)

   a. Adjective   b. Adverb   c. Preposition   d. Verb

___ 3. The syllabus can be your <u>salvation</u>. (Levine-Finley 118)

    a. Noun   b. Verb   c. Adjective   d. Adverb

___ 4. Disappointing grades <u>are</u> just one hint that the approach many students took in high school won't work in college. (Levine-Finley 118)

    a. Action verb   b. Linking verb   c. Helping verb

___ 5. Choose the item that is a complete sentence.

    a. When you begin working on your paper.

    b. When you begin working on your paper, you should make a schedule.

    c. When you begin working on your paper the night before it is due.

17

Make Sentences Complete:

Avoiding Fragments

| Learning Outcomes | In this chapter, you will learn to |

- Recognize complete and incomplete sentences.
- Build complete sentences by checking for five types of fragments.
- Edit for complete sentences.

In ordinary conversations, we don't always need to use complete sentences. Consider the following exchange:

> *Mallory*: Why didn't you do the homework assignment?
> *Ben*: Because I didn't understand it. [By itself, this statement is not complete.]
> *Mallory*: You could have asked me for help.
> *Ben*: Nah — didn't want to. I can figure it out later. [By itself, the first group of words is incomplete; the word *I* is missing.]

The standards for college and professional writing, however, are different from the rules we follow in conversations. In academic or professional contexts, incomplete sentences may confuse readers or slow down the reading process, and they may suggest to readers that the writer is careless or sloppy. In this chapter, you will learn how to test sentences for completeness.

Recognize Complete and Incomplete Sentences

You learned in Chapter 16 that an independent clause is complete if it contains the following: a *subject,* a *verb,* and *a sense of completion* (it does not need to be attached to another sentence to make sense). When one of these elements is missing, the sentence is called a **fragment**. Like its name suggests, a fragment is a piece of a sentence but cannot be a sentence by itself. (In the examples that follow, subjects are underlined, and verbs are double-underlined.)

Sentence	<u>I</u> <u>was</u> hungry, so <u>I</u> <u>ate</u> some cold pizza and <u>drank</u> a soda.
Fragment	<u>I</u> <u>was</u> hungry, so <u>I</u> <u>ate</u> some cold pizza. And drank a soda.

[*And drank a soda* contains a verb (*drank*) but no subject.]

When you edit your writing, especially in academic and professional situations, make sure that your sentences are complete.

Build Complete Sentences

To make sure you have written complete sentences, look for the five trouble spots identified in this chapter. They often signal fragments.

When you find a fragment in reading your own writing, you can usually correct it in one of two ways:

1. Add what is missing (a subject, a verb, or both).

2. Attach the fragment to the sentence before or after it.

1. Fragments That Start with Prepositions

Remember from Chapter 16 that a prepositional phrase contains a preposition and a noun. By itself, a prepositional phrase is not a complete sentence; it does not have a verb. Whenever you begin a sentence with a preposition, check for both a subject and a verb. If the group of words is missing either of these, it is a fragment. (For a list of common prepositions, see Chapter 16, p. 333.)

Fragment	I <u>pounded</u> as hard as I could. Against the door.

[*Against the door* lacks both a subject and a verb.]

Correct a fragment that starts with a preposition by connecting it to the sentence either before or after it. If you connect such a fragment to the sentence after it, put a comma after the fragment to join it to the next sentence.

Finding and fixing fragments: Fragments that start with prepositions	**Find** I did not work on improving my grammar. (In) high school. 1. **Circle** any preposition at the beginning of a word group. 2. *Ask:* Does the word group have a subject? No. Does it have a verb? No. Underline the subject, and double-underline any verb. 3. *Ask:* Does the word group express a complete thought? No. 4. If the word group is missing a subject or verb or does not express a complete thought, it is a fragment. This word group is a fragment. **Fix** 5. **Correct** the fragment by joining it to the sentence before or after it. I did not work on improving my grammar. In high school.

2. Fragments That Start with Subordinating Words

A **subordinating word** is the first word in a dependent clause. A **dependent clause** has a subject and a verb, like all clauses do. But a dependent clause can never express a complete thought by itself; it depends on another clause (an independent clause) to make sense. When writers begin a sentence with a dependent clause, they must always attach that clause to an independent clause. Otherwise, they will have a fragment.

Sentence with a subordinating word	Although there <u>are</u> some relaxed and easygoing <u>teachers</u>, for the most part, <u>students</u> <u>are expected</u> to respect the teachers and to submit without question. (Rantung 256)

[The word *although* is a subordinating word that introduces a dependent clause. If you put a period after the word *teachers,* what happens? *Although there are some relaxed and easygoing teachers.* This sentence is a fragment. It is a dependent clause that is not connected to an independent clause.]

Whenever you see a subordinating word at the beginning of a sentence, check for a subject, a verb, and another clause (a complete thought).

Writing Note: In Chapters 7–15, you learned about using transition words in writing. One type of transition is a **subordinating conjunction**. Subordinating conjunctions are subordinating words (see the chart below). Be careful when you are creating transitions in your writing. If you use a subordinating conjunction, you must make sure there is also an independent clause so that your sentence is complete.

Fragment	*Since I moved.* I have eaten out every day.

[*Since I moved* has a subject (*I*) and a verb (*moved*), but it does not express a complete thought.]

Corrected	Since I moved, I have eaten out every day.

Subordinating Words

after	although	as/as if/as though
as long as	as soon as	because
before	even if/even though	if/if only
now that	once	since
so that	that	though
unless	until	when/whenever
where/wherever	whether	which/whichever
while	who/whom/whose	

 Language note: When a word group starts with *who, whose,* or *which,* it is not a complete sentence unless it is a question.

Fragment	That woman is the police officer. *Who gave me a ticket last week.*
Question	*Who* gave you a ticket last week?
Fragment	He is the goalie. *Whose team is so bad.*
Question	*Whose* team are you on?
Fragment	Sherlene went to the HiHo Club. *Which does not serve alcohol.*
Question	*Which* club serves alcohol?

Correct a fragment that starts with a subordinating word by connecting it to the sentence before or after it. If you join a dependent clause to the sentence after it, put a comma after the dependent clause. (See the "Finding and Fixing" box on the next page for an example.)

> **PRACTICE 17–1**   **Correcting Fragments That Start with Prepositions or Subordinating Words**
>
> Read the following paragraph, and identify the ten fragments that start with prepositions or subordinating words. Be prepared to correct the fragments.

Staying focused at an office job can be difficult Because of these jobs' many distractions. After making just a few changes. Workers will find that they are less distracted and more productive. A good first step is to clear away clutter, such as old paperwork. from the desk. Once the workspace is cleared. It is helpful to make a list of the most important tasks for the day. It is best for workers to do brain-demanding tasks when they are at their best. Which is often the start of the day. Workers can take on simpler tasks, like filing. When they are feeling less energetic. While they are doing something especially challenging. workers might want to disconnect themselves from email and turn off their cell phones. Although it is tempting to answer emails and phone calls immediately. They are among the worst workplace distractions. Some people set up a special electronic folder. For personal emails. They check this folder only while they are on break or between tasks. Finally, it is important for workers to remember the importance of breaks. Which recharge the mind and improve its focus.

Finding and fixing fragments:

Fragments that start with subordinating words

Find

(Because) research takes a lot of time. Students should make a schedule to follow during the process.

1. **Circle** any subordinating words at the beginning of a word group.

2. *Ask:* Does the word group beginning with a subordinating word have a subject? Yes. Does it have a verb? Yes. **Underline** the subject, and **double-underline** any verb.

3. *Ask:* Does the word group express a complete thought? No.

4. If the word group is missing a subject or verb or does not express a complete thought, it is a fragment. This word group is a fragment.

Fix

5. **Correct** the fragment by joining it to the sentence before or after it. Add a comma if the dependent clause comes first.

    Because research takes a lot of time. ~~Students~~ , students should make a schedule to follow during the process.

3. Fragments That Start with -ing Verb Forms

A verb that ends in *-ing*— *walking, writing, running*— can be used at the beginning of a complete sentence when it is a **gerund**, a verb form used as a noun.

Sentence   Writing takes a lot of practice.

[We know that *writing* is used as a noun here because we can replace it with a pronoun: *Is writing hard? Yes,* **it** *takes a lot of practice.*]

Sometimes, an *-ing* verb form introduces a phrase that **modifies** (describes) an independent clause. The phrase by itself is not a complete sentence. Whenever an *-ing* verb form starts what you think is a sentence, stop and check for a subject, a verb, and a complete thought.

Fragment   I worked as hard as I could. *Hoping to get a good grade.*

[*Hoping to get a good grade* does not have a subject or a complete verb.]

Correct a fragment that starts with an *-ing* verb form either by adding what-ever sentence elements are missing (usually a subject and a helping verb) or by connecting the fragment to the sentence before or after it. You will usually need to put a comma before or after the fragment to join it to the complete sentence. (For more on using *–ing* phrases in sentences, see pp. 485–86, Chapter 24.)

PRACTICE 17–2	Correcting Fragments That Start with *-ing* Verb Forms

Circle any *-ing* verb that appears at the beginning of a word group in the paragraph. Then read the word group to see if it has a subject and a verb and expresses a complete thought. Not *all* the word groups that start with an *-ing* verb are fragments, so read carefully. In the space provided, record the numbers of the word groups that are fragments. Then correct each fragment either by adding the missing sentence elements or by connecting it to the sentence before or after it.

Which word groups are fragments? _____

1 People sometimes travel long distances in unusual ways trying to set new world records. **2** Walking is one unusual way to set records. **3** In 1931, Plennie Wingo set out on an ambitious journey **4** Walking backward around the world. **5** Wearing sunglasses with rearview mirrors, he started his trip early one morning. **6** After eight thousand miles, Wingo's journey was interrupted by a war in Pakistan. **7** Ending his ambitious journey. **8** Hans Mullikan spent more than two years in the late 1970s traveling to the White House by crawling from Texas to Washington, D.C. **9** Taking time out to earn money as a logger and a Baptist minister. **10** Alvin Straight, suffering from poor eyesight, traveled across the Midwest on a lawn mower. **11** Looking for his long-lost brother.

Finding and fixing fragments:

Fragments that start with -ing verb forms

Find

I ran as hard as I could. (Hoping) for a good position in line.

1. **Circle** any -ing verb form that begins a word group.

2. *Ask:* Does the word group have a subject? No. Does it have a verb? No. Underline any subject, and double-underline any verb.

3. *Ask:* Does the word group express a complete thought? No.

4. If the word group is missing a subject or verb or does not express a complete thought, it is a fragment. This is a fragment.

Fix

5. **Correct** the fragment by joining it to the sentence before or after it. If you put the word group with the -ing verb form first, add a comma after it. **Alternative:** Add the missing sentence elements.

               , hoping
I ran as hard as I could. ~~Hoping~~ for a good position in line.

                     I was hoping
I ran as hard as I could. ~~Hoping~~ for a good position in line.

4. Fragments That Start with To *and a Verb*

You learned in Chapter 16 that an *infinitive* (a word group that begins with *to* and a verb) can be used as a subject or direct object in a sentence. It can also be used as an adverb, showing the purpose of an action. In each of these cases, however, the infinitive by itself is not a complete sentence. When you read a sentence beginning with an infinitive, you need to make sure it is not a fragment.

Fragment	Each day, I check freecycle.org. *To see if it has anything I need.*
Corrected	Each day, I check freecycle.org to see if it has anything I need.

If a word group begins with *to* and a verb (an infinitive), it must have another verb; if it doesn't, it is not a complete sentence. Whenever you see a word group that begins with an infinitive, first check to see if there is another verb. If there is no other verb, the word group is a fragment.

Sentence	To run a complete marathon <u><u>was</u></u> my goal.
	[*To run* is the subject; *was* is the verb.]
Fragment	<u>Cheri <u>got</u></u> underneath the car. *To change the oil.*
	[No other verb appears in the word group that begins with *To change*.]

To correct a fragment that starts with *to* and a verb, join it to the sentence before or after it, or add the missing sentence elements.

> **PRACTICE 17–3**   **Correcting Fragments That Start with Infinitives**
>
> Circle any *to*-plus-verb combination that appears at the beginning of a word group in the paragraph. Then read the word group to see if it has a subject and a verb and expresses a complete thought. Not *all* the word groups that start with *to* and a verb are fragments, so read carefully. In the space provided, record the numbers of the word groups that are fragments. Then correct each fragment either by adding the missing sentence elements or by connecting it to the sentence before or after it.
>
> Which word groups are fragments? _____

1 For people older than twenty-five, each hour spent watching TV lowers life expectancy by nearly twenty-two minutes. **2** This finding is the result of Australian researchers' efforts **3** To investigate the health effects of TV viewing. **4** To put it another way, watching an hour of television is about the same as smoking two cigarettes. **5** The problem is that most people are inactive while watching TV. **6** They are not doing anything, like walking or playing sports. **7** To strengthen their heart and maintain a healthy weight. **8** Fortunately, it is possible **9** To counteract some of TV's negative health effects. **10** To increase their life expectancy by three years. **11** People need to exercise just fifteen minutes a day. **12** To accomplish this goal, they might exchange a ride in an elevator for a climb up the stairs. **13** Or they might walk around the block during a lunch break at work.

Finding and fixing fragments:

Fragments that start with *to* and a verb

Find

> Cheri got underneath the car. To change the oil.

1. **Circle** any infinitives that start a word group.

2. *Ask:* Does the word group have a subject? No. Does it have a verb? No. (Remember that an infinitive can never be a complete verb in a sentence.) Underline any subject, and double-underline any verb.

3. *Ask:* Does the word group express a complete thought? No.

4. If the sentence is missing a subject or verb or does not express a complete thought, it is a fragment. This word group is a fragment.

Fix

5. **Correct** the fragment by joining it to the sentence before or after it. If you put the infinitive first, add a comma after it. **Alternative:** Add the missing sentence elements.

> *to*
> Cheri got underneath the car. ~~To~~ change the oil.

> *To change the oil,*
> Cheri got underneath the car. ~~To change the oil~~.

> *She needed to*
> Cheri got underneath the car. ~~To~~ change the oil.

5. Fragments That Are Examples or Explanations

Effective writing provides readers with examples, lists, and explanations to support general statements. As you edit your writing, pay special attention to those examples or explanations, especially when they refer back to information you presented in a previous sentence. They may be fragments.

Fragment	More and more people are reporting food allergies. *For example, allergies to nuts or milk.*
Fragment	My body reacts to wheat-containing foods. *Such as bread or pasta.*

[*For example, allergwies to nuts or milk* and *Such as bread or pasta* are not complete thoughts.]

This last type of fragment is harder to recognize because there is no single word or kind of word to look for. The following words may signal a fragment, but fragments that are examples or explanations do not always start with these words:

especially	for example	like	such as

When a group of words gives an example or explanation connected to the previous sentence, stop to check it for a subject, a verb, and a complete thought.

Fragment	I have found great things at freecycle.org. *Like a nearly new computer.*
Fragment	Freecycle.org is a good site. *Especially for household items.*
Fragment	It lists many gently used appliances. *Such as toaster ovens.*
	[*Like a nearly new computer, Especially for household items,* and *Such as toaster ovens* are not complete thoughts.]

Correct a fragment that starts with an example or explanation by connecting it to the sentence before or after it. Sometimes, you can add whatever sentence elements are missing (a subject, a verb, or both) instead. When you connect the fragment to a sentence, you may need to change some punctuation. For example, fragments that are examples are often set off by a comma.

PRACTICE 17-4 **Correcting Fragments That Are Examples or Explanations**

Circle word groups that are examples or explanations. Then read the word group to see if it has a subject and verb and expresses a complete thought. In the space provided, record the numbers of the word groups that are fragments. Then correct each fragment either by adding the missing sentence elements or by connecting it to the sentence before or after it.

Which word groups are fragments? _____

1 Being a smart consumer can be difficult **2** Especially when making a major purchase. **3** At car dealerships, for example, important information is often in small type **4** Like finance charges or preparation charges. **5** Advertisements also put negative information in small type. **6** Such as a drug's side effects. **7** Credit-card offers often use tiny, hard-to-read print for the terms of the card. **8** Like interest charges and late fees, which can really add up. **9** Phone service charges can also be hidden in small print. **10** Like limits on text messaging and other functions. **11** Especially now, as businesses try to make it seem as if you are getting a good deal, it is important to read any offer carefully.

Finding and fixing fragments: Fragments that are examples or explanations	**Find** Freecycle.com recycles usable items. (Such as clothing.) 1. **Circle** the word group that is an example or explanation. 2. *Ask:* Does the word group have a subject, a verb, and a complete thought? No. 3. If the word group is missing a subject or verb or does not express a complete thought, it is a fragment. This word group is a fragment.

Fix

4. **Correct** the fragment by joining it to the sentences before or after it or by adding the missing sentence elements.

   such
   Freecycle.org recycles usable items/ ~~Such~~ as clothing.
                                       ^

   I should list some things on freecycle.org. The sweaters I never
   could keep others warm.
   wear.

Edit for Complete Sentences

Use the information in this chapter to help you complete the practice exercise in this section and edit your own writing.

> **PRACTICE 17-5**   **Editing Fragments**

Find and correct seven fragments in the following paragraph.

Over the past decades, school systems around the country have embraced educational standards. After all, everyone agrees that students should meet important requirements. Before they can graduate. A national standard for wall American students has many supporters, too.

If the requirements for graduation in Oregon and Tennessee are the same. Everyone with a high school diploma gets a similar education. There is a catch, of course. After reviewing proposed standards. Many educators, administrators, and parents disagree about what they should include. Mathematics and writing are important, but so are music and physical education. How can decision makers find standards that everyone accepts? Agreeing on the standards. Is not the final step in the process. Educators must determine how students will prove they have met the standards. To measure students' proficiency. Many states have passed laws requiring tests for eighth graders and high school juniors. These tests are standardized. Which means all of the students taking a grade test in a particular state are given the same test. Both individual students and their school districts are evaluated by the scores. The parents of a student learn what their child's score is. And how the school compares with others around the state. Then children who need extra help are supposed to receive it, and schools with very low scores year after year become eligible for additional resources.

Chapter 17 Review

1. What are the three elements required in an independent clause?
2. What is a fragment?
3. What are five trouble spots that signal possible fragments?
4. What are two basic ways to correct a fragment?

Chapter 17 Quiz

Indicate the correct choice for each of the following items.

___ 1. If an underlined portion of this word group is incorrect, select the revision that fixes it. If the word group is correct as written, choose d.

Natalie did not <u>go on</u> our bike <u>trip. Because</u> she could not <u>ride a</u> bike.
                               a   *b*   *c*

    a. go. On   c. ride; a

    b. trip because   d. No change is necessary.

___ 2. Choose the item that has no errors.

   a. Since Gary is the most experienced hiker here, he should lead the way.

   b. Since Gary is the most experienced hiker here. He should lead the way.

   c. Since Gary is the most experienced hiker here; he should lead the way.

___ 3. If an underlined portion of this passage is incorrect, select the revision that fixes it. If the passage is correct as written, choose d.

   Planting fragrant **flowers will** attract **wildlife. Such** as butterflies.
   <u>a</u>   <u>b</u>   <u>c</u>

   a. When planting   c. wildlife, such

   b. flowers; will   d. No change is necessary.

___ 4. Choose the item that has no errors.

   a. To get to the concert hall; take exit 5 and drive for three miles.

   b. To get to the concert hall. Take exit 5 and drive for three miles.

   c. To get to the concert hall, take exit 5 and drive for three miles.

___ 5. If an underlined portion of this passage is incorrect, select the revision that fixes it. If the passage is correct as written, choose d.

   Buying many unnecessary **groceries. Can** result **in wasted food**
                              <u>a</u>   <u>b</u>

   and **wasted money.**
        <u>c</u>

   a. groceries can   c. : wasted money.

   b. : in wasted food   d. No change is necessary.

___ 6. If an underlined portion of this passage is incorrect, select the revision that fixes it. If the passage is correct as written, choose d.

   Some scientists **predict that** people will **soon take** vacation
                    <u>a</u>   <u>b</u>

   cruises. Into space.
        <u>c</u>

   a. predict, that   c. cruises into

   b. soon; take   d. No change is necessary.

___ 7. Choose the item that has no errors.

    a. Walking for ten miles after her car broke down. Pearl became tired and frustrated.

    b. Walking for ten miles after her car broke down; Pearl became tired and frustrated.

    c. Walking for ten miles after her car broke down, Pearl became tired and frustrated.

___ 8. Choose the item that has no errors.

    a. Many people find it hard. To concentrate during stressful times.

    b. Many people find it hard to concentrate during stressful times.

    c. Many people find it hard, to concentrate during stressful times.

___ 9. If an underlined portion of this sentence is incorrect, select the revision that fixes it. If the sentence is correct as written, choose d.

> <u>**Growing suspicious,**</u> the secret <u>**agent discovered**</u> a tiny recording
>   *a*   *b*
> device <u>**inside a flower vase.**</u>
>   *c*

    a. Growing, suspicious   c. inside, a flower vase.

    b. agent. Discovered   d. No change is necessary.

___ 10. If an underlined portion of this passage is incorrect, select the revision that fixes it. If the passage is correct as written, choose d.

> <u>**Early in their training,**</u> <u>**doctors learn**</u> that there is a fine
>   *a*   *b*
> line. <u>**Between**</u> life and death.
>   *c*

    a. Early, in   c. line between

    b. doctors. Learn   d. No change is necessary.

Join Sentences Accurately:

Correcting Run-ons

In this chapter, you will learn to

- Recognize accurate sentence combinations.
- Join sentences accurately.
- Watch for run-ons in two common writing situations.
- Edit your writing for run-ons.

In our everyday conversations, we don't have to worry about how we combine sentences. After all, we do not use punctuation when we are speaking! In writing, however, joining sentences accurately and carefully is important; when sentences are not joined accurately, they may be misread or judged negatively by readers. When you take the time to join sentences accurately, readers are more likely to focus on the ideas and not on the grammar.

Recognize Accurate Sentence Combinations

In Chapter 16, you learned that a sentence must contain at least one *independent clause* or a group of words with a subject and a verb that expresses a complete thought. Sometimes, writers join two independent clauses together to create compound sentences. When they do so, they connect these clauses according to specific rules. In this chapter, you will learn about these rules so that you can avoid a common writing mistake, the run-on.

Sentences with two independent clauses

[The college offers financial aid], and [it encourages students to apply].

[Wasps wove a horn-shaped hive one year], but [we smoked them away with swords of rolled up newspapers lit with matches]. (Soto 166)

Each independent clause is in brackets. Subjects are underlined, and verbs are double-underlined.

[I once <u>tried</u> going a whole week without telling a lie], and [it <u>was</u> paralyzing]. (Ericsson 212)

A **run-on** occurs when two independent clauses are joined incorrectly as one sentence. There are two kinds of run-ons: fused sentences and comma splices.

- A **fused sentence** is two complete sentences joined without a coordinating conjunction or any punctuation:

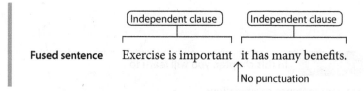

Fused sentence   Exercise is important it has many benefits.

- A **comma splice** is two complete sentences joined only by a comma:

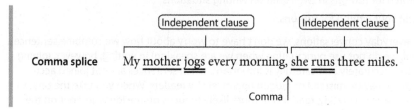

Comma splice   My <u>mother jogs</u> every morning, <u>she runs</u> three miles.

When you join two independent clauses (sentences), you must use proper punctuation.

Corrections   Exercise is important, and it has many benefits.

My mother jogs every morning; she runs three miles.

Join Sentences Accurately

To make sure sentences are accurately joined when you read through and edit your own writing, focus on one sentence at a time, looking for fused sentences and comma splices.

PRACTICE 18–1   Finding Run-ons

Identify the four run-ons in this paragraph. In the space provided, record the sentence numbers of the run-ons.

Which word groups are run-ons? _____

1 For many years, I did not take control of my life, I just drifted without any goals. **2** realized one day as I met with my daughter's guidance counselor that I hoped my daughter would have a better life than I do. **3** From that moment, I decided to do something to help myself and others. **4** I set a goal of becoming a teacher. **5** To begin on that path, I took a math course at night school, then I took another course in science. **6** I passed both courses with hard work, I know I can do well in the Cambridge College program. **7** I am committed to the professional goal I finally found it has given new purpose to my whole life.

Once you have found a fused sentence or a comma splice, there are five ways to correct it. Each of the methods represents a **sentence pattern** that you can use to improve your writing.

IC = independent clause

DC = dependent clause

ca = conjunctive adverb

cc = coordinating conjunction

sc = subordinating conjunction

S = subject

V = verb

Five Ways to Correct Run-on Sentences

Strategy	Example	Pattern
1. Add a period.	. He I saw the man he did not see me.	IC. IC. (S + V. S + V.)
2. Add a semicolon.	; he I saw the man he did not see me.	IC; IC. (S + V; S + V.)
3. Add a semicolon, a conjunctive adverb, and a comma.	; however, he I saw the man he did not see me.	IC; ca, IC. (S + V; ca, S + V.)
4. Add a comma and a coordinating conjunction.	, but he I saw the man he did not see me.	IC, cc IC. (S + V, cc S + V.)
5. Add a subordinating conjunction (subordinating word).	when I The man did not see me+saw him. When I , he +saw the man he did not see me.	IC DC. DC, IC. (S + V + sc + S + V.) (sc + S + V, S + V.)

Notice that the corrections are the same for both fused sentences and comma splices. Some students mistakenly believe that they can correct a fused sentence by adding a comma. What happens if you add a comma to a fused sentence?

Fused sentence	I saw the man he saw me.

If you answered that adding a comma creates a comma splice, you are correct.

Comma splice	I saw the man, he saw me.

Adding a comma does not correct the fused sentence; you must use one of the five strategies listed in the preceding chart. Let's look at these strategies in more detail.

Add a Period

You can correct run-ons by adding a period to make two separate sentences; in other words, you may decide that the two sentences should not be joined at all. After adding the period, capitalize the letter that begins the new sentence.

Pattern 1: IC. IC.

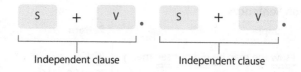

Fused sentence (corrected)	I interviewed a candidate for a job ~~she~~ . She gave me the "dead fish" handshake.
Comma splice (corrected)	The "dead fish" is a limp handshake~~,~~ . The person plops her hand into yours.

Add a Semicolon

A second way to correct run-ons is to use a semicolon (;) to join the two sentences. Joining two independent clauses this way is one way to create a **compound sentence**. Use a semicolon only when the two independent clauses express closely related ideas. Also, remember that a semicolon only works between independent clauses; if you cannot correct the sentence by adding a period, you cannot correct it with a semicolon, either.

Pattern 2: IC; IC.

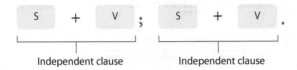

Pattern 2 is an example of **coordination**: using two independent clauses in a single sentence. (For more information on coordination, see Chapter 24, pp. 480–82)

Do not capitalize the word that follows a semicolon unless it is the name of a specific person, place, or thing , such as *Mel, Iowa,* or *Pop's.*

Fused sentence (corrected)	Slouching creates a terrible impression _{; it} ~~it~~ makes a person seem uninterested, bored, or lacking in self-confidence.
Comma splice (corrected)	It is important in an interview to hold your head up , it is just as important to sit up straight.

Add a Semicolon, a Conjunctive Adverb, and a Comma

A third way to join independent clauses is to add a semicolon followed by a conjunctive adverb and a comma. Many of the transitional expressions listed in the chapters in Part 2 were conjunctive adverbs: *however, moreover, in fact,* among others. Pay attention to the punctuation required for conjunctive adverbs when you use them to join independent clauses.

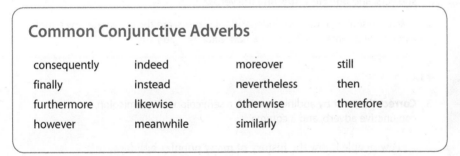

Common Conjunctive Adverbs

consequently	indeed	moreover	still
finally	instead	nevertheless	then
furthermore	likewise	otherwise	therefore
however	meanwhile	similarly	

Pattern 3: IC; ca, IC.

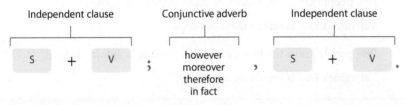

Like Pattern 2, Pattern 3 is an example of coordination: a sentence that contains two independent clauses.

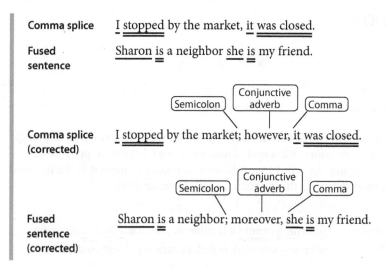

Comma splice — I stopped by the market, it was closed.

Fused sentence — Sharon is a neighbor she is my friend.

Comma splice (corrected) — I stopped by the market; however, it was closed.

Semicolon   Conjunctive adverb   Comma

Fused sentence (corrected) — Sharon is a neighbor; moreover, she is my friend.

Finding and fixing run-ons:

Adding a period; a semicolon; or a semicolon, a conjunctive adverb, and a comma

Find

Few people know the history of many popular holidays

Valentine's Day is one of these holidays.

1. To see if there are two independent clauses in a sentence, **underline** the subjects, and **double-underline** the verbs.

2. *Ask:* If the sentence has two independent clauses, are they separated by either a period or a semicolon? No. *The sentence is a run-on.*

Fix

3. **Correct** the error by adding a period; a semicolon; or a semicolon, a conjunctive adverb, and a comma.

Few people know the history of many popular holidays.

Valentine's Day is one of these holidays.

Few people know the history of many popular holidays;

Valentine's Day is one of these holidays.

Few people know the history of many popular holidays. Indeed,

Valentine's Day is one of these holidays.

PRACTICE 18-2   **Correcting Run-ons by Adding a Period or a Semicolon**

For each of the following items, indicate in the space to the left whether it is a fused sentence (FS) or a comma splice (CS). Then correct the error by adding a period or a semicolon. Capitalize the letters as necessary to make two sentences.

Example: _FS_ Being a farmer can mean dealing with all types of challenges; one of the biggest ones comes from the sky.
                                                    ^

_____ 1.   Farmers have been trying to keep hungry birds out of their

crops for centuries, the first scarecrow was invented for this

reason.

_____ 2.   Some farmers have used a variety of chemicals, other farmers

have tried noise, such as small cannons.

_____ 3.   Recently, a group of berry farmers tried something new, they

brought in bigger birds called falcons.

_____ 4.   Small birds, such as starlings, love munching on berries each

year they destroy thousands of dollars' worth of farmers' berry

crops.

_____ 5.   Because these starlings are frightened of falcons, they fly away

when they see these birds of prey in the fields they need to

get to where they feel safe.

Add a Comma and a Coordinating Conjunction

A fourth way to join independent clauses correctly is to add a comma and a coordinating conjunction. A coordinating conjunction is one of these seven words: *and, but, for, nor, or, so,* and *yet.* Some people remember the coordinating conjunctions by thinking of **FANBOYS:** *for, and, nor, but, or, yet, so.*

To correct a fused sentence this way, add a comma and a coordinating conjunction. A comma splice already has a comma, so just add a coordinating conjunction that makes sense in the sentence. As the name *coordinating conjunction* suggests, when you connect two independent clauses using this pattern, you are using coordination.

Pattern 4: IC, cc IC.

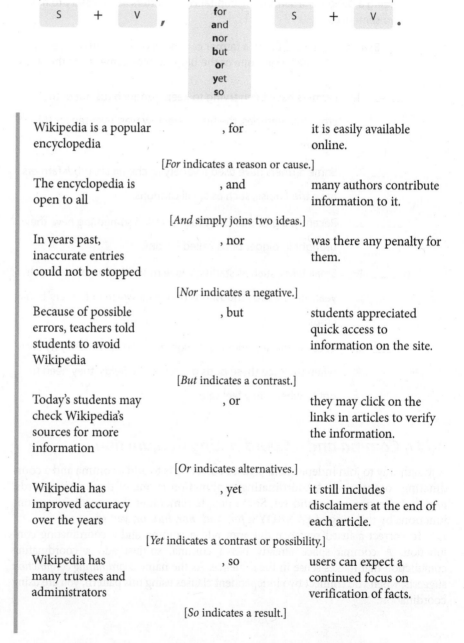

Wikipedia is a popular encyclopedia

, for

it is easily available online.

[*For* indicates a reason or cause.]

The encyclopedia is open to all

, and

many authors contribute information to it.

[*And* simply joins two ideas.]

In years past, inaccurate entries could not be stopped

, nor

was there any penalty for them.

[*Nor* indicates a negative.]

Because of possible errors, teachers told students to avoid Wikipedia

, but

students appreciated quick access to information on the site.

[*But* indicates a contrast.]

Today's students may check Wikipedia's sources for more information

, or

they may click on the links in articles to verify the information.

[*Or* indicates alternatives.]

Wikipedia has improved accuracy over the years

, yet

it still includes disclaimers at the end of each article.

[*Yet* indicates a contrast or possibility.]

Wikipedia has many trustees and administrators

, so

users can expect a continued focus on verification of facts.

[*So* indicates a result.]

Be careful to choose an appropriate coordinating conjunction when you are connecting independent clauses.

Fused sentence	Nekeisha was qualified for the job she hurt her chances by mumbling.
Illogical correction	Nekeisha was qualified for the job, and she hurt her chances by mumbling.
Logical correction	Nekeisha was qualified for the job, but she hurt her chances by mumbling.

Coordinating conjunctions are used to connect two independent clauses. You cannot use a coordinating conjunction between an independent clause and a *dependent clause*, a group of words that begins with a subordinating conjunction or other subordinating word. (For more information on dependent clauses, see Chapter 17, pp. 352–55.)

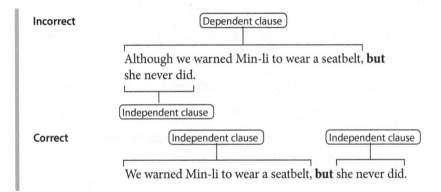

Incorrect

Dependent clause

Although we warned Min-li to wear a seatbelt, **but** she never did.

Independent clause

Correct

Independent clause   Independent clause

We warned Min-li to wear a seatbelt, **but** she never did.

Finding and fixing run-ons:

Using a comma and/or a coordinating conjunction

Find

Foods <u>differ</u> from place to place your favorite <u>treat</u> <u>might disgust</u> someone from another culture.

1. To see if there are two independent clauses in a sentence, **underline** the subjects, and **double-underline** the verbs.

2. *Ask:* If the sentence has two independent clauses, are they separated by either a period or a semicolon? No. The sentence is a run-on.

Fix

3. **Correct** a fused sentence by adding a comma and a coordinating conjunction between the two independent clauses. Correct a comma splice by adding just a coordinating conjunction.

Foods differ from place to place ~~your~~ *, and your* favorite treat might disgust someone from another culture.

PRACTICE 18–3 **Correcting Run-ons by Adding a Comma and/or a Coordinating Conjunction**

Correct each of the following run-ons by adding a comma, if necessary, and an appropriate coordinating conjunction. First, underline the subjects and double-underline the verbs.

Example: Most <u>Americans</u> <u>do</u> not <u>like</u> the idea of eating certain kinds
and
of food, <u>most</u> of us <u>would</u> probably <u>reject</u> horse meat.

1. In most cultures, popular foods depend on availability and tradition people tend to eat old familiar favorites.

2. Sushi shocked many Americans thirty years ago, today some young people in the United States have grown up eating raw fish.

3. In many societies, certain foods are allowed to age this process adds flavor.

4. Icelanders bury eggs in the ground to rot for months, these aged eggs are considered a special treat.

5. As an American, you might not like such eggs the thought of eating them might even revolt you.

Add a Subordinating Word

A fifth way to join clauses correctly and avoid run-ons is to make one of the independent clauses a dependent clause by adding a **subordinating word** (a subordinating conjunction or a relative pronoun), such as *after, because, before, even though, if, that, though,* or *which*. (For a complete list of subordinating words, see Chapter 17, p. 353.)

A subordinating word shows the relationship between the two clauses. We can turn one of the independent clauses into a dependent clause when it is less important than the other clause or explains it in some way.

Two sentences: Suggests both sentences express ideas of equal importance

<u>I'll</u> <u>get</u> to the train station. <u>I</u> <u>will call</u> Josh.

One sentence: Suggests idea in dependent clause is less important or adds explanation

When <u>I</u> <u>get</u> to the train station, <u>I</u> <u>will call</u> Josh.

The italicized clause is dependent (or subordinate) because it explains when the most important idea in the sentence — calling Josh — will happen. It begins with the subordinating word *When*.

Because a dependent clause is not a complete sentence — because it does not express a complete thought — it can be joined to an independent clause without creating a run-on. When the dependent clause is the first clause in a sentence, it is followed by a comma. When the dependent clause is the second clause in the sentence, you usually do not need to separate the clauses with a comma (unless the dependent clause shows contrast).

Two sentences

Halloween was originally a religious holiday. People worshipped the saints.

Dependent clause: no comma needed

Halloween was originally a religious holiday when people worshipped the saints.

Dependent clause showing contrast: comma needed

Many holidays have religious origins, though some celebrations have moved away from their religious roots.

Pattern 5, Option 1: IC DC.

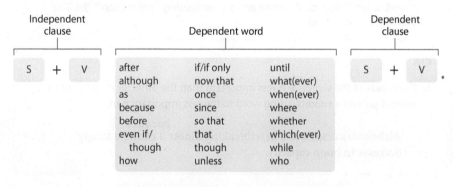

Independent clause	Dependent word			Dependent clause
S + V	after	if/if only	until	S + V .
	although	now that	what(ever)	
	as	once	when(ever)	
	because	since	where	
	before	so that	whether	
	even if/	that	which(ever)	
	though	though	while	
	how	unless	who	

Fused sentence (corrected)

Your final statement should express your interest in the , although position you do not want to sound desperate.

[The dependent clause *although you do not want to sound desperate* shows contrast, so a comma comes before it.]

Comma splice (corrected)

It is important to end an interview on a positive note because that final impression is what the interviewer will remember.

Pattern 5, Option 2: DC, IC.

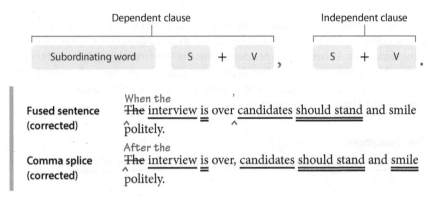

Fused sentence (corrected)	When the ~~The~~ interview is over candidates should stand and smile politely.
Comma splice (corrected)	After the ~~The~~ interview is over, candidates should stand and smile politely.

Finding and fixing run-ons:

Making a dependent clause

Find

> Alzheimer's disease is a heartbreaking illness, it causes a steady decrease in brain capacity.

1. To see if there are two independent clauses in a sentence, **underline** the subjects, and **double-underline** the verbs.

2. *Ask:* If the sentence has two independent clauses, are they separated by a period, a semicolon, or a comma and a coordinating conjunction? No. The sentence is a run-on.

Fix

3. If one part of the sentence is less important than the other, or if you want to make it so, add a subordinating word to the less important part.

> because
 Alzheimer's disease is a heartbreaking illness it causes a steady decrease in brain capacity.

> **PRACTICE 18–4**   **Correcting Run-ons by Adding a Subordinating Word**

Correct run-ons by adding a subordinating word to make a dependent clause. First, underline the subjects and double-underline the verbs. Although these run-ons can be corrected in different ways, in this exercise correct them by adding subordinating words. You may want to refer to the preceding graphics.

When bilingual speakers

Example: ~~Bilingual speakers~~ switch between two languages in the

same conversation it is called code-switching.

1. Code-switching is common wherever languages or dialects are in contact, not everyone thinks the habit is a good idea.

2. Some educators discourage code-switching in the classroom, they want students to practice English.

3. Students code-switch during group writing projects, they may actually solve writing problems.

4. Teachers know a lot more about code-switching today researchers began to study it in the 1980s.

5. Researchers have discovered a lot about code-switching they still have questions about how it can help bilingual students in elementary and middle school classrooms.

Special Considerations: Two Situations That Cause Run-ons

Using the word *then* and introducing quotes are two situations that can cause run-ons.

The Word Then

Many run-ons are caused by the word *then*. You can use *then* to join two independent clauses, but you must use correct punctuation when you do (Patterns 1–4). Otherwise, you will have a run-on sentence. Many writers use a comma alone to connect independent clauses with *then*. Unfortunately, this makes a comma splice.

| **Comma splice** | I picked up my laundry, then I went home. |

Examples of correcting this error using Patterns 1, 2, 4, and 5 are illustrated below.

. Then
I picked up my laundry, then I went home.

;
I picked up my laundry, then I went home.

and
I picked up my laundry, then I went home.

before
I picked up my laundry then I went home.

[The subordinating conjunction *before* is added to make "I went home" a dependent clause.]

Introducing a Quotation

In Chapters 7 and 10, you learned that you can include a reference to another writer's words in your own writing. When you introduce a quotation with a signal phrase, the signal phrase is followed by a comma.

Amy Tan says, "For Christmas I prayed for this blond-haired boy, Robert, and a slim new American nose." (118)

The introductory phrase has a subject (*Amy Tan*) and a verb (*says*), but it is not an independent clause (a complete thought). You can also introduce a quote with an independent clause.

Amy Tan explains that she was unhappy with her Chinese appearance: "For Christmas I prayed for this blond-haired boy, Robert, and a slim new American nose." (118)

In this sentence, an independent clause explains what a reader will find in the quote that follows. The reader is prompted to look for evidence that Tan was not happy with the fact that she looked Chinese.

Be careful when you introduce a quote with an independent clause. If you join an independent clause to a quote with a comma alone, you create a comma splice.

Comma splice   Amy Tan explains that she was unhappy with her Chinese appearance, "For Christmas I prayed for this blond-haired boy, Robert, and a slim new American nose." (118)

This kind of comma splice is usually corrected with a colon rather than with one of the patterns listed in this chapter. For more on colons, see, Chapter 28, pp. 549–50.

Edit for Run-ons

Use the information in this chapter to help you complete the practice exercise in this section and edit your own writing.

> **PRACTICE 18-5** **Editing Run-ons**
>
> The following student assignment contains five run-on sentences. Find and correct each one.
>
> In her essay "The Ways We Lie," Stephanie Ericsson discusses types of lies, and she argues that each type carries negative consequences, even if the lie seems innocent or common. One of the types of lies she discusses is stereotype or cliché this is of course when someone judges someone else without getting to know that person fully. I understand Ericsson's point when she calls a stereotype a lie, stereotypes do a lot of damage. My brother, for example, is a high school dropout. People always assume that he is not intelligent or that he won't understand instructions. The truth is that he is much smarter than the average high school graduate he dropped out because of peer pressure and social problems, not academic issues. I agree with Ericsson when she points out just how bad stereotypes are, "They are always dangerous" (215). On the other hand, I am not sure that a stereotype is a lie. When people form an opinion without enough information, I don't think they intend to mislead anyone; they are just being stupid. Stereotyping proves a person is not thinking, it doesn't mean a person is deceptive.

Chapter 18 Review

1. What is a fused sentence?

2. What is a comma splice?

3. List the five ways to correct run-ons.

4. What are two special situations to watch for when editing for run-ons?

Chapter 18 Quiz

Indicate the correct choice for each of the following items.

___ 1. Choose the item that has no errors.

    a. Please fill this prescription for me, it is for my allergies.

    b. Please fill this prescription for me. It is for my allergies.

    c. Please fill this prescription for me it is for my allergies.

___ 2. If an underlined portion of this sentence is incorrect, select the revision that fixes it. If the sentence is correct as written, choose d.

    Harlan is busy <u>now ask</u> <u>him if</u> he can do his <u>report next</u> week.
                     a   *b*   *c*

    a. now, so ask   c. report; next

    b. him, if   d. No change is necessary.

___ 3. Choose the item that has no errors.

    a. You cut all the onion slices to the same thickness, they will finish cooking at the same time.

    b. You cut all the onion slices to the same thickness they will finish cooking at the same time.

    c. If you cut all the onion slices to the same thickness, they will finish cooking at the same time.

___ 4. Choose the correct answer to fill in the blank.

    I have told Jervis several times not to tease the baby _____ he never listens.

    a. ,   c. No additional word or punctuation is necessary.

    b. , but

___ 5. Choose the item that has no errors.

    a. I can't get to the campus bookstore I order my textbooks online.

    b. I can't get to the campus bookstore, I order my textbooks online.

    c. When I can't get to the campus bookstore, I order my textbooks online.

___ 6. If an underlined portion of this sentence is incorrect, select the revision that fixes it. If the sentence is correct as written, choose d.

    Many people think a tomato is a vegetable it is really a fruit.
        _a_   _b_   _c_

    a. Many, people   c. really; a

    b. vegetable; it   d. No change is necessary.

___ 7. Choose the item that has no errors.

    a. Although air conditioning makes hot days more comfortable, it will increase your energy bills.

    b. Air conditioning makes hot days more comfortable it will increase your energy bills.

    c. Air conditioning makes hot days more comfortable, it will increase your energy bills.

___ 8. If an underlined portion of this sentence is incorrect, select the revision that fixes it. If the sentence is correct as written, choose d.

    In northern Europe, bodies that are thousands of years old have been
                                                 _a_

    found in swamps, some bodies are so well preserved that they look like
                 _b_   _c_

    sleeping people.

    a. old, have   c. look, like

    b. swamps. Some   d. No change is necessary.

___ 9. Choose the item that has no errors.

    a. Do not be shy about opening doors for strangers, courtesy is always appreciated.

    b. Do not be shy about opening doors for strangers; courtesy is always appreciated.

    c. Do not be shy about opening doors for strangers courtesy is always appreciated.

___ 10. Choose the correct answer to fill in the blank.

    You can ride with me to work _____ you can take the train.

    a. , or   c. No additional word or punctuation is necessary.

    b. if

19

Make Subjects and Verbs Match:

Solving Agreement Problems

In Chapter 16, you learned to identify subjects and verbs. You may have also noticed that a verb often changes if the subject changes:

Jamal practices his passing routes on Tuesdays and Thursdays.

His receivers practice with him on those days.

When you change verb forms based on the subject of the sentence, you are making the subject and verb **agree**.

 Language note: Some varieties of English follow different subject-verb agreement rules than those presented in this chapter. When you are editing for subject-verb agreement, consider your audience, purpose, and context to determine the most appropriate verb form.

Recognize Subject-Verb Agreement

In any sentence, the *subject and the verb must match — or agree —* in number. If the subject is singular (one person, place, or thing), the verb must also be singular. If the subject is plural (more than one), the verb must also be plural.

Language note: The word *they* is grammatically plural, but it may be used to refer to a single individual, as in this sentence: *When a volunteer works on the campaign, they are assigned to a paid employee's department.*

Singular	The <u>skydiver</u> <u>jumps</u> out of the airplane.
Plural	The <u>skydivers</u> <u>jump</u> out of the airplane.

Regular verbs (with forms that follow a fixed pattern) have two forms in the present tense: one that ends in *-s* and one that has no ending. The third-person subjects — *he, she, it* — and singular nouns always use the form that ends in *-s*. First-person subjects (*I*), second-person subjects (*you*), and plural subjects use the form with no ending.

Regular Verbs, Present Tense

Present Tense	Singular	Plural
First person	I walk.	We walk.
Second person	You walk.	You walk.
Third person	He (she, it) walks.	They walk.
	Joe walks.	Joe and Alice walk.
	The student walks.	The students walk.

Make Subjects and Verbs Agree

To make sure that subjects and verbs agree in your own writing, look for five trouble spots that often signal problems.

1. The Verb Is a Form of Be, Have, or Do

The verbs *be, have,* and *do* have special rules for forming singular and plural forms; they are **irregular verbs**. (For more on irregular verb forms, see Chapter 20.)

Forms of the Verb *Be*

Present Tense	Singular	Plural
First person	I am	we are
Second person	you are	you are
Third person	she, he, it is	they are
	the student is	the students are

Past Tense	Singular	Plural
First person	I was	we were
Second person	you were	you were
Third person	she, he, it was	they were
	the student was	the students were

Forms of the Verb *Have*, Present Tense

Present Tense	Singular	Plural
First person	I have	we have
Second person	you have	you have
Third person	she, he, it has	they have
	the student has	the students have

Forms of the Verb *Do*, Present Tense

Present Tense	Singular	Plural
First person	I do	we do
Second person	you do	you do
Third person	she, he, it does	they do
	the student does	the students do

are
They ~~is~~ sick today.

has
Joan ~~have~~ the best jewelry.

does
Carlos ~~do~~ the laundry every Wednesday.

Finding and fixing problems with subject-verb agreement:

Making subjects and verbs agree when the verb is *be*, *have*, or *do*

Find

My father have a new car.

1. **Underline** the subject.

2. *Ask:* Is the subject in the first (*I*), second (*you*), or third person (*he / she*)?
   Third person

3. *Ask:* Is the subject singular or plural? Singular

Fix

4. **Choose** the verb by matching it to the form of the subject (third person, singular).

   My father has a new car.

PRACTICE 19–1   **Identifying Problems with Subject-Verb Agreement**

Find the four problems with subject-verb agreement in this cover letter. Then, in the space provided, record the numbers of the sentences that have subject-verb agreement problems.

Which sentences have subject-verb agreement problems? _____

1 I am applying for the landscaping intern position. **2** I have been working for three years at A and G Landscaping Company. **3** This company, which is highly respected, handle lawn care needs for several businesses and commercial properties in our community. **4** When I began at the company, I was a crew member assigned to a residential team, but since then, I have risen to be a crew manager. **5** Crew managers makes sure that the client are satisfied with the level of service. **6** The members of my crew has given me excellent reviews. **7** As a result, my boss continues to give me new responsibilities. **8** I am confident that I am ready to extend my training in a new way at the college. **9** The experience of working with new crew members at the college will help me take another step toward my dream: owning my own landscaping company.

2. Words Come between the Subject and the Verb

When the subject and verb are not directly next to each other, it is more difficult to find them to make sure they agree. Most often, either a prepositional phrase or a dependent clause comes between the subject and the verb.

Prepositional Phrase between the Subject and the Verb

A *prepositional phrase* starts with a preposition and ends with a noun or pronoun:

> I took my bag *of books* and threw it *across the room*.

The subject of a sentence is *never* in a prepositional phrase. When you are looking for the subject of a sentence, you can cross out any prepositional phrases:

> Our <u>need</u> ~~for vast amounts of information in nanoseconds~~ has made the stereotype vital to modern communication. (Ericsson 213)

| **Finding and fixing problems with subject-verb agreement:** Making subjects and verbs agree when they are separated by a prepositional phrase | **Find**

    <u>Learners</u> ~~with dyslexia~~ faces many challenges.

1. **Underline** the subject.
2. **Cross out** any prepositional phrase that follows the subject.
3. *Ask:* Is the subject singular or plural? Plural

Fix

4. **Choose** the form of the verb that matches the subject.

    Learners with dyslexia face many challenges. |

PRACTICE 19–2   **Making Subjects and Verbs Agree When They Are Separated by a Prepositional Phrase**

In each of the following sentences, cross out the prepositional phrase between the subject and the verb, and circle the correct form of the verb. Remember that the subject of a sentence is never in a prepositional phrase.

Example: Tomatoes ~~from the supermarket~~ (is / (are)) often tasteless.

1. Experts in agriculture and plant science (identifies / identify) several reasons for flavorless tomatoes.

2. First, many commercial growers in the United States (chooses / choose) crop yield over taste.

3. Specially engineered breeds of tomatoes (produces / produce) many more bushels per planting than traditional breeds do.

4. Unfortunately, the tomatoes inside each bushel (tastes / taste) nothing like their sweet, juicy homegrown relatives.

5. Growing conditions at commercial farms also (contributes / contribute) to the problem.

Dependent Clause between the Subject and the Verb

A *dependent clause* has a subject and a verb, but it does not express a complete thought. When a dependent clause comes between the subject and the verb, it usually starts with the word *who, whose, whom, that,* or *which.* Dependent clauses that start with these words are called **relative clauses**. The subject of a sentence is *never* in a dependent clause. When you are looking for the subject of a sentence, you can cross out any dependent clauses:

The chile plants, ~~which also saved him from giving up his hot, sweaty quarters~~, were propped up with sticks to support an abundance of red fruit. (Soto 166)

Finding and fixing problems with subject-verb agreement:

Making subjects and verbs agree when they are separated by a dependent clause

Find

The security <u>systems</u> ~~that shopping sites on the Internet provide~~ is surprisingly effective.

1. **Underline** the subject.

2. **Cross out** any dependent clause that follows the subject. (Look for the words *who, whose, whom, that,* and *which* because they can signal such a clause.)

3. *Ask:* Is the subject singular or plural? Plural

Fix

4. **Choose** the form of the verb that matches the subject.

The security systems that shopping sites on the Internet provide are surprisingly effective.

PRACTICE 19–3   Making Subjects and Verbs Agree When They Are Separated by a Dependent Clause

In each of the following sentences, cross out any dependent clauses. Then correct any problems with subject-verb agreement. If the subject and the verb agree, write "OK" next to the sentence.

have

Example: My cousins ~~who immigrated to this country from Ecuador has~~ jobs in a fast-food restaurant.

1. The restaurant that hired my cousins are not treating them fairly.

2. People who work in the kitchen has to report to work at 7:00 a.m.

3. The boss who supervises the morning shift tells the workers not to punch in until 9:00 a.m.

4. The benefits that full-time workers earn have not been offered to my cousins.

5. Ramón, whose hand was injured slicing potatoes, need to have physical therapy.

3. *The Sentence Has a Compound Subject*

A **compound subject** is two (or more) subjects joined by *and, or,* or *nor*.

And/Or Rule: If two subjects are joined by *and*, use a plural verb. If two subjects are joined by *or* (or *nor*), they are considered separate, and the verb should agree with the subject it is closer to.

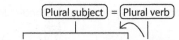

The teacher *and* her aide grade all the exams.

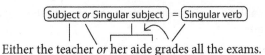

Either the teacher *or* her aide grades all the exams.

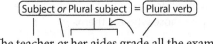

The teacher *or* her aides grade all the exams.

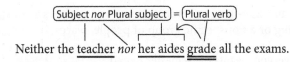

Neither the teacher *nor* her aides grade all the exams.

Finding and fixing problems with subject-verb agreement: Making subjects and verbs agree in a sentence with a compound subject	**Find**
	Watermelon or cantaloupe make a delicious and healthy snack.
	1. **Underline** the subjects.
	2. **Circle** the word between the subjects.
	3. *Ask:* Does that word join the subjects to make them plural or keep them separate? It keeps them separate.
	4. *Ask:* Is the subject that is closer to the verb singular or plural? Singular
	Fix
	5. **Choose** the verb form that agrees with the subject that is closer to the verb.
	Watermelon or cantaloupe makes a delicious and healthy snack.

> **PRACTICE 19–4**   **Choosing the Correct Verb in a Sentence with a Compound Subject**

In each of the following sentences, underline the word (*and* or *or*) that joins the parts of the compound subject. Then circle the correct form of the verb.

Example: My mother <u>and</u> my sister (has / (have)) asked a nutritionist for advice on a healthy diet.

1. A tomato and a watermelon (shares / share) more than just red-colored flesh.

2. A cooked tomato or a slice of watermelon (contains / contain) a nutrient called lycopene that seems to protect the human body from some diseases.

3. Fruits and vegetables (is / are) an important part of a healthy diet, most experts agree.

4. Nutrition experts and dietitians (believes / believe) that eating a variety of colors of fruits and vegetables is best for human health.

5. Collard greens or spinach (provides / provide) vitamins, iron, and protection from blindness to those who eat them.

4. The Subject Is an Indefinite Pronoun

An **indefinite pronoun**, such as *anyone*, *everyone*, and *no one*, replaces a nonspecific person, place, or thing or a nonspecific group of people, places, or things.

Singular	Everyone <u>wants</u> the semester to end.
Singular	<u>Either</u> of the meals <u>is</u> good.
Plural	<u>Many</u> <u>want</u> the semester to end.

Indefinite pronouns are often singular, although there are some exceptions, as shown in the chart below.

Indefinite Pronouns

Always Singular			May Be Singular or Plural
another	everybody	no one	all
anybody	everyone	nothing	any
anyone	everything	one (of)	none
anything	much	somebody	some
each (of)*	neither (of)*	someone	
either (of)*	nobody	something	

*When one of these words is the subject, mentally replace it with the word *one*. *One* is singular and takes a singular verb.

Often, an indefinite pronoun is followed by a prepositional phrase or a dependent clause. Remember that the verb of a sentence must agree with the subject of the sentence, and the subject of a sentence is *never* in a prepositional phrase or dependent clause. To choose the correct verb, cross out the prepositional phrase or dependent clause:

Everyone ~~in all the classes~~ (want / **wants**) the term to end.

Several ~~who have to take the math exam~~ (is / **are**) studying together.

Finding and fixing problems with subject-verb agreement: Making subjects and verbs agree when the subject is an indefinite pronoun	**Find** One ~~of my best friends~~ live in California. 1. **Underline** the subject. 2. **Cross out** any prepositional phrase or dependent clause that follows the subjects. 3. *Ask:* Is the subject singular or plural? Singular **Fix** 4. **Choose** the verb form that agrees with the subject. One of my best friends lives in California.

PRACTICE 19–5   **Choosing the Correct Verb When the Subject Is an Indefinite Pronoun**

In each of the following sentences, cross out any prepositional phrase or dependent clause that comes between the subject and the verb. Then underline the subject, and circle the correct verb.

> **Example:**   One ~~of the strangest human experiences~~ (**results**) / result) from the "small-world" phenomenon.

1. Everyone (**remembers** / remember) an example of a "small-world" phenomenon.

2. Someone whom you have just met (**tells** / tell) you a story.

3. During the story, one of you (realizes / realize) that you are connected somehow.

4. One of your friends (lives / live) next door to the person.

5. Someone in your family (knows / know) someone in the person's family.

5. *The Verb Comes before the Subject*

In most sentences, the subject comes before the verb. Sometimes, however, a writer reverses this order for emphasis: *Most inspiring of all were her speeches on freedom.*

Two other kinds of sentences that often reverse the usual subject-verb order are questions and sentences that begin with *here* or *there*. In these two types of sentences, check carefully for errors in subject-verb agreement.

Questions

In questions, the verb or part of the verb comes before the subject. To find the subject and verb, you can turn the question around as if you were going to answer it:

> "What would Robert think of our shabby Chinese Christmas?" (Tan 118)
> Robert would think . . .
>
> "Why are the students having a party?"
> The students are having a party because . . .

> **Language note:** For information on how to form questions, see the section on questions in Chapter 16, pp. 344–45.

Sentences That Begin with **Here** or **There**

When a sentence begins with *here* or *there*, the subject often follows the verb. Sometimes, you can turn the sentence around to find the subject and verb:

> Here is your copy of the study guide. / Your copy of the study guide is here.
> There are four copies on the desk. / Four copies are on the desk.

Notice the subjects (underlined once) and the verbs (underlined twice) in the following sentences:

> There are an additional 5,042 current K–12 CAMP qualifying students who were at one time active in the GaMEP program (Bello Escobar 287)
>
> But there is a world of difference between telling functional lies and living a lie. (Ericsson 216)

Finding and fixing problems with subject-verb agreement:

Making subjects and verbs agree when the verb comes before the subject

Find

What classes are the professor teaching?

There is two good classes in the music department.

1. If the sentence is a question, **turn the question into a statement**: *The professor (is / are) teaching the classes.*

2. If the sentence begins with *here* or *there,* **turn it around**: *Two good classes (is / are) in the music department.*

3. **Identify** the subject in each of the two new sentences. It is "professor" in the first sentence and "classes" in the second.

4. *Ask:* Is the subject singular or plural? "Professor" is singular; "classes" is plural.

Fix

5. **Choose** the form of the verb in each sentence that matches the subject.

What classes is the professor teaching?

There are two good classes in the music department.

PRACTICE 19–6   **Correcting a Sentence When the Verb Comes before the Subject**

Correct any problems with subject-verb agreement in the following sentences. If a sentence is already correct, write "OK" next to it.

      does
Example: What electives ~~do~~ the school offer?
      ^

1. What are the best reason to study music?

2. There is several good reasons.

3. There is evidence that music helps students with math.

4. What is your favorite musical instrument?

5. Here is a guitar, a saxophone, and a piano.

Language note: When the complete verb in a sentence contains a modal auxiliary verb (*can, could, should, would, may, might, must,* or *will*), there is no *-s* at the end of the modal verb or the main verb of the sentence.

	modal auxiliary

Incorrect   My teacher cans speak four languages.

	main verb

Incorrect   My teachers can speaks four languages.

Correct   My teacher can speak four languages.

Watch for Subject-Verb Agreement in Partial Quotations

In some types of writing, you may need to quote a sentence or part of a sentence from another writer. When you choose to include a partial quote in your writing, pay attention to subject-verb agreement.

Incorrect   Stephanie Ericsson says that a stereotype — such as the idea that all truck drivers use foul language — "take a single tree and make it a landscape." (215)

Correct   Stephanie Ericsson says that stereotypes — such as the idea that all truck drivers use foul language — "take a single tree and make it a landscape." (215)

Correct   Stephanie Ericsson says that a stereotype — such as the idea that all truck drivers use foul language — can "take a single tree and make it a landscape." (215)

Edit for Subject-Verb Agreement

Use the information in this chapter to help you complete the practice exercise in this section and edit your own writing.

PRACTICE 19–7   **Editing for Subject-Verb Agreement**

Find and correct ten fragments in the following paragraph.

In his essay "A Learning Tool Whose Time Has Come," Jason Yilmaz argues we should use social media in the classroom because such online interaction "make students feel more confident and connected" (297). This argument makes sense; after all, each one of the students in this class have talked about the ways the discussion board helps the class understand the material and feel more empowered to express opinions. On the other hand, Shari Beck raises a legitimate concern in her essay "A Classroom Distraction — and Worse." Beck, who is a mom to young teenagers, say she does not want to see social network platforms in a class because "students' postings on Facebook or Twitter might compromise their privacy" (298). There is several choices that students and teachers can make to receive the benefits of social networks while reducing the privacy problems. For example, our English course use the BlackBoard platform, and only students who are registered in the class gets to see what is posted there. Teachers and assistants with administrative control of the site sets the rules and the guidelines. But if a student group wants to avoid the oversight of a teacher, it cans create a private Facebook group. Only members of the group can see the content on the site. Unfortunately, a private group without the presence of teachers make cheating easier, as Shari Beck points out in her essay. If a site is created by the students and for the students, the teacher cannot controls what happens on the site. Maybe the best solution is for the teacher to offer a private but dynamic media platform for students so that students won't see a need to create a separate discussion space.

PRACTICE 19–8   **Editing a Cover Letter**

Reread the cover letter in Practice 19-1 (p. 385). You may have already identified the subject-verb agreement errors; if not, do so now. Next, using what you have learned in this chapter, correct each error.

Chapter 19 Review

1. The _____ and the _____ in a sentence must agree (match) in terms of number. They must both be _____, or they must both be plural.

2. Five trouble spots (provided below) can cause errors in subject-verb agreement:
   - When the verb is a form of _____ , _____ , or _____
   - When a _____ or a _____ comes between the subject and the verb
   - When the sentence has a _____ subject joined by *and, or,* or *nor*
   - When the subject is an _____ pronoun
   - When the _____ comes _____ the subject

Chapter 19 Quiz

Indicate the correct choice for each of the following items.

___ 1. If an underlined portion of this sentence is incorrect, select the revision that fixes it. If the sentence is correct as written, choose d.

> **There is only certain times when you can call to get**
> $\quad\quad\quad$ a $\quad\quad\quad\quad\quad\quad\quad\quad\quad\quad\quad$ b $\quad\quad$ c
> **technical support for this computer.**

    a. There are   c. getting

    b. you could   d. No change is necessary.

___ 2. Choose the correct word to fill in the blank.

> **Dana's dog Bernard _____ just a puppy, but he moves so slowly that he seems old.**

    a. be   c. being

    b. am   d. is

___ 3. If an underlined portion of this sentence is incorrect, select the revision that fixes it. If the sentence is correct as written, choose d.

> **The umpire was not happy to see that everyone were watching**
> $\quad\quad\quad$ a $\quad\quad\quad\quad\quad\quad\quad\quad\quad\quad\quad\quad\quad\quad\quad\quad$ b
> **him argue with the baseball player.**
> $\quad\quad\quad$ c

    a. umpire were   c. argues with

    b. everyone was   d. No change is necessary.

___ 4. Choose the correct word to fill in the blank.

> **The woman who rented us our kayaks _____ now paddling her own kayak down the river.**

a. are   b. be   c. is

___ 5. Choose the item that has no errors.

a. Alex and Dane likes to travel now that they have retired from their jobs.

b. Alex and Dane liking to travel now that they have retired from their jobs.

c. Alex and Dane like to travel now that they have retired from their jobs.

___ 6. Choose the correct word to fill in the blank.

> **The builders of this house _____ used the best materials they could find.**

a. have   b. having   c. has

___ 7. Choose the correct word to fill in the blank.

> **The calm before hurricanes _____ most people with anxiety.**

a. fill   b. filling   c. fills

___ 8. Choose the item that has no errors.

a. Sheryl and her sons go to the beach whenever they can find the time.

b. Sheryl and her sons goes to the beach whenever they can find the time.

c. Sheryl and her sons is going to the beach whenever they can find the time.

___ 9. Choose the correct word to fill in the blank.

> **Where _____ the children's wet swimsuits?**

a. are   b. is   c. be

___ 10. If an underlined portion of this sentence is incorrect, select the revision that fixes it. If the sentence is correct as written, choose d.

> **Anybody who <u>can</u> speak several languages <u>are</u> in great demand**
>   a   b
>
> **to <u>work</u> for the government, especially in foreign embassies.**
>   c

a. could   c. working

b. is   d. No change is necessary.

20

Indicate Time Clearly:

Addressing Verb Problems

- Recognize verb tenses in sentences.
- Identify the principal parts of verbs.
- Use simple, progressive, and perfect verbs correctly.
- Use passive verbs and modal verbs correctly.
- Check verb forms for accuracy and consistency.
- Edit your own writing for verb tense.

One of the most important things we communicate when we are speaking or writing is the time frame during which events occur. In addition to time words like *now* or *yesterday*, English requires that the main verb in a clause include time information. When verbs do not show time consistently or accurately, readers may misinterpret what is written.

Recognize Verb Tense

Verb tense tells *when* an action happened: in the past, in the present, or in the future. Verb tense can also show **aspect**, which tells us if an action is in progress or complete. Verbs change their **base form** (the simple form that appears in a dictionary) or use the helping verbs *have, be,* or *will* to indicate different tenses. (Subjects are underlined, and verbs are double-underlined.)

Present	Damon's mother's special <u>dressing combines</u> her own turkey broth with giblets and bits of the neck and boiled egg. (Okona 263)
Past	On April 24, New Orleans city <u>employees began</u> the process of removing four Confederate monuments. (Brophy 320)
Future	<u>Some</u> of you <u>will judge</u> me for that. (Whitmer 142)

The following sections will teach you about verb tenses and give you practice with using them. You should also pay attention to the verb tenses in your reading. Select paragraphs from your reading, circle the verbs, and think about the way the tenses are used. You can also read the paragraphs out loud, focusing on pronouncing and hearing yourself say the verb forms.

The Principal Parts of Verbs

All of the English tenses are formed from one of the three principal parts of a verb: the base (or first) form, the past (or second) form, or the past participle (third form). For many English verbs, known as *regular verbs*, it is easy to predict these forms. The base form is the simplest form, the one we would find in a dictionary. The second and third forms for regular verbs are the same: both have an *-ed* ending. Here are the principal parts for the regular verbs *walk* and *smile*:

Base (First) Form	Past (Second) Form	Past Participle (Third Form)
walk	walked	walked
smile	smiled	smiled

Many common English verbs, however, are **irregular** — they do not form the past (second) and past participle (third) forms by adding *-ed*. The past tense and past participle of irregular verbs usually involve a change in spelling, although some irregular verbs, such as *cost, hit,* and *put,* do not change their spelling. The most common irregular verbs are *be* and *have*. As you write and edit, refer to the following chart to make sure you have the correct form of irregular verbs.

Irregular Verbs

Base (First) Form	Past (Second) Form	Past Participle (Third Form)
be (am/are/is)	was/were	been
become	became	become
begin	began	begun
bite	bit	bitten
blow	blew	blown
break	broke	broken
bring	brought	brought
build	built	built
buy	bought	bought
catch	caught	caught
choose	chose	chosen
come	came	come
cost	cost	cost
dive	dived, dove	dived
do	did	done
draw	drew	drawn
drink	drank	drunk
drive	drove	driven
eat	ate	eaten
fall	fell	fallen
feed	fed	fed
feel	felt	felt
fight	fought	fought
find	found	found
fly	flew	flown
forget	forgot	forgotten
get	got	gotten
give	gave	given
go	went	gone
grow	grew	grown
have/has	had	had
hear	heard	heard
hide	hid	hidden

Base (First) Form	Past (Second) Form	Past Participle (Third Form)
hit	hit	hit
hold	held	held
hurt	hurt	hurt
keep	kept	kept
know	knew	known
lay	laid	laid
lead	led	led
leave	left	left
let	let	let
lie	lay	lain
light	lit	lit
lose	lost	lost
make	made	made
mean	meant	meant
meet	met	met
pay	paid	paid
put	put	put
quit	quit	quit
read	read	read
ride	rode	ridden
ring	rang	rung
rise	rose	risen
run	ran	run
say	said	said
see	saw	seen
seek	sought	sought
sell	sold	sold
send	sent	sent
shake	shook	shaken
show	showed	shown
shrink	shrank	shrunk
shut	shut	shut
sing	sang	sung
sink	sank	sunk

→

Base (First) Form	Past (Second) Form	Past Participle (Third Form)
sit	sat	sat
sleep	slept	slept
speak	spoke	spoken
spend	spent	spent
stand	stood	stood
steal	stole	stolen
stick	stuck	stuck
sting	stung	stung
strike	struck	struck, stricken
swim	swam	swum
take	took	taken
teach	taught	taught
tear	tore	torn
tell	told	told
think	thought	thought
throw	threw	thrown
understand	understood	understood
wake	woke	woken
wear	wore	worn
win	won	won
write	wrote	written

Use Verbs Correctly: The Simple Tenses

The simple tenses consist of the simple present, simple past, and simple future.

Simple Present Tense

The **simple present tense** is used to describe situations that exist now, including facts, habits, schedules, and preferences. The simple present tense is the base form of the verb with either an -s ending or no ending, as illustrated in the following chart:

-s Ending	No Ending
jumps	jump
lives	live
walks	walk

Use the *-s* ending when the subject is in the third person (*he, she, it,* or the name of one person or thing). Use no ending for all other subjects. (For more information on making subjects and verbs match in the present tense, see the section "Make Subjects and Verbs Agree" in Chapter 19, pp. 383–94.)

PRACTICE 20-1   **Using Present-Tense Regular Verbs**

In each of the following sentences, first underline the subject and then circle the appropriate verb form.

Example: I (tries / try) to keep to my budget.

1. My classes (requires / require) much of my time these days.

2. In addition to attending school, I (works / work) twenty hours a week in the college library.

3. The other employees (agrees / agree) that the work atmosphere is pleasant.

4. Sometimes, we even (manages / manage) to do homework at the library.

5. The job (pays / pay) a fairly low wage, however.

Present Tense of Be *and* Have

The present tense of the verbs *be* and *have* is irregular, as shown in the following chart:

Present Tense of *Be* and *Have*

Be		Have	
Singular	**Plural**	**Singular**	**Plural**
I am	we are	I have	we have
you are	you are	you have	you have
he, she, it is	they are	he, she, it has	they have
the editor is	the editors are		
DJ is	DJ and Ling are		

PRACTICE 20-2   **Using *Be* and *Have* in the Present Tense**

In each of the following sentences, fill in the correct present-tense form of the verb indicated in parentheses.

Example: Because of my university's internship program, I ‗am‗ (*be*) able to receive academic credit for my summer job.

1. I ____ (*have*) a job lined up with a company that provides private security to many local businesses and residential developments.

2. The company ___ (*have*) a good record of keeping its clients safe from crime.

3. The company _ (*be*) part of a fast-growing industry.

4. Many people no longer ____ (*have*) faith in the ability of the police to protect them.

5. People with lots of money ___ (*be*) willing to pay for their own protection.

⊕ **Language note:** All simple present tense verbs except *be* require *do/does* in negative statements and questions. In negative statements and questions with forms of the helping verb *do*, use the base form of the main verb:

Incorrect	John doesn't works on Saturday.
Correct	John doesn't work on Saturday.
Incorrect	Does this teacher requires a presentation?
Correct	Does this teacher require a presentation?

The Simple Past

Use the **simple past** (the second form of the verb) to describe situations that began and ended in the past. In regular verbs, the simple past has an *-ed* ending. To find the past form of irregular verbs, refer to the "Irregular Verbs" chart on pages 400–02.

	Simple Present Tense	Simple Past Tense
First person	I avoid her.	I avoided her.
Second person	You help me.	You helped me.
Third person	He walks quickly.	He walked quickly.

Past Tense of Be

The past tense of the verb *be* is tricky because it has two different forms: *was* and *were*.

Past Tense of *Be*

	Singular	Plural
First person	I was	we were
Second person	you were	you were
Third person	she, he, it was	they were
	the student was	the students were

 Language note: All simple past tense verbs except *be* use the helping verb *did* to form negatives and questions. In negatives and questions with *did*, use the base form of the verb:

Incorrect	She did not wanted money for helping.
Correct	She did not **want** money for helping.
Incorrect	Did she saw anything strange?
Correct	Did she **see** anything strange?

For more on negatives and questions, see Chapter 16, pages 340–41.

> | PRACTICE 20-3 | Using Regular and Irregular Verbs in the Past Tense |
> | --- | --- |
>
> Read the following paragraph, and write the correct past tense of the verb. If you are unsure of the past-tense forms of irregular verbs, refer to the "Irregular Verbs" chart on pages 402–04.
>
> For years, Homer and Langley Collyer _____ (*be*) known for their strange living conditions. Neighbors who _____ (*pass*) by the brothers' New York City townhouse _____ (*see*) huge piles of trash through the windows. At night, Langley _____ (*roam*) the streets in search of more junk. In March 1947, an anonymous caller _____ (*tell*) the police that someone had died in the Collyers' home. In response, officers _____ (*break*) through a second-floor window and _____ (*tunnel*) through mounds of newspapers, old umbrellas, and other junk. Eventually, they _____ (*find*) the body of Homer Collyer, who _____ (*seem*) to have died of starvation. But where _____ (*be*) Langley? In efforts to locate him, workers _____ (*spend*) days removing trash from the house — more than one hundred tons' worth in total. They _____ (*bring*) a strange variety of items to the curb, including medical equipment, bowling balls, fourteen pianos, and the frame of a Model T car. In early April, a worker finally _____ (*discover*) Langley's body. It _____ (*lie*) just 10 feet from where Homer had been found. Apparently, Langley _____ (*die*) while bringing food to his disabled brother. As he tunneled ahead, a pile of trash _____ (*fall*) on him and _____ (*crush*) him. This trash was part of a booby trap that Langley had created to stop intruders. Not long after the brothers' deaths, the city _____ (*demolish*) their former home. In 1965, community leaders _____ (*do*) something that might have surprised Homer and Langley: where the trash-filled home once _____ (*stand*), workers _____ (*create*) a neat and peaceful park. In the 1990s, this green space _____ (*become*) the Collyer Brothers Park.

The Simple Future

The simple future refers to actions that will begin in the future. It is very easy to form: for all subjects, use the modal verb *will* plus the base form of the verb:

I/You/She/He/We/They <u>*will eat*</u> pizza tonight.

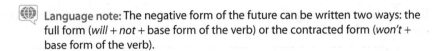 **Language note:** The negative form of the future can be written two ways: the full form (*will* + *not* + base form of the verb) or the contracted form (*won't* + base form of the verb).

Language note: Do not use the future tense in a dependent clause beginning with a time word, even if the action occurs in the future. (For more on dependent clauses, see Chapters 18 and 24.)

Incorrect	After he will retire, my *father* will move to Florida.
	The students are planning to celebrate after they will finish exams.
Correct	After he retires, my father will move to Florida.
	The students are planning to celebrate after they finish exams.

Common Time Words (Subordinating Conjunctions)

after   as soon as   before   when   while

Use Verbs Correctly: The Progressive Tenses

A **progressive tense** is used to describe ongoing actions in the past, present, or future. The progressive tenses are often used to show background actions in progress at a specific time. All progressive tenses are formed by combining a form of the word *be* and the *-ing* form of another verb.

Present Progressive

The **present progressive** represents an action in progress at the time that someone is writing or speaking:

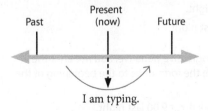

To form the present progressive, use the correct present tense form of *be* and the *-ing* form of the verb:

(Present of *be (am / is / are)*) + (Base verb ending in *-ing*) = (Present progressive)

I **am typing**.   We **are typing**.

You **are typing**.   They **are typing**.

She/He **is typing**.

🌐 **Language note:** To make the present progressive negative, add *not* after the form of *be*. To make a question, move the form of *be* to the beginning of the sentence.

Negative   We are not typing.

Question   Are you typing?

Past Progressive

The **past progressive** represents an action in progress at a specific time in the past or at the moment another action occurred in the past:

To form the past progressive, use the correct past tense form of *be* and the *-ing* form of the verb:

(Present of *be (was / were)*) + (Base verb ending in *-ing*) + (Past progressive)

I/He/She/It was working at 9:00 last night.

You/We/They were working at 9:00 last night.

🌐 **Language note:** To make the past progressive negative, add *not* after the form of *be*. To make a question, move the form of *be* to the beginning of the sentence.

Negative   They were not working at 9:00 last night.

Question   Were you working at 9:00 last night?

Future Progressive

The **future progressive** represents an action that will be in progress at a specific time in the future:

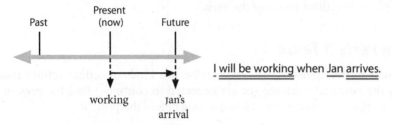

I will be working when Jan arrives.

Form the future progressive with *will be* and the *-ing* form of the verb:

(*will be*) + (Base verb ending in *-ing*) = (Future progressive)

I/You/He/She/It/We/They will be sleeping at midnight.

> 🌐 Language note: To make the future progressive negative, add *not* between *will* and the form of *be*. To make a question, move *will* to the beginning of the sentence.
>
> **Negative**   They will not be sleeping at midnight.
>
> **Question**   Will you be sleeping at midnight?

> 🌐 Language note: Some English verbs do not generally occur in the progressive tense. These verbs are nonaction verbs; they usually describe states, possession, or opinion.
>
> **Incorrect**   My mother is owning a house at the beach.
>
> I am needing a haircut.
>
> **Correct**   My mother owns a house at the beach.
>
> I need a haircut.

Common Nonaction Verbs

believe	need	possess	seem
like	own	prefer	

Use Verbs Correctly: The Perfect Tenses

The perfect tenses consist of the present perfect, past perfect, and future perfect. Perfect tense verbs are formed by combining a form of the helping verb *have* and the past participle (third form) of the verb.

Present Perfect Tense

The **present perfect tense** is used to describe two kinds of action: actions that began in the past and continue (or are expected to continue) into the present, and actions that occurred at an unknown time before the present:

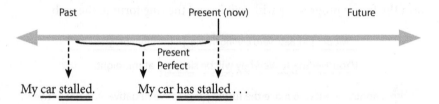

Present perfect tense   My <u>car</u> <u>has</u> <u>stalled</u> several times recently.

[This sentence says that the stalling began in the past and may continue into the present or future.]

Past tense   My <u>car</u> <u>stalled</u> this morning on the way to work.

[This sentence says that the car stalled once; it's finished, and we don't expect it to happen again.]

Present perfect tense   <u>I</u> <u>have</u> <u>read</u> all seven books in the *Harry Potter* series.

[This sentence says that some time before now the speaker read the books, but that time is not specified.]

Past tense   <u>I</u> <u>read</u> *Harry Potter and the Order of the Phoenix* three years ago.

[This sentence describes an action that was completed at a specific time before now.]

Form the present perfect using the correct present tense form of *have* and the past participle:

(have/has) + (Past participle) = (Present perfect)

I/You/We/They <u>have seen</u> three new movies.

He/She/It <u>has seen</u> three new movies.

Language note: To make the present perfect sentences negative, add *not* between *has/have* and the past participle. To make a question, move *has/have* to the beginning of the sentence. Many writers add the word *yet* with the present perfect in negative statements and questions.

Negative   We <u>have</u> not <u>seen</u> the museum (yet).

Question   <u>Has</u> he <u>seen</u> the museum (yet)?

Language note: The words *since* and *for* often signal that the present perfect is required. We do not use the simple present or present progressive to describe actions that began in the past and continue into the present.

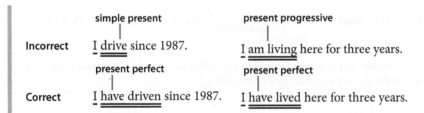

	simple present	present progressive
Incorrect	I <u>drive</u> since 1987.	I <u>am living</u> here for three years.
	present perfect	present perfect
Correct	I <u>have driven</u> since 1987.	I <u>have lived</u> here for three years.

PRACTICE 20-4   Using the Present Perfect Tense

In each of the following sentences, circle the appropriate verb.

Example: Because of the pandemic, many gyms and health clubs [closed]/have closed during the summer of 2020.

1. Sales of home exercise equipment (increased/have increased) in June, July, and August of 2020.

2. Companies (reported/have reported) strong sales since that time.

3. Danera Campbell (purchased/has purchased) a bike and (joined/has joined) a virtual exercise group in January 2021.

4. Danera (lost/has lost) 15 pounds since she began working out with the virtual group.

5. Before she joined the group, Danera (didn't know/hasn't known) how to find the motivation to stick with an exercise plan.

Past Perfect Tense

The **past perfect tense** is used to show the relationship between two actions in the past: One action began and ended in the past before the other action began:

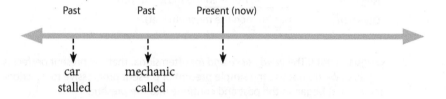

| Past perfect tense | My <u>car had stalled</u> several times before I called the mechanic. |

[This sentence says that both the *stalling* and *calling the mechanic* happened in the past but that the stalling happened before the calling.]

To form the past perfect, use *had* and the past participle of the verb:

$$\boxed{had} + \boxed{\text{Past participle}} = \boxed{\text{Past perfect}}$$

<u>I/You/He/She/It/We/They had bought</u> the book.

🌐 Language note: To make past perfect sentences negative, add *not* between *had* and the past participle. To make a question, move *had* to the beginning of the sentence. Many writers add the word *yet* with the past perfect in negative statements and questions.

| **Negative** | We <u>had not bought</u> the book (yet). |
| **Question** | <u>Had</u> he <u>bought</u> the book (yet)? |

🌐 Language note: The past perfect is used only to emphasize that one action happened before another. It should not be used for events that occurred at the same time as each other or for the main events in a story.

Incorrect	Yesterday, I had seen my teacher. She told me about the quiz next week.
Correct	Yesterday, I saw my teacher. She told me about the quiz next week.

Notice the way Amy Tan uses the past perfect in her essay "Fish Cheeks":

past perfect

When I found out that my parents had invited the minister's family over for

simple past

Christmas dinner, I cried.

The main event in this story is the moment that Tan learns about the Christmas plans and cries. Tan uses the past perfect only for the action that happened before the main event of the story: the invitation to the minister's family.

PRACTICE 20–5   **Using the Past Perfect Tense**

In each of the following sentences, circle the correct verb tense.

Example: When musician Ray Charles was born in September 1930, the Great Depression already (caused /(had caused)) many Americans to lose hope.

1. His family (was / had been) poor even before the Great Depression started.

2. Until he was four years old, Ray (enjoyed / had enjoyed) normal vision.

3. However, by the time he was seven, he (became / had become) totally blind.

4. When he (tripped / had tripped) over furniture and asked for his mother's help, often she just watched him and remained silent.

5. In this way, she (encouraged / had encouraged) him to learn how to help himself get back up.

The Future Perfect

Use the **future perfect** to describe situations that begin and end before another situation begins:

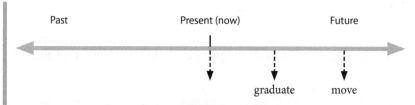

I / You / She / He / We / They *will have graduated* before moving.

[This sentence says that graduation will occur before moving.]

Use this formula to form the future perfect tense:

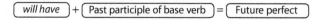

will have + Past participle of base verb = Future perfect

🌐 Language note: To make future perfect sentences negative, add *not* between *will* and *have*. To make a question, move *will* to the beginning of the sentence.

Negative   We will not have bought the book on the first day of class.

Question   Will he have bought the book?

Use Verbs Correctly: Passive Voice

A sentence that is written in the **passive voice** has a subject that does not perform an action. Instead, the subject is acted upon. To create a passive verb, combine a form of the verb *be* with a past participle:

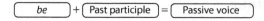

be + Past participle = Passive voice

Passive voice   The newspaper was thrown onto the porch.

[The subject (newspaper) did not throw itself onto the porch. Some unidentified person threw the newspaper.]

Read this passive sentence from Steven Thrasher's essay "Confederate Memorials Have No Place in American Society. Good Riddance" (pp. 317–19):

| Passive voice | When the Confederate <u>flag</u> <u>was taken</u> down in South Carolina, <u>it was done</u> with such pomp and circumstance it was like the <u>thing was being given</u> a state funeral. |

[In this sentence, the subjects (*flag, it, the thing*) are not acting. Instead, someone else is acting on the subjects.]

Writers use the passive voice when no one specific performed an action, when they do not know who performed the action, or when they want to emphasize the receiver of the action. In Thrasher's example, the emphasis is on the flag and the process of its removal — not the specific workers who did the job.

Writers generally do not use passive verbs when they know who performed the action or when they want to emphasize the action itself. Instead, they use verbs in the **active voice**, which means the subject performs the action. Notice how Thrasher uses active verbs in these sentences:

Active voice	But <u>we're</u> still <u>treating</u> these relics of the Confederacy with an absurd amount of care.
	[Here, the subject (*we*) performs the action of treating.]
Active voice	<u>U.S. governments</u> <u>will spend</u> money preserving these Confederate monuments.
	[Here, the subject (*governments*) performs the action of spending.]

(For additional discussion of the passive voice, see Chapter 13, p. 265.)

PRACTICE 20-6 **Changing the Passive Voice to the Active Voice**

Rewrite the following sentences, changing them from the passive voice to the active voice.

> The legislature cut funding
> **Example:** ~~Funding~~ for animal shelters ~~was cut by the legislature~~.
> ^

1. Some shelters were going to be closed by the owners.

2. What would become of the animals was unknown.

3. A campaign was started by animal lovers.

4. Interviews were given by the owners and volunteers at shelters.

5. The animals were filmed by news teams.

Use Verbs Correctly: Modal Verbs

Modal verbs (or **modal auxiliary verbs**) are helping verbs that can express possibility, probability, advice, necessity, or expectations. The following chart illustrates the eight most common modal verbs:

Modal (Helping) Verbs

General Formulas	STATEMENTS
For all modal verbs	[Subject] + [Modal verb] + [Base verb] Dumbo　　　　　can　　　　　fly. NEGATIVES [Subject] + [Modal verb + *not*] + [Base verb] Dumbo　　　　cannot　　　　fly. QUESTIONS [Modal verb] + [Subject] + [Base verb] Can　　　　Dumbo　　　fly?
Can Means *ability* For past-tense forms, see *could*.	**Present:** DJ can run in marathons. **Past:** DJ could run in marathons when she was younger.
Could Means *possibility* It can also be the past tense of *can*.	**Present:** DJ could run in the marathon if she wanted to. **Past:** DJ could have run in the marathon if she had wanted to.
May Means *permission* or *possibility* For past-tense forms, see *might*.	You may borrow my car. It may rain today.
Might Means *possibility* It can also be the past tense of *may*.	STATEMENTS **Present:** Lou might be asleep. **Past:** Lou might have been asleep. **Future:** Lou might sleep after work. 🌐 Language note: *Might* is not generally used in questions; questions with *might* occur only in the most formal situations.

Must	STATEMENTS
Means *necessary*	**Present:** They must buy a new car.
Must + *have* + past participle means a logical conclusion about the past based on evidence.	**Past (Logical Conclusion):** I don't see their old van; they must have bought a new car.
To talk about necessities or requirements in the past, use *had to* + the base form of the verb.	**Past:** They had to buy a new car.
	Language note: Questions with *must* are unusual and very formal. Most questions are formed with *have to* + the base form of the verb:
	Do you have to work next week?
Should	STATEMENTS
Means *duty* or *expectation*	**Present:** They should call.
Should + *have* + past participle shows a duty in the past that was not completed.	**Past (with):** They should have called. (They didn't call.)
Will	STATEMENTS
Means *intend to* (future)	**Future:** I will succeed.
For past-tense forms, see *would*.	
Would	STATEMENTS
Means *prefer*	**Present:** I would like to travel.
In question form, it can be a *request*.	**Request/Question:** Would you take me home after class?
It is often called the past tense of *will* because it is used to report statements with *will*.	**Reported Speech:** Ling: I will take you home.
It is also used in *conditional sentences*:	**Daneisha:** What did she say?
(Condition) *if* + subject + past tense verb	**Kenyon:** She said she would take you home.
(Result) subject + *would* + base form	**Condition:** If I had the money, I would travel.
(Condition) *if* + subject + past perfect verb	**Condition:** If I had had the money, I would have traveled.
(Result) subject + *would* + *have* + past participle of the verb	

🌐 **Language note:** Watch for these common problems in using modal verbs.

Using more than one helping verb:

Incorrect	They <u>will can help</u>.
Correct	They <u>will help</u>. [future intention]
	They <u>can help</u>. [are able to]

Using *to* between the modal verb and the main (base) verb:

Incorrect	Emilio <u>might to come</u> with us.
Correct	Emilio <u>might come</u> with us.

Forgetting to change *can* to *could* to form the past negative:

Incorrect	Last night, <u>I cannot sleep</u>.
Correct	Last night, <u>I could not sleep</u>.

Forgetting to use *have* with *could/should/would* to form the past tense:

Incorrect	Tara <u>should called</u> last night.
Correct	Tara <u>should have called</u> last night.

Using *will* instead of *would* to express a preference in the present tense:

Incorrect	<u>I will like</u> to travel.
Correct	<u>I would like</u> to travel.

Using *-s* on verbs that follow modals:

Incorrect	Ivan <u>can speaks</u> French.
Correct	Ivan <u>can speak</u> French.

Use Verbs Correctly: Editing Help

Effective writing builds sentences with strong verbs; it is important to consider the verbs in each sentence when you are editing.

Accurate Verb Forms

Remember that the past participle (third form) of irregular verbs and the *-ing* form of verbs must occur with a helping verb when they are used as the main verb in the sentence. These forms cannot occur by themselves:

Incorrect	That author written a new book.
Correct	That author has written a new book. (That author wrote a new book.)
Incorrect	We seen him at the park.
Correct	We saw him at the park. (We have seen him at the park before.)
Incorrect	Our class having a party next week after the final.
Correct	Our class is having a party next week after the final.

In formal writing situations, make sure you use the correct past participle form:

Incorrect	Mrs. Childers has went to the store.
Correct	Mrs. Childers has gone to the store.

Consistency of Verb Tense

Consistency of verb tense means that all actions in a sentence that happen (or happened) at the same time are in the same tense. If all the actions happen in the present or happen all the time, use the present tense for all verbs in the sentence. If all the actions happened in the past, use the past tense for all verbs:

Inconsistent	The movie started just as we take our seats.

[The actions both happened at the same time, but *started* is in the past tense, and *take* is in the present tense.]

Consistent, past tense	The movie started just as we took our seats.

[The actions *started* and *took* both happened in the past, and both are in the past tense.]

Use different tenses only when you are referring to different times:

My daughter hated math as a child, but now she loves it.

[The sentence uses two different tenses because the first verb (*hated*) refers to a past condition, whereas the second verb (*loves*) refers to a present one.]

> **PRACTICE 20-7**   **Using Consistent Verb Tense**

In each of the following sentences, double-underline the verbs, and correct any unnecessary shifts in verb tense. Write the correct form of the verb in the blank space provided.

Example: *have* Although some people dream of having their picture taken by a famous photographer, not many ~~had~~ the chance.

1. _____ Now, special stores in malls take magazine-quality photographs of anyone who wanted one.

2. _____ The founder of one business got the idea when she hear friends complaining about how bad they looked in family photographs.

3. _____ She decide to open a business to take studio-style photographs that did not cost a lot of money.

4. _____ Her first store included special lighting and offers different sets, such as colored backgrounds and outdoor scenes.

5. _____ Now, her stores even have makeup studios for people who wanted a special look for their pictures.

Edit for Verb Problems

Use the information in this chapter to help you complete the practice exercises in this section and edit your own writing.

> **PRACTICE 20-8**   **Identifying and Correcting Verb Errors**

Identify and correct eight verb errors in the following student draft.

Since I had failed my first English class two years ago, I have realize that college success is an investment. Yes, I could make more money by working full-time, but then I would not earn my degree. As Mr. Holloway saying in class, "If we stop learning, we are stuck." I need a plan for success so that I won't be stuck. First, I need to attend class, and I done that regularly since last fall. In fact, I keep perfect attendance since last October. Second, I must spend more time studying than I done two years ago. Third, I must ask for help when I don't understand. I still working part-time each week, but I have promise myself that I will go to the tutoring center at least one hour a week. I have a plan, and I know I will make it this time.

> **PRACTICE 20–9**   **Editing for Verb Problems**

In the following paragraph, find and correct ten problems with verb tense, verb form, and subject-verb agreement.

During the Covid-19 pandemic in 2020 and 2021, many Americans experienced frustration and anger, and as a society, we did not always express that frustration in positive ways. Under the stress of lockdown, we had seen people lose control of their emotions. For example, a subway rider was slam to the ground and forced to leave because he wasn't wear a mask. Sadly, in stores, there were some customers who get mad and push clerks against the wall because the store did not has toilet paper in stock. And other workers lost their composure because they were exhausted. The question for our country now is whether we can learns from our experiences and handle our frustration better in the future. We must to control what we say and what we do when we are tired or afraid. According to therapists, this sort of control begins when we listen to our bodies and rest when we will need to. And we should also forgive ourselves — and others — when we done something wrong.

Chapter 20 Review

1. What are the principal parts of verbs?

2. What are the three simple tenses?

3. How is a progressive verb formed?

4. How is a perfect verb formed?

5. How is a passive verb formed?

6. What is the difference between verbs in the active and passive voice?

Chapter 20 Quiz

Indicate the correct choice for each of the following items.

___ 1. If an underlined portion of this sentence is incorrect, select the revision that fixes it. If the sentence is correct as written, choose d.

> It has <u>became</u> difficult to tell whether Trisha <u>is</u> tired of her work or
>   *a*   *b*
>
> <u>tired</u> of her boss.
> *c*

   a. become   c. tiring

   b. be   d. No change is necessary.

___ 2. Choose the item that has no errors.

   a. By the time we arrived, Michelle already gave her recital.

   b. By the time we arrived, Michelle had already given her recital.

   c. By the time we arrived, Michelle has already given her recital.

___ 3. If an underlined portion of this sentence is incorrect, select the revision that fixes it. If the sentence is correct as written, choose d.

> I <u>likes</u> Manuel's new car, but I <u>wish</u> he wouldn't park it in my
>   *a*   *b*
>
> space when he <u>comes</u> home from work.
>   *c*

   a. like   c. came

   b. wishing   d. No change is necessary.

___ 4. Choose the item that has no errors.

   a. Patrick has such a bad memory that he has to write down everything he is supposed to do.

   b. Patrick had such a bad memory that he has to write down everything he is supposed to do.

   c. Patrick had such a bad memory that he having to write down everything he is supposed to do.

___ 5. Choose the correct word(s) to fill in the blank.

> **For many years, Steven _____ the manual typewriter his grandfather had given to him.**

   a. keeped   b. kept   c. was keeping

___ 6. Choose the item that has no errors.

   a. I have be cutting back on the amount of coffee I drink.

   b. I has been cutting back on the amount of coffee I drink.

   c. I have been cutting back on the amount of coffee I drink.

___ 7. Choose the correct word(s) to fill in the blank.

> **We had intended to visit Marina's parents while we _____ in town, but we did not have time.**

   a. was   b. had were   c. were

___ 8. Choose the correct word(s) to fill in the blank.

> **Each family _____ a dish and brought it to our knitting club's annual dinner.**

   a. prepares   b. prepared   c. have prepared

___ 9. If an underlined portion of this sentence is incorrect, select the revision that fixes it. If the sentence is correct as written, choose d.

> **The boy <u>jumped</u> out of the way just before the car <u>is</u> about to <u>hit</u> him.**
>   *a*   *b*   *c*

   a. jumping   c. hitted

   b. was   d. No change is necessary.

___ 10. Choose the correct word to fill in the blank.

> **Who has _____ the train to New York before?**

   a. taken   b. take   c. taked

Part 4

Editing for Clarity, Cohesion, and Conventions

Word Choice

Selecting Accurate and Specific Nouns and Verbs

In this chapter, you will learn to

- Choose specific, accurate, and appropriate nouns and verbs for your writing.
- Use articles accurately to indicate definite and indefinite nouns.

Effective writing uses pronouns, nouns, and verbs to refer to specific people, places, things, ideas, actions, or situations in ways that readers can clearly follow. When we edit for **word choice**, we make sure that the words we use to designate and describe a person, place, action, and so on are accurate, specific, and appropriate.

Find the Right Word: Nouns and Verbs

The sentence patterns you learned about in Chapter 16 contain slots for various sentence parts: subject, verb, direct object, indirect object, and so on. Subject and direct and indirect object slots can be filled with a wide variety of nouns; verb slots can be filled with any of a number of verb choices. Effective writers select nouns and verbs that are specific and concrete to fill these slots, and they choose adjectives and adverbs carefully to describe nouns and verbs.

Specific Words

Compare the following sentences:

Vague and general:	An old man walked down the street.
Concrete and specific:	An eighty-seven-year-old priest limped and stumbled along the sidewalks on Main Street.

While the first version does show who did what, it does not create a strong image for the reader. The second version provides more specific references for the reader, who is thus able to visualize the scene. The noun *man* has been narrowed to *priest*, while the verb *walked* has been replaced with the more specific verbs *limped* and *stumbled*.

| PRACTICE 21–1 | **Making Nouns and Verbs More Specific** |

For each of the following general nouns and verbs, find at least three words with similar but more specific references.

Nouns	Verbs
Book:	Work:
Device:	Think:
House:	Study:

Accurate Words

Specific words help writers communicate effectively, but if a specific word is not accurate, it can be more confusing than helpful. Consider the following example from a student's argument essay:

> Americans from both political sects struggle to maintain a basic level of severity.

The student was attempting to describe how difficult it can be to hold a polite conversation with someone with different political views. The student used a thesaurus to try to find a more specific word than *group*; the word *sect* seemed like a good choice. But *sect* usually refers to a religious group, not a political party. In addition, *sect* can have negative **connotations**—or associations—for readers. *Sect* is not the right word for this sentence.

Similarly, the word *severity* is not the right word for the sentence. Here the student was uncertain of how to spell a word—*civility*. After making a guess, the writer let autocorrect take care of the rest. Technology—just like a thesaurus—can be a useful tool in writing. But always check the results to make sure that the words are not only specific but also accurate: does the sentence say what you want and mean for it to say?

Appropriate Words

Words that are accurate and specific may still not be appropriate for the audience and purpose of the paper. Consider the following sentences:

Informal/slang:	Hey Prof, I'm gonna drop out of your class cuz I don't have time to write all the papers you want us to. Theres no frickin way to hand it all in on time without pulling all-nighters, and I gotta work.
Overly formal:	Dear professor, I am writing to inform you that I intend to withdraw from your course, primarily due to the amount of time I am compelled to devote to the completion of writing assignments. I am unable to submit the work on time unless I abandon sleep for multiple nights, and this solution is untenable, for I must be gainfully employed and earn a salary.
Formal/professional:	Dear Professor, I am writing to let you know that I am going to withdraw from your class because of time issues. I cannot complete writing assignments on time and still get enough sleep to function at my job, which I must keep for financial reasons.

The words you choose should fit the formality of the situation. While an email to an instructor is certainly not the place to use slang or casual language, it probably does not require highly formal word choice. Readers will make judgments about writers based on the appropriateness of their word choices.

In addition to avoiding slang in professional or formal writing, you can also pay attention to **phrasal verbs**, or two-word verbs, which consist of a general verb plus a preposition.

Common Phrasal Verbs and Their Meanings

call off (cancel)	They *called off* the party.
call on (ask for a response/chooses)	The teacher always *calls on* me.
drop in/by (visit)	*Drop in* the next time you are around.
drop off (deliver/leave)	Juan will *drop off* the car for service.
drop out of (quit/withdraw from)	Many students *drop out* of school.
fight against (combat)	He tried to *fight against* the proposal.
fight for (defend)	We will *fight for* our rights.
fill out (complete)	Please *fill out* the form.
find out (discover)	Did you *find out* the answer?
give up (forfeit)	Do not *give up* your chance to succeed.
go by (visit, pass by)	I may *go by* the store on my way home.

go over (review)	Please *go over* your notes before the test.
grow out of (outgrow, lose)	Children may *grow out of* their childhood fears.
hand in (submit)	Please *hand in* your homework.
lock up (secure)	*Lock up* the apartment before leaving.
look up (find/check)	*Look up* the meaning in the dictionary.
pick out (choose)	*Pick out* a good apple.
pick up (buy, take, collect)	Please *pick up* some drinks.
put off (postpone)	Do not *put off* starting your paper.
sign in (register)	*Sign in* when you arrive.
sign out (borrow)	You can *sign out* a book from the library.
sign up (register)	I want to *sign up* for the contest.
think about (consider)	Simon *thinks about* moving.
turn in (submit)	Please *turn in* your homework.

Conversational English relies heavily on phrasal verbs for communication, and these verbs are usually considered informal. In addition, they can be difficult for English learners to master because the meaning of the combination is not usually the meaning that the verb and the preposition would each have on their own.

> My mother **turned up** at my door on Friday.
>
> [*Turned up* means "appeared unexpectedly."]
>
> I **turned down** their offer.
>
> [*Turned down* means "refused."]

If you want to raise the formality of your writing, use one-word verbs instead of phrasal verbs.

 Language note: Some verb/preposition pairs can be separated by an object:

Correct (verb + preposition, not separated) I had to fill out a form.

Correct (verb + preposition, separated) I had to fill a form out.

Other verb/preposition pairs cannot be separated by an object.

Correct (verb + preposition, not separated) We need to go over your notes.

Incorrect (verb + preposition, separated) We need to go your notes over.

Note: Use an ESL dictionary to identify the meaning of phrasal verbs and to determine whether the verb and preposition are separable or inseparable.

> **PRACTICE 21-2**   **Choosing Appropriate Words**

Paragraph 4 of Morgan Xiong's essay on pages 113–14 mixes both formal and informal word choice. Rewrite the paragraph twice, first for a more formal audience (perhaps a scholarship selection committee) and then for a more casual audience (a note of encouragement to students at her former high school).

Make References to Nouns Clear

Once writers have selected specific, accurate, and appropriate words, they need to make sure additional references to those words are clear throughout the work, especially references to nouns. Two tools writers use to manage references to nouns are *articles*, which introduce nouns, and *pronouns*, which substitute for them. In this chapter you will learn how articles help readers understand reference and why effective writers edit carefully for them. In Chapter 22, you will learn about keeping references clear by using pronouns carefully and strategically.

Definite and Indefinite Articles

Articles announce a noun, and they can also point out if a specific noun is known to both the reader and writer of a text. English uses only three articles—*a, an,* and *the.*

The is a **definite article** and is used before a specific person, place, or thing. *The* is also used before a noun that is specifically known to both a reader and a writer. *A* and *an* are **indefinite articles** and are used with a person, place, or thing whose specific identity is not known.

Definite article:	*The* car crashed into the building.
	[A specific car crashed into the building. Both reader and writer know which car is referred to.]
Indefinite article:	*A* car crashed into the building.
	[Some car—we don't know which one exactly—crashed into the building.]
Indefinite article followed by definite article:	*A* car crashed into the building. Later, a tow-truck removed *the* car.
	[In the first sentence, the writer introduces the car with *a* because the reader does not know which car crashed; in the second sentence, *the* is used because the reader now knows that it is the car that crashed into the building that is referred to.]

When the word following the article begins with a vowel sound (*a, e, i, o, u*), use *an* instead of *a.*

An old car crashed into the building.

 Language note: Pay attention to words that begin with *u*. When the *u* is pronounced like the consonant *y,* use the article *a:*

My mother works at a university.

When the *u* sounds like a vowel, use the article *an:*

Do you need an umbrella?

Refer to the dictionary if you are not sure how to pronounce the *u* at the beginning of a word.

Count and Noncount Nouns

To use the correct article, you need to know what count and noncount nouns are. **Count nouns** name things that can be counted, and they can be made plural, usually by adding *-s* or *-es*. **Noncount nouns** name things that cannot be counted, and they are usually singular. They cannot be made plural.

Count noun—singular	I got a **ticket** for the concert.
Count noun—plural	I got two **tickets** for the concert.
Noncount noun	The Internet has all kinds of **information**.

[You would not say, "The Internet has all kinds of informations."]

 Language note: The following is a brief list of count and noncount nouns. All English nouns are either count or noncount. Most ESL dictionaries include this information in entries for nouns.

Count	Noncount	
apple/apples	beauty	milk
chair/chairs	flour	money
dollar/dollars	furniture	postage
letter/letters	grass	poverty
smile/smiles	grief	rain
tree/trees	happiness	rice
	health	salt
	homework	sand
	honey	spaghetti
	information	sunlight
	jewelry	thunder
	mail	wealth

Use the chart that follows to determine when to use *a, an, the,* or no article.

Articles with Count and Noncount Nouns

Count Nouns	Article Used
Singular	
Specific	*the*
	I want to read **the** book on taxes that you recommended.
	[The sentence refers to one particular book: the one that was recommended.]
	I cannot stay in **the** sun very long.
	[There is only one sun.]
Not specific	*a* or *an*
	I want to read **a** book on taxes.
	[It could be any book on taxes.]
Plural	
Specific	*the*
	I enjoyed **the** books that we read.
	[The sentence refers to a particular group of books: the ones that we read.]
Not specific	no article or *some*
	I usually enjoy books.
	[The sentence refers to books in general.]
	She found **some** books.
	[The reader does not know which books she found.]

Noncount Nouns	Article Used
Singular	
Specific	*the*
	I put away **the** food that we bought.
	[The sentence refers to particular food: the food that we bought.]
Not specific	no article or *some*
	There is food all over the kitchen.
	[The reader does not know what food the sentence refers to.]
	Give **some** food to the neighbors.
	[The sentence refers to an indefinite quantity of food.]

PRACTICE 21–3   **Using Articles Correctly**

Fill in the correct article (*a*, *an*, or *the*) in each of the following sentences. If no article is needed, write "no article."

> **Example:**   Children who go to <u>no article</u> preschool have several advantages over those who do not.

1. First, ___ good preschool will help students learn about letters and numbers.

2. These skills can make ___ big difference when preschoolers move on to kindergarten.

3. Research shows that ___ prereading and math skills of children who have attended preschool are stronger than those of kids who have not.

4. Additionally, preschoolers learn everyday information, such as ___ names of the days of the week.

5. But ___ biggest advantage of preschool is that it teaches social skills.

PRACTICE 21–4   **Recognizing Nouns and Articles**

Read the following paragraph from Stephanie Ericsson's essay "The Ways We Lie." Underline each noun in the paragraph, and put a check over each noun that is introduced by an article. Compare your answers with a classmate, and discuss why Ericsson used the articles that she did. How do the articles help you understand what you are reading?

But facades can be destructive because they are used to seduce others into an illusion. For instance, I recently realized that a former friend was a liar. He presented himself with all the right looks and the right words and offered lots of new consciousness theories, fabulous books to read, and fascinating insights. Then I did some business with him, and the time came for him to pay me. He turned out to be all talk and no walk. I heard a plethora of reasonable excuses, including in-depth descriptions of the big break around the corner. In six months of work, I saw less than a hundred bucks. When I confronted him, he raised both eyebrows and tried to convince me that I'd heard him wrong, that he'd made no commitment to me. A simple investigation into his past revealed a crowded graveyard of disenchanted former friends.

Chapter 21 Review

1. When we edit for _____, we make sure that the words we use are specific, accurate, and appropriate.

2. _____ are two-word verbs and are usually considered informal.

3. Articles may be _____ or _____.

4. Give an example of a count noun.

5. Give an example of a noncount noun.

Chapter 21 Quiz

Indicate the correct choice for each of the following items.

___ 1. Choose the item that has specific, accurate, and appropriate words.

    a. The girl cried because the man said he wanted a discount.

    b. The chick teared up because the old geezer harassed her about a discount.

    c. My daughter let the tears flow after a cranky seventy-five-year-old yelled at her and demanded a discount.

___ 2. Choose the best words to fill in the blank. You are writing a professional email.

    I am afraid that all your hard work did not _____.

    a. solve our problem   b. do the trick   c. do it for us

___ 3. Which word in the following sentence is vague?

    Kevin was extremely arrogant about stuff he was doing at the mayor's office.

    a. arrogant   b. office   c. stuff

___ 4. Choose the item that describes Nikki's actions the most specifically.

    a. I like that thing Nikki does whenever she scores a goal.

    b. I like the way Nikki goes nuts whenever she scores a goal.

    c. I like the way Nikki does a backflip whenever she scores a goal.

___ 5. Which sentence uses articles correctly?

    a. A woman at library said I needed a better information for the paper Dr. Smith assigned.

    b. A woman at the library said I needed better information for the paper Dr. Smith assigned.

    c. The woman at the library said I needed the better information for the paper Dr. Smith assigned.

22

Pronouns

Keeping Reference Clear

Learning Outcomes | In this chapter, you will learn to

- Identify pronouns and their antecedents.
- Make sure that pronouns agree with their antecedents.
- Make pronoun reference clear.
- Use the right type of pronoun.
- Make pronouns consistent.

A **pronoun** is used in place of a noun or another pronoun mentioned earlier. Pronouns enable writers to avoid repeating nouns and pronouns, and when they are used effectively, they make sentences and paragraphs clear and engaging for readers.

> Sheryl got into ~~Sheryl's~~ her, car.
>
> I like Mario. ~~Mario~~ He is a good dancer.

The noun or pronoun that a pronoun replaces is called the **antecedent**. In most cases, a pronoun refers to a specific antecedent nearby.

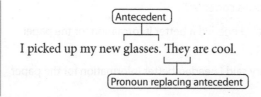

Problems in pronoun usage cause confusion for readers.

Nina told Jackie *she* needed to change shoes.

Who is being referred to in this sentence? Is it Nina who needs to change shoes or Jackie?

Identify Pronouns and Antecedents

Learning to identify pronouns and their antecedents is important for both writing and reading. If you do not match pronouns and their antecedents accurately, you may misunderstand what you read or confuse others.

Take a minute to review the chart of common pronouns that follows.

Common Pronouns

Personal Pronouns	Possessive Pronouns	Indefinite Pronouns	
I	my	all	much
me	mine	any	neither (of)
you	your/yours	anybody	nobody
she/he	her/hers/his	anyone	none (of)
her/him	her/hers/his	anything	no one
it	its	both	nothing
we	our/ours	each (of)	one (of)
us	our/ours	either (of)	some
they	their/theirs	everybody	somebody
them	their/theirs	everyone	someone
		everything	something
		few (of)	

PRACTICE 22-1   Identifying Pronouns

In each of the following sentences, identify the pronoun and the noun that the pronoun refers to.

> **Example:** But his favorite tree was the avocado because it offered hope and the promise of more years. (Soto, 165)

The word it (pronoun) refers to avocado.

1. Now a graduating senior, Trevino, 22, realizes she got bum advice. (Levine-Finley, 186)

2. Telling a friend he looks great when he looks like hell can be based on a decision that the friend needs a compliment more than a frank opinion. (Ericsson, 212)

3. It's a historical fact that black soldiers and sailors who fought overseas in World War II came home to Southern cities where they had to ride in the back of the bus. . . . (Robinson, 236)

4. Just like today, cornbread was used in dressing because it was a staple in the typical Southern diet. (Okona, 263)

5. Relative to their glummer peers, happier people are more satisfied with their jobs; they also receive greater social support from coworkers and better performance evaluations from supervisors. (Walsh, Boehm, and Lyubomirski, 290)

6. As a historian myself, I am mindful of preserving the history of the country, no matter how awful, violent and racist it is. (Thrasher, 318)

Once you have practiced identifying pronouns and antecedents, make sure that you are using pronouns in ways that are clear and easy for a reader to understand. Also make sure that your pronoun use is respectful and inclusive.

Check for Pronoun Agreement

Traditionally, writers have made pronouns agree with (match) the noun or pronoun they refer to in number, either singular (one) or plural (more than one). Also, in traditional grammars, writers have matched singular pronouns to the gender of the antecedent as well (*he, she,* or *it*).

Magda sold *her* old television set.
[*Her* agrees with *Magda* because both are singular and feminine.]

The Wilsons sold *their* old television set.
[*Their* agrees with *the Wilsons* because both are plural.]

More recent editing guides have updated pronoun agreement guidelines so that they are flexible, respectful, and inclusive. For example, some people may tell you which pronouns they prefer (*he/him/his, she/her/her*, or *they/them/their*), and you should respect those requests. In addition, most recent style guides accept *they/them/their* as appropriate for singular nouns. Use *they/them/their* to refer to a single person when gender is not specified or relevant ("the applicant") or when someone asks you to use these pronouns to refer to them.

In many traditional editing guidelines, writers were told not to use *they/them/their* to refer to a singular generic noun referring to a person; they were encouraged to use *he/him/his* or *she/her/her*. But when writers pick a gendered pronoun, the result may sound sexist:

> **Inappropriate:**   The successful applicant will be given *his* own office.

A more appropriate and inclusive option is to make nouns plural where possible, and when this is not feasible, either rewrite to avoid the pronoun or use *they/their/them* instead of a gendered pronoun.

> **Appropriate:**   Successful applicants will be given *their* own offices.
>
> **Appropriate:**   The successful applicant will be given *their* own office.
>
> **Appropriate:**   The successful applicant will be given *a private* office.

Indefinite Pronouns

Two types of words often cause problems in pronoun agreement: *indefinite pronouns* and *collective nouns*. An **indefinite pronoun** does not refer to a specific person, place, or thing: it is general. Traditionally, indefinite pronouns have taken singular verbs, but usage is changing to make the language more inclusive. Consider the following sentences:

> Everyone boarding the plane must present *his* boarding pass.
> Everyone boarding the plane must present *his or her* boarding pass.

The wording in both cases is problematic: the first example excludes women; the second excludes people who may not identify as either male or female. There are three possible revisions:

1. Make the antecedent plural:

   ~~Everyone~~ Passengers boarding the plane must present ~~his~~ their boarding ~~pass~~ passes.

2. Eliminate the pronoun so that there is no agreement problem:

   ~~Everyone boarding the plane~~ Passengers must present ~~his~~ a boarding pass.

3. Use plural pronouns to refer to the singular antecedent:

their

Everyone boarding the plane must present ~~his~~ boarding pass.
^

Indefinite Pronouns

Always Singular			May Be Plural or Singular
another	everyone	nothing	all
anybody/anyone	everything	one (of)	any
anything	much	somebody	none
each (of)	neither (of)	someone	some
either (of)	nobody	something	
everybody	no one		

PRACTICE 22–2   Agreement with Indefinite Pronouns

In each of the following sentences, first underline the indefinite pronoun. Then revise the word(s) in italics. You may change the pronoun or use another type of word. You may also need to change a verb form. If no revisions are needed, write OK in the blank. More than one option may be acceptable. The first sentence is done for you.

1 <u>Anyone</u> who wants to start *his own* <u>a; their own</u> business had better be prepared to work hard. **2** <u>One</u> may find, for example, that *his or her* _____ work is never done. **3** <u>Something</u> is always waiting, with *their* _____ own peculiar demands. **4** <u>Nothing</u> gets done on *its* _____ own. **5** <u>Anybody</u> who expects to have more freedom now that *he or she* _____ no longer works for a boss may be disappointed. **6** After all, when you work as an employee for a company, <u>someone</u> above you makes decisions as *he* _____ sees fit. **7** When you are your own boss, <u>no one</u> else places *themselves* _____ in the position of final responsibility.

8 <u>Somebody</u> starting a business may also be surprised by how much tax *she* _____ must pay. **9** <u>Each</u> employee at a company pays only about half as much toward social security as what *they* _____ would pay if self-employed. **10** A medical or dental policy is not cheap, and <u>neither</u> of them can be obtained as inexpensively as *it* _____ can when a person is an employee at a corporation.

PRACTICE 22–3   **Revising for Pronoun Usage**

Revise the sentences in Practice 22-2 by eliminating the need for pronoun agreement or by making the subjects plural.

Collective Nouns

A **collective noun** names a group that acts as a single unit.

> ### Common Collective Nouns
>
> | | | |
> |---|---|---|
> | audience | company | group |
> | class | crowd | jury |
> | college | family | society |
> | committee | government | team |

Collective nouns are usually singular, so when you use a pronoun to refer to a collective noun, it is also usually singular.

> ⟵ ‾its
> The team had ~~their~~ sixth consecutive win of the season.
>   ^

If the people in a group are acting as individuals, however, the noun is plural and should be used with a plural pronoun.

> The class brought *their* papers to read.

Finding and fixing pronoun problems: Using collective nouns and pronouns	**Find**
	The <u>committee</u> changed their meeting time.
	1. **Underline** any collective nouns.
	2. *Ask:* Is the collective noun singular (a group acting as a single unit) or plural (people in a group acting as individuals)? Singular
	Fix
	3. **Choose** the pronoun that agrees with the subject.
	The committee changed (its)/~~their~~) meeting time.

PRACTICE 22-4   **Using Collective Nouns and Pronouns**

Fill in the best pronoun (*it, its,* or *their*) in each of the following sentences.

Example: The Vidocq Society is known for __its__ unusual approach to investigating unsolved murders, or "cold cases."

1. The Philadelphia-based club got _____ name from Eugène François Vidocq, a French detective who also worked on unsolved crimes.

2. A police department with a cold case may find that _____ can benefit from the Vidocq Society's services.

3. During the society's monthly meetings, a team of crime investigators, psychologists, scientists, and others bring _____ varied skills to such cases.

4. When guests with knowledge about a case speak to the society, the audience gives _____ full attention to the information.

5. A group of police officers who worked a particular murder case might describe _____ original findings in detailed presentations.

Make Pronoun Reference Clear

It is important to ensure that your reader understands what each pronoun you use refers to.

Ambiguous Pronoun Reference

In an **ambiguous pronoun reference**, the pronoun could refer to more than one noun.

Ambiguous:	Enrico told Jim that *he* needed a better résumé.
	[Did Enrico tell Jim that Enrico himself needed a better résumé? Or did Enrico tell Jim that Jim needed a better résumé?]
Edited:	Jim revised his résumé based on Enrico's advice.
Ambiguous:	I put the glass on the shelf, even though *it* was dirty.
	[Was the glass dirty? Or was the shelf dirty?]
Edited:	I put the dirty glass on the shelf.

Vague Pronoun Reference

In a **vague pronoun reference**, the pronoun does not refer clearly to any particular person, place, or thing. To edit a vague pronoun reference, use a more specific noun instead of the pronoun.

Vague:	When Tom got to the clinic, *they* told him it was closed.
	[Who told Tom the clinic was closed?]
Edited:	When Tom got to the clinic, the nurse told him it was closed.
Vague:	Before I finished printing my report, *it* ran out of paper.
	[What ran out of paper?]
Edited:	Before I finished printing my report, the printer ran out of paper.

Finding and fixing pronoun problems:

Avoiding ambiguous or vague pronoun references

Find

The <u>cashier</u> said that (they) were out of milk.

1. **Underline** the subject.

2. **Circle** the pronoun.

3. *Ask:* Who or what does the pronoun refer to? No one. "They" does not refer to "cashier."

Fix

4. **Correct** the pronoun reference by revising the sentence to make the pronoun more specific.

                  the store was
The cashier said that ~~they were~~ out of milk.
                         ^

PRACTICE 22-5   **Avoiding Ambiguous or Vague Pronoun References**

Edit each sentence to eliminate ambiguous or vague pronoun references. Some sentences may be revised in more than one way.

    Example: I am always looking for good advice on controlling my
                            experts
             weight, but ~~they~~ have provided little help.
               ^

1. My doctor referred me to a physical therapist, and she said that I

    needed to exercise more.

2. I joined a workout group and did exercises with the members, but it did not solve my problem.

3. I tried a lower-fat diet along with the exercising, but it did not really work either.

4. They used to say that eliminating carbohydrates is the easiest way to lose weight.

5. Therefore, I started eating fats again and stopped consuming carbs, but this was not a *permanent solution*.

Repetitious Pronoun Reference

In a **repetitious pronoun reference**, the pronoun repeats a reference to a noun rather than replacing the noun.

> The nurse at the clinic ~~he~~ told Keyan that it was closed.

> The newspaper,~~ it~~ says that the new diet therapy is promising.

Finding and fixing pronoun problems:

Avoiding repetitious pronoun references

Find

Television advertising (it) sometimes has a negative influence on young viewers.

1. **Underline** the subject, and **double-underline** the verb.
2. **Circle** any pronouns in the sentence.
3. *Ask:* What noun does the pronoun refer to? Advertising
4. *Ask:* Do the noun and the pronoun that refers to it share the same verb? Yes
   Does the pronoun just repeat the noun rather than replace it? Yes If the answer to one or both questions is yes, the pronoun is repetitious.

Fix

5. **Correct** the sentence by deleting the repetitious pronoun.

   Television advertising ~~it~~ sometimes has a negative influence on young viewers.

PRACTICE 22–6   Avoiding Repetitious Pronoun References

Correct any repetitious pronoun references in the following sentences.

> **Example:**   Car commercials ~~they~~ want viewers to believe that buying
> a certain brand of car will bring happiness.

1. Young people they sometimes take advertisements too literally.

2. In a beer advertisement, it might suggest that drinking alcohol makes
    people more attractive and popular.

3. People who see or hear an advertisement they have to think about the
    message.

4. Parents should help their children understand why advertisements
    they do not show the real world.

5. A recent study, it said that parents can help kids overcome the
    influence of advertising.

Use the Right Type of Pronoun

Three important types of pronouns are *subject pronouns, object pronouns,* and
possessive pronouns. Notice their uses in the following sentences:

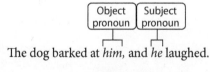

The dog barked at *him,* and *he* laughed.

As Josh walked out, *his* phone started ringing.

Pronoun Types

	Subject	Object	Possessive
First-person singular/plural	I/we	me /us	my, mine/ our, ours
Second-person singular/plural	you/you	you /you	your, yours/ your, yours
Third-person singular	he, she, it who	him, her, it whom	his, her, hers, its whose
Third-person plural	they who	them whom	their, theirs whose

> When Andreas earned an A on <u>Andreas's</u> final exam, <u>Andreas</u> was proud of himself, and the teacher congratulated <u>Andreas</u>.

Subject Pronouns

Subject pronouns serve as the subject of a verb.

> *You* live next door to a coffee shop.
>
> *I* opened the door too quickly.

Object Pronouns

Object pronouns either receive the action of a verb or are part of a prepositional phrase.

> **Object of the verb:**   Javier gave *me* his watch.
>
> **Object of the preposition:**   Javier gave his watch to *me*.

Possessive Pronouns

Possessive pronouns show ownership.

Dave is *my* uncle.

Other Pronoun Types

Other types of pronouns include *intensive, reflexive, relative, interrogative, demonstrative,* and *reciprocal.* The chart below shows what each of these pronoun types does and provides an example.

Other Pronoun Types

Pronoun Types	What They Do	Examples
Intensive pronouns	They emphasize a noun or another pronoun.	The club members *themselves* have offered to support the initiative.
Reflexive pronouns	They are used when the performer of an action is also the receiver of the action.	He taught *himself* how to play the guitar.
Relative pronouns (*who, whom, whose, which, that*)	They refer to a noun already mentioned and introduce a group of words that describe this noun.	Tomatoes, *which* are popular worldwide, were first grown in South America.
Interrogative pronouns (*who, whom, whose, which, what*)	They begin questions.	*What* did the senator say at the meeting?
Demonstrative pronouns (*this, these, that, those*)	They specify which noun is being referred to.	Have you seen *this* simple budgeting app? Yes, I saw *that* a few weeks ago.
Reciprocal pronouns (*each other, one another*)	They refer to individuals when the antecedent is plural.	My friend and I could not see *one another* in the crowd.

Three trouble spots—compound subjects and objects; comparisons; and sentences that need *who* or *whom*—may make it difficult to know what type of pronoun to use.

Pronouns with Compound Subjects and Objects

A **compound subject** has more than one subject joined by *and* or *or*. A **compound object** has more than one object joined by *and* or *or*.

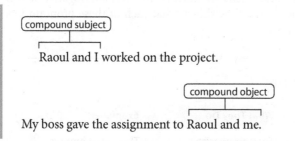

compound subject

Raoul and I worked on the project.

compound object

My boss gave the assignment to Raoul and me.

To decide what type of pronoun to use in a compound construction, try leaving out the other part of the compound and the *and* or *or*. Then say the sentence aloud to yourself.

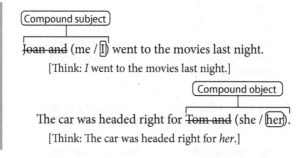

Compound subject

~~Joan and~~ (me / I) went to the movies last night.

[Think: *I* went to the movies last night.]

Compound object

The car was headed right for ~~Tom and~~ (she / her).

[Think: The car was headed right for *her*.]

If a pronoun is part of a compound object in a prepositional phrase, use an object pronoun.

Compound object

I will keep that information between you and (I / me).

[*Between you and me* is a prepositional phrase, so an object pronoun, *me*, is required.]

Finding and fixing pronoun problems:

Using pronouns in compound constructions

Find

~~My friend and~~ me <u>talk</u> at least once a week.

1. **Underline** the subject, **double-underline** the verb, and **circle** any object or objects.

2. *Ask:* Does the sentence have a compound subject or object? *Yes —"friend and me" is a compound subject.*

3. *Ask:* Do the nouns in the compound construction share a verb? *Yes —"talk"*

4. **Cross out** one of the subjects so that only the pronoun remains.

5. *Ask:* Does the sentence sound correct with just the pronoun as the subject? *No*

Fix

6. **Correct** the sentence by replacing the incorrect pronoun with the correct one.

My friend and ~~me~~ I talk at least once a week.

PRACTICE 22–7   **Editing Pronouns in Compound Constructions**

Correct any pronoun errors in the following sentences. If a sentence is correct, write a "C" next to it.

Example: Marie Curie made several major contributions to science, but in 1898, ~~her~~ she and her husband, Pierre Curie, announced their greatest achievement: the discovery of radium.

1. Before this discovery, Marie and Pierre understood that certain sub- stances gave off rays of energy, but them and other scientists were just beginning to learn why and how.

2. Eventually, the Curies made a discovery that intrigued they and, soon afterward, hundreds of other researchers.

3. Two previously unknown elements, radium and polonium, were responsible for the extra radioactivity; fascinated by this finding, Marie began thinking about the consequences of the work that she and her husband had done.

4. As them and other researchers were to discover, radium was especially valuable because it could be used in X-rays and for other medical purposes.

5. Marie was deeply moved when, in 1903, the scientific community honored she and Pierre with the Nobel Prize in physics.

Pronouns in Comparisons

Using the right type of pronoun in comparisons is particularly important because using the wrong type changes the meaning of the sentence. Editing comparisons can be tricky because they often imply (suggest the presence of) words that are not actually included in the sentence.

DB trusts Daneisha more than *I*.

[This sentence means that DB trusts Daneisha more than I trust her. The implied words are *trust her*.]

DB trusts Daneisha more than *me*.

[This sentence means that DB trusts Daneisha more than he trusts me. The implied words are *he trusts*.]

To decide whether to use a subject pronoun or an object pronoun in a comparison, try adding the implied words and saying the sentence aloud.

The registrar is much more efficient than (us / we).

[Think: The registrar is much more efficient than *we are*.]

Susan rides her bicycle more than (he / him).

[Think: Susan rides her bicycle more than *he does*.]

Finding and fixing pronoun problems:	**Find**
Using pronouns in comparisons	The other band attracts a bigger audience (than) us on Friday nights.

Finding and fixing pronoun problems:

Using pronouns in comparisons

Find

The other band attracts a bigger audience (than) us on Friday nights.

1. **Circle** the word that indicates a comparison.

2. *Ask:* What word or words that would come after the comparison word are implied but missing from the sentence? *"Do"*

3. *Ask:* If you add the missing word or words, does the pronoun make sense? No

Fix

4. **Correct** the sentence by replacing the incorrect pronoun with the correct one.

                                                      we (do)

The other band attracts a bigger audience than ~~us~~ on Friday nights.

PRACTICE 22-8   Editing Pronouns in Comparisons

Correct any pronoun errors in the following sentences. If a sentence is correct, write a "C" next to it.

   Example: The camping trip we planned did not seem dangerous to
                     Hannah, so she was not as nervous about it as ~~me~~.

1. In addition, I was nowhere near as well equipped for camping as her.

2. In the store, Hannah rather than me did all the talking.

3. At the campground, I could see that some of the other camping

    groups were not as prepared as we.

4. The park ranger chatted with the other campers more than we.

5. He seemed to believe that we were more experienced than them.

Choosing between Who *and* Whom

Who is always a subject; *whom* is always an object. If a pronoun performs an action, use the subject form *who*. If a pronoun does not perform an action, use the object form *whom*.

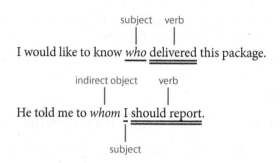

In sentences other than questions, when the pronoun is followed by a verb, use *who*. When the pronoun is followed by a noun or pronoun, use *whom*.

The pianist (who/whom) played was excellent.
[The pronoun is followed by the verb *played*. Use *who*.]

The pianist (who/whom) I saw was excellent.
[The pronoun is followed by another pronoun: *I*. Use *whom*.]

Finding and fixing problems with *who* and *whom*:
Using pronouns in questions and adjective clauses

Find

I contacted the assistant (whom) helped me complete the paperwork.

1. **Circle** *who* or *whom*.

2. *Ask:* Is this word a subject? Is the next word a verb? Yes If the answer is "yes," use "who."

3. *Ask:* Is this word an object? Is the next word a noun or pronoun? No If the answer is "yes," use "whom."

Fix

4. **Correct** the sentence by replacing the incorrect pronoun with the correct one.
                                                    who
   I contacted the assistant ~~whom~~ helped me complete the paperwork.
                                    ^

PRACTICE 22–9   **Choosing between *Who* and *Whom***

In each sentence, choose the correct word: *who* or *whom*.

> **Example:**   In some college classrooms professors (who/whom) are
> worried about the distractions caused by social media
> have placed restrictions on using phones and laptops
> during class sessions.

1. Other instructors argue that these technology bans actually hurt the students (who/whom) they are designed to help.

2. These instructors cite research to show that students (who/whom) use these tools may actually be more active and engaged in the class.

3. On the other hand, Daniel Willingham, (who/whom) is a professor from the University of Virginia, has investigated how successfully students can multitask, especially when they are using technology.

4. Professor Willingham's research suggests that students (who/whom) say they are multitasking are actually shifting rapidly between one task and another, and they are actually studying less effectively and efficiently.

5. Professor Willingham, (who/whom) many recognize as a leader in the science of learning, recommends focusing on a single task when studying.

6. Professors do not need to ban technology in the classroom, but they can encourage students (who/whom) use it to turn notifications off and keep distractions to a minimum while studying.

Make Pronouns Consistent in Person

Person is the point of view writers use—the perspective from which they write. Pronouns may be in the first person (*I* or *we*), second person (*you*), or third person (*he, she,* or *it*). (See the "Pronouns Type" chart on p. 446.)

Inconsistent:	As soon as *a shopper* walks into the store, *you* can tell it is a weird place.
	[The sentence starts with the third person (*a shopper*) but shifts to the second person (*you*).]
Consistent, singular:	As soon as you walk into the store, *you* can tell it is a weird place.
Consistent, plural:	As soon as *shoppers* walk into the store, *they* can tell it is a weird place.

Finding and fixing pronoun problems:

Making pronouns consistent in person

Find

I had the correct answer, but to win the tickets (you) had to be the ninth caller.

1. **Underline** all the subject nouns and pronouns in the sentence.
2. **Circle** any pronouns that refer to another subject noun or pronoun in the sentence.
3. *Ask:* Is the subject noun or pronoun that the circled pronoun refers to in the first (*I* or *we*), second (*you*), or third person (*he, she,* or *it*)? First person
4. *Ask:* What person is the circled pronoun in? Second person

Fix

5. **Correct** the sentence by changing the pronoun to be consistent with the noun or pronoun it refers to.

I had the correct answer, but to win the tickets ~~you~~ ^I^ had to be the ninth caller.

PRACTICE 22–10 **Making Pronouns Consistent in Person**

In the following sentences, correct the shifts in person. There may be more than one way to correct some sentences.

Example: Many college students have access to a writing center
where ~~you~~ ^they^ can get tutoring.

1. A writing tutor has to understand writing assignments so you can help any student who comes in.

2. I have gone to the writing center at my school because sometimes you need a second pair of eyes to look over a paper.

3. Students signing up for tutoring at the writing center may not be in your first semester of college.

4. Even a graduate student may need help with your paper.

5. When I go to the writing center, the tutors explain the problems, but they won't edit your papers.

PRACTICE 22-11   Editing Paragraphs for Pronoun Problems

The following paragraph contains seven examples of the pronoun problems you have reviewed in this chapter. Find and correct these mistakes.

Ask people who have moved to a city, and he or she will tell you that, at first, life can feel pretty lonely. Fortunately, it is possible to make friends just about anywhere. One good strategy is to get involved in a group that interests you, such as a sports team or arts club. In many cases, a local baseball team or theater group will open their arms to new talent. Joining in on practices, games, or performances is a great way to build friendships with others whom have interests like yours. Also, most community organizations are always in need of volunteers. It is a great way to form new friendships while doing something positive for society.

Getting a pet or gardening, it is another great way to meet new people. In many cities, you can walk down the street for a long time and never be greeted by another person. If you are walking a dog, though, it is likely that others will say hello. Some may even stop to talk with you and pet your dog. Also, gardeners tend to draw other gardeners. If you are planting flowers and other flower growers stop by to chat, them and you will have plenty to talk about.

To sum up, newcomers to any city do not have to spend all their nights alone in front of the TV. You have plenty of opportunities to get out and feel more connected.

Chapter 22 Review

1. What are pronouns?

2. Traditionally, a pronoun agrees with (matches) the noun or pronoun it replaces
   in _____ and _____. Nowadays, writers use three strategies to make their
   writing respectful and inclusive:

3. What is the problem with ambiguous pronoun reference?

4. Give an example of each of the following: subject pronouns, object pronouns,
   relative pronouns, and demonstrative pronouns.

5. What are three trouble spots in pronoun use?

Chapter 22 Quiz

Indicate the best choice for each of the following items.

___ 1. Which sentence uses pronouns correctly?

    a. Miguel didn't study for the test as much as me.

    b. Miguel didn't study for the test as much as I.

___ 2. Choose the most appropriate word(s) to fill in the blank.

    **Everyone hopes that the jury will deliver _____ verdict by
the end of this week.**

    a. his or her   b. their   c. its

___ 3. If an underlined portion of this sentence is problematic, select the best
revision. If the sentence is effective as written, choose d.

    She is the one who Jake always calls whenever he wants a favor.
            a   *b*   *c*

    a. Her   b. him   c. whom   d. No change is necessary.

___ 4. Choose the sentence that is most inclusive.

    a. Somebody has left his camera here.

    b. Somebody has left his or her camera here.

    c. Someone has left a camera here.

___ 5. Choose the item that avoids ambiguous pronoun reference.

    a. Becky told Lydia that she needed to help clean up after the party.

    b. Becky told Lydia to help clean up after the party.

    c. Becky told Lydia that she needed to help clean up after it.

___ 6. Choose the item that uses pronouns consistently.

    a. When I applied for the tour operator job, I was told that you needed a special certificate.

    b. When I applied for the tour operator job, you were told that you needed a special certificate.

    c. When I applied for the tour operator job, I was told that I needed a special certificate.

___ 7. Choose the best word(s) to fill in the blank.

    Nicole's _____ must be lonely because _____ keeps calling me.

    a. brother / he   b. brother / him   c. sister / he

___ 8. Choose the best words to fill in the blank.

    The other players in my soccer club like me because _____ agree on the importance of teamwork.

    a. they and I   b. them and me   c. them and I

___ 9. If an underlined portion of this sentence is problematic, select the best revision. If the sentence is appropriate as written, choose d.

    I think that <u>my next-door</u> neighbor has mice in <u>him house</u> because
                        a   *b*

    he keeps asking me to <u>lend him</u> my cat.
                            c

    a. me next-door

    b. his house

    c. lend he

    d. No change is necessary.

___ 10. Choose the item that is most inclusive.

    a. Any lifeguard can tell you about a scary experience he has had on the job.

    b. Any lifeguard can tell you about a scary experience she has had on the job.

    c. Most lifeguards can tell you about a scary experience they have had on the job.

23

Description

Modifying Nouns and Verbs

| Learning Outcomes | In this chapter, you will learn to |

- Identify adjectives and adverbs.
- Choose between adjectives and adverbs in writing.
- Select specific adjectives and adverbs.
- Use adjectives and adverbs effectively in comparisons.
- Recognize and edit for misplaced and dangling modifiers.

You learned in Chapters 21 and 22 that writers help readers visualize and understand information by using words that are specific, accurate, and appropriate, and by making sure that references to those words are clear. Sometimes the best way to make a reference specific and accurate is by adding a description. The words we add to nouns or verbs to provide additional description are called **modifiers**. Modifiers can be single words, like adjectives or adverbs, or they may be longer phrases. In this chapter, you will learn how to recognize modifiers when you are reading and to use modifiers accurately and clearly in writing.

Identify Adjectives and Adverbs

Adjectives are modifiers that describe nouns (words that name people, places, things, or ideas) and pronouns (words that replace nouns). They add information about *what kind, which one,* or *how many.*

Consider the following sentences from Amy Tan's narrative "Fish Cheeks." In each sentence, the adjectives are in *italics*, and the nouns that these adjectives describe are in **bold**.

The kitchen was littered with *appalling* **mounds** of *raw* **food**: A *slimy* **rock cod** with *bulging* **eyes** that pleaded not to be thrown into a pan of *hot* **oil**. Tofu, which looked like *stacked* **wedges** of *rubbery white* **sponges**. A bowl soaking *dried* **fungus** back to life.

> 🌐 **Language note:** In English, adjectives do not indicate whether the words they describe are singular or plural.
>
> | **Incorrect:** | The three babies are *adorables*. |
> |---|---|
> | | [The adjective *adorables* should not end in -*s*.] |
> | **Correct:** | The three babies are *adorable*. |

Adverbs describe or modify verbs (words that tell what happens in a sentence), adjectives, or other adverbs. They add information about *how, how much, when, where, why,* or *to what extent*.

Look at the following sentences from Stephanie Ericsson's "The Ways We Lie." The adverbs are underlined.

I discovered that telling the truth all the time is <u>nearly</u> impossible.
As I said <u>earlier</u>, it's not easy to <u>entirely</u> eliminate lies from our lives.
The new diocese was aware of Father Porter's obsession with children, but they needed priests and <u>recklessly</u> believed treatment had cured him.

Adjectives usually come before the words they modify; adverbs come before or after. You can use more than one adjective or adverb to modify a word.

> 🌐 **Language note:** The -*ed* and -*ing* forms of verbs (known as *participles*) can be used as adjectives. Common examples include *bored/boring, interested/interesting,* and *excited/exciting*. Usually, the -*ed* form describes a person's reaction, while the -*ing* form describes the thing that causes the reaction.
>
> | **Incorrect:** | Some students are *boring* in their grammar classes. |
> |---|---|
> | **Correct:** | Some students are *bored* in their grammar classes. |
> | **Correct:** | Grammar classes can be *boring* for students. |
> | | Some students find their grammar classes *boring*. |

Use Adjectives and Adverbs Effectively

How and when to use adjectives and adverbs depends on the words you are describing and whether you are making a comparison.

Choosing between Adjectives and Adverbs

Many adverbs are formed by adding *-ly* to the end of an adjective.

Adjective	Adverb
She received a *quick* answer.	Her sister answered quickly.
Our *new* neighbors just got married.	The couple is newly married.
That is an *honest* answer.	Please answer honestly.

To decide whether to use an adjective or an adverb, find the word being described. If that word is a noun or pronoun, use an adjective. If it is a verb, an adjective, or another adverb, use an adverb.

> **PRACTICE 23-1** **Choosing between Adjectives and Adverbs**
>
> In each sentence, underline (or highlight) the word that is being described or modified. Then circle the correct word in parentheses.
>
> **Example:** People are (common / commonly) aware that smoking causes health risks.
>
> 1. Many smokers are (stubborn / stubbornly) about refusing to quit.
>
> 2. Others who are thinking about quitting may decide (sudden / suddenly) that the damage from smoking has already been done.
>
> 3. In such cases, the (typical / typically) smoker sees no reason to stop.
>
> 4. The news about secondhand smoke may have made some smokers stop (quick / quickly) to save the health of their families.
>
> 5. Research now shows that pet lovers who smoke can have a (terrible / terribly) effect on their cats.

Choosing Specific Adjectives and Adverbs

Adjectives make nouns more specific by describing them in concrete or vivid ways. Be careful when selecting adjectives to avoid words that are vague or non-specific, as in the following sentence (the adjectives are in *italics*):

My neighbor is a very *nice old* woman who lives in a *small* house.

By choosing more concrete adjectives, we can make this sentence more vivid for a reader:

> My neighbor is a *white-haired* ninety-year-old whose *wrinkled* face is always smiling, even though she lives in a *three-room* house.

Like adjectives, adverbs can make other words more specific, but writers should be careful and precise when selecting adverbs. Some adverbs, like the word *very*, are vague and do not give readers specific information about a word.

Vague Adjectives

amazing	cute	nice	small
awesome	dumb	ok	terrible
bad	good	old	young
beautiful	great	pretty	
big	happy	sad	

Using Adjectives and Adverbs in Comparisons

To compare two people, places, or things, use the **comparative** form of adjectives or adverbs. Comparisons often use the word *than*.

> Najee ran *faster* than I did.
> Johan is *more intelligent* than his sister.

To compare three or more people, places, or things, use the **superlative** form of adjectives or adverbs.

> Najee ran the *fastest* of all the runners.
> Johan is the *most intelligent* of the five children.

If an adjective or adverb is short (one syllable), add the endings *-er* to form the comparative and *-est* to form the superlative. Also use this pattern for adjectives that end in *-y* (but change the *-y* to *-i* before adding *-er* or *-est*).

For all other adjectives and adverbs, add the word *more* (or *less*) to make the comparative and the word *most* (or *least*) to make the superlative.

Forming Comparatives and Superlatives

Adjective or Adverb	Comparative	Superlative
Adjectives and adverbs of one syllable		
tall	taller	tallest
fast	faster	fastest
Adjectives ending in -y		
happy	happier	happiest
silly	sillier	silliest
Other adjectives and adverbs		
graceful	more/less graceful	most/least graceful
gracefully	more/less gracefully	most/least gracefully
intelligent	more/less intelligent	most/least intelligent
intelligently	more intelligently	most/least intelligently

Use *either* an ending (*-er* or *-est*) *or* an extra word (*more* or *less, most* or *least*) to form a comparative or superlative, but *not* both at once.

David Ortiz is the ~~most~~ greatest designated hitter in the team's history.

PRACTICE 23-2   **Using Adjectives and Adverbs in Comparisons**

For each sentence, write the correct form of the adjective or adverb in parentheses. You may need to add *more* or *most* to some adjectives and adverbs.

Example: It was one of the <u>scariest</u> (scary) experiences of my life.

1. I was driving along Route 17 and was _____ (relaxed) than I ought to have been.

2. Knowing it was a busy highway, I was _____ (careful) than usual to make sure my cell phone was ready in case of an accident.

3. I had run the cord for the phone's earbud over my armrest, where it would be in the _____ (easy) place to reach if the phone rang.

4. I was in the _____ (heavy) traffic of my drive when the cell phone rang.

5. I saw that the earbud was _____ (hard) to reach than before because the cord had fallen between the front seats of the car.

Using Good, Well, Bad, and Badly

Four common adjectives and adverbs have irregular forms: *good, well, bad,* and *badly.*

Forming Irregular Comparatives and Superlatives

	Comparative	Superlative
Adjective		
good	better	best
bad	worse	worst
Adverb		
well	better	best
badly	worse	worst

People often get confused about whether to use *good* or *well*. *Good* is an adjective, so use it to describe a noun or pronoun. *Well* is an adverb, so use it to describe a verb or an adjective.

| **Adjective** | She has a *good* job. |
| **Adverb** | He works *well* with his colleagues. |

Well can also be an adjective to describe someone's health: I am not *well* today.

> **PRACTICE 23-3**   Using *Good* and *Well*

Complete each sentence by choosing the correct word in parentheses. Identify the word that *good* or *well* modifies.

> **Example:**   A (good)/ well) <u>pediatrician</u> spends as much time talking with parents as he or she does examining patients.

1. The ability to communicate (good / well) is something that many parents look for in a pediatrician.

2. With a firstborn child, parents see a doctor's visit as a (good / well) chance to ask questions.

3. Parents can become worried when their infant does not sleep (good / well) because the child cannot say what the problem is.

4. Doctors today have (good / well) diagnostic tools, however.

5. Otoscopes help doctors see (good / well) when they look into their patients' ears.

> **PRACTICE 23-4**   Using Comparative and Superlative Forms of *Good* and *Bad*

Complete each sentence by choosing the correct comparative or superlative form of *good* or *bad* in parentheses.

> **Example:**   According to some critics, the (worse /(worst)) film in the DC film franchise is the 2016 film *Suicide Squad*.

1. The (better / best) explanation for the film's problems is that the story does not do justice to the characters or the actors who play them.

2. Another film that was (worse / worst) than audiences expected was *Wonder Woman 1984*, released in 2020.

3. But fans should not give up on the DC franchise; Gal Godot's first *Wonder Woman*, released in 2017, is considered not only the (better / best) film in the series, but one of the most outstanding superhero films ever made.

4. Although fans may be more familiar with the movies *Justice League* and *Man of Steel*, some critics think that the 2019 film *Shazam* is (better / best) than both of these.

5. The (worse / worst) character in *Shazam* is its predictable villain, Dr. Sivana, but audiences and critics alike love its heroes, who improve on the DC standard.

PRACTICE 23–5   ### Editing Paragraphs for Correct Adjectives and Adverbs

Find and correct seven adjective and adverb errors in the following paragraphs.

Every day, many people log on to play one of the popularest computer games of all time, *World of Warcraft*. This multiplayer game was first introduced by Blizzard Entertainment in 1994 and has grown quick ever since. More than 11 million players participate in the game every month, according to the recentest figures.

Computer game experts call *World of Warcraft* a "massively multiplayer online role-playing game," or MMORPG for short. Players of this game select a realm in which to play. They choose from among four differently realms. Each realm has its own set of rules and even its own language. Players also choose if they want to be members of the Alliance or the Horde, which are groups that oppose each other. Each side tends to think that it is gooder than the other one.

In *World of Warcraft*, questing is one of the funnest activities. Questing players undertake special missions or tasks to earn experience and gold. The goal is to trade these earnings for better skills and equipment. Players must proceed careful to stay in the game and increase their overall power and abilities.

Recognize Misplaced and Dangling Modifiers

Adjectives and adverbs modify nouns and verbs, but there are other types of modifiers that describe nouns and verbs as well. Read the following sentences from Gary Soto's "The Grandfather" (p. 165):

> You could see the moon at night, and the stars were *clear* points all the way to the horizon. And wind reached all the way from the sea, <u>which was *blue* and *clean*</u>, unlike the *oily* water **sloshing against a San Francisco pier**.

In addition to the adjectives (in italics) in these sentences, there is an *–ing* or **participial phrase modifier** (*sloshing against a San Francisco pier*) as well as a **relative clause modifier** (*which was blue and clean*). The participial modifier describes the word *water*, while the relative clause modifier describes the word *sea*.

Finding and Correcting Misplaced Modifiers

A **misplaced modifier** describes the wrong word or words because it is in the wrong place in a sentence. Modifiers should be near the word or words that they modify; otherwise, the sentence can be confusing or, in some cases, unintentionally funny.

To correct a misplaced modifier, place the modifier as close as possible to the word or words it modifies, often directly before it.

> Wearing my bathrobe,
> I went outside to chat with the neighbor. ~~wearing my bathrobe.~~
>   ^

Four constructions often lead to misplaced modifiers:

1. **Modifiers such as *only, almost, hardly, nearly,* and *just***
   These adverbs need to be placed immediately before—not just close to—the words or phrases they modify.

   > only
   > I ~~only~~ found two old photos in the drawer.
   >   ^
   >
   > [The intended meaning is that just two photos were in the drawer.]
   >
   >   almost
   > Joanne ~~almost~~ ate the whole cake.
   >   ^
   >
   > [Joanne actually ate; she did not "almost" eat.]
   >
   >   nearly
   > Xavier ~~nearly~~ spent two hours waiting for the bus.
   >   ^
   >
   > [Xavier spent close to two hours waiting; he did not "nearly" spend them.]

2. **Modifiers that are prepositional phrases**

> *from the cash register*
> The cashier found money ^ on the floor. ~~from the cash register~~.

[The floor was not from the cash register; the money was.]

> *in plastic cups*
> Jen served punch to the seniors. ~~in plastic cups.~~
> ^

[The seniors were not in plastic cups; the punch was.]

3. **Modifiers that start with -*ing* verbs**

> *Using jumper cables,*
> Darshane started the car. ~~using jumper cables.~~
> ^

[The car was not using jumper cables; Darshane was.]

> *Wearing flip-flops,*
> Yvonne climbed the mountain. ~~wearing flip-flops.~~
> ^

[The mountain was not wearing flip-flops; Javier was.]

4. **Modifier clauses that start with *who, whose, that,* or *which* (relative clause modifiers)**

> *that was infecting my hard drive*
> Pablo found the computer virus attached to an email message.
> ~~that was infecting my hard drive.~~

[The email did not infect the hard drive; the virus did.]

> *who was crying*
> The baby on the bus ~~who was crying~~ had curly hair.
> ^

[The bus was not crying; the baby was.]

Finding and fixing problems with misplaced modifiers: Making sure modifiers are next to the word that they modify	**Find**
	I saw the ⬚professor⬚ at the theater <u>who gave me an A.</u>
	1. **Underline** modifiers in your sentence, including adverbs, prepositional phrases, *-ing* words, or clauses with *who, whose, which,* or *that.*
	2. *Ask:* Who or what does this modifier describe? **Circle** this word. professor
	3. *Ask:* Is the modifier next to the word it describes? No
	Fix
	4. **Move** the modifier so that it is next to the word it modifies.
	I saw the professor who gave me an A at the theater.
	At the theater, I saw the professor who gave me an A.

PRACTICE 23–6   **Correcting Misplaced Modifiers**

Find and correct misplaced modifiers in the following sentences.

> **Example:**   I write things in my blog that I used to ~~only~~ tell ^only^ my best friends.

1. I used to write about all kinds of personal things and private observations. in a diary.

2. Now, I nearly write the same things in my blog.

3. Any story might show up in my blog that is entertaining.

4. The video I was making was definitely something I wanted to write about in my blog of my cousin Tim's birthday.

5. I had invited to the birthday party my loudest, wildest friends wanting the video to be funny.

Finding and Correcting Dangling Modifiers

A **dangling modifier** "dangles" because the word or word group it modifies is not in the sentence. Dangling modifiers usually appear at the beginning of a sentence and seem to modify the noun or pronoun that immediately follows them, but they are really modifying another word or group of words.

> **Dangling:**   *Rushing to class*, the books fell out of my bag.
>
>   [The books were not rushing to class.]
>
> **Clear:**   *Rushing to class*, I dropped my books.

There are two basic ways to correct dangling modifiers. Use the one that makes more sense. One way is to add the word being modified immediately after the opening modifier so that the connection between the two is clear.

> Trying to eat a hot dog, ~~my bike~~ I swerved on my bike.

Another way is to add the word being modified in the opening modifier itself.

> While I was trying
> ~~Trying~~ to eat a hot dog, my bike swerved.

Finding and fixing problems with dangling modifiers:

Making sure the sentence contains the noun or pronoun the modifier describes

Find

Watching the debate, the questions did not make sense.

1. **Underline** the modifier in your sentence.
2. *Ask:* Who or what does this modifier describe? "I"
3. *Ask:* Does this word appear in the sentence? *No. This is a dangling modifier.*

Fix

4. **Add** the word in the modifying phrase or next to the modifier.

Watching the debate, I realized the questions did not make sense.

PRACTICE 23–7   **Correcting Dangling Modifiers**

Find and correct any dangling modifiers in the following sentences. If a sentence is correct, write a "C" next to it. It may be necessary to add new words or ideas to some sentences.

> *Because I had invited*
Example: ~~Inviting~~ my whole family to dinner, the kitchen was filled
> ^
> with all kinds of food.

1. Preparing a big family dinner, the oven suddenly stopped working.

2. In a panic, we searched for Carmen, who can solve any problem.

3. Trying to help, the kitchen was crowded.

4. Looking into the oven, the turkey was not done.

5. Discouraged, the dinner was about to be canceled.

PRACTICE 23–8   **Editing Paragraphs for Misplaced and Dangling Modifiers**

Find and correct any misplaced or dangling modifiers in the following paragraphs.

Carrying overfilled backpacks is a common habit, but not necessarily

a good one. Bulging with books, water bottles, and sports equipment and weighing an average of 14 to 18 pounds, students' backs can gradually become damaged. Because they have to plan ahead for the whole day and often need books, extra clothes, and on-the-go meals, backpacks get heavier and heavier. An increasing number of doctors, primarily physical therapists, are seeing young people with chronic back problems.

Researchers have recently invented a new type of backpack from the University of Pennsylvania and the Marine Biological Laboratory. Designed with springs, the backpack moves up and down as a person walks. This new backpack creates energy, which is then collected and transferred to an electrical generator. Experiencing relief from the wear and tear on muscles, the springs make the pack more comfortable.

What is the purpose of the electricity generated by these new backpacks? Needing electricity for their night-vision goggles, the backpacks could solve a problem for soldiers. Soldiers could benefit from such an efficient energy source to power their global positioning systems and other electronic gear. Instead of being battery operated, the soldiers could use the special backpacks and would not have to carry additional batteries.

For the average student, these backpacks might one day provide convenient energy for laptops, tablets, and cell phones. Designed with this technology, kids would just have to look both ways before crossing the street.

Chapter 23 Review

1. What do modifiers such as adjectives or adverbs do?
2. What is one common way to form adverbs?
3. What is the difference between comparative and superlative adjectives (or adverbs)?
4. What are misplaced and dangling modifiers?
5. Which four constructions often lead to misplaced modifiers?

Chapter 23 Quiz

Indicate the correct choice for each of the following items.

___ 1. Choose the correct word to fill in the blank.

We performed _____ in the debate, so we will have to be better prepared next time.

   a. bad   b. worse   c. badly

___ 2. If an underlined portion of this sentence is incorrect, select the revision that fixes it. If the sentence is correct as written, choose d.

After the beautiful wedding, the groom danced happy down the
          a   b

church's stone steps.
                c

   a. beautifully   b. happily   c. stonily   d. No change is
                                                        necessary.

___ 3. Choose the item that has no errors.

   a. Sarah's foot is healing well, and she is making a good recovery.

   b. Sarah's foot is healing good, and she is making a good recovery.

   c. Sarah's foot is healing good, and she is making a well recovery.

___ 4. Choose the correct word(s) to fill in the blank.

With Kenneth's wild imagination, he is a _____ choice than Connor for writing the play's script.

   a. gooder   b. better   c. more good

___ 5. If an underlined portion of this sentence is incorrect, select the revision that fixes it. If the sentence is correct as written, choose d.

When asked about the thoughtfulest person I know, I immediately
                                    a

gave the name of my best friend, who is kind to everyone.
                        b   c

   a. most thoughtful

   b. bestest

   c. kindest

   d. No change is necessary.

—   6. If an underlined portion of this sentence is incorrect, select the revision that fixes it. If the sentence is correct as written, choose d.

> **Annoyed by the flashing cameras, the limousine drove the celebrity**
> ⎯⎯⎯⎯⎯⎯⎯   ⎯⎯⎯⎯⎯⎯⎯⎯⎯⎯⎯⎯
>   *a*   *b*
>
> **away from the crowd in front of the restaurant.**
>   ⎯⎯⎯⎯⎯⎯⎯⎯⎯⎯⎯⎯⎯⎯⎯⎯
>   *c*

   a. Annoying

   b. the celebrity got into the limousine, which drove

   c. the restaurant in front of

   d. No change is necessary.

—   7. Choose the sentence that has no errors.

   a. The thief found the code in the bank clerk's desk for the alarm system.

   b. The thief found the code for the alarm system in the bank clerk's desk.

   c. For the alarm system, the thief found the code in the bank clerk's desk.

—   8. If an underlined portion of this sentence is incorrect, select the revision that fixes it. If the sentence is correct as written, choose d.

> **Talking on his cell phone, his shopping cart rolled over my foot.**
> ⎯⎯⎯⎯⎯ ⎯⎯⎯⎯⎯⎯⎯ ⎯⎯⎯⎯⎯⎯⎯⎯⎯⎯⎯
>   *a*   *b*   *c*

   a. Talking and concentrating too much

   b. his cell phones

   c. he rolled his shopping cart

   d. No change is necessary.

—   9. If an underlined portion of this sentence is incorrect, select the revision that fixes it. If the sentence is correct as written, choose d.

> **I only bought two tickets to the game, so one of the three of us**
> ⎯⎯⎯⎯⎯⎯⎯⎯ ⎯⎯⎯⎯⎯⎯⎯⎯⎯ ⎯⎯⎯⎯⎯⎯⎯⎯⎯
>   *a*   *b*   *c*
>
> **cannot go.**

   a. bought only

   b. to go to the game

   c. of the us three of

   d. No change is necessary.

Balance and Rhythm
Making Sentences Easy to Read

In this chapter, you will learn to

- Use parallel structures with pairs and lists, comparisons, and correlative conjunctions.
- Vary sentence styles using coordination and subordination.
- Join or lengthen sentences using -*ing* verbs, past participles, appositives, and adjective clauses.
- Vary sentence openers, using adverbs, prepositional phrases, or infinitives.

After you have revised a draft for unity, coherence, and development (see Chapter 6), you will edit that draft to make sure the sentences work together, communicating effectively and clearly to your reader. One strategy for editing in this way is to read your draft aloud (or have someone else read it to you) and listen to the sound of the sentences.

Try this editing strategy by reading the following paragraph aloud. As you read, ask yourself these questions:

- Does it sound right?
- Does each sentence flow smoothly to the next, or are the transitions choppy?
- Is there variety and balance in the style and rhythm of the sentences?

Many people do not realize how important their speaking voice and style are. Speaking style can make a difference, particularly in a job interview. What you say is important. How you say it is nearly as important. Your speaking voice creates an impression. Mumbling is a bad way of speaking. It makes the speaker appear sloppy and lacking in confidence. Mumbling also makes it difficult for the interviewer to hear what is being said. Talking too fast is another bad speech behavior. The speaker runs his or her ideas together. The interviewer cannot follow them or distinguish what is important. A third common bad speech behavior concerns verbal "tics." Verbal tics are empty filler phrases like "um," "like," and "you know." Practice for an interview. Sit up straight. Look the person to whom you are speaking directly in the eye. Speak up. Slow down. One good way to find out how you sound is to leave yourself a message. If you sound bad to yourself, you need practice speaking aloud. Do not let poor speech behavior interfere with creating a good impression.

Now compare the first version with the one that follows.

Many people do not realize how important their speaking voice and style are, particularly in a job interview. What you say is important, but how you say it is nearly as important in creating a good impression. For example, mumbling is a bad way of speaking. Not only does it make the speaker appear sloppy and lacking in confidence, but mumbling also makes it difficult for the interviewer to hear what is being said. Talking too fast is another bad speech behavior. The speaker runs his or her ideas together, and the interviewer cannot follow them or distinguish what is important. A third common bad speech behavior is called verbal "tics," empty filler expressions, such as "um," "like," and "you know." When you practice for an interview, sit up straight, look the person to whom you are speaking directly in the eye, speak up, and slow down. One good way to find out how you sound is to leave yourself a message. If you sound bad to yourself, you need practice speaking aloud. Do not let poor speech behavior interfere with creating a good impression.

Do you see a difference? Do you hear a difference? When writers are in a hurry, they may not take time to read their work aloud and consider the sound and rhythm of the sentences.

This chapter will focus on creating balance through parallel structures, as well as on techniques for lengthening sentences and changing sentence openers. As you learn about these techniques, you will see that writers must make choices about rhythm and emphasis in sentences; there is no perfect way to write a sentence or paragraph. Look for examples of balance and rhythm in the essays that you have read. Make a note of the ways in which other writers have used these techniques to keep their writing both balanced and varied.

Create Balance with Parallel Structures

Parallelism in writing means that similar parts in a sentence, or similar sentences, have the same structure: the parts or sentences are balanced. Look at the following sentences from Katie Horn's essay "A Beginner's Guide to Movie Night," pages 181–82. What do the underlined parts in each sentence have in common? (For more on parallel structures, see Chapter 11, pp. 215–16.)

- Most theaters will have at least <u>one action movie</u>, <u>one sappy romantic movie</u>, and <u>one family-friendly movie</u>.

- As a last resort, you can make yourself unappealing to potential neighbors by <u>using the seatbacks as a footrest</u>, <u>chewing open-mouthed</u>, and <u>laughing noisily</u>—annoying behaviors that must be halted as soon as the movie begins.

In each case, the parts that are underlined share a similar grammatical structure: nouns are grouped with nouns, verbs with verbs, and gerunds (the *-ing* form of a verb used as a noun) with gerunds. Parallelism is particularly important when you present items in a series, make comparisons, or use paired words. When items in pairs, lists, and comparisons are parallel, they appear balanced; as a result, they are easier to read.

Parallelism in Pairs and Lists

When two or more items in a series are joined by *and* or *or*, use a similar form for each item.

Not parallel:	The professor assigned <u>readings</u>, <u>practices</u>, and <u>we had to write a paper</u>.
	[*Readings* and *practices* are nouns. *We had to write a paper* is a clause, not a noun.]
Parallel:	The professor assigned <u>readings</u>, <u>practices</u>, and <u>a paper</u>.
Not parallel:	The story was <u>in the newspaper</u>, <u>on the radio</u>, and <u>the television</u>.
	[*In the newspaper* and *on the radio* are prepositional phrases. *The television* is not.]
Parallel:	The story was <u>in the newspaper</u>, <u>on the radio</u>, and <u>on television</u>.

Finding and fixing problems with parallel structure in pairs and lists:

Making sure combinations of two or more items are grammatically parallel

Find

Pre-game drills include <u>stretches</u>, <u>sprints</u>, <u>push-ups</u>, and <u>we have to do some free-throws.</u>

1. **Underline** items in a pair or list.

2. *Ask:* What is the grammatical structure of each item? *Stretches, sprints, push-ups are nouns. We have to do some free throws is a clause with subject and verb.*

3. *Ask:* Do all the items have the same structure? No

Fix

4. **Change** any item that does not have the same structure.

Pre-game drills include stretches, sprints, push-ups, and some free-throws.

PRACTICE 24–1   **Using Parallelism in Pairs and Lists**

In each sentence, identify the parts of the sentence that should be parallel. Then edit the sentence to make it parallel.

Example: Coyotes roam the <u>western mountains</u>, the <u>central plains</u>, and ~~they are in the suburbs of~~ the East Coast ~~of the United States.~~
    suburbs.

1. Wild predators, such as wolves, are vanishing because people hunt them and are taking over their land.

2. Coyotes are surviving and they do well in the modern United States.

3. The success of the coyote is due to its varied diet and adapting easily.

4. Coyotes are sometimes vegetarians, sometimes scavengers, and sometimes they hunt.

5. Today, they are spreading and populate the East Coast for the first
   time.

Parallelism in Comparisons

Comparisons often use the word *than* or *as*. When you edit for parallelism, make
sure the items on either side of those words have parallel structures.

Not parallel:	Taking the bus downtown is as fast as the drive there.
Parallel:	Taking the bus downtown is as fast as driving there.
Not parallel:	To admit a mistake is better than denying it.
Parallel:	To admit a mistake is better than to deny it.
	Admitting a mistake is better than denying it.

Sometimes you need to add or delete a word or two to make the parts of a
sentence parallel.

Not parallel:	A tour package is less expensive than arranging every travel detail yourself.
Parallel, word added:	*Buying* a tour package is less expensive than arranging every travel detail yourself.
Not parallel:	The sale price of the shoes is as low as paying half of the regular price.
Parallel, words added:	The sale price of the shoes is as low as half of the regular price.

Finding and fixing problems with parallel structures in comparisons:

Making sure items in comparisons have the same grammatical structure

Find

When it comes to learning a new language, <u>an online program</u> is not (as) effective (as) <u>working with a real person</u>.

1. **Circle** comparison words, such as *than* or *as*.

2. **Underline** words being compared with *than* or *as*.

3. *Ask:* Do the words being compared have the same structure? *No. An online program is a noun, but working with a real person is an -ing form (gerund).*

Fix

4. **Change** the words being compared so they have the same structure.

When it comes to learning a new language, an online program is not as effective as a real person.

When it comes to learning a new language, practicing with an on-line program is not as effective as working with a real person.

PRACTICE 24–2   **Using Parallelism in Comparisons**

In each sentence, identify the parts of the sentence that should be parallel. Then edit the sentence to make it parallel.

    Example: <u>Leasing</u> a new car may be less expensive than ~~to buy~~ one. *(buying)*

1. Car dealers often require less money down for leasing a car than for the purchase of one.

2. The monthly payments for a leased car may be as low as paying for a loan.

3. You should check the terms of leasing to make sure they are as favor-able as to buy.

4. You may find that to lease is a safer bet than buying.

5. You will be making less of a financial commitment by leasing a car than to own it.

Parallelism with Correlative Conjunctions

Certain paired words, called **correlative conjunctions**, link two equal elements and show the relationship between them.

Correlative Conjunctions

both ... and   either ... or   neither ... nor

not only ... but also   rather ... than

Make sure the items joined by correlative conjunctions are parallel.

Not parallel:	Vu wants *both* <u>freedom</u> *and* <u>to be wealthy</u>.
	[*Both* is used with *and*, but the items joined by them are not parallel.]
Parallel:	Vu wants *both* <u>freedom</u> *and* <u>wealth</u>.
Parallel:	Vu wants *both* <u>to have freedom</u> *and* <u>to be wealthy</u>.
Not parallel:	He can *neither* <u>fail the course</u> and <u>quitting his job</u> is also impossible.
Parallel:	He can *neither* <u>fail the course</u> *nor* <u>quit his job</u>.

> **PRACTICE 24–3**   **Using Parallelism with Certain Paired Words**

In each sentence, circle or highlight the paired words, and identify the parts of the sentence that should be parallel. Then edit the sentence to make it parallel. You may need to change one of the paired elements to make the sentence parallel.

Example: A cell phone can be ⟨either⟩ a lifesaver ⟨or⟩ ~~it can be annoying~~. *an annoyance*

1. Twenty years ago, most people neither had cell phones nor did they want them.

2. Today, cell phones are not only used by people of all ages but also are carried everywhere.

3. Cell phones are not universally popular: Some commuters would rather ban cell phones on buses and trains than being forced to listen to other people's conversations.

4. No one denies that a cell phone can be both useful and convenience is a factor.

5. A motorist stranded on a deserted road would rather have a cell phone than to walk to the nearest gas station.

> **PRACTICE 24-4**   **Editing for Parallelism Problems**

Find and correct the parallelism errors in the following sentences.

On a mountainous island between Norway and the North Pole is a special underground vault. It contains neither gold and other currency. Instead, it is full of a different kind of treasure: seeds. They are being saved for the future in case something happens to the plants that people need to grow for food.

The vault has the capacity to hold 4.5 million types of seed samples. Each sample contains an average of five hundred seeds, which means that up to 2.25 billion seeds can be stored in the vault. To store them is better than planting them. Stored, they are preserved for future generations to plant. On the first day that the vault's storage program began, 268,000 different seeds were deposited, put into sealed packages, and collecting into sealed boxes. Some of the seeds were for maize (corn), while others were for rice, wheat, and barley.

Although some people call it the "Doomsday Vault," many others see it as a type of insurance policy against starvation in the case of a terrible natural disaster. The vault's location keeps it safe from floods, earthquakes, and storming. Carefully storing these seeds not only will help ensure people will have food to eat plus make sure important crops never go extinct.

Variation in Sentence Styles

In addition to creating balance through parallel structures, writers can adjust the rhythm of sentences by varying sentence length and sentence introductions.

Joining Ideas to Lengthen Sentences: Coordination

Coordination means joining two (or more) independent clauses to form a compound sentence. In Chapter 18, you learned three methods of joining independent clauses correctly.

Method 1: Add a Comma and a Coordinating Conjunction (IC, cc IC.)

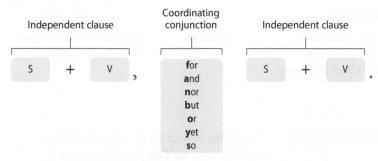

Wikipedia is a popular encyclopedia, for it is easily available online.

[The word *for* indicates a reason or cause.]

The encyclopedia is open to all, and anyone can add information to it.

[The word *and* simply joins two ideas.]

Method 2: Add a Semicolon (IC; IC.)

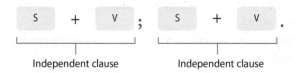

There was no sleep for me that night; the events of the day made sure of that (Healy 161).

Method 3: Add a Semicolon, a Conjunctive Adverb, and a Comma (IC; ca, IC.)

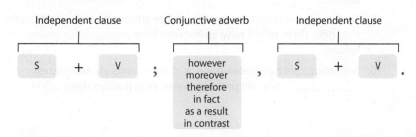

Antarctica is largely unexplored;	as a result,	it is unpopulated.
It receives little rain;	also,	it is incredibly cold.
It is may hold clues to animal life from thousands of years ago;	therefore,	scientists are becoming more interested in it.

> **PRACTICE 24–5**   **Choosing the Correct Coordinating Conjunction or Conjunctive Adverb**

Fill in each blank with a coordinating conjunction or conjunctive adverb that makes sense in the sentence. Make sure to add the correct punctuation.

> **Example:**   Rebates sound like a good deal ___ *, but* ___ they rarely are.

1. Rebate offers are common _____ you have probably seen many of them on packages for appliances and electronics.

2. These offers may promise to return hundreds of dollars to consumers _____ many people apply for them.

3. Applicants hope to get a lot of money back soon _____ they are often disappointed.

4. They might have to wait several months _____ they might not get their rebate at all.

5. Rebate applications are not short _____ are they easy to fill out.

6. One applicant compared completing a rebate form to filling out tax forms _____ he spent more than an hour on the process.

7. Manufacturers sometimes use rebates to move unpopular products off the shelves _____ they can replace these products with newer goods.

8. Only about 10 to 30 percent of people who apply for a rebate eventually get it _____ consumer groups are warning people to be careful.

9. Problems with rebates are getting more attention _____ companies that offer them might have to improve their processes for giving refunds.

10. Manufacturers have received a lot of complaints about rebates _____ they will probably never stop making these offers.

Joining Ideas: Subordination

Subordination means joining ideas by making one of the ideas a dependent or subordinate clause. You learned in Chapter 18 that a dependent clause begins with a subordinating conjunction, such as *because, after, although,* or *when.*

Subordination, Option 1: IC DC.

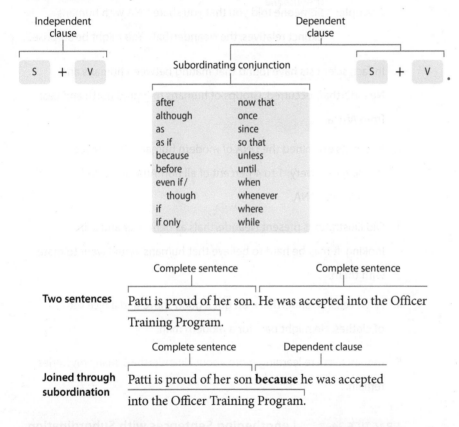

| Two sentences | Complete sentence — Patti is proud of her son. | Complete sentence — He was accepted into the Officer Training Program. |

| Joined through subordination | Complete sentence — Patti is proud of her son | Dependent clause — **because** he was accepted into the Officer Training Program. |

Subordination, Option 2: DC, IC.

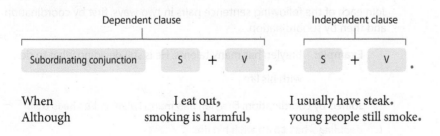

| When | I eat out, | I usually have steak. |
| Although | smoking is harmful, | young people still smoke. |

| PRACTICE 24–6 | Combining Sentences Using Subordination |

Combine each pair of sentences into a single sentence by adding an appropriate subordinating conjunction either between (Option 1) or at the beginning of the two sentences (Option 2). Use a subordinating conjunction that makes sense with the two sentences, and add commas where necessary.

Example: *If someone*
~~Someone~~ told you that you share DNA with humans'
extinct relatives, the Neanderthals, *, you* ~~You~~ might be surprised.

1. In fact, scientists have found that mating between humans and Neanderthals occurred. Groups of humans migrated north and east from Africa.

2. Scientists examined the DNA of modern humans. They made a startling discovery: 1 to 4 percent of all non-Africans' DNA is Neanderthal DNA.

3. Old illustrations present Neanderthals as bent over and primitive looking. It may be hard to believe that humans would want to mate with them.

4. However, a Neanderthal man got a good shave and a nice set of clothes. He might pass for a modern man.

5. Researchers are learning more about Neanderthals. Many mysteries remain.

| PRACTICE 24–7 | Lengthening Sentences with Subordination and Coordination |

Join each of the following sentence pairs in two ways, first by coordination and then by subordination.

Example: Braylen has many talents. He is still deciding what to do with his life.

Joined by coordination: Braylen has many talents, but he is still deciding what to do with his life.

Joined by subordination: Although Braylen has many talents, he is still deciding what to do with his life.

1. Braylen rides a unicycle. He can juggle four oranges.

    Joined by coordination:

    Joined by subordination:

2. A trapeze school opened in our town. Braylen signed up immediately.

    Joined by coordination:

    Joined by subordination:

3. Braylen is now at the top of his class. He worked hard practicing trapeze routines.

    Joined by coordination:

    Joined by subordination:

4. Braylen asks me for career advice. I try to be encouraging.

    Joined by coordination:

    Joined by subordination:

5. He does not want to join the circus. He could study entertainment management.

    Joined by coordination:

    Joined by subordination:

Other Ways to Join Ideas and Lengthen Sentences

In addition to coordination and subordination, you can also combine sentences using an *-ing* verb, a past participle, an appositive, or an adjective clause.

Using an *-ing* Verb

One way to combine sentences is to turn the less important of the two sentences into a phrase by adding *-ing* to the verb and deleting the subject.

Two sentences:	A pecan roll from our bakery is not a health food. It contains 800 calories.
Joined with *-ing* verb form:	*Containing* 800 calories, a pecan roll from our bakery is not a health food.

You can add the *-ing* phrase to the beginning or the end of the other sentence, depending on what makes more sense.

The fat content is also high. ~~It equals~~ *, equaling* the fat in a huge country breakfast.

If you add the *-ing* phrase to the beginning of a sentence, you will usually need to put a comma after it. If you add the phrase to the end of a sentence, you will usually need to put a comma before it. A comma should *not* be used if the *-ing* phrase is essential to the meaning of the sentence.

Two sentences:	Experts examined the effects of exercise on arthritis patients. The experts found that walking, jogging, or swimming could reduce pain.
Joined without commas:	Experts examining the effects of exercise on arthritis patients found that walking, jogging, or swimming could reduce pain. [The phrase *examining the effects of exercise on arthritis patients* is essential to the meaning of the sentence.]

If you put a phrase starting with an *-ing* verb at the beginning of a sentence, be sure the word that the phrase modifies follows immediately. Otherwise, you will create a dangling modifier. (For more on dangling modifiers, see Chapter 23.)

Two sentences:	I ran through the rain. My raincoat got all wet.
Dangling modifier:	Running through the rain, my raincoat got all wet.
Edited:	Running through the rain, I got my raincoat all wet.

PRACTICE 24-8   **Joining Ideas Using an *-ing* Verb**

Combine each pair of sentences into a single sentence by using an *-ing* verb. Add or delete words as necessary.

> **Example:** Some people read faces amazingly well. ~~They interpret~~ , interpreting
>
> nonverbal cues that other people miss.

1. A recent study tested children's abilities to interpret facial expressions. The study made headlines.

2. Physically abused children participated in the study. They saw photographs of faces changing from one expression to another.

3. The children told researchers what emotion was most obvious in each face. The children chose among fear, anger, sadness, happiness, and other emotions.

4. The study also included nonabused children. They served as a control group for comparison with the other children.

5. All the children in the study were equally good at identifying most emotions. They all responded similarly to happiness or fear.

Using a Past Participle

Another way to combine sentences is to use a past participle (often, a verb ending in *-ed*) to turn the less important of the two sentences into a phrase. (For more information about past participles, see Chapter 20.)

Two sentences:	Henry VIII was a powerful English king. He is *remembered* for his many wives.
Joined with a past participle:	*Remembered* for his many wives, Henry VIII was a powerful English king.

Past participles of irregular verbs do not end in *-ed*; they take different forms.

Two sentences:	Tim Treadwell was *eaten* by a grizzly bear. He showed that wild animals are unpredictable.
Joined with a past participle:	*Eaten* by a grizzly bear, Tim Treadwell showed that wild animals are unpredictable.

Notice that sentences can be joined this way when one of them has a form of *be* along with a past participle (*is remembered* in the first Henry VIII example and *was eaten* in the first Tim Treadwell example). By deleting that subject and *be* form, you create a phrase that can be added to the beginning or the end of the other sentence, depending on what makes more sense.

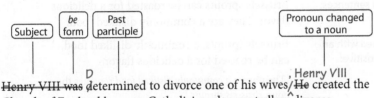

If you add a phrase that begins with a past participle to the beginning of a sentence, put a comma after it. If you add the phrase to the end of the sentence, put a comma before it.

> ### PRACTICE 24–9   Joining Ideas Using a Past Participle
>
> Combine each pair of sentences into a single sentence by using a past participle.
>
> **Example:**   ~~The oil company was forced~~ *Forced* to take the local women's
>   objections seriously/~~The~~ *, the oil* company had to close for ten days
>   during their protest.
>
> 1. The women of southern Nigeria were angered by British colonial rule in 1929. They organized a protest.
>
> 2. Nigeria is now one of the top ten oil-producing countries. The nation is covered with pipelines and oil wells.
>
> 3. The oil is pumped by American and other foreign oil companies. The oil often ends up in wealthy Western economies.
>
> 4. The money from the oil seldom reaches Nigeria's local people. The cash is stolen by corrupt rulers in many cases.
>
> 5. The Nigerian countryside is polluted by the oil industry. The land then is becoming a wasteland.

Using an Appositive

An **appositive** is a noun or noun phrase that renames a noun or pronoun. Appositives can be used to combine two sentences into one.

Two sentences:	Brussels sprouts can be roasted for a delicious flavor. They are a commonly disliked food.
Joined with an appositive:	Brussels sprouts, a commonly disliked food, can be roasted for a delicious flavor.
	[The phrase *a commonly disliked food* renames the noun *Brussels sprouts.*]

Notice that the sentence that renames the noun was turned into a noun phrase by dropping the subject and the verb (*They* and *are*). Also, commas set off the appositive. (For more information about appositives in writing, see Chapter 10, p. 189.)

PRACTICE 24–10   **Joining Ideas Using an Appositive**

Combine each pair of sentences into a single sentence by using an appositive. Be sure to use a comma or commas to set off the appositive.

Example: Levi's jeans have looked the same for well over a century. ~~They are perhaps the most famous work clothes in the world.~~

, perhaps the most famous work clothes in the world,

1. Jacob Davis was a Russian immigrant working in Reno, Nevada. He was the inventor of Levi's jeans.

2. Davis came up with an invention that made work clothes last longer. The invention was the riveted seam.

3. Davis bought denim from a wholesaler. The wholesaler was Levi Strauss.

4. In 1870, he offered to sell the rights to his invention to Levi Strauss for the price of the patent. Patents then cost about $70.

5. Davis joined the firm in 1873 and supervised the final development of its product. The product was the famous Levi's jeans.

Using an Adjective Clause

An **adjective clause**, also called a **relative clause**, is a group of words with a subject and a verb that describes a noun. An adjective clause often begins with the word *who, which,* or *that,* and it can be used to combine two sentences into one.

Two sentences:	Lauren has won many basketball awards. She is captain of her college team.
Joined with an adjective clause:	Lauren, *who is captain of her college team,* has won many basketball awards.

To join sentences this way, use *who, which,* or *that* to replace the subject in a sentence that describes a noun in the other sentence. You now have an adjective clause that you can move so that it follows the noun it describes. The sentence with the more important idea (the one you want to emphasize) should become the main clause. The less important idea should be in the adjective clause.

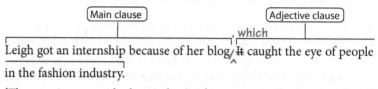

Leigh got an internship because of her blog, It caught the eye of people in the fashion industry.

[The more important idea here is that Leigh got an internship because of her blog. The less important idea is that the blog caught the eye of people in the fashion industry.]

Note: If an adjective clause can be taken out of a sentence without completely changing the meaning of the sentence, put commas around it.

Latoya, *who is captain of her college team,* has won many basketball awards.

[The phrase *who is captain of her college team* adds information about Latoya, but it is not essential.]

If an adjective clause is an essential part of a sentence, do not put commas around it.

Latoya is an award-winning basketball player who overcame childhood cancer.

[*Who overcame childhood cancer* is an essential part of this sentence.]

PRACTICE 24-11   Joining Ideas Using an Adjective Clause

Combine each pair of sentences into a single sentence by using an adjective clause beginning with *who, which,* or *that.*

Example: My friend Erin had her first child last June. ~~She has been going to college for the past three years.~~ , who has been going to college for the past three years,

1. While Erin goes to classes, her baby boy stays at a day-care center. The day-care center costs Erin about $100 a week.

2. Twice when her son was ill, Erin had to miss her geology lab. The lab is an important part of her grade for that course.

3. Occasionally, Erin's parents come up and watch the baby while Erin is studying. They live about 70 miles away.

4. Sometimes Erin feels discouraged by the extra costs. The costs have come from having a child.

5. She believes that some of her professors are not very sympathetic. These professors are the ones who have never been parents themselves.

6. Erin understands that she must take responsibility for both her child and her education. She wants to be a good mother and a good student.

7. Her grades have suffered somewhat since she had her son. They were once straight A's.

8. Erin wants to graduate with honors. She hopes to go to graduate school someday.

9. Her son is more important than an A in geology. He is the most important thing to her.

10. Erin still expects to have a high grade point average. She has simply given up expecting to be perfect.

Strategies for Changing Sentence Openers

In addition to combining or lengthening sentences to achieve rhythm and variety, you may also consider changing how you begin a sentence. Most student writers follow a basic pattern, beginning each sentence with a subject. In this section, we will explore other ways to begin a sentence.

Starting with Adverbs

Adverbs are words that describe verbs, adjectives, or other adverbs; they often end with *-ly*. As long as the meaning is clear, adverbs can be placed at the beginning of a sentence instead of in the middle. Adverbs at the beginning of a sentence are usually followed by a comma. (For more on adverbs, see Chapter 23.)

Adverb in middle:	Stories about haunted houses *frequently* surface at Halloween.
Adverb at beginning:	*Frequently,* stories about haunted houses surface at Halloween.
Adverb in middle:	These stories *often* focus on ship captains lost at sea.
Adverb at beginning:	*Often,* these stories focus on ship captains lost at sea.

Starting with Prepositions or Infinitives

You may also begin a sentence with a prepositional phrase or an infinitive.

Prepositional phrase at the end:	Zaria and her team celebrated *after their final match.*
Prepositional phrase at the beginning:	*After their final match,* Zaria and her team celebrated.
Infinitive phrase at the end:	Ximena signed up for a math class *to help her daughter with algebra homework.*
Infinitive phrase at the beginning:	*To help her daughter with algebra homework,* Ximena signed up for a math class.

Notice that when you begin a sentence with a prepositional phrase or an infinitive, the phrase is usually followed by a comma.

> **PRACTICE 24–12** **Starting Sentences with Prepositional Phrases or Infinitives**
>
> Practice changing sentence structure by moving the prepositional phrase or the infinitive phrase to the beginning of each sentence. Pay attention to punctuation.
>
> **Example:** To help reduce the amount of vehicle traffic in the city, Washington, D.C., began a public bicycle-sharing program.
> ~~to help reduce the amount of vehicle traffic in the city.~~

1. The idea has been popular in Europe for years.

2. Citizens must pay $7 a day, $25 a month, or $75 a year to join the program in Washington.

3. They have access to more than one thousand bikes for that fee.

4. They must return the bikes to a local station after each use.

5. A number of stations are located in Washington, D.C., and Arlington, Virginia, to make sure all riders can have convenient access to the bicycles.

6. Cycling has become much more popular throughout the United States in recent years.

7. People are turning to bicycles to save money on fuel costs.

PRACTICE 24-13   **Editing Sentences for Sentence Variety**

Create sentence variety in the following paragraphs by joining at least two sentences in each of the paragraphs. Use several of the techniques covered in this chapter. More than one correct answer is possible.

Few people would associate the famous English poet and playwright William Shakespeare with prison. However, Shakespeare has taken on an important role in the lives of certain inmates. They are serving time at the Luther Luckett Correctional Complex in Kentucky. These inmates were brought together by the Shakespeare Behind Bars program. They spend nine months preparing for a performance of one of the great writer's plays.

Recently, prisoners at Luckett performed *The Merchant of Venice*. It is one of Shakespeare's most popular plays. Many of the actors identified with Shylock. He is a moneylender who is discriminated against because he is Jewish. When a rival asks Shylock for a loan to help a friend, Shylock drives a hard bargain. He demands a pound of the rival's flesh if the loan is not repaid. One inmate shared his views of this play with a newspaper reporter. The inmate said, "It deals with race. It deals with discrimination. It deals with gambling, debt, cutting people. It deals with it all. And we were all living that someway, somehow."

Chapter 24 Review

1. What is parallel structure in writing, and what are three situations when writers must pay attention to it?

2. What are five ways to vary sentence styles?

3. What are three patterns for joining ideas through coordination?

4. What is subordination?

5. What is an appositive?

6. What is an adjective (relative) clause?

Chapter 24 Quiz

Indicate the correct choice for each of the following items.

—   1. If an underlined portion of this sentence is incorrect, select the revision that fixes it. If the sentence is correct as written, choose d.

> For our home renovation, we are planning to <u>expand the kitchen,</u>
> a
> <u>retile the bathroom,</u> and <u>we also want to add a bedroom.</u>
>   *b*   *c*

    a. add space to the kitchen

    b. replace the tile in the bathroom

    c. add a bedroom

    d. No change is necessary.

—   2. Choose the correct word(s) to fill in the blank.

> In my personal ad, I said that I like taking long walks on the beach, dining over candlelight, and _____ sculptures with a chain saw.

    a. to carve   b. carving   c. carved

___ 3. If an underlined portion of this sentence is incorrect, select the revision that fixes it. If the sentence is correct as written, choose d.

> **To get her elbow back into shape, she wants exercising and not**
>   *a*   *b*
>
> **to take pills.**
>   *c*

    a. To getting   c. taking pills

    b. to do exercises   d. No change is necessary.

___ 4. Choose the correct word(s) to fill in the blank.

> **I have learned that _____ a pet is better than buying one from a pet store.**

    a. adopting   b. have adopted   c. to adopt

___ 5. Choose the correct words to fill in the blank.

> **You can travel by car, by plane, or _____.**

    a. boating is fine   b. by boat   c. on boat

___ 6. Choose the option below that best combines these two independent clauses— "Luis straightened his tie" and "he waited to be called in for his job interview"—into a single sentence:

    a. Straightened his tie, Luis waited to be called in for his job interview.

    b. Straightening his tie, Luis waited to be called in for his job interview.

___ 7. Choose the correct word(s) to fill in the blank.

> **_____ the candidate stepped up to the podium, a group of protesters began to shout criticisms of her.**

    a. So that   b. As if   c. As

___ 8. Choose the option below that best combines these two independent clauses—"My niece is a star softball player" and "she loves to watch baseball on TV"—into a single sentence:

    a. My niece, a star softball player, loves to watch baseball on TV.

    b. Starring as a softball player, my niece loves to watch baseball on TV.

___ 9. Choose the correct word(s) to fill in the blank.

> **_____ you are sure that the lightning has stopped, don't let the kids get back into the pool.**

    a. Until   b. Before   c. As if

___ 10. Choose the option below that best combines these two independent clauses—"The lawyer believed passionately in his client's innocence" and "he convinced the jury to come to a verdict of not guilty"—into a single sentence:

a. The lawyer, who believed passionately in his client's innocence, convinced the jury to come to a verdict of not guilty.

b. The lawyer believed passionately in his client's innocence, yet he convinced the jury to come to a verdict of not guilty.

___ 11. Choose the correct word(s) to fill in the blank.

Matt speaks out against glorifying college sports _____ he himself is the star of our football team.

a. until   b. even though   c. unless

___ 12. Choose the correct word(s) to fill in the blank.

I did not like the teacher's criticism of my paper; _____ I must admit that everything she said was right.

a. as a result,   b. in addition,   c. still,

___ 13. Choose the correct word to fill in the blank.

Jenna is the best speaker in the class, _____ she will give the graduation speech.

a. or   b. so   c. yet

___ 14. Choose the correct word(s) to fill in the blank.

There were now neat rows of suburban homes _____ there had once been orange groves.

a. where   b. as if   c. before

___ 15. Choose the correct word to fill in the blank.

_____ we bought a snowblower, my son has not complained about having to shovel after storms.

a. Since   b. Where   c. Unless

25

Capitalization, Apostrophes ❯ , and Spelling

Learning Outcomes   In this chapter, you will learn to

- Capitalize sentences, names, dates, and titles correctly.
- Use apostrophes accurately to show ownership and contractions.
- Use strategies to edit and improve spelling.

Conventions are expected ways of doing something, whether it's allowing faster drivers to pass in the left lane or standing for certain prayers within a church. Conventions develop over time within a group, and they may even be formalized (written down) into rules or laws. Writers who work in an academic setting know that readers will have certain expectations about the ways words, sentences, and paragraphs are presented. In the editing stages of writing, effective writers make sure that each word in their developing text matches their readers' expectations. In other words, they edit for the conventions of written English. In this chapter, you will study three such conventions: capitalization, apostrophes, and spelling.

Capitalization

Capital letters (*A, B, C*) are generally bigger than lowercase letters (*a, b, c*), and they may have a different form. In English, capitals are used to indicate the beginnings of sentences; proper nouns (or names, like John Lennon, the Mississippi River, Wednesday, and the Fourth of July); and titles of books, TV shows, newspapers, songs, and so on (like *The Catcher in the Rye,* the *Los Angeles Times, Parks and Recreation,* and "Rain on Me"). Careful use of capitalization provides visual help to readers, and academic readers expect writing to follow capitalization conventions.

Most problems in capitalization can be avoided by following these three rules:

1. Capitalize the first letter of every new sentence.
2. Capitalize the names of specific people, places, dates, and things.
3. Capitalize important words in titles.

Capitalizing Sentences

Capitalize the first letter of each new sentence, including the first word of a direct quotation.

The superintendent was surprised. He asked, "What is going on here?"

Capitalizing Proper Nouns

The general rule is to capitalize the first letter in the names of specific people, places, dates, and organizations, nationalities, and religions. Do not capitalize a generic (or *common*) noun, such as *college*, but do capitalize a specific (or *proper*) noun, such as *Carroll State College*. Look at the following examples for each group.

People

Capitalize the first letter in the names of specific people and in the titles used with the names of specific people.

Specific	Not Specific
Eunsook Yu	my neighbor
Professor Fitzgerald	your math professor
Dr. Cornog	the doctor
Aunt Pat, Mother	my aunt, your mother

The name of a family member is capitalized when the family member is being addressed directly: Happy Birthday, *Mother*. In other instances, do not capitalize: It is my *mother's* birthday.

The word *president* is not capitalized unless it comes directly before a name as part of that person's title: *President* Joe Biden.

Places

Capitalize the first letter in the names of specific buildings, streets, cities, states, regions, and countries.

Specific	Not Specific
Bolton Town Hall	the town hall
Arlington Street	our street
Dearborn Heights	my hometown
Arizona	this state
the South	the southern region
Spain	that country

Do not capitalize directions in a sentence.

Drive *south* for five blocks.

Dates

Capitalize the first letter in the names of days, months, and holidays. Do not capitalize the names of the seasons (winter, spring, summer, fall).

Specific	Not Specific
Wednesday	tomorrow
June 25	summer
Thanksgiving	my birthday

🌐 **Language note:** Some languages, such as Spanish, French, and Italian, do not capitalize days, months, and languages. In English, such words must be capitalized.

Incorrect:	I study russian every monday, wednesday, and friday from january through may.
Correct:	I study *Russian* every *Monday, Wednesday,* and *Friday* from *January* through *May.*

Organizations, Companies, and Groups

Specific	Not Specific
Taft Community College	my college
Microsoft	a software company
Alcoholics Anonymous	the self-help group

Languages, Nationalities, and Religions

Specific	Not Specific
English, Greek, Spanish	my first language
Christianity, Buddhism	your religion

Courses

Specific	Not Specific
Composition 101	a writing course
Introduction to Psychology	my psychology course

The names of languages should be capitalized even if you aren't referring to a specific course.

> I am taking psychology and *Spanish.*

Commercial Products

Specific	Not Specific
Diet Pepsi	a diet cola
Skippy peanut butter	peanut butter

Capitalizing Titles

When you write the title of a book, movie, television program, magazine, newspaper, article, story, song, paper, poem, and so on, capitalize the first and last words and all important words in between. The only words that do not need to be capitalized (unless they are the first word) are *the, a,* and *an;* coordinating conjunctions (*and, but, for, nor, or, so, yet*); and prepositions.

> *I Love Lucy* was a long-running television program.
> *For Whom the Bell Tolls* is a classic novel.
> Both *USA Today* and the *New York Times* are popular newspapers.
> "Once More to the Lake" is one of Diego's favorite essays.

PRACTICE 25–1   Editing Paragraphs for Capitalization

Edit the following paragraphs by capitalizing as needed and removing any unnecessary capitalization.

in Robert louis Stevenson's 1886 novella "the strange case of dr. jekyll and mr. hyde," a doctor uses Himself as the subject of an experiment, and the results are Disastrous. The novella was a Great Success, but stevenson didn't originate the idea of Doctors experimenting on themselves.

one of the earliest known examples of self-experimentation goes back to the sixteenth Century, when santorio santorio, of padua, italy, weighed himself every Day for thirty Years. By weighing everything he ate and drank as well as his Bodily Discharges, Santorio discovered that the Human body continually and imperceptibly loses large amounts of Fluid. today, that Loss, called *insensible perspiration,* is routinely measured in Hospital patients.

A Key Breakthrough to the modern age of Cardiology was made in 1929 by a german, dr. werner forssmann, who as a Surgical Resident at a medical facility called the august victoria home, near berlin, conducted a daring self-experiment by inserting a thin tube into one of his Veins and slid the tube into his own Heart. This idea was later developed by other Researchers into the Technique of cardiac catheterization. Dr. forssmann, who used catheters on himself nine times, shared a nobel prize in 1956 for his Pioneering Experiments.

Apostrophes '

Like capitalization, the use of apostrophes within words is an important convention of written English. An **apostrophe** (') is a punctuation mark that shows ownership (*Susan's*) or indicates that a letter has been intentionally left out to form a contraction (*I'm, that's, they're*). Apostrophes can also be used to make numbers and letters plural.

Apostrophes to Show Ownership

Add -'s to a singular noun to show ownership even if the noun already ends in -s.

> *Shaniyah's* apartment is on the South Side.
>
> *Javier's* roommate is looking for him.
>
> *Ross's* house is on the market right now.

If a noun is plural and ends in -s, just add an apostrophe. If it is plural but does not end in -s, add -'s.

> My *books'* covers are falling off.
>
> [more than one book]

> The *twins'* father was building them a playhouse.
>
> [more than one twin]

> The *children's* toys were broken.
>
> The *men's* locker room is being painted.

The placement of an apostrophe makes a difference in meaning.

> My *sister's* six children are at my house for the weekend.
>
> [one sister who has six children]

> My *sisters'* six children are at my house for the weekend.
>
> [two or more sisters who together have six children]

Do not use an apostrophe to form the plural of a noun.

> Gina went camping with her *sister's* and their children.
>
> All the *highway's* to the airport are under construction.

Do not use an apostrophe with a possessive pronoun. These pronouns already show ownership (possession).

> Is that bag *your's*?   No, it is *our's*.

Possessive Pronouns

my	his	its	their
mine	her	our	theirs
your	hers	ours	whose
yours			

The single most common error with apostrophes and pronouns is confusing *its* (a possessive pronoun) with *it's* (a contraction meaning "it is"). Whenever you write *it's*, test correctness by replacing it with *it is* and reading the sentence aloud to hear if it makes sense. (For more on *its/it's*, see p. 514.)

Apostrophes in Contractions

A **contraction** is formed by joining two words and leaving out one or more of the letters. When writing a contraction, put an apostrophe where the letter or letters have been left out. Contractions are generally viewed as a marker of informal writing; students are often expected to avoid contractions in formal writing situations. If you are not sure whether or not contractions are acceptable, be sure to ask your instructor.

Common Contractions

aren't = are not

can't = cannot

couldn't = could not

didn't = did not

don't = do not

he'd = he would, he had

he'll = he will

he's = he is, he has

I'd = I would, I had

I'll = I will

I'm = I am

I've = I have

isn't = is not

it's = it is, it has

let's = let us

she'd = she would, she had

she'll = she will

she's = she is, she has

there's = there is

they'd = they would, they had

they'll = they will

they're = they are

they've = they have

who'd = who would, who had

who'll = who will

who's = who is, who has

won't = will not

wouldn't = would not

you'd = you would, you had

you'll = you will

you're = you are

you've = you have

She's on her way. = She is on her way.

I'll see you there. = I will see you there.

Be sure to put the apostrophe in the correct place.

It doesn't really matter

Apostrophes with Letters, Numbers, and Time

Use -'s to make letters and numbers plural. The apostrophe prevents confusion or misreading.

Tip: To shorten the full year to only the final two numbers, replace the first two numbers with an apostrophe: the year 2021 becomes '21.

In Scrabble games, there are more e's than any other letter.

In women's shoes, size 8's are more common than size 10's.

Use an apostrophe or -'s in certain expressions in which time nouns are treated as if they possess something.

> She took four *weeks'* maternity leave after the baby was born.
>
> This *year's* graduating class is huge.

PRACTICE 25-2   **Editing Paragraphs for Apostrophes**

Edit the following paragraphs by adding two apostrophes where needed and crossing out five incorrectly used apostrophes.

Have you noticed many honeybee's when you go outside? If not, it is'nt surprising. For reasons that scientists still don't quite understand, these bees have been disappearing all across the country. This mass disappearance is a problem because bees are an important part of growing a wide variety of flowers, fruits, vegetables, and nuts as they spread pollen from one place to another.

In the past year, more than one-third, or billions, of the honeybees in the United States' have disappeared. As a consequence, farmers have been forced either to buy or to rent beehives for their crops. Typically, people who are in the bee business ship hives to farmers fields by truck. The hives often have to travel hundreds of miles.

Scientist's have been trying to find out what happened to the once-thriving bee population. They suspect that either a disease or chemicals harmed the honeybee's.

Spelling

Spelling is one of the most basic conventions of written language, and it is also a challenge for many people, including some who are extremely intelligent. Standard spellings used today have evolved over hundreds of years as English has changed, and these spellings reflect different patterns and pronunciations; as a result, they can be difficult to master. Fortunately, most writers can address spelling challenges by practicing strategies for finding and correcting spelling mistakes (including careful use of technology) and using a list of commonly misspelled and confused words, such as the ones on pages 511–18.

Using a Dictionary

When proofreading your papers, consult a dictionary whenever you are unsure about the spelling of a word. Dictionaries (both online and print) can help you determine the correct spelling and allow you to check the meaning of the word at the same time.

Using a Spell Checker—with Caution

Use a **spell checker** after you have completed a piece of writing but before you print it out. This word-processing tool finds and highlights a word that may be misspelled, suggests other spellings, and gives you the opportunity to change the spelling of the word.

However, you should never rely on a spell checker to do your editing for you. Because a spell checker ignores anything that it recognizes as a word, it will not help you find words that are misused or misspelled words that are also words. For example, a spell checker will not recognize an error if you make a mistake with any of the commonly confused words listed later in this chapter, such as *to*, *two*, and *too*.

Using Proofreading Techniques

Use some of the following proofreading techniques to focus on the spelling of one word at a time. Try them all. Then decide which ones work best for you.

- Print out your paper before proofreading. (Many writers find it easier to detect errors on paper than on screen.)
- Put a piece of paper under the line that you are reading.
- Proofread your paper backward, one word at a time.
- Print out a version of your paper that has larger words, larger margins, or triple-spaced lines.
- Read your paper aloud. This strategy will help you if you tend to leave words out.
- Have someone else read your paper aloud. You may hear where you have used a word incorrectly or left a word out.

Making a Personal Spelling List

Set aside a section of your course notebook or learning journal for your spelling list. Every time you edit a paper, write down the words that you misspelled. Every couple of weeks, go back to your spelling list to see if your problem words have changed. Are you misspelling fewer words in each paper?

For each word on your list, create a memory aid to help you remember the correct spelling. You might, for example, choose a different pronunciation to help you remember the word. If you have trouble spelling *definitely*, you might remember the spelling by pronouncing the word so that the second and third syllables rhyme with "eye." Another memory trick is to sing the spelling to a familiar tune: d-e-f-i-n-i-t-e-l-y spells *definitely* (sung to the tune of "Twinkle, Twinkle, Little Star").

Building Spelling Skills Over Time

Here are four good strategies for improving your spelling skills over time:

1. Learn the six spelling rules that follow.
2. Learn the exceptions when forming plurals.
3. Consult a list of commonly misspelled words.
4. Master commonly confused words.

Learn Six Spelling Rules

If you can remember the following six rules, you can correct many of the spelling errors in your writing.

First, here is a quick review of vowels and consonants.

Vowels:	*a, e, i, o,* and *u*
Consonants:	*b, c, d, f, g, h, j, k, l, m, n, p, q, r, s, t, v, w, x,* and *z*

The **letter *y*** can be either a vowel or a consonant. It is a vowel when it sounds like the *y* in *fly* or *hungry*. It is a consonant when it sounds like the *y* in *yellow*.

Rule 1 "*I* before *e*, except after *c* or when sounding like *a*, as in *neighbor* or *weigh*." Many people repeat this rhyme to themselves as they decide whether a word is spelled with an *ie* or an *ei*.

piece (*i* before *e*)
receive (except after *c*)
eight (sounds like *a*)

Exceptions: *either, neither, foreign, height, seize, society, their, weird*

Rule 2

a. Drop the final *e* when adding an ending that begins with a vowel.

> hope + ing = hoping
> imagine + ation = imagination

b. Keep the final *e* when adding an ending that begins with a consonant.

> achieve + ment = achievement
> definite + ly = definitely

Exceptions: *argument, awful, judgment, simply, truly*

Rule 3

a. When adding an ending to a word that ends in *y*, change the *y* to *i* when a consonant comes before the *y*.

> lonely + est = loneliest   apology + ize = apologize
> happy + er = happier   likely + hood = likelihood

b. Do not change the *y* when a vowel comes before the *y*.

> boy + ish = boyish   survey + or = surveyor
> pay + ment = payment   buy + er = buyer

Exceptions:

1. When adding *-ing* to a word ending in *y*, always keep the *y*, even if a consonant comes before it: stu**dy** + ing = studying.

2. Other exceptions include *daily, dryer, said,* and *paid*.

Rule 4   When adding an ending that starts with a vowel to a one-syllable word, follow these rules:

a. Double the final consonant only if the word ends with a consonant-vowel-consonant.

> tra**p** + ed = trapped   kni**t** + ed = knitted
> dri**p** + ed = dripped   fa**t** + er = fatter

b. Do not double the final consonant if the word ends with some other combination.

Vowel-Vowel-Consonant	Vowel-Consonant-Consonant
clean + est = cleanest	slick + er = slicker
poor + er = poorer	teach + er = teacher
clear + ed = cleared	last + ed = lasted

Rule 5 When adding an ending that starts with a vowel to a word with two or more syllables, follow these rules:

a. Double the final consonant only if the word ends with a consonant-vowel-consonant and the stress is on the last syllable.

submit + ing = submitting   prefer + ed= preferred

b. Do not double the final consonant in other cases.

understand + ing = understanding   offer + ed = offered

Rule 6

a. Add -s to most nouns to form the plural, including words that end in *o* preceded by a vowel.

Most Words	Words That End in Vowel Plus *o*
book + s = books	video + s = videos
college + s = colleges	stereo + s = stereos

b. Add -es to words that end in *o* preceded by a consonant and words that end in *s, sh, ch,* or *x*.

Words That End in Consonant Plus *o*	Words That End in *s, sh, ch,* or *x*
potato + es = potatoes	class + es = classes
hero + es = heroes	push + es = pushes
tomato + es = tomatoes	bench + es = benches
	fax + es = faxes

Learn the Exceptions When Forming Plurals

A **compound noun** is formed when two nouns are joined with a hyphen (*in-law*), a space (*life vest*), or no space (*keyboard, stockpile*). Plurals of compound nouns are generally formed by adding an *-s* to the end of the last noun (*in-laws, life vests*) or to the end of the combined word (*keyboards, stockpiles*). Some hyphenated compound words such as *mother-in-law* or *hole-in-one* form plurals by adding an *-s* to the chief word (*mothers-in-law, holes-in-one*).

Some words form plurals in different ways, as in the following list.

Different Types of Plurals

Singular	Plural	Singular	Plural
analysis	analyses	loaf	loaves
bacterium	bacteria	louse	lice
bison	bison	man	men
cactus	cacti	medium	media
calf	calves	mouse	mice
child	children	phenomenon	phenomena
deer	deer	roof	roofs
die	dice	sheep	sheep
focus	foci	shelf	shelves
foot	feet	thief	thieves
goose	geese	tooth	teeth
half	halves	vertebra	vertebrae
hoof	hooves	wife	wives
knife	knives	wolf	wolves
leaf	leaves	woman	women

Consult a List of Commonly Misspelled Words

Use a list like the one below as an easy reference to check your spelling.

One Hundred Commonly Misspelled Words

absence	convenient	harass	receive
achieve	cruelty	height	recognize
across	daughter	humorous	recommend
aisle	definite	illegal	restaurant
a lot	describe	immediately	rhythm
already	develop	independent	roommate
analyze	dictionary	interest	schedule
answer	different	jewelry	scissors
appetite	disappoint	judgment	secretary
argument	dollar	knowledge	separate
athlete	eighth	license	sincerely
awful	embarrass	lightning	sophomore
basically	environment	loneliness	succeed
beautiful	especially	marriage	successful
beginning	exaggerate	meant	surprise
believe	excellent/excellence	muscle	truly
business	exercise	necessary	until
calendar	fascinate	ninety	usually
career	February	noticeable	vacuum
category	finally	occasion	valuable
chief	foreign	perform	vegetable
column	friend	physically	weight
coming	government	prejudice	weird
commitment	grief	probably	writing
conscious	guidance	psychology	written

Master Commonly Confused Words

What follows is a list of twenty-seven sets of words that are commonly confused because they sound similar, such as *write* and *right*. Mastering this list will help you avoid many spelling mistakes.

a / an / and

a: used before a word that begins with a consonant sound

A friend of mine just won the lottery.

an: used before a word that begins with a vowel sound

An old friend of mine just won the lottery.

and: used to join two words

My friend *and* I went out to celebrate.

A friend *and* I ate at *an* Italian restaurant.

accept / except

accept: to agree to receive or admit (verb)

I will *accept* the job offer.

except: but, other than (preposition)

All the stores are closed *except* the Quik-Stop.

I *accept* all the job conditions *except* the low pay.

advice / advise

advice: opinion (noun)

I would like your *advice* before I make a decision.

advise: to give an opinion (verb)

Please *advise* me what to do.

Please *advise* me what to do; you always give me good *advice*.

affect / effect

affect: to make an impact on, to change something (verb)

The whole city was *affected* by the hurricane.

effect: a result (noun)

What *effect* will the hurricane have on the local economy?

Although the storm will have many negative *effects*, it will not *affect* the price of food.

are / our

are: a form of the verb *be*

The workers *are* about to go on strike.

our: a pronoun showing ownership

> The children played on *our* porch.

My relatives *are* staying at *our* house.

by / buy / bye

by: next to, before, or past (preposition)

> Meet me *by* the entrance.

> Make sure the bill is paid *by* the fifteenth of the month.

> The motorcycle raced *by* me.

buy: to purchase (verb)

> I would like to *buy* a new laptop.

bye: an informal way to say *goodbye*

> "Bye, Grandma!"

Terence heard his wife say, *"Bye"* as he ran out to go *buy* milk at the convenience store *by* the highway.

conscience / conscious

conscience: a personal sense of right and wrong (noun)

> Jake's *conscience* would not allow him to cheat.

conscious: awake, aware (adjective)

> The coma patient is now *conscious*.

> I am *conscious* that it is getting late.

The judge was *conscious* that the accused had acted according to his *conscience* even though he had broken the law.

fine / find

fine: of high quality (adjective); feeling well (adjective); a penalty for breaking a law (noun)

> This jacket is made of *fine* leather.

> After a day in bed, Jacob felt *fine*.

> The *fine* for exceeding the speed limit is $50.

find: to locate, to discover (verb)

> Did Clara *find* her glasses?

I *find* gardening to be a *fine* pastime.

its / it's

its: a pronoun showing ownership

The dog chased *its* tail.

it's: a contraction of the words *it is*

It's about time you got here.

It's very hard for a dog to keep *its* teeth clean.

knew / new / know / no

knew: understood; recognized (past tense of the verb *know*)

I *knew* the answer, but I could not think of it.

new: unused, recent, or just introduced (adjective)

The building has a *new* security code.

know: to understand; to have knowledge of (verb)

I *know* how to bake bread.

no: used to form a negative

I have *no* idea what the answer is.

I never *knew* how much a *new* car costs.

loose / lose

loose: baggy; relaxed; not fixed in place (adjective)

In hot weather, people tend to wear *loose* clothing.

lose: to misplace; to forfeit possession of (verb)

Every summer, I *lose* about three pairs of sunglasses.

If the ring is too *loose* on your finger, you might *lose* it.

mind / mine

mind: to object to (verb); the thinking or feeling part of one's brain (noun)

Toby does not *mind* if I borrow his tool chest.

Estela has a good *mind*, but often she does not use it.

mine: belonging to me (pronoun); a source of ore and minerals (noun)

That coat is *mine*.

My uncle worked in a coal *mine* in West Virginia.

That writing problem of *mine* was on my *mind*.

of / have

of: coming from; caused by; part of a group; made from (preposition)

The leader *of* the band played bass guitar.

have: to possess (verb; also used as a helping verb)

I *have* one more course to take before I graduate.

I should *have* started studying earlier.

The president *of* the company should *have* resigned.

Note: Do not use *of* after *would, should, could,* and *might.* Use *have* after those words (*would have, should have*).

passed / past

passed: went by or went ahead (past tense of the verb *pass*)

We *passed* the hospital on the way to the airport.

past: time that has gone by (noun); gone by, over, just beyond (preposition)

In the *past,* I was able to stay up all night and not be tired.

I drove *past* the burning warehouse.

This *past* school year, I *passed* all my exams.

peace / piece

peace: no disagreement; calm (noun)

Could you quiet down and give me a little *peace*?

piece: a part of something larger (noun)

May I have a *piece* of that pie?

The feuding families found *peace* after they sold the *piece* of land.

principal / principle

principal: main (adjective); head of a school or leader of an organization (noun)

Brush fires are the *principal* risk in the hills of California.

Ms. Edwards is the *principal* of Memorial Elementary School.

Corinne is a *principal* in the management consulting firm.

principle: a standard of beliefs or behaviors (noun)

Although tempted, she held on to her moral *principles.*

The *principal* questioned the delinquent student's *principles.*

quiet / quite / quit

quiet: soft in sound; not noisy (adjective)

The library was *quiet*.

quite: completely; very (adverb)

After cleaning all the windows, Alex was *quite* tired.

quit: to stop (verb)

She *quit* her job.

After the band *quit* playing, the hall was *quite quiet*.

right / write

right: correct; in a direction opposite from left (adjective)

You definitely made the *right* choice.

When you get to the stoplight, make a *right* turn.

write: to put words on paper (verb)

Will you *write* your phone number for me?

Please *write* the *right* answer in the space provided.

set / sit

set: a collection of something (noun); to place an object somewhere (verb)

Paul has a complete *set* of Johnny Cash records.

Please *set* the package on the table.

sit: to rest in a chair or other seatlike surface; to be located in a particular place (verb)

I need to *sit* on the sofa for a few minutes.

The shed *sits* between the house and the garden.

If I *sit* down now, I will not have time to *set* the plants outside.

suppose / supposed

suppose: to imagine or assume to be true (verb)

I *suppose* you would like something to eat.

Suppose you won a million dollars.

supposed: past tense of *suppose*; intended

Karen *supposed* Thomas was late because of traffic.

I *suppose* you know that Rita was *supposed* to be home by 6:30.

than / then

than: a word used to compare two or more people, places, or things (conjunction)

It is colder inside *than* outside.

then: at a certain time; next in time (adverb)

I got out of the car and *then* realized the keys were still in it.

Clara ran more miles *than* she ever had before, and *then* she collapsed.

their / there / they're

their: a pronoun showing ownership

I borrowed *their* clippers to trim the hedges.

there: a word indicating location or existence (adverb)

Just put the keys *there* on the desk.

There are too many lawyers.

they're: a contraction of the words *they are*

They're about to leave.

There is a car in *their* driveway, which indicates that *they're* home.

though / through / threw

though: however; nevertheless; in spite of (conjunction)

Though he is short, he plays great basketball.

through: finished with (adjective); from one side to the other (preposition)

I am *through* arguing with you.

The baseball went right *through* the window.

threw: hurled; tossed (past tense of the verb *throw*)

She *threw* the basketball.

Even *though* it was illegal, she *threw* the empty cup *through* the window onto the road.

to / too / two

to: a word indicating a direction or movement (preposition); part of the infinitive form of a verb

Please give the message *to* Sharon.

It is easier *to* ask for forgiveness than *to* get permission.

too: also; more than enough; very (adverb)

I am tired *too*.

Dan ate *too* much and felt sick.

That dream was *too* real.

two: the number between one and three (noun)

The lab had only *two* computers.

They went *to* a restaurant and ordered *too* much food for *two* people.

use / used

use: to employ or put into service (verb)

How do you plan to *use* that blueprint?

used: past tense of the verb *use*. *Used to* can indicate a past fact or state, or it can mean "familiar with."

He *used* his lunch hour to do errands.

He *used* to go for a walk during his lunch hour.

She is also *used* to improvising in the kitchen.

She *used* to be a chef, so she knows how to *use* all kinds of kitchen gadgets.

who's / whose

who's: a contraction of the words *who is*

Who's at the door?

whose: a pronoun showing ownership

Whose car is parked outside?

Who's the person *whose* car sank in the river?

your / you're

your: a pronoun showing ownership

Did you bring *your* wallet?

you're: a contraction of the words *you are*

You're not telling me the whole story.

You're going to have *your* third exam tomorrow.

PRACTICE 25–3   Editing Paragraphs for Commonly Confused Words

Edit the following paragraphs to correct eighteen errors in word use.

More and more women are purchasing handguns, against the advise of law enforcement officers. Few of these women are criminals or plan to commit crimes. They no the risks of guns, and they except those risks. They buy weapons primarily because their tired of feeling like victims. They do not want to contribute too the violence in are society, but they also realize that women are the victims of violent attacks far to often. Many women loose they're lives because they cannot fight off there attackers. Some women have made a conscience decision to arm themselves for protection.

But does buying a gun make things worse rather then better? Having a gun in you're house makes it three times more likely that someone will be killed there—and that someone is just as likely to be you or one of your children as a criminal. Most young children cannot tell the difference between a real gun and a toy gun when they fine one. Every year, their are tragic examples of children who accidentally shoot and even kill other youngsters while they are playing with guns. A mother who's children are injured while playing with her gun will never again think that a gun provides piece of mind. Reducing the violence in are society may be a better solution.

Chapter 25 Review

1. What are conventions?

2. What are three situations that require capital letters?

3. Give two reasons to include an apostrophe.

4. To show ownership, add _____ to a singular noun, even if the noun already ends in -s. For a plural noun, add an _____ alone if the noun ends in -s; add _____ if the noun does not end in -s.

5. What are two important tools for finding and correcting spelling mistakes?

6. What strategies can you use to become a better speller?

Chapter 25 Quiz

For each sentence, write the letter that identifies the correct spelling of the word that goes in the blank.

___ 1. Choose the item that has no errors.

a. My daughter's school, Spitzer High School, no longer sells pepsi and other sodas in its vending machines.

b. My daughter's school, Spitzer high school, no longer sells pepsi and other sodas in its vending machines.

c. My daughter's school, Spitzer High School, no longer sells Pepsi and other sodas in its vending machines.

___ 2. If an underlined portion of this sentence is incorrect, select the revision that fixes it. If the sentence is correct as written, choose d.

Will our company **President** speak at the **annual meeting**, or will
                         a   b

Dr. Anders?
       c

a. president

b. Annual Meeting

c. doctor Anders

d. No change is necessary.

___ 3. Choose the item that has no errors.

a. Which Library do you go to, Hill Library or Barry Township Library?

b. Which library do you go to, Hill Library or Barry Township Library?

c. Which library do you go to, Hill library or Barry Township library?

___ 4. If an underlined portion of this sentence is incorrect, select the revision that fixes it. If the sentence is correct as written, choose d.

In my **english 99** class **last summer,** we read some interesting
        a   b

essays by famous authors.
         c

a. English 99

b. last Summer

c. Famous Authors

d. No change is necessary.

___ 5. If an underlined portion of this sentence is incorrect, select the revision that fixes it. If the sentence is correct as written, choose d.

        Of the states in the <u>East</u>, one can travel the farthest <u>North</u> in <u>Maine</u>.
                        a   *b*   *c*

    a. east
    b. north
    c. maine
    d. No change is necessary.

___ 6. If an underlined portion of this sentence is incorrect, select the revision that fixes it. If the sentence is correct as written, choose d.

        I've always believed that <u>its</u> a crime to use software that you <u>haven't</u>
         a   *b*   *c*
        paid for.

    a. Ive
    b. it's
    c. havent
    d. No change is necessary.

___ 7. Choose the item that has no errors.

    a. The thieves boldness made them a lot of money, but it eventually landed them in jail.

    b. The thieves's boldness made them a lot of money, but it eventually landed them in jail.

    c. The thieves' boldness made them a lot of money, but it eventually landed them in jail.

___ 8. Choose the item that has no errors.

    a. By playing that slot machine, your throwing away money.

    b. By playing that slot machine, you're throwing away money.

    c. By playing that slot machine, youre' throwing away money.

___ 9. If an underlined portion of this sentence is incorrect, select the revision that fixes it. If the sentence is correct as written, choose d.

        The house is now <u>Renee's</u>, but <u>she'll</u> regret having an address with
                                    a   *b*
        five <u>3s</u> in it.
             c

    a. Renees
    b. sh'ell
    c. 3's
    d. No change is necessary.

___ 10. Choose the item that has no errors.

    a. Her eighteen months' service overseas has somehow made her seem older.

    b. Her eighteen month's service overseas has somehow made her seem older.

    c. Her eighteen months service overseas has somehow made her seem older.

___ 11. Choose the correct word to complete the sentence.

    Your joining us for dinner is a pleasant _____.

    a. suprise   b. surprize   c. surprise

___ 12. Choose the correct word to complete the sentence.

    When can I expect to _____ the package?

    a. recieve   b. receive   c. reeceive

___ 13. Choose the correct word to complete the sentence.

    The solar technology program is _____ many new students.

    a. admiting   b. admitting   c. addmitting

___ 14. Choose the correct word to complete the sentence.

    Keyara's roommate is _____ weird.

    a. definately   b. definitely   c. definitly

___ 15. Choose the correct word to complete the sentence.

    After my doctor diagnosed my injury, she _____ me to a physical therapist.

    a. refered   b. reffered   c. referred

26

Commas **,**

Learning Outcomes   In this chapter, you will learn to

- Use commas correctly in sentences.
- Recognize other common uses for commas.
- Identify commas that are not necessary.

Commas (,) are punctuation marks that help readers understand a sentence. Read aloud the following three sentences. How does the use of commas change the meaning?

No comma:	When you call Savion I will start cooking.
One comma:	When you call Savion, I will start cooking.
Two commas:	When you call, Savion, I will start cooking.

To get your intended meaning across to your readers, it is important that you understand when and how to use commas.

Use Commas Correctly

Writers use commas to separate information within sentences in a variety of different ways in order to ensure readers can follow their thoughts.

Commas between Items in a Series

Use commas to separate the items in a series (three or more items), including the last item in the series, which usually has *and* before it.

item **,** item **,** item **,** and item

524 Chapter 26 • Commas

> To get from South Dakota to Texas, we will drive through *Nebraska,*
> *Kansas,* and *Oklahoma.*
>
> We can *sleep in the car, stay in a motel,* or *camp outside.*
>
> As I drive, I see many beautiful sights, such as *mountains, plains,* and
> *prairies.*

Items in lists should be parallel. See Chapter 24 for more on parallel structure.

Note: Writers do not always use a comma before the final item in a series. In college writing, however, it is best to include it.

Commas with Coordinate and Cumulative Adjectives

Coordinate adjectives are two or more adjectives that independently modify the same noun and are separated by commas.

> Connor ordered a *big, fat, greasy* burger.
>
> The diner food was *cheap, unhealthy,* and *delicious.*

Do *not* use a comma between the final adjective and the noun it describes.

> **Incorrect:** Joelle wore a *long, clingy, red,* dress.
>
> **Correct:** Joelle wore a *long, clingy, red* dress.

Cumulative adjectives describe the same noun but are not separated by commas because they form a unit that describes the noun. You can identify cumulative adjectives because separating them by *and* does not make any sense.

> The store is having its *last storewide clearance* sale.
>
> [Putting *and* between *last* and *storewide* and between *storewide* and *clearance* would make an odd sentence:
>
> The store is having its *last* and *storewide* and *clearance* sale.
>
> The adjectives in the sentence are cumulative and should not be separated by commas.]

In summary:

- **Do** use commas to separate two or more **coordinate adjectives**.
- **Do not** use commas to separate **cumulative adjectives**.

> **PRACTICE 26-1**   **Using Commas in Series and with Adjectives**
>
> Edit the following sentences by identifying the items in the series and adding commas where they are needed. If a sentence is already correct, put a "C" next to it.
>
> **Example:**   In 1935, the U.S. government hired writers, teachers, historians, and others to work for the Federal Writers' Project (FWP).

1. The FWP was part of an effort to create jobs during the long devastating economic crisis known as the Great Depression.

2. Many famous writers, such as John Cheever Ralph Ellison and Zora Neale Hurston, joined the FWP.

3. The FWP's Folklore Unit dedicated itself to interviewing ordinary Americans writing down their stories and bringing together this information so that it could be shared with the public.

4. Folklore Unit workers were able to collect not only life stories but also songs folktales and superstitions.

5. The director of the Folklore Unit hoped that by publishing this information, the FWP might make Americans more accepting of fellow citizens whose experiences, beliefs, and interests were different from their own.

Commas in Compound Sentences

A **compound sentence** contains two complete sentences joined by a coordinating conjunction: *and, but, for, nor, or, so,* and *yet.* Use a comma before the joining word to separate the two complete sentences.

┌──────────┐   ┌─────────────────────────┐   ┌──────────┐
│ Sentence │ , │ and, but, for, nor, or, so, yet │   │ Sentence │ .
└──────────┘   └─────────────────────────┘   └──────────┘

I called my best friend, and she agreed to drive me to work.

I asked my best friend to drive me to work, but she was busy.

I can take the bus to work, or I can call another friend.

 Language note: A comma alone cannot separate two sentences in English. Using a comma in this way creates a run-on. (See Chapter 18.)

PRACTICE 26–2   Using Commas in Compound Sentences

Edit the following compound sentences by adding commas where they are needed. If a sentence is already correct, put a "C" next to it.

Example: Marika wanted to get a college education, but her husband
                                                    ^
                 did not like the idea.

1. Marika's hospital volunteer work had convinced her to become a
   physical therapist, but she needed a college degree to qualify.

2. Deciding to apply to college was difficult for her so she was excited
   when she was admitted.

3. She had chosen the college carefully for it had an excellent program in
   physical therapy.

4. Marika knew that the courses would be difficult but she had not
   expected her husband to oppose her plan.

5. They had been married for twelve years, and he was surprised that she
   wanted a career.

Editing for correct comma usage:

Using commas in compound sentences

Find

Many college <u>students</u> <u>are</u> the first in their families to go to college (and) these students' <u>relatives</u> <u>are</u> proud of them.

1. To determine if the sentence is compound, **underline** the subjects, and **double-underline** the verbs.

2. *Ask:* Is the sentence compound? Yes

3. **Circle** the word that joins them.

Edit

4. **Put a comma** before the word that joins the two sentences.

Many college students are the first in their families to go to college, and these students' relatives are proud of them.

Commas after Introductory Words

Use a comma after an introductory word, phrase, or clause. The comma lets your readers know when the main part of the sentence is starting.

(Introductory word or word group) , (Main part of sentence) .

Introductory word:	*Yesterday,* I went to the game.
Introductory phrase:	*By the way,* I do not have a babysitter for tomorrow.
Introductory clause:	*While I waited outside,* Susan went backstage.

PRACTICE 26-3 **Using Commas after Introductory Word Groups**

In each item, identify the introductory word or word group. Then add a comma where it is needed. If a sentence is already correct, put a "C" next to it.

Example: In the 1960s, John Mackey became famous for his speed and strength as a tight end for the Baltimore Colts football team.

1. In his later years the National Football League Hall-of-Famer was in the news for another reason: he suffered from dementia possibly linked to the head blows he received on the football field.

2. According to medical experts, repeated concussions can severely damage the brain over time, and they are especially harmful to young people, whose brains are still developing.

3. Based on these warnings and on stories like John Mackey's athletic associations, coaches, and parents of young athletes are taking new precautions.

4. For example more football coaches are teaching players to tackle and block with their heads up, reducing the chance that they will receive a blow to the top of the head.

5. Also when players show signs of a concussion—such as dizziness, nausea, or confusion—more coaches are taking them out of the game.

Commas around Appositives and Interrupters

An **appositive** comes directly before or after a noun or pronoun and renames it.

> Lily, *a senior,* will take her nursing exam this summer.
> The prices are outrageous at Beans, *the local coffee shop.*

An **interrupter** is an aside or transition that interrupts the flow of a sentence and does not affect its meaning.

> My sister, *incidentally,* has good reasons for being late.
> Her child had a fever, *for example.*

Putting commas around appositives and interrupters tells readers that these elements give extra information but are not essential to the meaning of a sentence. If an appositive or interrupter is in the middle of a sentence, set it off with a pair of commas, one before and one after. If an appositive or interrupter comes at the beginning or end of a sentence, separate it from the rest of the sentence with one comma.

> *By the way,* your proposal has been accepted.
>
> Your proposal, *by the way,* has been accepted.
>
> Your proposal has been accepted, *by the way.*

Note: Sometimes, an appositive is essential to the meaning of a sentence. When a sentence would not have the same meaning without the appositive, the appositive should not be set off with commas.

> The actor *Michael Keaton* has never won an Oscar.
>
> [The sentence *The actor has never won an Oscar* does not have the same meaning.]

For additional examples of commas with appositives, see the "Grammar for Process Analysis" section in Chapter 10, page 189.

Editing for correct comma usage:

Using commas to set off appositives and interrupters

Find

Tamara my sister-in-law moved in with us last week.

1. **Underline** the subject.

2. **Circle** any appositive (which renames the subject) or interrupter (which interrupts the flow of the sentence).

3. *Ask:* Is the appositive or interrupter essential to the meaning of the sentence? No

Edit

4. If it is not essential, **set it off with commas.**

Tamara, my sister-in-law, moved in with us last week.

PRACTICE 26-4   **Using Commas to Set Off Appositives and Interrupters**

Identify all the appositives and interrupters in the following sentences. Then use commas to set them off.

Example: Harry, an attentive student, could not hear his teacher because the radiator in the classroom made a constant rattling.

1. Some rooms in fact are full of echoes, dead zones, and mechanical noises that make it hard for students to hear.

2. The American Speech-Language-Hearing Association experts on how noise levels affect learning abilities has set guidelines for how much noise in a classroom is too much.

3. The association recommends that background noise the constant whirring or whining sounds made by radiators, lights, and other machines be no more than 35 decibels.

4. That level 35 decibels is about as loud as a whispering voice fifteen feet away.

5. One study found a level of 65 decibels the volume of a vacuum cleaner in a number of classrooms around the country.

Commas around Adjective Clauses

An **adjective clause** is a group of words that begins with *who, which,* or *that*; has a subject and a verb; and describes a noun right before it in a sentence. (For more information on writing with adjective clauses, see Chapter 24.)

If an adjective clause can be taken out of a sentence without completely changing the meaning of the sentence, put commas around the clause.

Noun , Adjective clause not essential to meaning , Rest of sentence .

Lola, *who is my cousin,* will take her nursing exam this summer.

Beans, *which is the local coffee shop,* charges outrageous prices.

I complained to Mr. Kranz, *who is the shop's manager.*

If an adjective clause is essential to the meaning of a sentence, do not put commas around it.

| Noun | | Adjective clause essential to meaning | | Rest of sentence | .

You can tell whether a clause is essential by taking it out and seeing if the meaning of the sentence changes significantly, as it would if you took the clauses out of the following examples:

The only grocery store *that sold good bread* went out of business.

Students *who do internships* often improve their hiring potential.

Salesclerks *who sell liquor to minors* are breaking the law.

Editing for correct comma usage:

Using commas to set off adjective clauses

Find

The woman <u>who had octuplets</u> received much publicity.

1. **Underline** any adjective clause (a word group that begins with *who, which,* or *that*).

2. **Read** the sentence without this clause.

3. *Ask:* Does the meaning change significantly without the clause? Yes

Edit

3. If the meaning *does* change, as in this case, **do not put in commas**. (Add commas only if the meaning *does not* change.)

The woman who had octuplets received much publicity.

PRACTICE 26–5   Using Commas to Set Off Adjective Clauses

Identify the adjective clauses in the following sentences. Then put commas around these clauses where they are needed. Remember that if an adjective clause is essential to the meaning of a sentence, commas are not necessary. If a sentence is already correct, put a "C" next to it.

Example: Daniel Kish, who has been blind since the age of one, has changed many people's ideas about what blind people can and cannot do.

1. Kish who runs the organization World Access for the Blind regularly rides his bike down busy streets and goes on long hikes.

2. His system for "seeing" his surroundings which is known as echolocation uses sound waves to create mental pictures of buildings, cars, trees, and other objects.

3. As Kish bikes around his neighborhood or hikes to sites that are deep in the wilderness, he clicks his tongue and listens to the echoes.

4. The echoes which differ depending on the distance and physical features of nearby objects allow him to map his surroundings in his mind.

5. This mental map which he constantly revises as he moves ahead helps him avoid running into cars, trees, and other obstacles.

Recognize Other Uses for Commas

Commas are also used to set off information in several different situations.

Commas with Quotation Marks

Quotation marks are used to show that you are repeating exactly what someone said. Use commas to set off the words inside quotation marks from the rest of the sentence.

> "Let me see your license," demanded the police officer.
> "Did you realize," she asked, "that you were going 80 miles per hour?"
> I exclaimed, "No!"

Notice that a comma never comes directly after a quotation mark.

When quotations are not attributed to a particular person, commas may not be necessary.

> "Pretty is as pretty does" never made sense to me.

Commas in Addresses

Use commas to separate the elements of an address included in a sentence. However, do not use a comma before a zip code.

> My address is 2512 Windermere Street, Jackson, Mississippi 40720.

If a sentence continues after a city-state combination or after a street address, put a comma after the state or the address.

> I moved here from Detroit, Michigan, when I was eighteen.
> I've lived at 24 Heener Street, Madison, since 1999.

Commas in Dates

Separate the day from the year with a comma when including a date in a sentence. If you give just the month and year, do not separate them with a comma.

> My daughter was born on November 8, 2004.
> The next conference is in August 2023.

If a sentence continues after the date, put a comma after the date.

> On April 21, 2028, the contract will expire.

Commas with Names

Put a comma after (and sometimes before) the name of someone being addressed directly.

> Diego, I want you to come look at this.
> Unfortunately, Marie, you need to finish the report by next week.

Commas with Yes or No

Put a comma after the word *yes* or *no* in response to a question.

> Yes, I believe that you are right.

| PRACTICE 26–6 | **Using Commas in Other Ways** |

Edit the following sentences by adding commas where they are needed. If a sentence is already correct, put a "C" next to it.

Example: On August 12, 2012, beachfront property was badly
                  ^   ^
                damaged by a fast-moving storm.

1. Some homeowners were still waiting to settle their claims with their insurance companies in January 2022.

2. Rob McGregor of 31 Hudson Street Wesleyville is one of those homeowners.

3. Asked if he was losing patience, McGregor replied "Yes I sure am."

4. "I've really had it up to here," McGregor said.

5. His wife said "Rob don't go mouthing off to any reporters."

Identify Commas That Are Not Necessary

Knowing where commas are required is important, but so is knowing where commas are *not* needed.

- **Don't separate a verb from the subject or the object with a comma.**

Incorrect:	My cousin and her family, are traveling to Europe this summer.
	[A comma separates the verb from the subject.]
Incorrect:	The websites will provide, exercises and other practice materials.
	[A comma separates the verb from its object.]

- **Don't separate compound subjects, verbs, or objects with a comma.**

Incorrect: Kayleigh, and her mother are shopping for the
                  holidays this afternoon.

                  [A comma separates the compound subject.]

Incorrect: After shopping, they will get dinner, and go to a movie.

                  [A comma separates the compound verb.]

Incorrect: Kayleigh hopes to find a fitness-tracker, and a
                  sweatshirt for her Dad.

                  [A comma separates the compound object of "find."]

- **Don't put a comma before the first item in a list.**

Incorrect: The team brought, water bottles, power bars, protein
                  powder, and chocolate to eat.

                  [A comma comes before the first item in the series.]

Incorrect: Information about, fitness, diet, weight reduction, and
                  muscle development can be found near the front of the
                  gym.

                  [A comma comes before the first item in the series.]

PRACTICE 26-7   **Editing Paragraphs for Commas**

Edit the following paragraphs by adding commas where they are needed.

Can you remember the last time you picked up a quick lunch from a
food truck? Think about what you got in addition to your food: a disposable
plate napkins a cup with a plastic straw plastic utensils and some packets of
condiments. Like most people you may have tossed all of those items into
the trash after eating. Do you know what happens to them after that?

Many states including California and Washington are concerned about
where these disposable items especially the plastic ones go after they are
discarded. Disposable plastic utensils and straws which are meant to be
used only once are known as "single-use" plastics and environmental scientists around the world are concerned about how they may impact the

environment. Specifically scientists worry because single-use plastics are not biodegradable.

The World Wildlife Fund estimates that 2.47 billion plastic straws end up in landfills in Australia and millions more drift into the ocean where they can harm fish and other marine animals. As a result the state of South Australia passed a ban on single-use plastic straws in 2020. However because of Covid-19 restrictions in restaurants the ban is not scheduled to be enforced until later in 2021.

Chapter 26 Review

1. How do you use commas if you have items in a series?
2. How do you use commas in compound sentences?
3. What are four other situations that require commas?
4. Where are commas *not* needed?

Chapter 26 Quiz

Indicate the correct choice for each of the following items.

_____ 1. If an underlined portion of this sentence is incorrect, select the revision that fixes it. If the sentence is correct as written, choose d.

The company <u>owners, for</u> your <u>information are</u> planning to inspect
                            a   *b*

our <u>department this</u> afternoon.
            c

  a. owners for   c. department, this

  b. information, are   d. No change is necessary.

_____ 2. Choose the item that has no errors.

  a. I used to hate parties but now I like to socialize with others.

  b. I used to hate parties, but now I like to socialize with others.

  c. I used to hate parties, but, now I like to socialize with others.

___ 3. Choose the item that has no errors.

    a. If you do not file your income tax forms by April 15, 2022 you could face penalties.

    b. If you do not file your income tax forms by April 15, 2022, you could face penalties.

    c. If you do not file your income tax forms by April 15 2022 you could face penalties.

___ 4. If an underlined portion of this sentence is incorrect, select the revision that fixes it. If the sentence is correct as written, choose d.

Henry's <u>favorite hobbies</u> <u>are watching birds,</u> collecting <u>stamps, and</u>
                  a   *b*   *c*

fixing up old cars.

    a. favorite, hobbies   c. stamps and

    b. are watching, birds   d. No change is necessary.

___ 5. Choose the item that has no errors.

    a. Roger, who teaches dance at a local studio, will be my partner for the ballroom competition.

    b. Roger who teaches dance at a local studio will be my partner for the ballroom competition.

    c. Roger who teaches dance at a local studio, will be my partner for the ballroom competition.

___ 6. If an underlined portion of this sentence is incorrect, select the revision that fixes it. If the sentence is correct as written, choose d.

Feeling <u>adventurous, Alexia</u> <u>tasted the</u> guava, <u>mango and</u> passion
                  a   *b*   *c*

fruit.

    a. adventurous Alexia   c. mango, and

    b. tasted, the   d. No change is necessary.

___ 7. Choose the item that has no errors.

    a. I discovered that Lansing, Michigan was the hometown of four people at the party.

    b. I discovered that Lansing Michigan, was the hometown of four people at the party.

    c. I discovered that Lansing, Michigan, was the hometown of four people at the party.

___ 8. If an underlined portion of this sentence is incorrect, select the revision that fixes it. If the sentence is correct as written, choose d.

Just to be different I decided to wear a top hat to all my classes
      _____ _____   _____
          a   b   c

today.

a. different, I

c. hat, to

b. decided, to

d. No change is necessary.

___ 9. Choose the item that has no errors.

a. "If you follow my instructions precisely" said the manager, "I will consider you for a promotion."

b. "If you follow my instructions precisely," said the manager "I will consider you for a promotion."

c. "If you follow my instructions precisely," said the manager, "I will consider you for a promotion."

___ 10. If an underlined portion of this sentence is incorrect, select the revision that fixes it. If the sentence is correct as written, choose d.

No Jaleel, I cannot swim, paddle a kayak, or steer a sailboat.
 _____   _____   _____
      a   b   c

a. No, Jaleel,

c. kayak or

b. swim paddle

d. No change is necessary.

27

Quotation Marks and Italics   " "

Learning Outcomes   **In this chapter, you will learn to**

- Use quotation marks for direct quotations.
- Use quotation marks in some titles.
- Use italics for titles, emphasis, and words as words.

Look at the following sentences from Samantha Levine-Finley's article, "Isn't It Time You Hit the Books?" (Chapter 10):

> Now a graduating senior, Trevino, 22, realizes she got bum advice. "In high school, I was so monitored to go to class, it was hard to miss," she says. "In college, you are responsible for your own actions and can't blame problems on someone else. It doesn't work like that."

In this passage, Levine-Finley includes words written or spoken by someone else. The convention that writers use to show that words come from another person is quotation marks.

Quotation marks (" ") always appear in pairs. They are used with **direct quotations**, which exactly repeat, word for word, what someone said or wrote, as in the example by Levine-Finley. They are also used to set off titles:

> My favorite song is "Sophisticated Lady."

In academic writing, it is important to use quotation marks correctly, especially when quoting sources in college papers: using someone else's words without giving them credit is considered plagiarism. Academic readers will also expect to see quotation marks used correctly to indicate the titles of short works, such as articles, poems, songs, and episodes of TV shows and podcasts.

Use Quotation Marks for Direct Quotations

When you write a direct quotation, use quotation marks around the quoted words. Quotation marks tell readers that the words used are exactly what was said or written.

> **Examples of Quotation Marks in Dialogue**
>
> - "I do not know what she means," I said to my friend Lina.
> - Lina asked, "Do you think we should ask a question?"
> - "Excuse me, Professor Soames," I called out, "but could you explain that again?"
> - "Yes," said Professor Soames. "Let me make sure you all understand."
> - After further explanation, Professor Soames asked, "Are there any other questions?"

(For more on using dialogue in narration, see "Third Basic: Secondary Support in Narration," pp. 105–6, in Chapter 7.)

When you are writing a paper that uses outside sources, use quotation marks to indicate where you quote the exact words of a source.

> **Example of Quotation Marks in a Research Paper**
>
> We all need to become more conscientious recyclers. A recent editorial in the *Bolton Common* reported, "When recycling volunteers spot-checked bags that were supposed to contain only newspaper, they found a collection of nonrecyclable items, such as plastic candy wrappers, aluminum foil, and birthday cards."

(For more on integrating outside sources, see Chapter 15, pp. 308–9.)

When quoting, writers usually use words that identify who is speaking, such as *I said to my friend Lina* in the first dialogue example above. The identifying words can come after the quoted words (as in that first example), before them (second example), or in the middle of them (third example). Here are some guidelines for capitalization and punctuation with quotation marks.

Guidelines for Capitalization and Punctuation When Quoting

- Capitalize the first letter in a complete sentence that is being quoted, even if it comes after some identifying words. (See the second example above.)
- Do not capitalize the first letter in a quotation if it is not the first word in a complete sentence (The word *but* in the third example above is not capitalized.)

- If it is a complete sentence and it is clear who the speaker is, a quotation can stand on its own. (See the second sentence in the fourth example on p. 540.)
- Identifying words must be attached to a quotation; they cannot be a sentence on their own.
- Use commas to separate any identifying words from quoted words in the same sentence.
- Always put quotation marks after commas and periods. Put quotation marks after question marks and exclamation points if they are part of the quoted sentence.

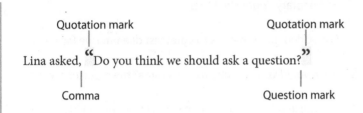

- If a question mark or an exclamation point is part of your own sentence, put it after the quotation mark.

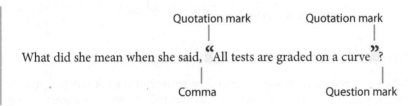

Setting Off a Quotation within Another Quotation

Sometimes, when you quote someone directly, part of what that person said quotes words that someone else said or wrote. Put single quotation marks (' ') around the quotation within a quotation so that readers understand who said what.

> Terry told his instructor, "I am sorry I missed the exam, but that is not a reason to fail me for the term. Our student handbook says, 'Students must be given the opportunity to make up work missed for legitimate reasons,' and I have a good reason."

PRACTICE 27–1   **Punctuating Direct Quotations**

Edit the following sentences by adding quotation marks and commas where needed.

Example: A radio journalist asked a nurse at a critical-care facility, "Do you believe that the medical community needlessly prolongs the life of the terminally ill?"

1. If I could answer that question quickly the nurse replied I would deserve an honorary degree in ethics.

2. She added But I see it as the greatest dilemma we face today.

3. How would you describe that dilemma? the reporter asked the nurse.

4. The nurse said It is a choice of when to use our amazing medical technology and when not to.

5. The reporter asked So there are times when you would favor letting patients die on their own?

No Quotation Marks for Indirect Speech

When you report what someone said or wrote but do not use the person's exact words, you are writing **indirect speech**, also called **reported speech**. Do not use quotation marks for indirect speech. Indirect speech often begins with the word *that*.

Indirect Speech	Direct Quotation
Sam said that there was a fire downtown.	Sam said, "There was a fire downtown."
The police told us to move along.	"Move along," directed the police.
Tara told me that she is graduating.	Tara said, "I am graduating."

PRACTICE 27–2   **Punctuating Direct and Indirect Quotations**

Edit the following sentences by adding quotation marks where needed and crossing out quotation marks that are used incorrectly. If a sentence is already correct, put a "C" next to it.

Example: Three days before her apartment was robbed, Jocelyn told

a friend,"I worry about the safety of this building."

1. Have you complained to the landlord yet? her friend asked.

2. Not yet, Jocelyn replied, although I know I should.

3. Jocelyn phoned the landlord and asked him to install a more secure lock on the front door.

4. The landlord said that "he believed that the lock was fine the way it was."

5. When Jocelyn phoned the landlord after the burglary, she said, I know this burglary would not have happened if that lock had been installed.

Use Quotation Marks for Titles of Shorter Works That Appear in Other, Longer Works

When you refer to a work that appears in another, longer work, such as an article in a magazine or newspaper; a chapter in a book; a web page on a website; a short story, essay, or poem in a collection; or an episode from a TV show or podcast, put quotation marks around the title of the work.

Newspaper article:	"Volunteers Honored for Service"
Short story:	"The Awakening"
Essay:	"Why Are We So Angry?"

Use Italics for Some Titles and Names, for Emphasis, and for Special Words

Italics refers to a feature of the fonts used for typing: in *italics,* the letters slant to the right.

Italics for Titles of Stand-alone Works and Some Names

Titles of longer, stand-alone works, such as books, magazines, newspapers, movies, websites, TV shows, and podcasts, are italicized.

Book:	*The Good Earth*
Newspaper:	*Washington Post*

The names of ships, trains, or spacecraft may also be italicized.

Ship:	*Titanic*
Train:	*Orient Express*
Spacecraft:	Space Shuttle *Challenger*

The titles of sacred books, such as the Bible or the Koran, are neither italicized nor surrounded by quotation marks.

If you are writing a paper with many outside sources, your instructor will probably refer you to a particular system of citing sources. Follow that system's guidelines when you use titles in your paper. (The Modern Language Association [MLA] system of documentation is explained in the Appendix, pp. 554–62.)

Note: Do not enclose in quotation marks or italicize the title of a paragraph or an essay that you have written when it appears at the beginning of your paper.

Italics for Emphasis, Words as Words, and Unfamiliar Words from Other Languages

Italics may also be used to emphasize a word or phrase, to focus on a word as a word (and not the meaning of the word), or to treat unfamiliar words and phrases from a different language. (Use your dictionary: If a word from another language is familiar enough to English speakers to be included in the dictionary, it does not need to be typed in italics.)

Emphasis:	Your paper is due *before* 5:00 p.m.
Words as words:	The words *to, two,* and *too* are often misspelled.
Foreign language:	He is my best friend, my number one fan, *mi abuelo.*

PRACTICE 27-3   **Editing Paragraphs for Quotation Marks**

Edit the following paragraphs by adding quotation marks and commas where needed. Highlight words that should be in italics.

Ruiz Sanchez is a success coach, which means he helps students with the challenges that keep them from being successful in their first year of college courses. I recently talked with Ruiz, who is a former student of mine, and I asked him about his work.

Ruiz said The two problems I see the most are poor time management and a fixed mindset. I asked him to explain more about these problems.

Sure, Profesora Ruiz answered. With time management, students don't plan ahead. They are always late because they don't know what to do or when to do it. I help them make a schedule, el horario. That way they don't wait until the last minute.

I asked So what sorts of tools do you give them?

Well, we use the calendar online, and we set reminders. And the very first thing is so simple! We just make a list—una lista, you know?

Then Ruiz explained that a mindset is the way people think about their own abilities. He mentioned a book by Carol Dweck called Mindset: The New Psychology of Success. That book describes two approaches to learning new things. A fixed mindset means you believe your talents and abilities are determined and unchanging, so you are good at some things and bad at others. But a growth mindset, on the other hand, thinks improvement is always possible. In fact, the key word for a growth mindset is yet. A person with a growth mindset says I haven't fully mastered these algebra problems yet, but I will get them soon.

Chapter 27 Review

1. Quotation marks look like _____. They always appear in (pairs / threes).

2. A direct quotation _____ exactly what someone (or some outside source) said or wrote. (Use / Do not use) quotation marks around direct quotations.

3. What is an indirect quotation? How is it punctuated?

4. How do you show a quotation within a quotation?

5. Which kind of titles require quotation marks?

6. When should you use italics?

Chapter 27 Quiz

Indicate the correct choice for each of the following items.

____ 1. If an underlined portion of this sentence is incorrect, select the revision that fixes it. If the sentence is correct as written, choose d.

> Do you think that <u>she</u> was serious when she <u>said, "Leave the</u>
>   *a*   *b*
>
> building <u>immediately?"</u>
>   *c*

  a. "she"   c. immediately"?

  b. said "Leave   d. No change is necessary.

____ 2. Choose the item that has no errors.

  a. "You need to strengthen that knee," Dr. Wheeler warned, "so be sure to do all your exercises".

  b. "You need to strengthen that knee," Dr. Wheeler warned, so be sure to do all your exercises.

  c. "You need to strengthen that knee," Dr. Wheeler warned, "so be sure to do all your exercises."

____ 3. Choose the item that has no errors.

  a. Eric pointed at an article titled 'New Alternative Fuel in Your Backyard.'

  b. Eric pointed at an article titled New Alternative Fuel in Your Backyard.

  c. Eric pointed at an article titled "New Alternative Fuel in Your Backyard."

____ 4. If an underlined portion of this sentence is incorrect, select the revision that fixes it. If the sentence is correct as written, choose d.

> The man said, "I'm sorry, <u>officer, but</u> did I hear you correctly
>
> a
>
> when you <u>said, "Drive</u> into that <u>ditch'?"</u>
>
> b   c

    a. officer, "but   c. ditch' "?

    b. said, 'Drive   d. No change is necessary.

____ 5. Choose the item that has no errors.

    a. Rafa chose to do a podcast instead of a traditional book report on *The Great Gatsby*.

    b. Rafa chose to do a podcast instead of a traditional book report on "The Great Gatsby."

    c. Rafa chose to do a podcast instead of a traditional book report on The Great Gatsby.

28

Other Punctuation ; : ( ) — -

Learning Outcomes | In this chapter, you will learn to

- Use semicolons correctly.
- Add colons when they are needed.
- Use parentheses correctly.
- Use dashes effectively.
- Place hyphens where they are needed.

Punctuation—like capitalization and spelling—is a convention that helps readers understand writing. In spoken conversations, we rely on sounds, pauses, intonation, facial expressions, and gestures to make sure our words are understood. Writers and readers, however, do not have those tools available, so they rely on punctuation.

This chapter covers five punctuation marks that help writers communicate a message effectively: *semicolons, colons, parentheses, dashes,* and *hyphens.* Understanding how these punctuation marks are used helps writers edit effectively, and it helps readers make sense of the texts they read.

Use Semicolons ;

Semicolons are used in two ways:

1. To join closely related sentences
2. To separate items in a list, when list items contain commas

To Join Closely Related Sentences

Use a semicolon to join two closely related sentences into one sentence.

In an interview, hold your head up and do not slouch; it is important to look alert.

Make good eye contact; looking down is not appropriate in an interview.

 Language note: Using a comma instead of a semicolon to join two sentences creates a run-on. (See Chapter 18.)

To Separate Items in a List When List Items Contain Commas

Use semicolons to separate items in a list that itself contains commas. Otherwise, it is difficult for readers to tell where one item ends and another begins.

For dinner, Noah ate an order of onion rings; a 16-ounce steak; a baked potato with sour cream, bacon bits, and cheese; a green salad; and a huge bowl of ice cream with fudge sauce.

Because one item, *a baked potato with sour cream, bacon bits, and cheese,* contains its own commas, all the other items in the series need to be separated by semicolons.

Use Colons :

Colons are used before lists, explanations, or examples, as well as in business correspondence and before subtitles.

Before Lists

Use a **colon** after an independent clause to introduce a list. An independent clause contains a subject, a verb, and a complete thought. It can stand on its own as a sentence.

The software conference fair featured a vast array of products: financial-management applications, games, educational CDs, college-application programs, and so on.

Before Explanations or Examples

Use a colon after an independent clause to let readers know that you are about to provide an explanation or example of what you just wrote.

> The conference was overwhelming: too much hype about too many things.

One of the most common misuses of colons is to use them after a phrase instead of an independent clause. Watch out especially for colons following the phrases *such as* and *for example*.

Incorrect:	Tonya enjoys sports that are sometimes dangerous. For example: white-water rafting, wilderness skiing, rock climbing, and motorcycle racing.
Correct:	Tonya enjoys sports that are sometimes dangerous: white-water rafting, wilderness skiing, rock climbing, and motorcycle racing.
Incorrect:	Saquon has many interests. They are: bicycle racing, sculpting, and building musical instruments.
Correct:	Saquon has many interests: bicycle racing, sculpting, and building musical instruments.

In Business Correspondence and before Subtitles

Use a colon after a greeting (called a *salutation*) in a business letter.

> Dear Mr. Hernandez:

Colons should also be used before subtitles—for example, "Running a Marathon: The Five Most Important Tips."

Use Parentheses ( )

Use **parentheses** to set off information that is not essential to the meaning of a sentence. Writers can also use parentheses to make side comments directly to a reader (**asides**) and to provide citations. Parentheses for added information and asides are generally considered less formal; pay attention to the context of writing before using parentheses extensively. Parentheses are always used in pairs.

> My grandfather's most successful invention (and also his first) was the electric blanket.
>
> When he died (at the age of ninety-six), he had more than 150 patents registered.

Use Dashes —

Dashes can be used like parentheses to set off additional information, particularly information that you want to emphasize. Make a dash by typing two hyphens together or by using the symbols available in word-processing programs. Do not put extra spaces around a dash.

The final exam—worth 25 percent of your total grade—will be next Thursday.

A dash can also indicate a pause, much like a comma does.

My uncle went on long fishing trips—without my aunt and cousins.

Use Hyphens -

Hyphens are used both to join words and to divide words when they break across a line.

To Join Words That Form a Single Description

Writers often use hyphens to join two or more words that together form a single description of a person, place, or thing.

Being a stockbroker is a high-risk career.
Tamari is a lovely three-year-old girl.

When writing out two-word numbers from twenty-one to ninety-nine, put a hyphen between the two words.

Seventy-five people participated in the demonstration.

To Divide a Word at the End of a Line

Use a hyphen to divide a word when part of the word must continue on the next line.

Critics accused the tobacco industry of increasing the amounts of nico-
tine in cigarettes to encourage addiction and boost sales.

If you are not sure where to break a word, look it up in a dictionary. The word's main entry will show you where you can break the word: *dic • tio • nary*. If you still are not confident that you are putting the hyphen in the correct place, do not break the word; write it all on the next line.

> **PRACTICE 28-1   Editing Paragraphs for Other Punctuation Marks**
>
> Edit the following paragraphs by adding semicolons, colons, parentheses, dashes, and hyphens when needed. In some places, more than one type of punctuation may be acceptable.
>
> When John Wood was on a backpacking trip to Nepal in 1998, he discovered something he had not expected only a few books in the nation's schools. He knew that if the students did not have the materials they needed, it would be much harder for them to learn. They did not need high tech supplies as much as they needed old fashioned books. Wood decided that he would find a way to get those books.
>
> Two years later, Wood founded Room to Read, an organization dedicated to shipping books to students who needed them. Since then, the group has donated more than three million books. One of Wood's first shipments was carried to students on the back of a yak. Many others arrived in a Cathay Pacific Airlines plane.
>
> Along with the books, Room to Read has also built almost three hundred schools and has opened five thousand libraries. Different companies donate books to the organization Scholastic, Inc., recently sent 400,000 books to Wood's group. Money to fund all these efforts comes through various fund-raisers read-a-thons, auctions, and coin drives.

Chapter 28 Review

1. What are two uses of semicolons?

2. Colons can be used in what four ways?

3. What kind of information is placed in parentheses?

4. What kind of information is set off with dashes?

5. Hyphens (-) can be used to join two or more words that do what?

Chapter 28 Quiz

Indicate the correct choice for each of the following items.

___ 1. Choose the item that has no errors.

    a. Our car trip took us through Pittsburgh, Pennsylvania, Wheeling, West Virginia, and Bristol, Tennessee.

    b. Our car trip took us through Pittsburgh, Pennsylvania; Wheeling, West Virginia; and Bristol, Tennessee.

    c. Our car trip took us through Pittsburgh; Pennsylvania, Wheeling; West Virginia, and Bristol; Tennessee.

___ 2. If an underlined portion of this sentence is incorrect, select the revision that fixes it. If the sentence is correct as written, choose d.

        Gary's dog <u>(a seventeen-year-old</u> easily won first prize in the
                          a

        Elderly Dog <u>Show; she</u> had the shiniest <u>coat and the</u> most
                b   *c*

        youthful step.

    a. (a seventeen-year-old)   c. coat: and

    b. Show-she   d. No change is necessary.

___ 3. Choose the item that has no errors.

    a. As our computer specialist, you have three tasks: fixing malfunctioning computers, teaching people to use their computers, and not making any problem worse.

    b. As our computer specialist: you have three tasks, fixing malfunctioning computers, teaching people to use their computers, and not making any problem worse.

    c. As our computer specialist, you have three tasks: fixing malfunctioning computers, teaching people to use their computers (and not making any problem worse).

___ 4. Choose the item that has no errors.

    a. Is there such a thing as a low-stress-job?

    b. Is there such a thing as a low-stress job?

    c. Is there such a thing as a low stress-job?

___ 5. If an underlined portion of this sentence is incorrect, select the revision that fixes it. If the sentence is correct as written, choose d.

        You will have <u>five and only five minutes to leave</u> the office <u>before the</u>
                   a   *b*   *c*

        alarm sounds.

    a. five—and only five—   c. before; the

    b. to: leave   d. No change is necessary.

Appendix

Citing Research Sources in MLA Style

Many assignments in college require that you research a topic before writing about it, using books, articles, websites, or other sources. When you write a paper with research, you will be required to **document**—or show—where you found your information. Different disciplines and majors use different styles of documentation. Humanities and English majors usually use MLA (Modern Language Association) style, while psychology majors and some other majors in the sciences and social sciences document sources in APA (American Psychological Association) style. Always check with your instructor to find out which style is required for a specific course. This appendix presents MLA style.

Beginning Well: Using College Resources and Taking Good Notes

It is always tempting to begin research by going to Google and copying information from the first search results that you find. But searching in this way actually sets you up for problems later. Once you have identified a research task (also called a **research question**), begin with the best resource that your school provides: the library. Talk with a librarian about an effective search strategy, and learn to use research tools in the library, including the library catalog and databases.

As you begin to find sources, it is important to do three things:

1. **Evaluate the credibility of your sources**. Can the source be trusted? How do you know? Whether you are using a search engine (like Google) or a database from the library website, you need to consider the quality and purpose of the information. Use the information in Chapter 15 (Argument), page 305, to help you assess the source for bias.

2. **Keep a source trail**. Make a note of what you found, how you found it, who wrote it, the date of publication and any other publication information (such as the volume and issue number for articles in journals or magazines), the DOI, permalink, or URL (if you found the source online), and the date you found it. You will need this information later.

3.   **Take careful notes to avoid plagiarism.** As you find information for your research essay, do not rely on your memory to recall details about your sources; take good notes from the start. It is usually a good idea to write a short summary of the source (see Chapter 1, pp. 18–20). You may also paraphrase a writer's words (see Chapter 1, pp. 14–15). If you copy the writer's exact words, be sure to enclose them in quotation marks (see Chapter 27, pp. 540–41). If the source you are using has page numbers, be sure to write down the page for any quotations or paraphrases in your notes.

Understanding Documentation: In-Text Citations

In-text citations signal to readers that information comes from a source. These citations may include two parts: a signal phrase (such as *Dr. Ann Leavell says*) and a parenthetical citation, which includes the author's last name (if it is not given in a signal phrase) and the page number for the quotation or paraphrase. Use first and last names in your first signal phrase for a work.

In-text Citation

Signal phrase   Page number

As Martin Luther King, Jr. wrote, "No American can afford to be apathetic about the problem of racial justice. It is a problem that meets every man at his front door" (67).

The following examples show in-text citations for different kinds of sources.

One Author

As David Shipler states, ". . ." (16).

The number of people who work and fall below the poverty line has increased dramatically (Shipler 16).

Two Authors

Use both authors' last names.

Olivia Quigley and James Morrison found that . . . (243).

Banks and credit card companies are charging many more fees . . . (Quigley and Morrison 243).

Three or More Authors

In a signal phrase, use the first author's name and the words *and others* or *and colleagues*. In a parenthetical citation, use *et al.*, which means "and others" in Latin.

> According to Keya Sen and colleagues, . . . (659).
>
> The overuse of antibiotics can result in . . . (Sen et al. 659).

Group, Corporation, or Government Agency

In a signal phrase, use the full name of the group, corporation, or government agency (the same name as in the works cited list). In the parenthetical citation, you can shorten the name.

> To reduce runoff into the Chesapeake Bay, the United States
> Environmental Protection Agency recommends that farmers not plant
> "high nutrient loading crops" (like corn) in sensitive areas (26).
>
> Avoid planting corn in environmentally sensitive areas near the
> Chesapeake Bay (Environmental Protection 26).

Author Not Named

Use the title in place of the author's name; you can shorten long titles in the parenthetical citation.

> The article "Medical Mysteries and Surgical Surprises" explains . . . (79).
>
> . . . ("Medical Mysteries" 79).

Encyclopedia or Other Reference Work

Use the name of the entry you are using as a source.

> In its entry on xeriscaping, the *Landscape Encyclopedia* claims that . . .
> ("Xeriscaping").
>
> Xeriscaping is often used in . . . ("Xeriscaping").

Understanding Documentation: The Works Cited List

A works cited list is a complete list, alphabetized by author, of the outside sources you use in your essay. This list follows the essay and starts on a new page.

The two most basic elements of any works cited entry are the author's name and the title of the work, both of which are followed by a period.

> Lutz, Iva. *The Passenger.* (novel)
>
> Coles, Kimberly Anne. "The Matter of Belief in John Donne's Holy Sonnets." (periodical)
>
> Levy, Shawn. *"Holly Jolly." (Episode of a TV series)*

In MLA style, after noting these two elements, you must indicate the larger work (if any) in which you found the material you are citing. If you cite a passage from a novel, the novel *is* the larger work. However, for an essay or article, the larger work might be a newspaper or magazine; for an online article, it could be a website; for a TV or podcast episode, it would be the TV series or podcast. Whatever the larger work, provide as many of the following elements as you can find or that apply to the source you are citing, in the order shown. Each of these items is followed by a comma, except the last one, which ends with a period.

- The title of the larger work
- The names of other contributors (such as editors, translators, and directors)
- The version (for example, revised edition, 2nd ed., or director's cut)
- The volume number for a multivolume work or the volume and issue numbers for a scholarly journal or magazine (if available)
- The publisher (such as the publishing company, network, or database)
- The date of publication (use day-month-year format and abbreviate names of all months longer than four letters: 6 Feb. 2018, 17 June 2018)
- Information locator (a page number, DOI, permalink, or URL)

In MLA style, a DOI (digital object identifier, a permanent code) is the preferred option; a permalink (unchanging URL) is second best. If the site provides no date of publication or update, add your access date at the end of your works cited entry.

> Coles, Kimberly Anne. "The Matter of Belief in John Donne's Holy
>   Sonnets." *Renaissance Quarterly*, vol. 68, no. 3, fall 2015, pp. 899–931.
>
> "Holly Jolly." *Stranger Things*, directed by Shawn Levy, written by Matt
>   and Ross Duffer, 21 Laps Entertainment/Monkey Massacre, 2016.
>   *Netflix*, www.netflix.com.
>
> Kiuchi, Tatsuro. *Tatsuro Kiuchi: News & Blog.* http://tatsurokiuchi.com/.
>   Accessed 3 Mar. 2016.
>
> Lutz, Iva. *The Passenger.* Simon and Schuster, 2016.

In some cases, the longer work you cite might itself be part of an even longer work. (For example, you might find an article from a scholarly journal in a database, as in the example below.) In that case, simply add the same information listed above for the larger work at the end of the citation.

> Coles, Kimberly Anne. "The Matter of Belief in John Donne's Holy
>   Sonnets." *Renaissance Quarterly*, vol. 68, no. 3, fall 2015, pp. 899–931.
>   *JSTOR*, https://doi.org/10.1086/683855.

Models and Examples

One Author

Author's Last Name, First Name. *Title of Book: Subtitle.* Name of Publisher, Publication Date.

> Doerr, Anthony. *All the Light We Cannot See.* Scribner, 2014.

Two Authors

Author's Last Name, First Name, and Other Author's First and Last Name. *Title of Book: Subtitle.* Name of Publisher, Publication Date.

> Kuang, Cliff, and Robert Fabricant. *User Friendly.* Picador, 2019.

Three or More Authors

Author's Last Name, First Name, et al. *Title of Book: Subtitle.* Name of Publisher, Publication Date.

> Roark, James L., et al. *The American Promise: A History of the United
>   States.* 8th ed., Macmillan Learning, 2020.

This example also includes a version number: "8th ed."

Group, Corporation, or Government Agency

Name of Group, Corporation, or Agency. *Title of Book: Subtitle.* Name of Publisher, Publication Date.

> Human Rights Watch. *World Report 2020: Events of 2019.* Seven Stories
>   Press, 2020.

Editor

Editor's Last Name, First Name, editor. *Title of Book: Subtitle*. Name of Publisher, Publication Date.

> Canellos, Peter S., editor. *The Last Lion: The Fall and Rise of Ted Kennedy*. Simon & Schuster, 2009.

Encyclopedia

Entry Author's Last Name, First Name. "Title of Entry." *Title of Encyclopedia*, Edition Number [1st, 2nd, 3rd] ed., Publisher, Date of publication, Location information (DOI, permalink, URL, or page number).

> Araya, Yoseph. "Ecology of Water Relations in Plants." *Encyclopedia of Life Sciences*, Wiley Online Library, 8 Aug. 2014, https://doi .org/10.1002/9780470015902.a0003201.pub2.
>
> "House Music." *Wikipedia: The Free Encyclopedia*, Wikimedia Foundation, 8 Apr. 2021, en.wikipedia.org/wiki/House_music.
>
> Robinson, Lisa Clayton. "Harlem Writers Guild." *Africana: The Encyclopedia of the African and African American Experience*, edited by Kwame Anthony Appiah and Henry Louis Gates Jr., 2nd ed., Oxford UP, 2005, p. 163.

The first example shows an online encyclopedia that names the writer of each article; this citation includes a DOI. The second example is for another online encyclopedia, *Wikipedia*, which does not name the authors of its articles, because it is crowdsourced and updated regularly; this citation includes a URL. The third example, from a printed book, includes a page number.

Magazine Article

Author's Last Name, First Name. "Title of Article." *Title of Magazine*, Volume (abbreviated *vol.*), Issue Number (abbreviated *no.*), Date, Page Number or URL.

> Guerrero, Desirée. "All Genders, Period." *The Advocate*, no. 1105, Oct.–Nov. 2019, p. 31. *ProQuest*, www.proquest.com.proxy3.noblenet.org /docview/2488268993.
>
> Leonard, Andrew. "The Surveillance State High School." *Salon*, 27 Nov. 2012, www.salon.com/2012/11/27/the_surveillance_state_high_school/.
>
> Misner, Rebecca. "How I Became a Joiner." *Condé Nast Traveler*, vol. 5, 2018, pp. 55–56.
>
> Owusu, Nadia. "Head Wraps." *The New York Times Magazine*, 7 Mar. 2021, p. 20.

The first example also includes database information.

Short Work from a Website

Author's Last Name, First Name. "Title of Work." *Website Title,* Site Sponsor (if different from Website Name), Publication Date, URL.

> Bali, Karan. "Shashikala." *Upperstall,* upperstall.com/profile/shashikala/. Accessed 22 Apr. 2021.
>
> Enzinna, Wes. "Syria's Unknown Revolution." *Pulitzer Center,* 24 Nov. 2015, pulitzercenter.org/projects/middle-east-syria-enzinna-war-rojava.

The first example is from a website that does not provide a date of publication or update, so access information is included at the end of the citation.

Newspaper Article

Author's Last Name, First Name. "Title of Article." *Title of Newspaper,* Publication Date, Page Numbers or URL

> Kemper, Tyler. "All Strikeouts and No Walks." *The New York Times,* 13 May 2021, www.nytimes.com/2021/05/13/sports/baseball/corbin-burnes-strikeouts.html?smid=url-share.
>
> Sherry, Allison. "Volunteers' Personal Touch Turns High-Tech Data into Votes." *The Denver Post,* 30 Oct. 2012, pp. 1A+.

If print articles do not appear on consecutive pages, use the first page number followed by a plus sign, as in the second example.

Article from a Scholarly Journal

Author's Last Name, First Name. "Title of Article." *Title of Journal,* Volume Number (abbreviated *vol.*), Issue Number (abbreviated *no.*), Publication Date, Page Numbers.

> Bryson, Devin. "The Rise of a New Senegalese Cultural Philosophy?" *African Studies Quarterly,* vol. 14, no. 3, Mar. 2014, pp. 33–56, asq.africa .ufl.edu/files/Volume-14-Issue-3-Bryson.pdf.
>
> Coles, Kimberly Anne. "The Matter of John Donne's Holy Sonnets." *Renaissance Quarterly,* vol. 68, no. 3, fall 2015, pp. 899–931. *JSTOR,* www.jstor.org/stable/10.1086/683855.
>
> Fountain, Glinda H. "Inverting the Southern Belle: Romance Writers Redefine Gender Myths." *Journal of Popular Culture,* vol. 41, no. 1, Feb. 2008, pp. 37–55.

The first and second journal articles were accessed from databases, so database name and DOI or URL are included.

Formatting a Works Cited List

To format a works cited list in MLA style, follow these rules:

- Begin the list of works cited on a new page at the end of the project.
- Center the title *Works Cited* (without boldface, italics, or quotation marks) one inch from the top of the page.
- Double-space the whole list.
- Alphabetize the entries by the last names of the authors; if a work has no author, alphabetize by the first word of the title other than *A, An,* or *The.*
- Do not indent the first line of each works cited entry, but indent any additional lines half an inch.
- If you include a URL in a works cited entry, copy the URL directly from your browser. If the entire URL moves to another line, you may leave it that way. Do not add any hyphens or spaces. (Professionally typeset works, such as this book, may introduce line breaks to avoid uneven lines.)

   You may shorten URLs longer than three lines on your works cited page, but leave at least the website host (for example, cnn.com or www.usda .gov) in the entry. If you plan to link URLs to the sources, though, do not shorten the URLs or delete the protocol (https:// or http://).

The following sample shows how to format a works cited list in MLA style.

Jacobs 6

Works Cited

Gillmor, Dan. *We the Media: Grassroots Journalism by the People, for the People.* O'Reilly Media, 2006.

Glaser, Mark. "NOLA.com Blogs and Forums Help Save Lives after Katrina." *OJR: The Online Journalism Review*, Knight Digital Media Center, 13 Sept. 2005, www.ojr.org/050913glaser/.

Hazinski, David. "Unfettered 'Citizen Journalism' Too Risky." *Atlanta Journal-Constitution*, 13 Dec. 2007, p. 23A. *General OneFile*, go.galegroup.com/ps/.

Jones, Alex S. *Losing the News: The Future of the News That Feeds Democracy.* Oxford UP, 2009.

Sapin, Rachel. "Credit-Shy: Younger Generation Is More Likely to Stick to a Cash-Only Policy." *The Denver Post*, 26 Aug. 2013, www.denverpost.com/ci_23929523/credit -shy-younger-generation-stick-cash-only-policy.

"The 2006 Pulitzer Prize Winners: Public Service." *The Pulitzer Prizes*, Columbia U, www.pulitzer.org/prize-winners-by -year/2006. Accessed 12 May 2021.

Weinberger, David. "Transparency Is the New Objectivity." *Joho the Blog*, 19 July 2009, www.hyperorg.com/blogger/2009/07/19/transparency -is-the-new-objectivity/.

Title *Works Cited* centered

Alphabetized by authors' last names (or title when a no author)

Database information included after publication information

Double-spaced throughout; first line of each entry at left margin, additional lines indented 1/2"

Access date used for a Web source that has no date of publication or update

Acknowledgments

Alfred Brophy, "Why the Case for the Removal of Confederate Memorials Isn't So Clear-cut," *The Conversation*, July 8, 2015. Copyright © 2015 by The Conversation. Distributed under Creative Commons Attribution License 4.0 (CC BY-ND 4.0) https://theconversation.com/why-the-case-for-the-removal-of-confederate-memorials-isnt-so-clear-cut-44218.

Lisa Currie, "Profile of Success: Lisa Currie" and "Letter to the State Budget Officials." Reprinted by permission.

Stephanie Ericsson, "The Ways We Lie." Copyright © 1992 by Stephanie Ericsson. Originally published by *The Utne Reader*. Reprinted by the permission of Dunham Literary Inc. as agents for the author.

Paola Garcia-Muniz, "Profile of Success: Paola Garcia-Muniz, Editorial Assistant" and "Submitting Reprint Collections." Reprinted by permission.

Juan C. Gonzalez, "Profile of Success: Juan C. Gonzalez, Vice Chancellor for Student Affairs, University of California, San Diego" and "Workplace Essay: Juan C. Gonzalez, Address to New Students." Reprinted by permission of the author.

Katie Horn (student), "A Beginner's Guide to Movie Night." Reprinted by permission.

Amanda Jacobowitz, "A Ban on Water Bottles: A Way to Bolster the University's Image." Posted by Amanda Jacobowitz on April 28, 2010. Forum Staff Columnists. Reprinted by permission.

Samantha Levine-Finley, "Isn't It Time You Hit the Books?" Originally published in *U.S. News and World Report's America's Best Colleges 2008*, August 17, 2007. Reprinted by permission. Copyrighted 2007. U.S. News & World Report. 277406:0918BC

Amanda Martinez, "To All the Boys I've Ghosted Before," *The Independent Florida Alligator*, May 28, 2019. Copyright © 2019 by The Independent Florida Alligator. Used with permission.

Nneka M. Okona, "Stuffing vs. Dressing: What You Call It Can Reveal Where You're From," *Huffington Post*, October 26, 2020. Copyright © 2020 by Huffington Post. All rights reserved. Used under license. https://huffpost.com/

Maria Olloqui, "The Five Main Types of Texters," *Washington Square News*, March 26, 2019. Copyright © 2019 by Washington Square News. Used with permission.

Rita Rantung (student), "Indonesian and U.S. School Systems." Reprinted by permission.

Eugene Robinson, "A Special Brand of Patriotism," *Washington Post*, July 4, 2008. Copyright © 2008 by Washington Post. All rights reserved. Used under license. https://www.washingtonpost.com//

James Roy, "Profile of Success: James Roy" and "Workplace Essay: James Roy, Police Report." Reprinted by permission.

Gary Soto, "The Grandfather" From A SUMMER LIFE, © 1990 by Gary Soto, Laurel Leaf, 1990. Used by permission of the author.

Amy Tan, "Fish Cheeks" © 1987 by Amy Tan. First appeared in *Seventeen Magazine*. Reprinted by permission of the author and the Sandra Dijkstra Literary Agency.

Steven Thrasher, "Confederate Memorials Have No Place in American Society. Good Riddance," *The Guardian*, April 25, 2017. Copyright © 2017 by Guardian News & Media Limited. Used with permission.

Margaret Troup, "Virtual Reality: Fun and Innovative Indoor Exercise," *Iowa State Daily*, July 8, 2020. Copyright © 2020 by Iowa State Daily. Used with permission.

Garth Vaz, "Profile of Success" and "Workplace Comparison and Contrast: Garth Vaz, Physician." Reprinted by permission.

Lisa C. Walsh, Julia K. Boehm, and Sonja Lyubomirsky, "Happiness Doesn't Follow Success: It's the Other Way Round," *Aeon*, May 24, 2019. This article was originally published at https://aeon.com and has been republished under Creative Commons Attribution-No Derivatives license (CC BY-ND).

Andrea Whitmer, "When Poor People Have Nice Things." *sooverthis.com*, June 18, 2012. Reprinted by permission.

Index

Useful Editing and Proofreading Marks

The marks and abbreviations below are those typically used by instructors when marking papers, but you can also mark your own work or that of your peers with these helpful symbols.

Standard symbol	How to revise or edit (numbers in boldface are chapters where you can find help)
adj	Use correct adjective form **Ch. 23**
adv	Use correct adverb form **Ch. 23**
agr	Correct subject-verb agreement or pronoun agreement **Chs. 19 and 22**
awk	Awkward expression: edit for clarity **Chs. 21 and 24**
cap or triple underline [example]	Use capital letter correctly **Ch. 25**
case	Use correct pronoun type (or *case*) **Ch. 22**
cliché	Replace overused phrase with fresh words
coh	Revise paragraph or essay for coherence **Ch. 6**
coord	Use coordination correctly **Ch. 24**
cs	Comma splice: join the sentences correctly **Ch. 18**
dev	Develop your paragraph or essay more completely **Chs. 4 and 6**
dm	Revise to avoid a dangling modifier **Ch. 23**
frag	Attach the fragment to a sentence or make it a sentence **Ch. 17**
fs	Fused sentence: join the two sentences correctly **Ch. 18**
ital	Use italics **Ch. 27**
lc or diagonal slash [Example]	Use lowercase **Ch. 25**
mm	Revise to avoid a misplaced modifier **Ch. 23**
pl	Use the correct plural form **Chs. 19 and 21**
ref	Make pronoun reference clear **Ch. 22**
ro	Run-on sentence: join the two sentences correctly **Ch. 18**
sp	Correct the spelling error **Ch. 25**
sub	Use subordination correctly **Ch. 24**
sup	Support your point with details, examples, or facts **Chs. 4 and 6**
tense	Correct the problem with verb tense **Ch. 20**
trans	Add a transition **Chs. 6 and 7–15**
wc	Reconsider your word choice **Ch. 21**
?	Make your meaning clearer **Ch. 6**
⌃ ,	Use comma correctly **Ch. 26**
; : ( ) — -	Use semicolon/colon/parentheses/dash/hyphen/correctly **Ch. 28**
" " ∨ ∨	Use quotation marks correctly **Ch. 27**
⌃	Insert something
✐ [exa͡mple]	Delete something
⌢ [words͡example]	Change the order of letters or words
¶	Start a new paragraph
# [example#words]	Add a space
⌒ [ex ⊃ample]	Close up a space